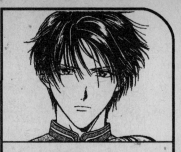

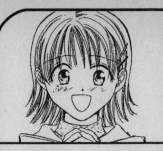

♥ Tanpopo Yamazaki, a freshman at Meio High School. Her goal is to enjoy her school life.

♥ Koki Kugyo, also a freshman at Meio. Koki comes from a very wealthy family.

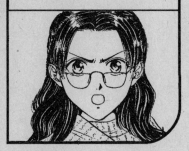

♥ Aoi Kyogoku, computer geek, class mate of Tanpopo and Koki.

♥ Tsukiko Saionji, vixen. Aspires to be Mrs. Koki Kugyo.

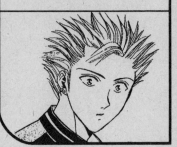

On a visit to Koki's house, Tanpopo learns that Koki's older brother, Yoji, disappeared two years before, and that Yoji's former fiancée, Erika Yanahara, is now engaged to Koki and living with him. Even so, Tanpopo and Koki gradually grow closer when they form the school's Planting Club together. Then Yoji suddenly shows up in Hokkaido, and things seem to be turning around for Tanpopo--until Erika decides to remain engaged to Koki! Worse still, Erika transfers to Meio and sticks to Koki like a leech. Tanpopo and Erika decide to settle the matter once and for all at the school's Rose Exchange event, but while Tanpopo works to see that everyone else has a rose to give to their crushes, Erika uses the opportunity to plant a very public kiss on Koki...

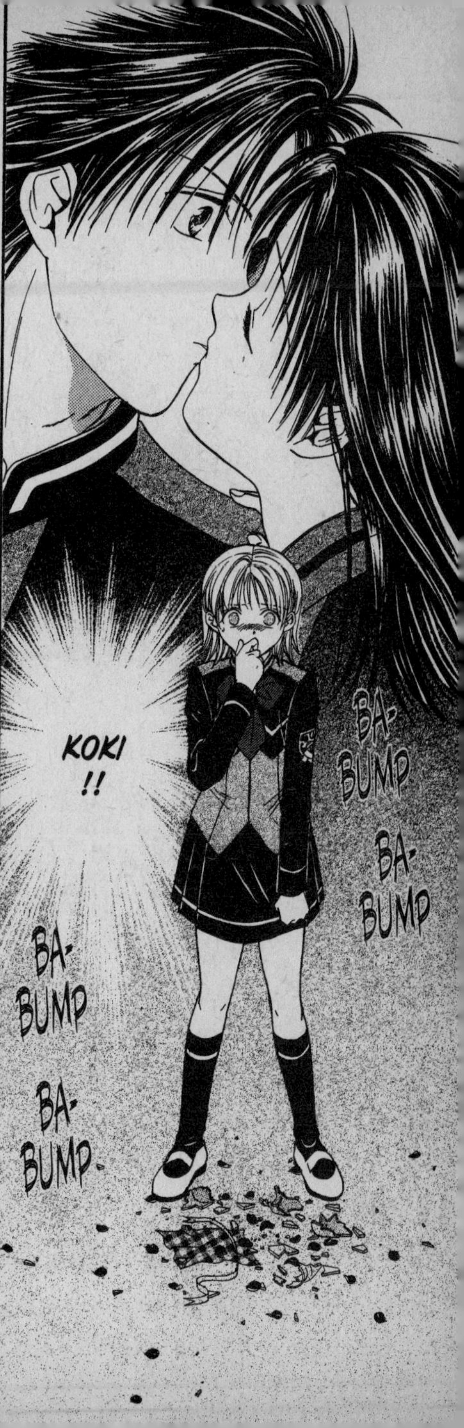
BA-BUMP
BA-BUMP
KOKI !!
BA-BUMP
BA-BUMP

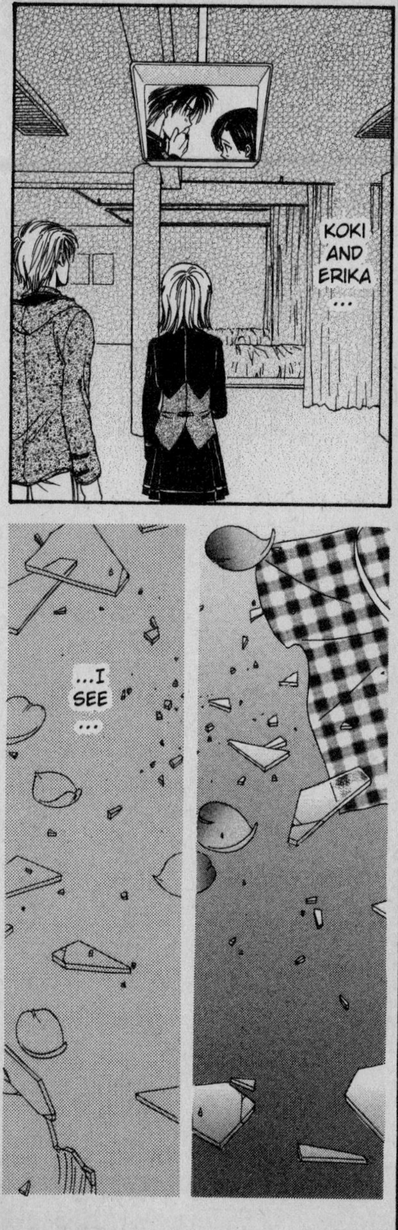
KOKI AND ERIKA ...
...I SEE ...

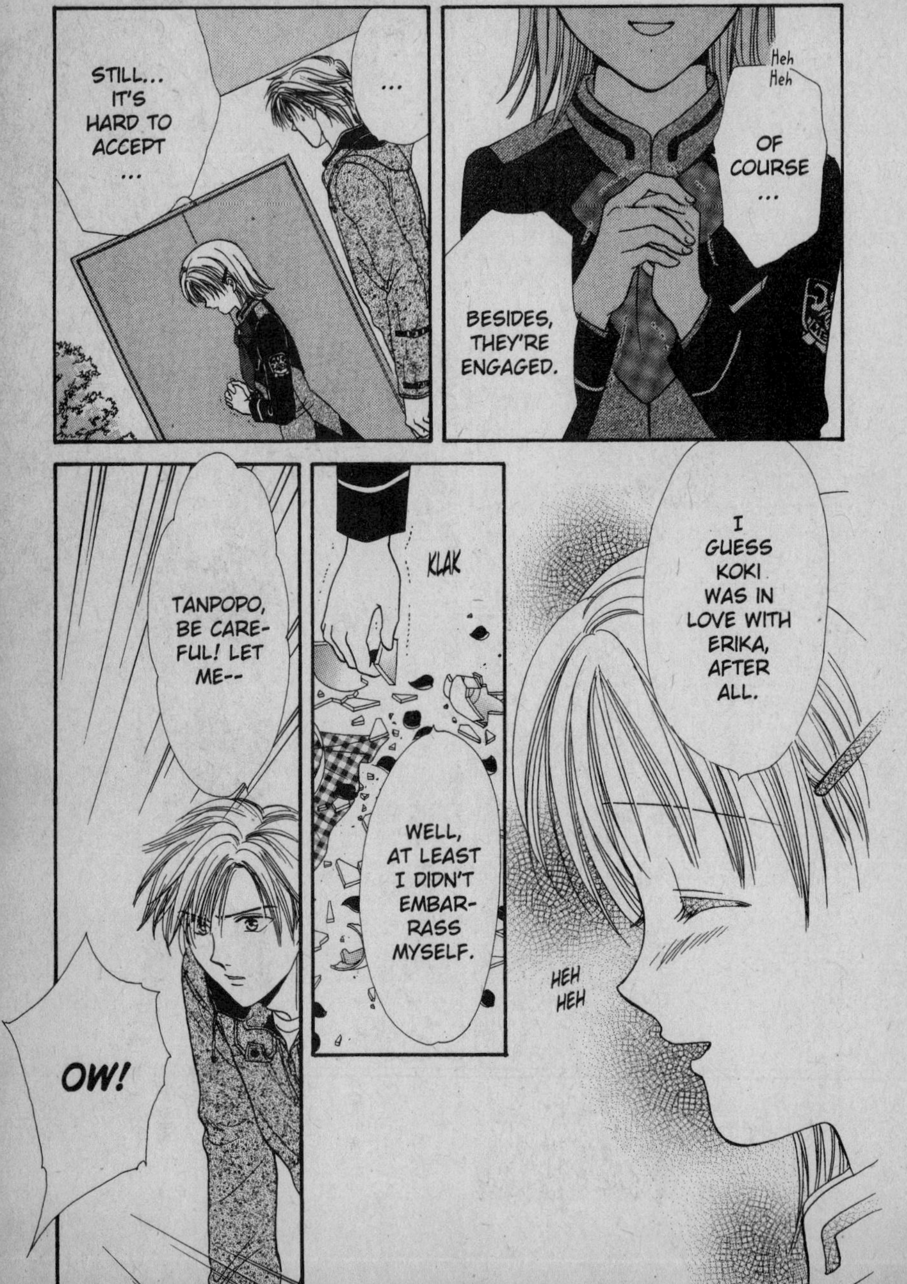
Heh Heh
OF COURSE ...
BESIDES, THEY'RE ENGAGED.
...
STILL... IT'S HARD TO ACCEPT ...
I GUESS KOKI WAS IN LOVE WITH ERIKA, AFTER ALL.
HEH HEH
KLAK
WELL, AT LEAST I DIDN'T EMBARRASS MYSELF.
TANPOPO, BE CAREFUL! LET ME--
OW!

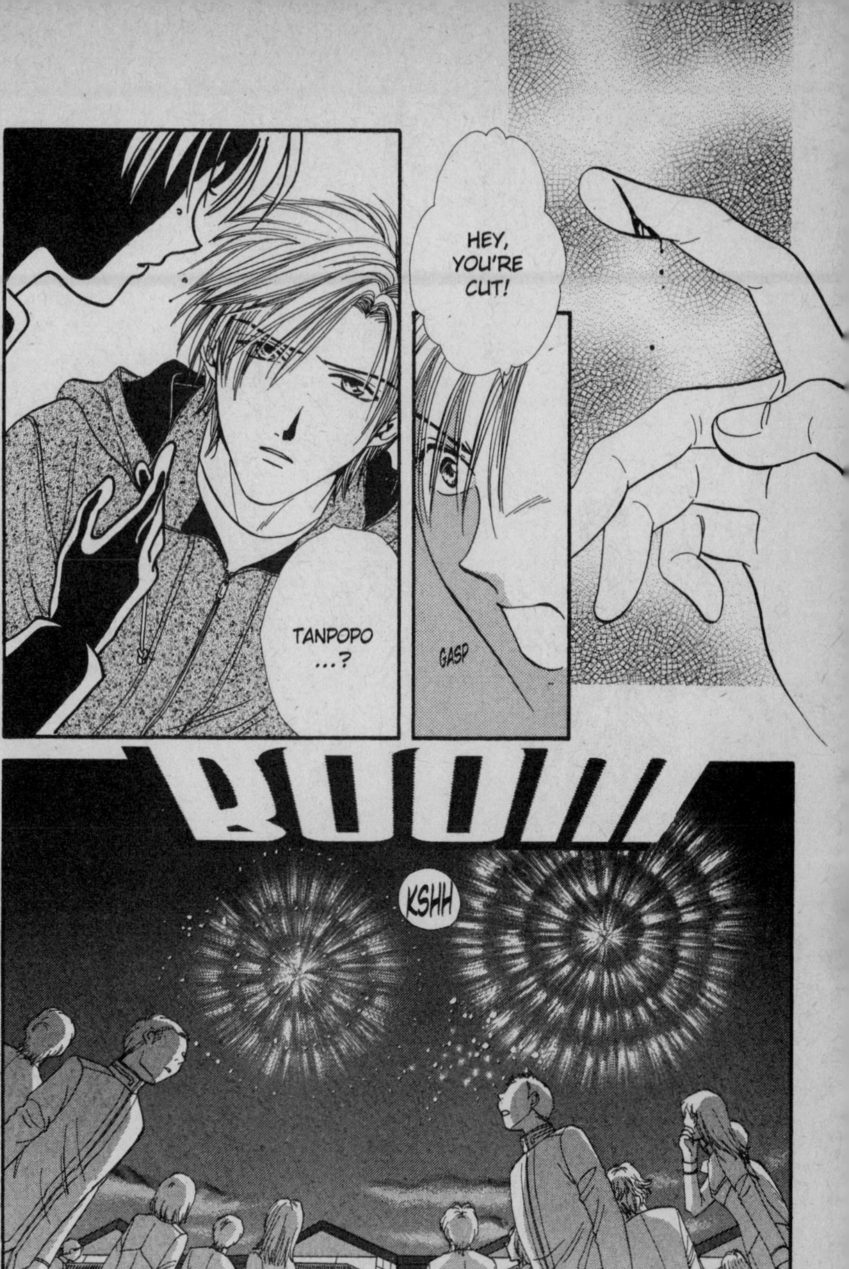
HEY, YOU'RE CUT!
GASP
TANPOPO ...?
BOOM
KSHH

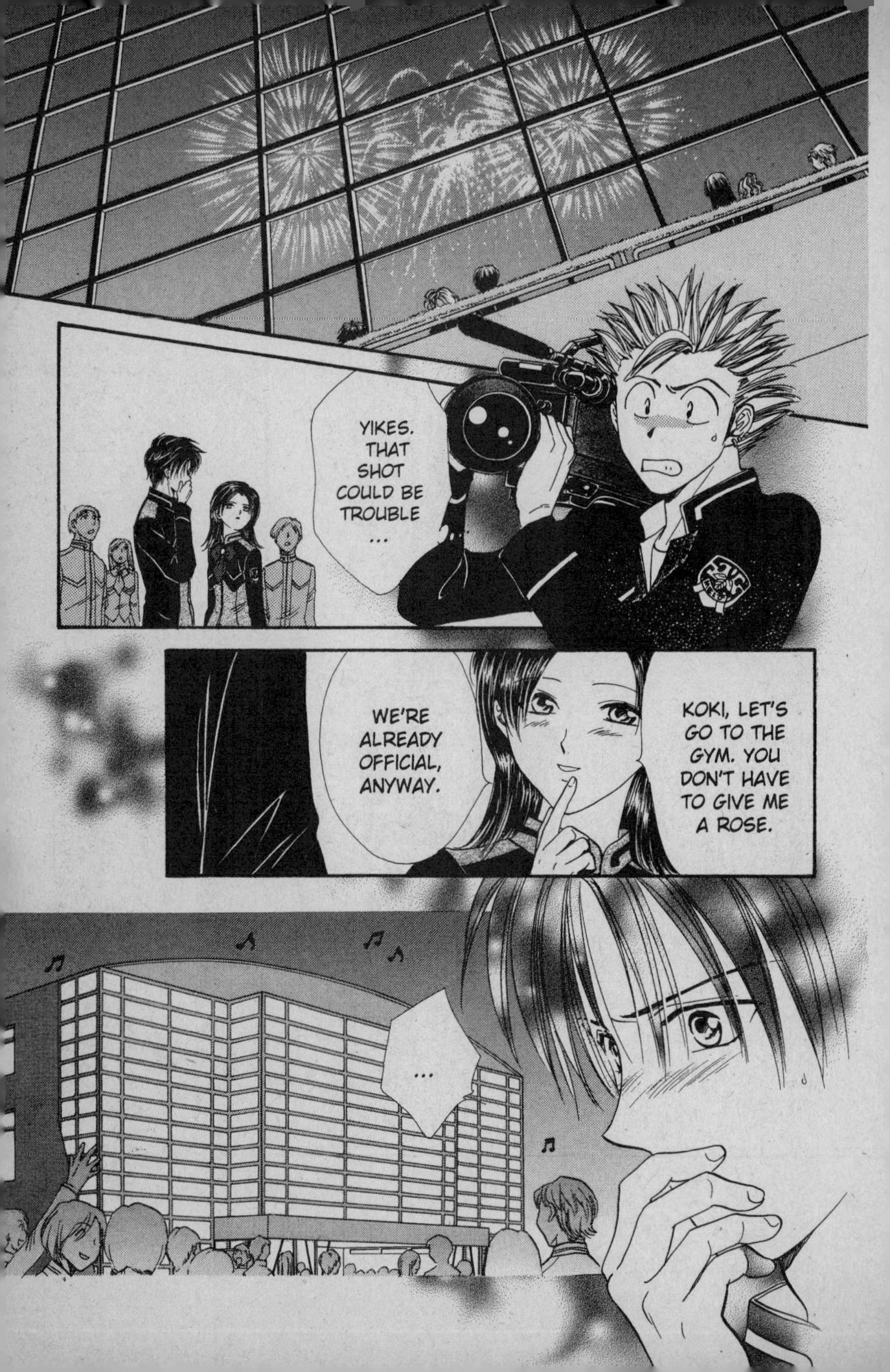
YIKES. THAT SHOT COULD BE TROUBLE ...
KOKI, LET'S GO TO THE GYM. YOU DON'T HAVE TO GIVE ME A ROSE.
WE'RE ALREADY OFFICIAL, ANYWAY.
...

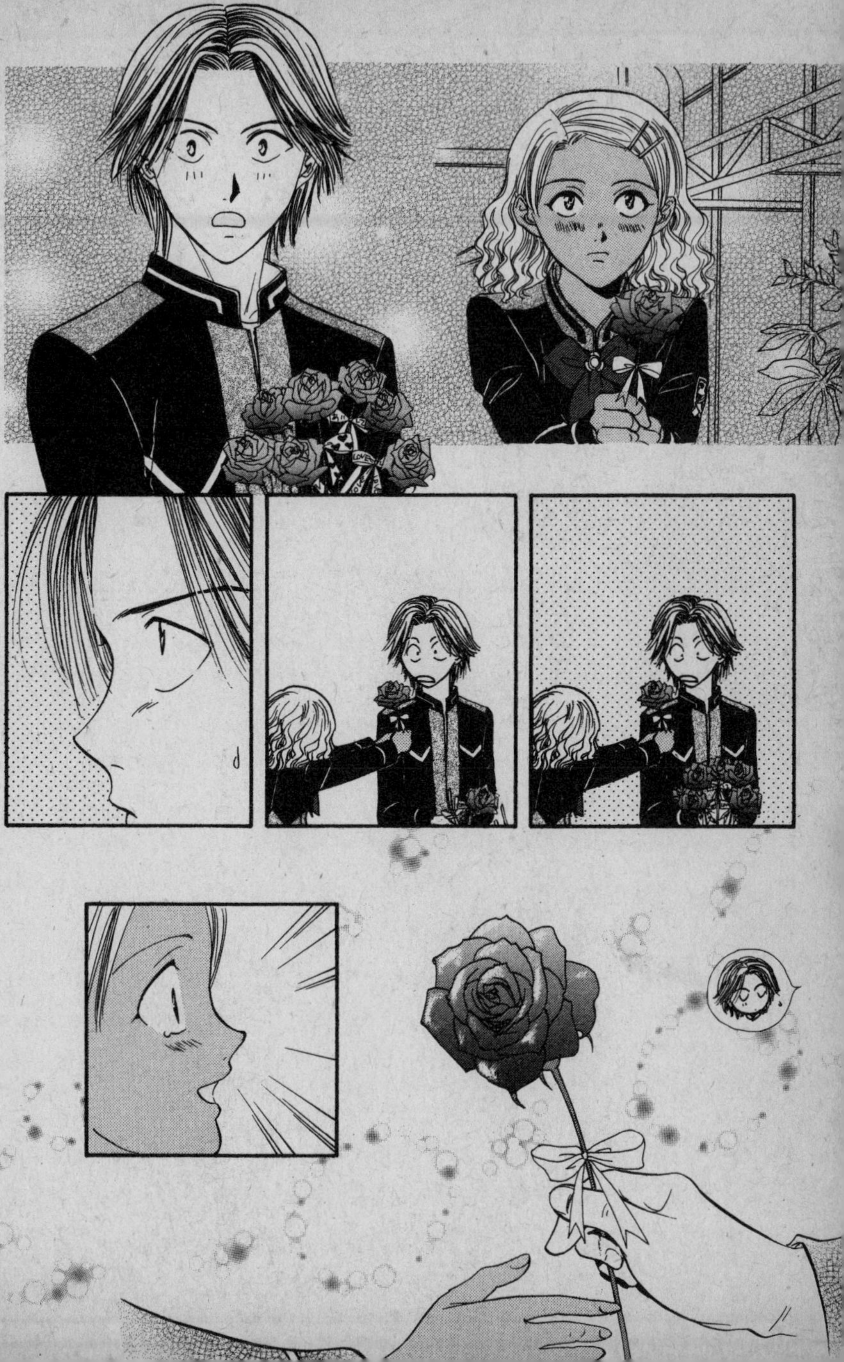

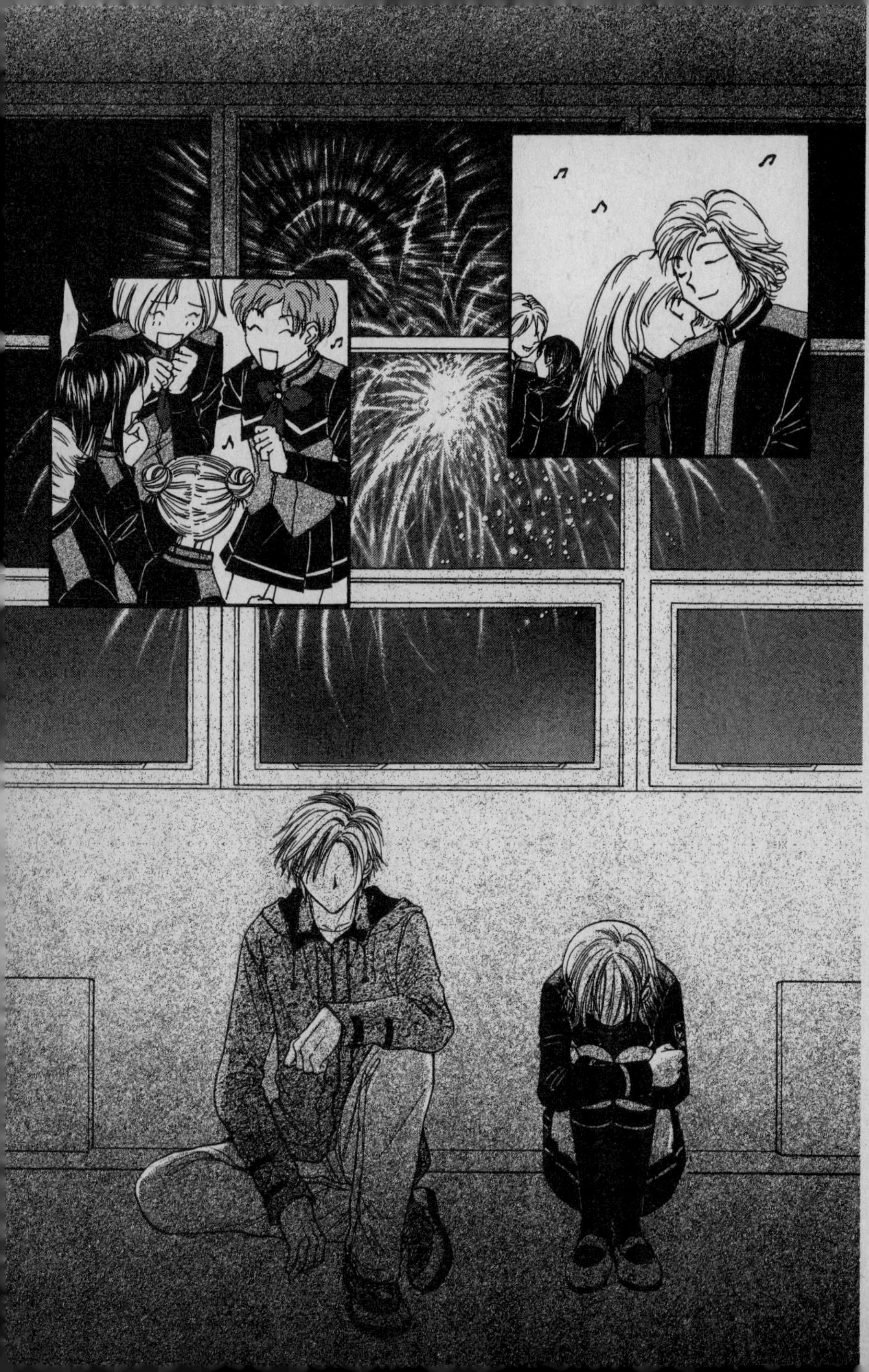

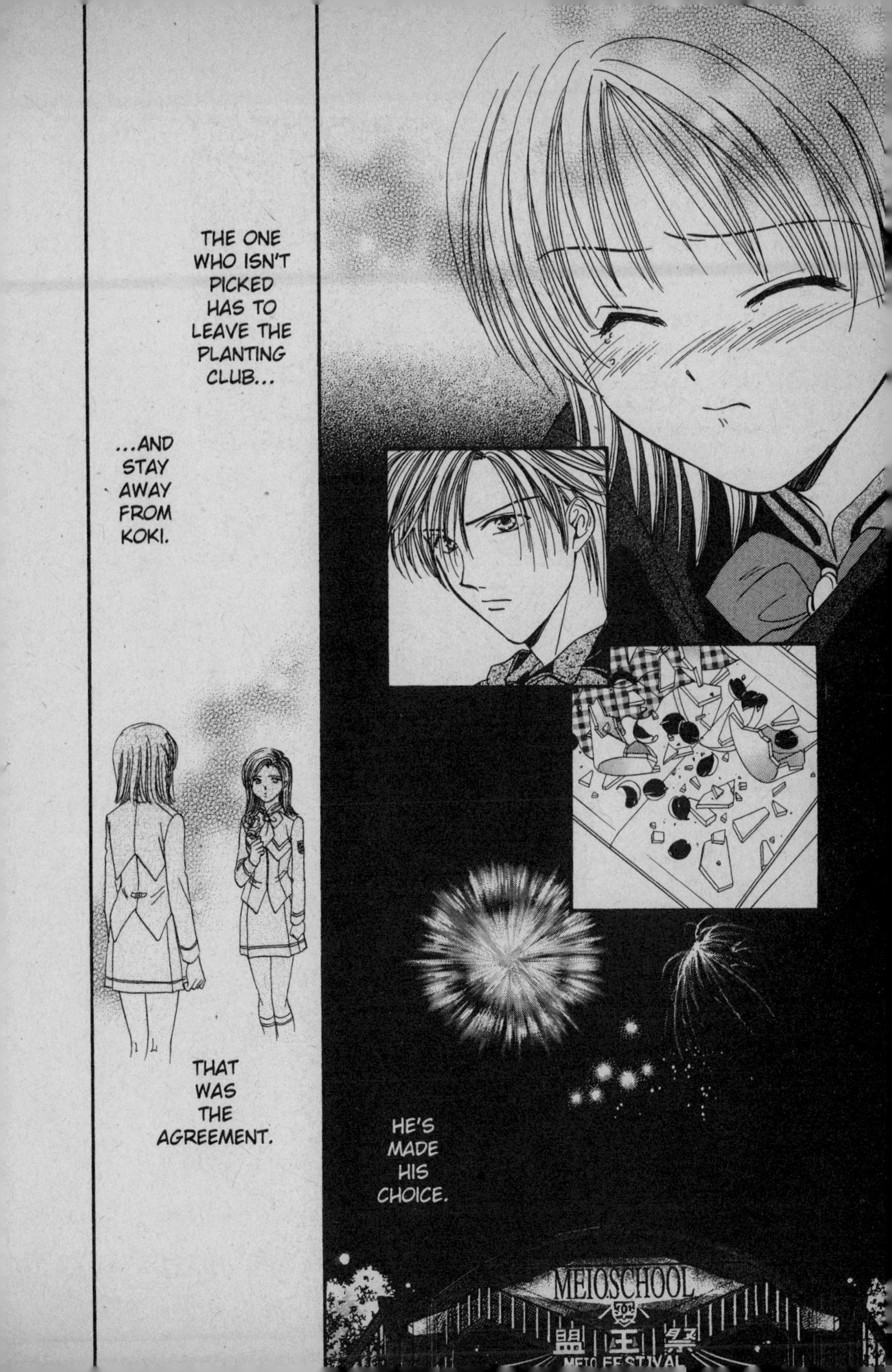
HE'S MADE HIS CHOICE.
MEIO SCHOOL
盟王祭
MEIO FESTIVAL
THE ONE WHO ISN'T PICKED HAS TO LEAVE THE PLANTING CLUB...
...AND STAY AWAY FROM KOKI.
THAT WAS THE AGREEMENT.

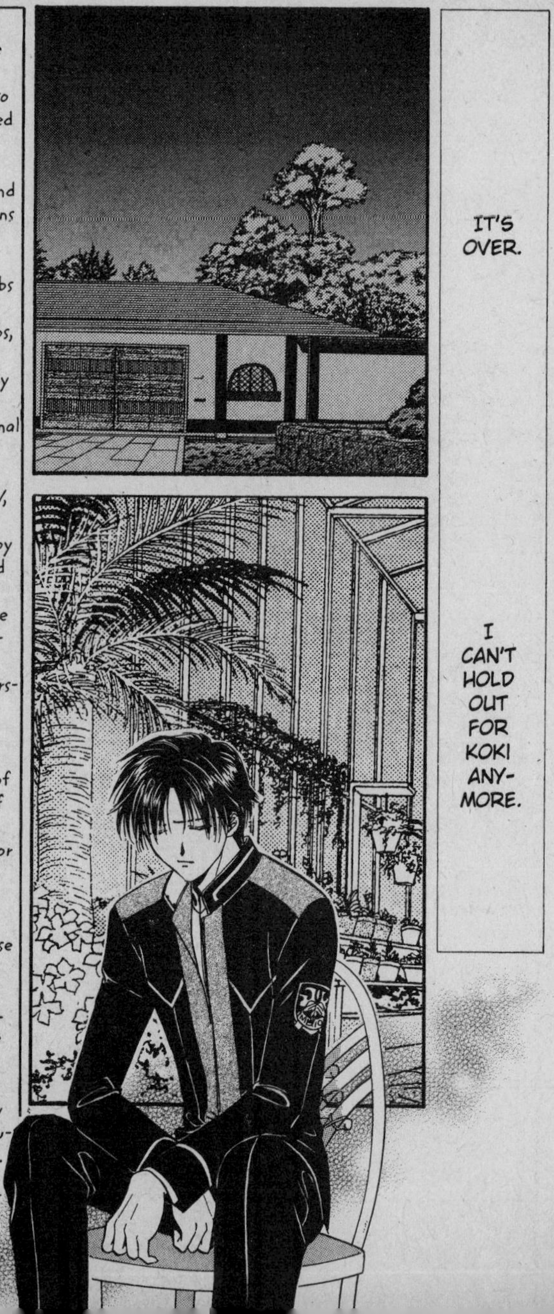
IT'S OVER.
I CAN'T HOLD OUT FOR KOKI ANYMORE.

Hi, welcome to Imadoki! 4.
I'm feeling so sleepy...Watase here.
It's strange. This is supposed to be my month off, but I've ended up working as much as ever!
Why is it my month off? I'll leave that question for now and answer a few readers' questions instead.
First, "Do you have a fan club?" I don't. Private fan clubs are okay, but I don't intend to authorize any official fan clubs, now or ever.
My friend's homepage is partly authorized (or am I just a visitor?), but you need a personal computer to check it out. ^^;
Long ago, when **Fushigi Yûgi** was made into an anime for TV, there was a Fushigi Yûgi Fan Club. But that was operated by Studio Pierrot, which produced the anime, so all I did was let them use my illustrations in the fan club newsletter. (I remember they had things like club membership cards and members-only merchandise...)
Of course, this fan club no longer exists.
Right now (you're really out of luck if you don't have a PC), if you go to Pierrot's homepage, there's a **Fushigi Yûgi** corner for fans. This is sort of like a fan club. There are links to info on your favorite characters.
I don't know much about these things myself. Hey, wait a minute.
By the way, I actually have a hard time answering questions about **Fushigi Yûgi**. I've already forgotten so many things. ^^; I've even forgotten bits of **Ayashi no Ceres**. (Only details, though.) That'll eventually happen with **Imadoki!** too. Hey! ☆

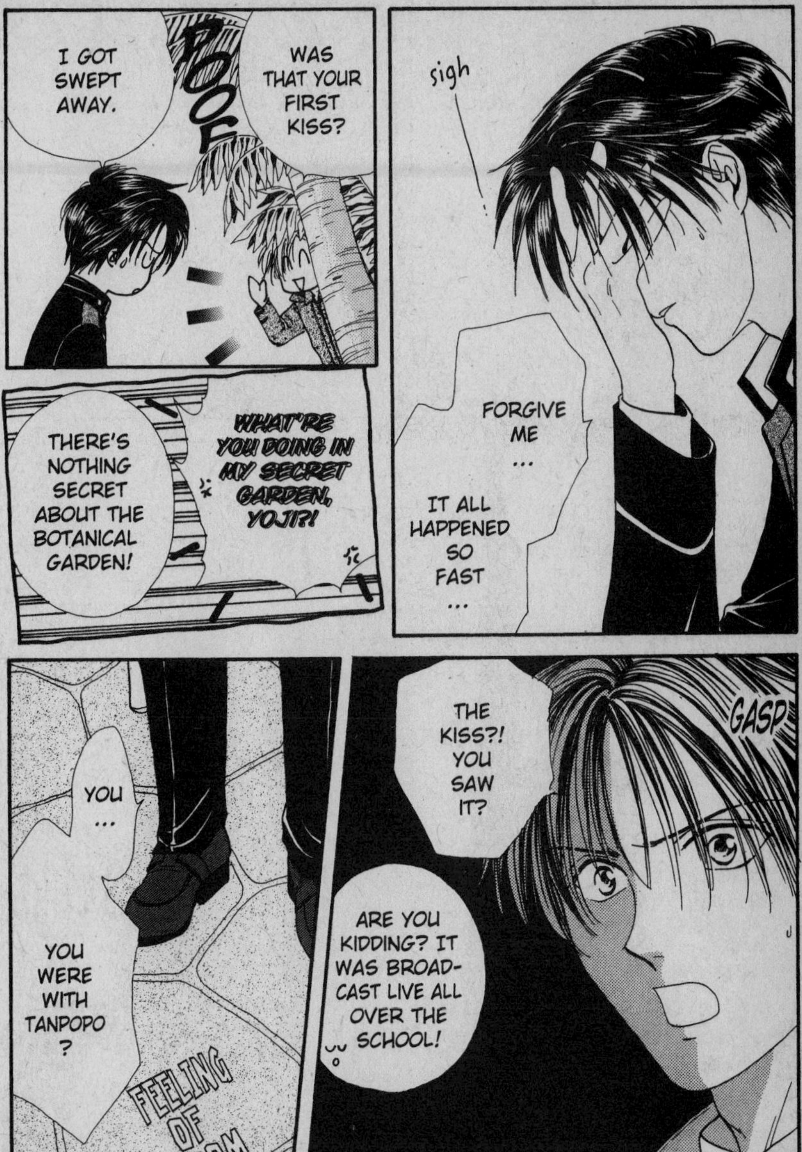
sigh
FORGIVE ME ...
IT ALL HAPPENED SO FAST ...
POOF
WAS THAT YOUR FIRST KISS?
I GOT SWEPT AWAY.
WHAT'RE YOU DOING IN MY SECRET GARDEN, YOJI?!
THERE'S NOTHING SECRET ABOUT THE BOTANICAL GARDEN!
GASP
THE KISS?! YOU SAW IT?
ARE YOU KIDDING? IT WAS BROAD-CAST LIVE ALL OVER THE SCHOOL!
YOU ...
YOU WERE WITH TANPOPO?
FEELING OF DOOM

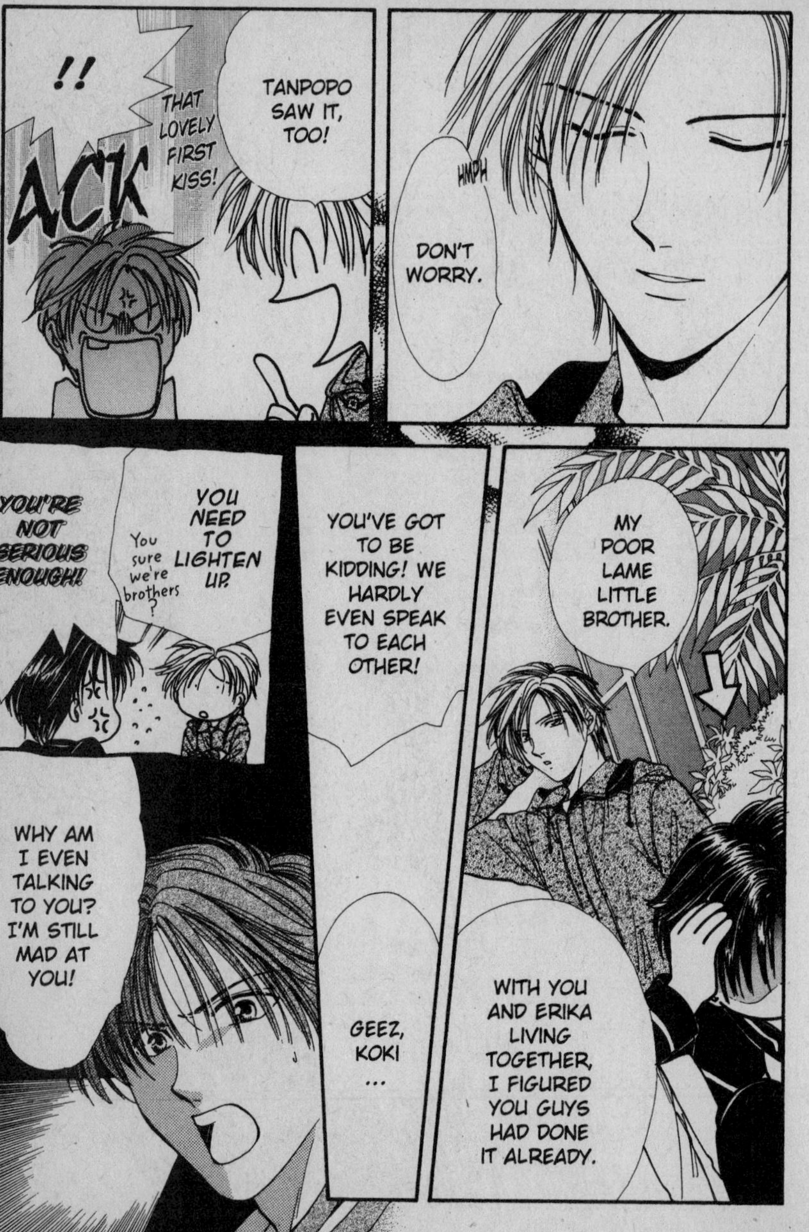
HMPH
DON'T WORRY.
TANPOPO SAW IT, TOO!
THAT LOVELY FIRST KISS!
ACK
!!
MY POOR LAME LITTLE BROTHER.
WITH YOU AND ERIKA LIVING TOGETHER, I FIGURED YOU GUYS HAD DONE IT ALREADY.
YOU'VE GOT TO BE KIDDING! WE HARDLY EVEN SPEAK TO EACH OTHER!
GEEZ, KOKI ...
YOU NEED TO LIGHTEN UP.
You sure we're brothers?
YOU'RE NOT SERIOUS ENOUGH!
WHY AM I EVEN TALKING TO YOU? I'M STILL MAD AT YOU!

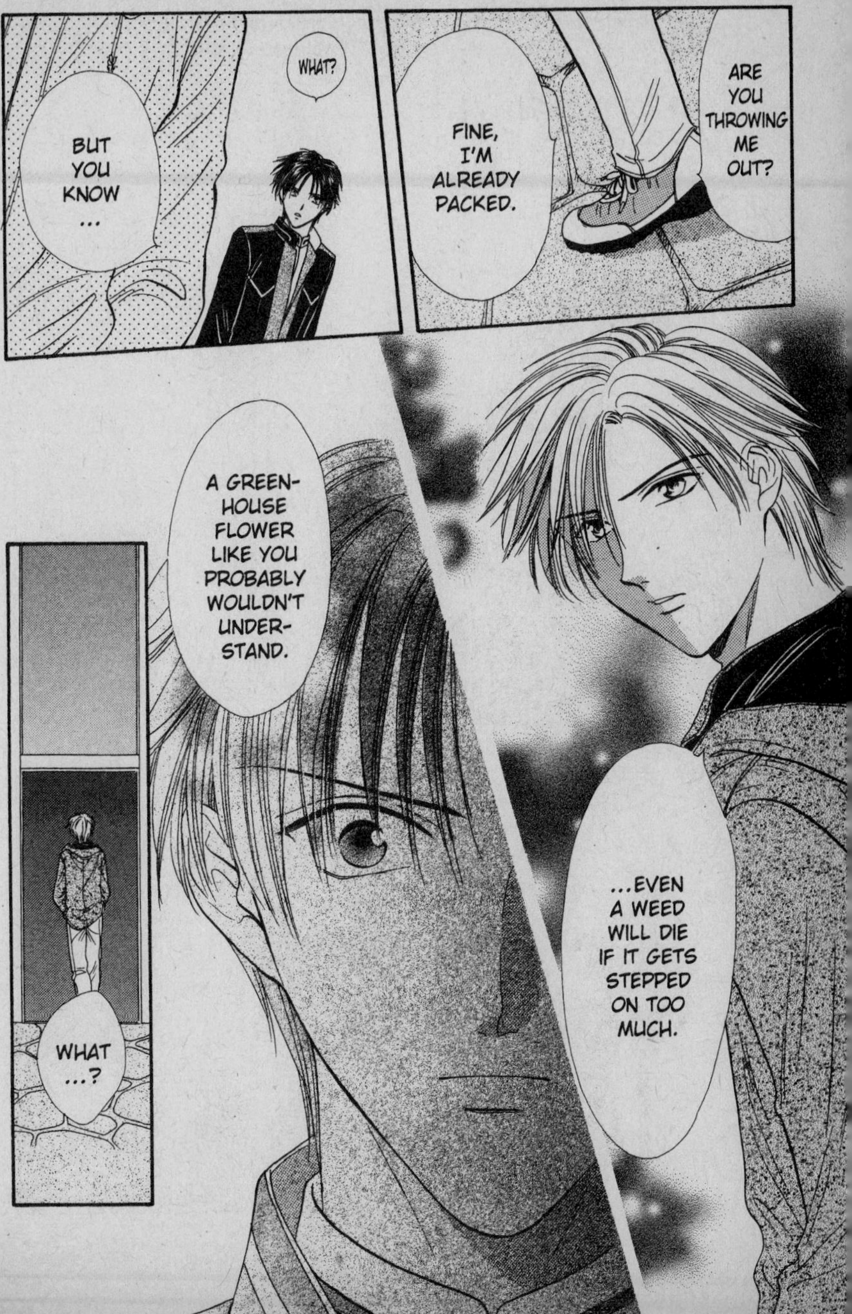
ARE YOU THROWING ME OUT?
FINE, I'M ALREADY PACKED.
WHAT?
BUT YOU KNOW ...
...EVEN A WEED WILL DIE IF IT GETS STEPPED ON TOO MUCH.
A GREEN-HOUSE FLOWER LIKE YOU PROBABLY WOULDN'T UNDER-STAND.
WHAT ...?

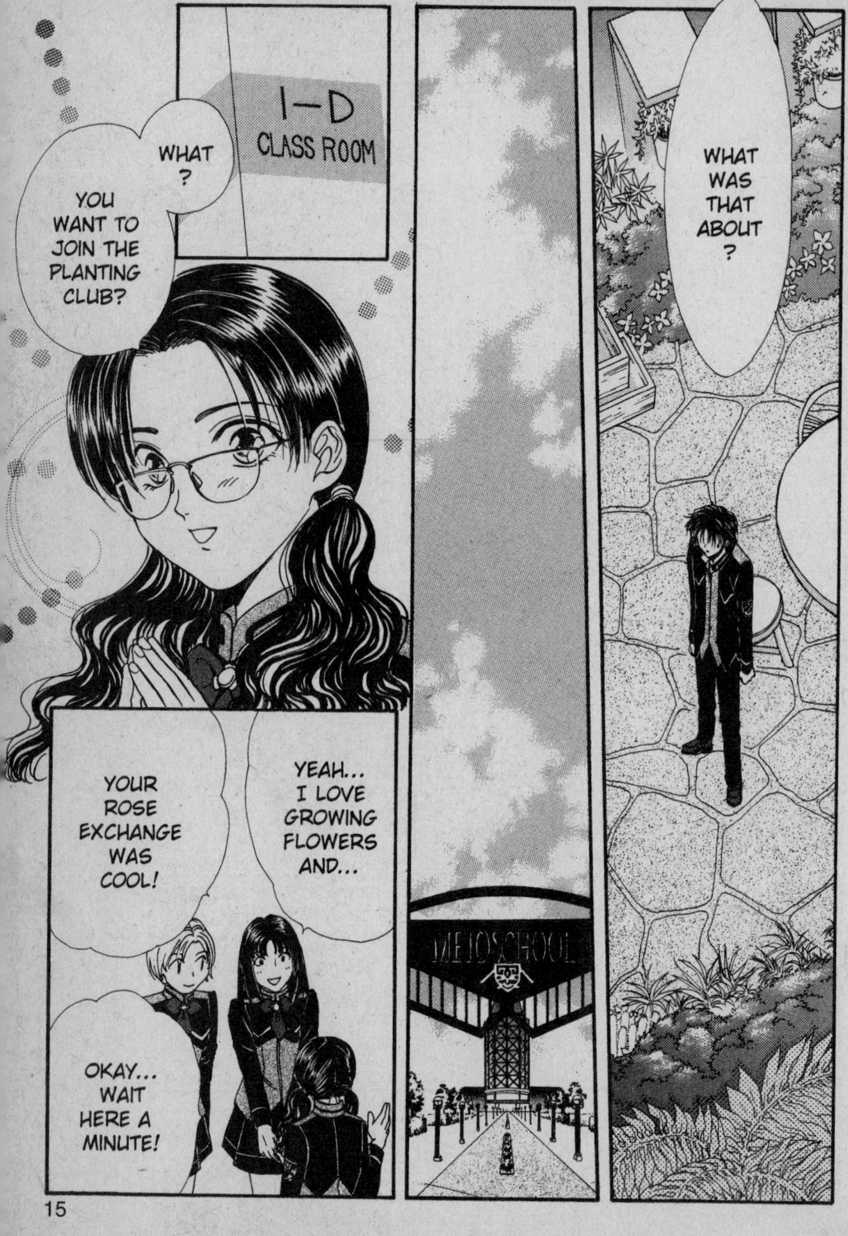
WHAT WAS THAT ABOUT?
I—D
CLASS ROOM
WHAT?
YOU WANT TO JOIN THE PLANTING CLUB?
YEAH... I LOVE GROWING FLOWERS AND...
YOUR ROSE EXCHANGE WAS COOL!
OKAY... WAIT HERE A MINUTE!

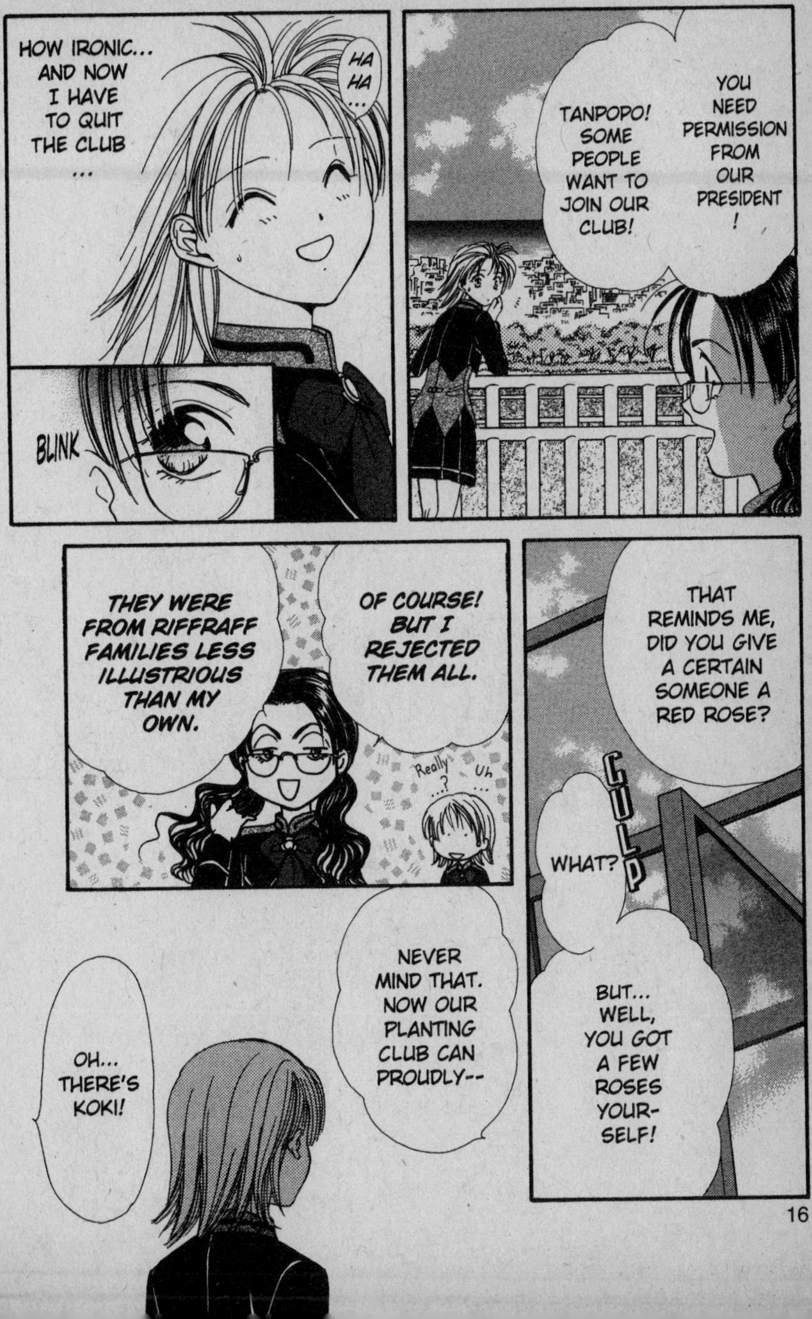
YOU NEED PERMISSION FROM OUR PRESIDENT!
TANPOPO! SOME PEOPLE WANT TO JOIN OUR CLUB!
HA HA ...
HOW IRONIC... AND NOW I HAVE TO QUIT THE CLUB ...
BLINK
THAT REMINDS ME, DID YOU GIVE A CERTAIN SOMEONE A RED ROSE?
GULP
WHAT?
BUT... WELL, YOU GOT A FEW ROSES YOURSELF!
OF COURSE! BUT I REJECTED THEM ALL.
THEY WERE FROM RIFFRAFF FAMILIES LESS ILLUSTRIOUS THAN MY OWN.
Uh ...
Really ...?
NEVER MIND THAT. NOW OUR PLANTING CLUB CAN PROUDLY--
OH... THERE'S KOKI!

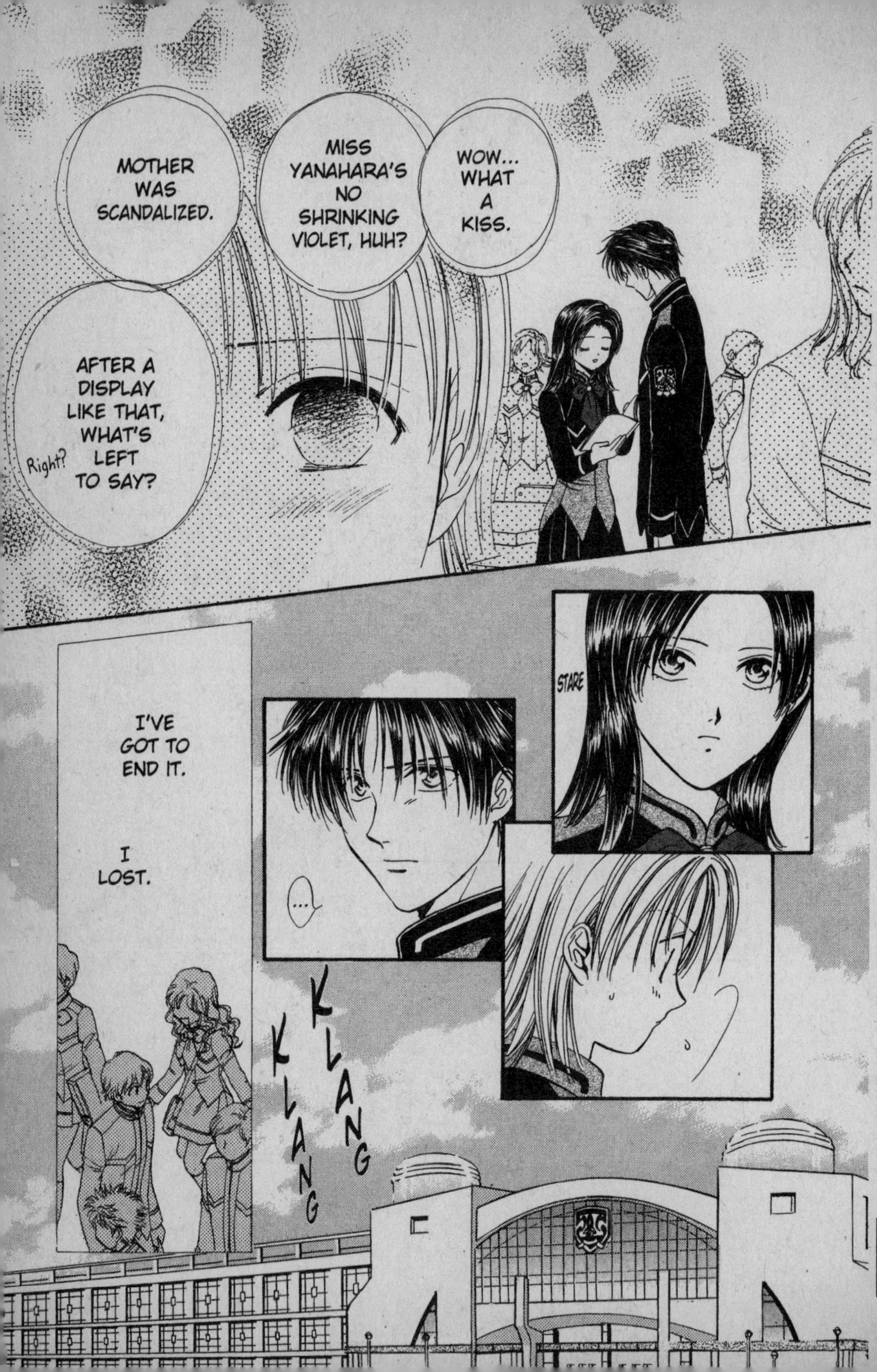
WOW... WHAT A KISS.
MISS YANAHARA'S NO SHRINKING VIOLET, HUH?
MOTHER WAS SCANDALIZED.
AFTER A DISPLAY LIKE THAT, WHAT'S LEFT TO SAY?
Right?
STARE
...
KLANG
KLANG
I'VE GOT TO END IT.
I LOST.

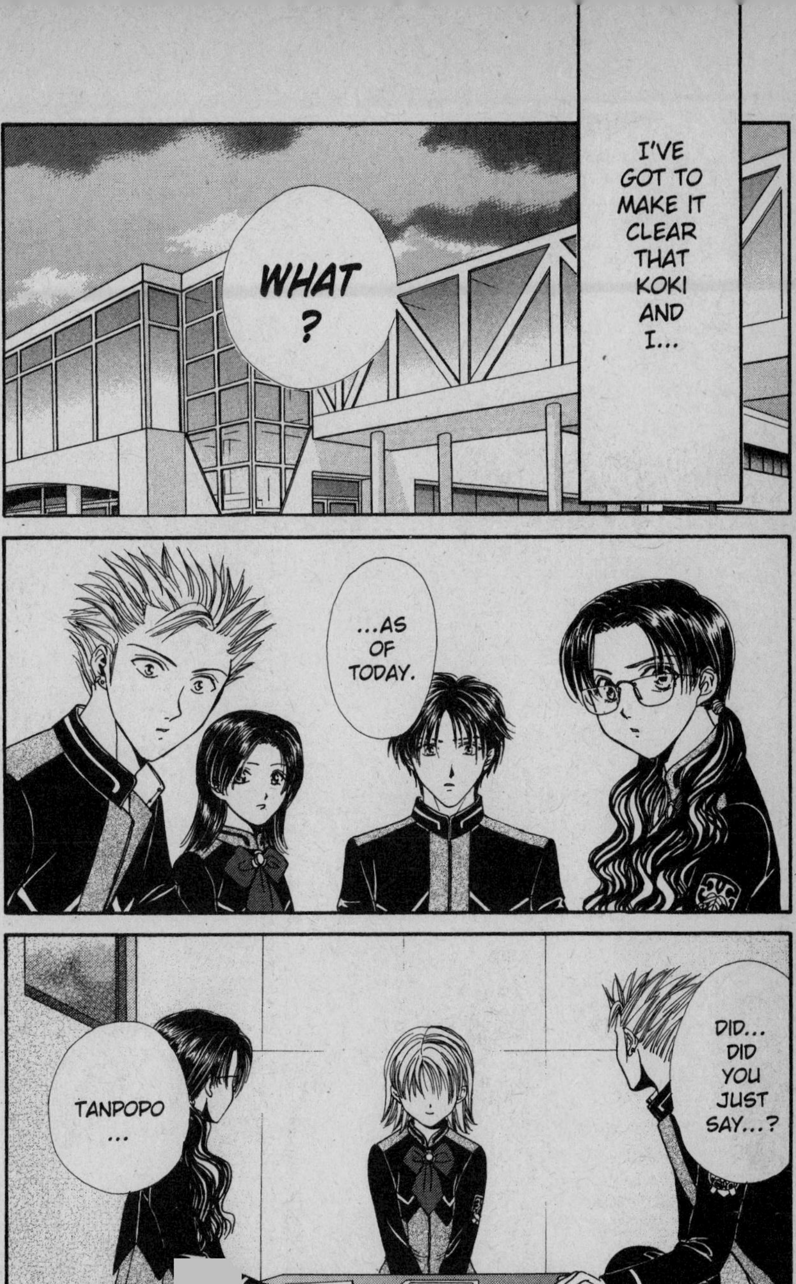
I'VE GOT TO MAKE IT CLEAR THAT KOKI AND I...
WHAT?
...AS OF TODAY.
DID... DID YOU JUST SAY...?
TANPOPO...

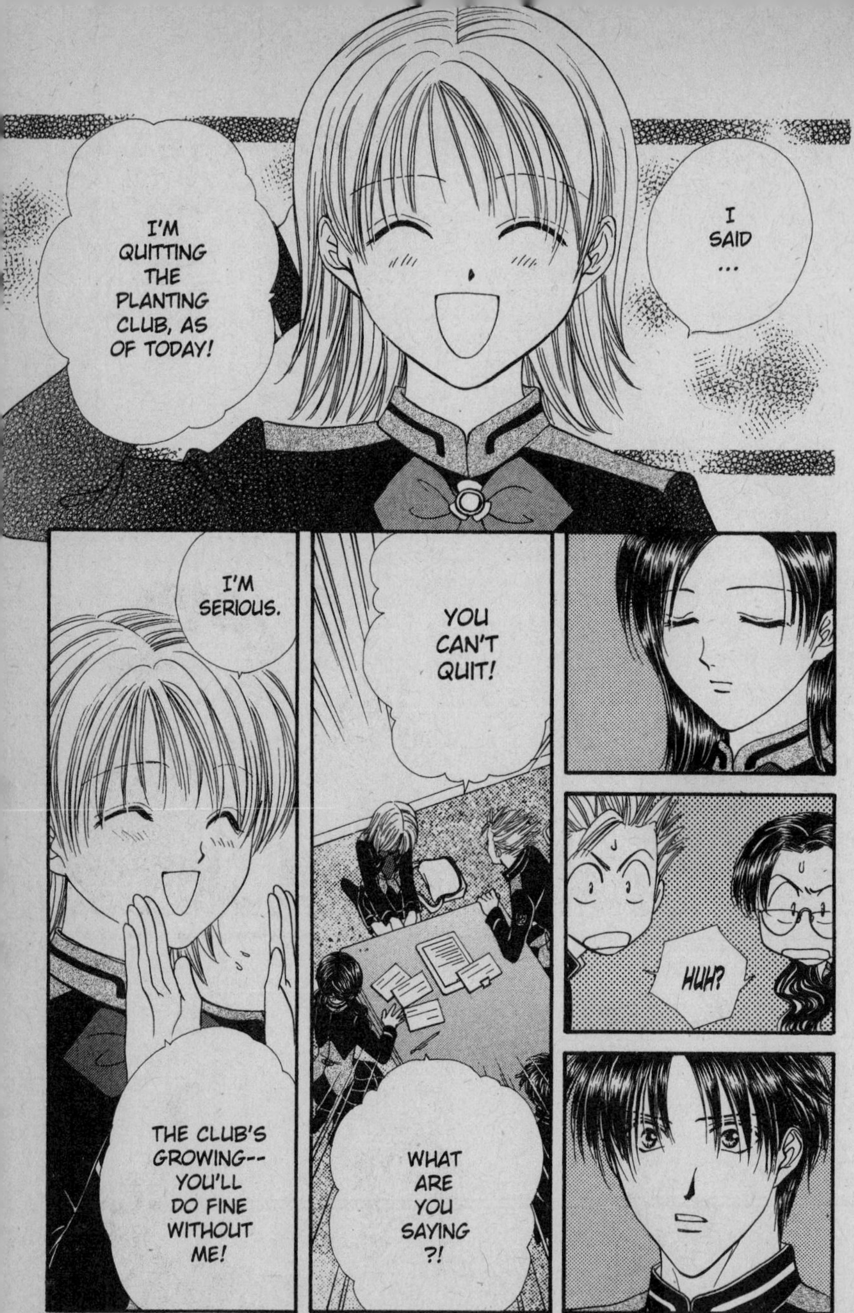

I SAID ...
I'M QUITTING THE PLANTING CLUB, AS OF TODAY!
HUH?
YOU CAN'T QUIT!
WHAT ARE YOU SAYING ?!
I'M SERIOUS.
THE CLUB'S GROWING-- YOU'LL DO FINE WITHOUT ME!

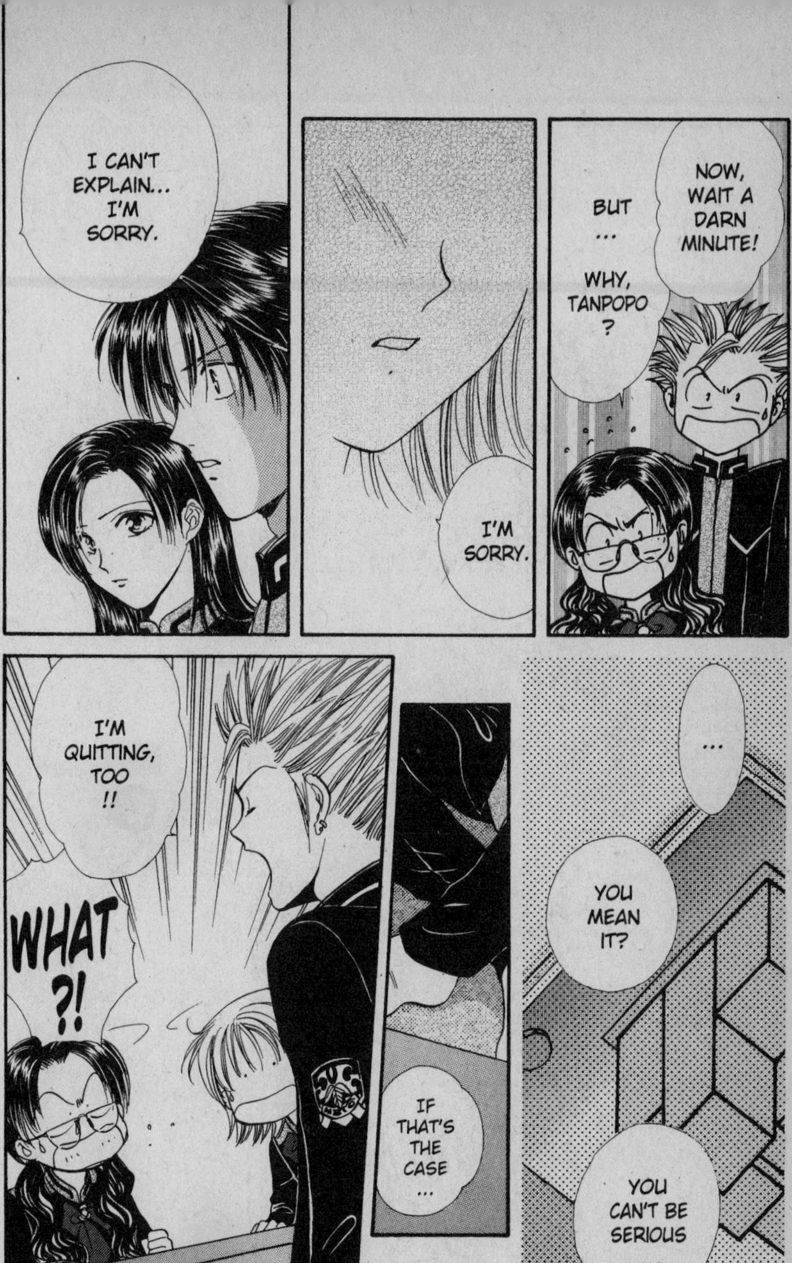
NOW, WAIT A DARN MINUTE!
BUT ... WHY, TANPOPO ?
I'M SORRY.
I CAN'T EXPLAIN... I'M SORRY.
...
YOU MEAN IT?
YOU CAN'T BE SERIOUS ...
IF THAT'S THE CASE ...
I'M QUITTING, TOO !!
WHAT ?!

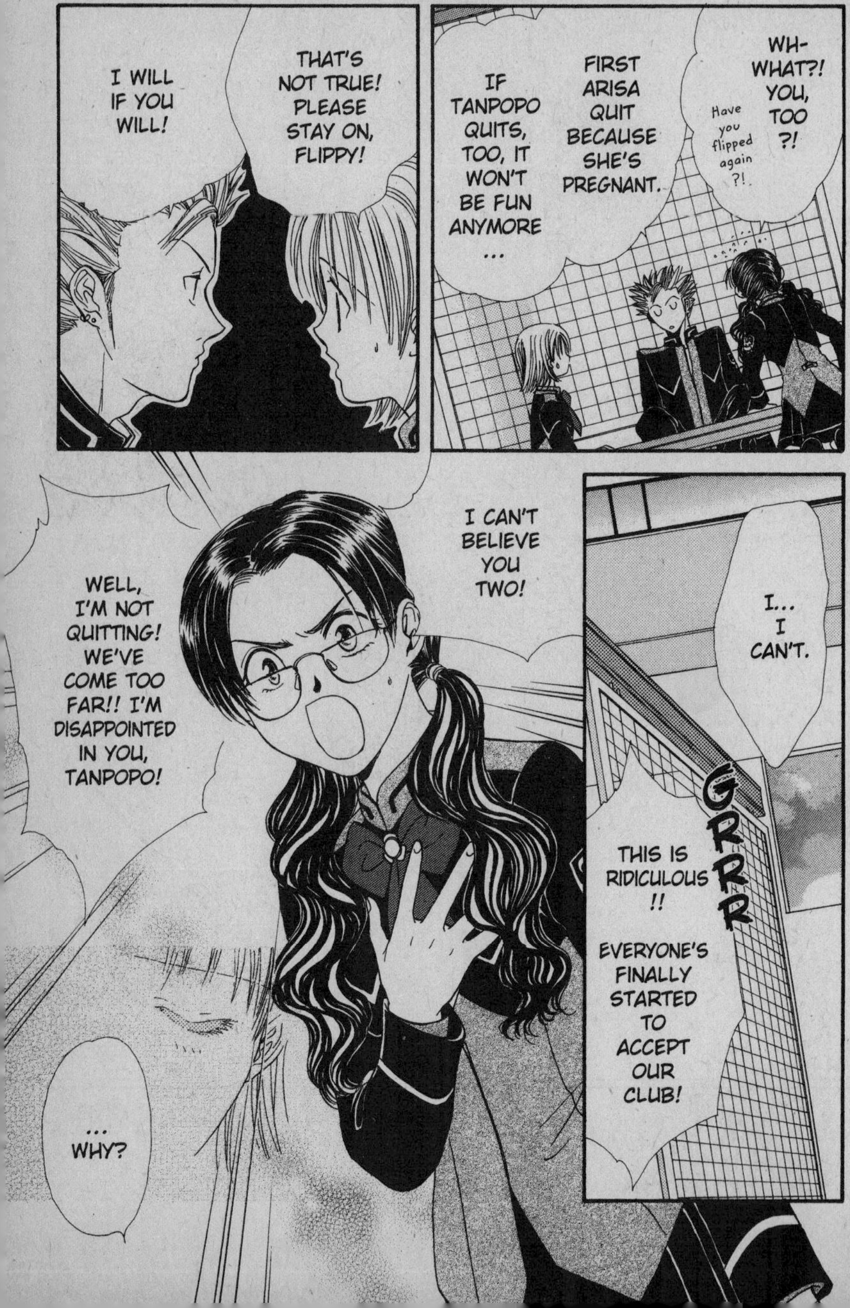
WH- WHAT?! YOU, TOO ?!
Have you flipped again ?!
FIRST ARISA QUIT BECAUSE SHE'S PREGNANT.
IF TANPOPO QUITS, TOO, IT WON'T BE FUN ANYMORE ...
THAT'S NOT TRUE! PLEASE STAY ON, FLIPPY!
I WILL IF YOU WILL!
I... I CAN'T.
GRRR
THIS IS RIDICULOUS !!
EVERYONE'S FINALLY STARTED TO ACCEPT OUR CLUB!
I CAN'T BELIEVE YOU TWO!
WELL, I'M NOT QUITTING! WE'VE COME TOO FAR!! I'M DISAPPOINTED IN YOU, TANPOPO!
... WHY?

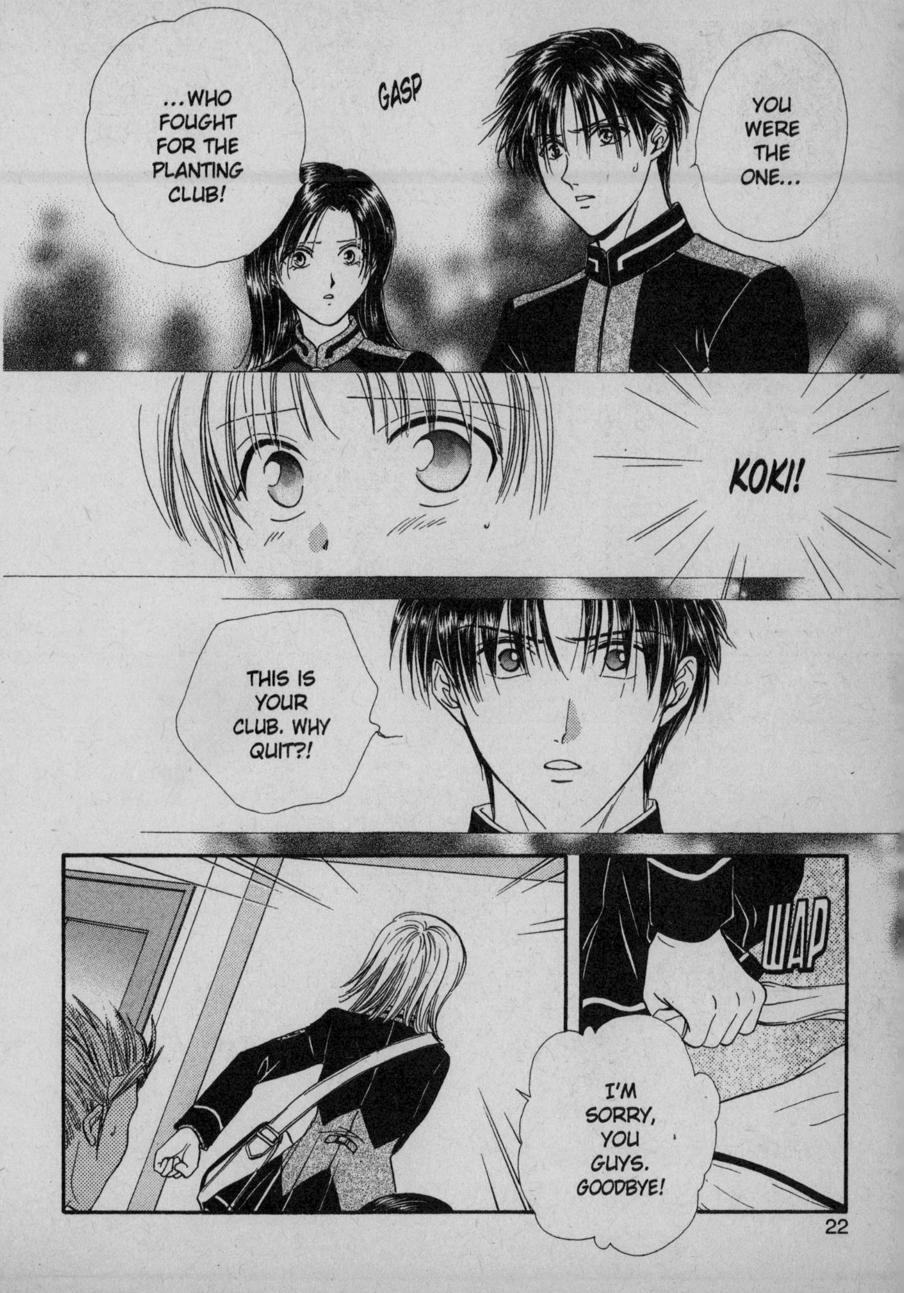
YOU WERE THE ONE...
GASP
...WHO FOUGHT FOR THE PLANTING CLUB!
KOKI!
THIS IS YOUR CLUB. WHY QUIT?!
WAP
I'M SORRY, YOU GUYS. GOODBYE!

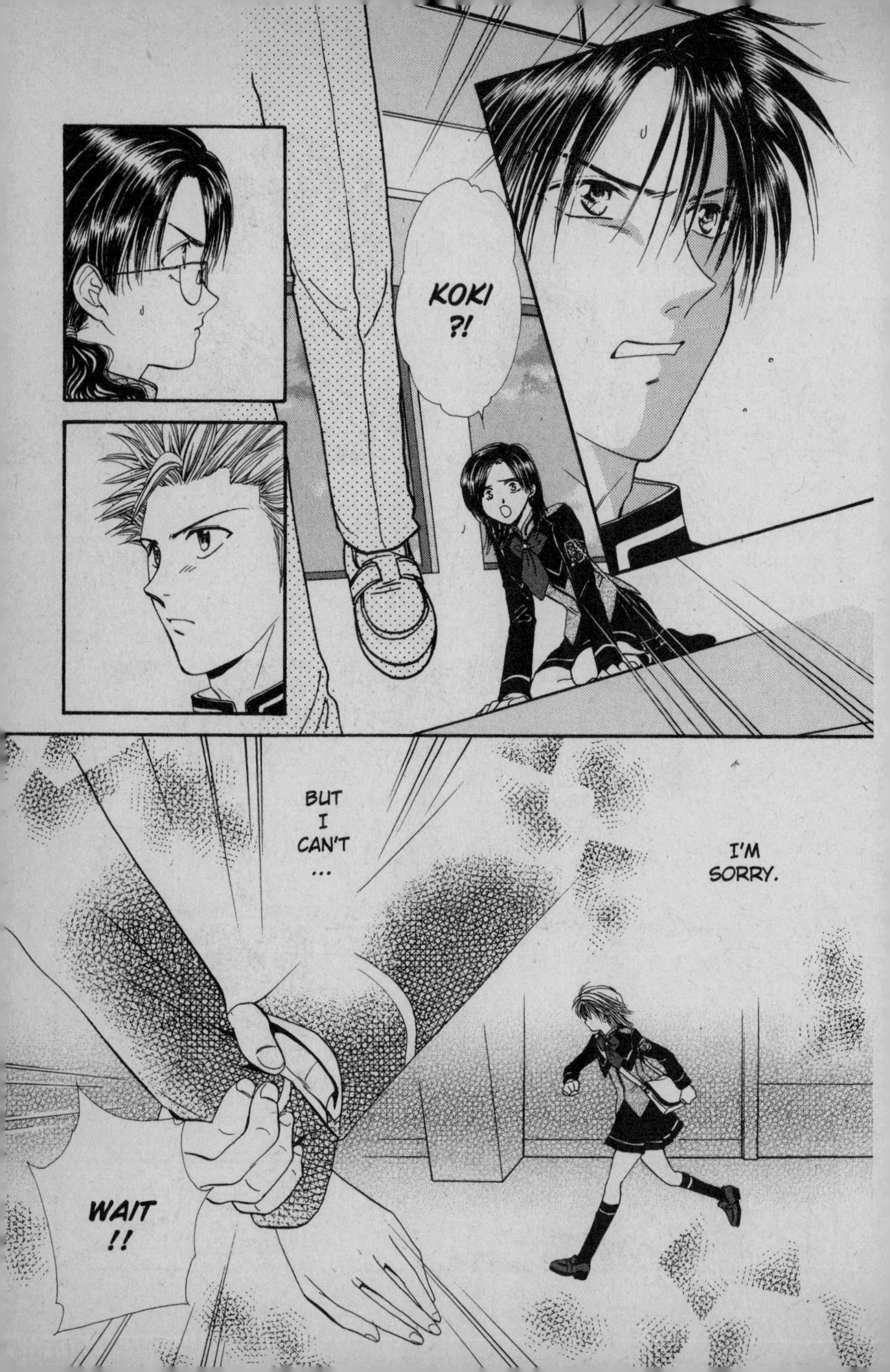
KOKI ?!
I'M SORRY.
BUT I CAN'T ...
WAIT !!

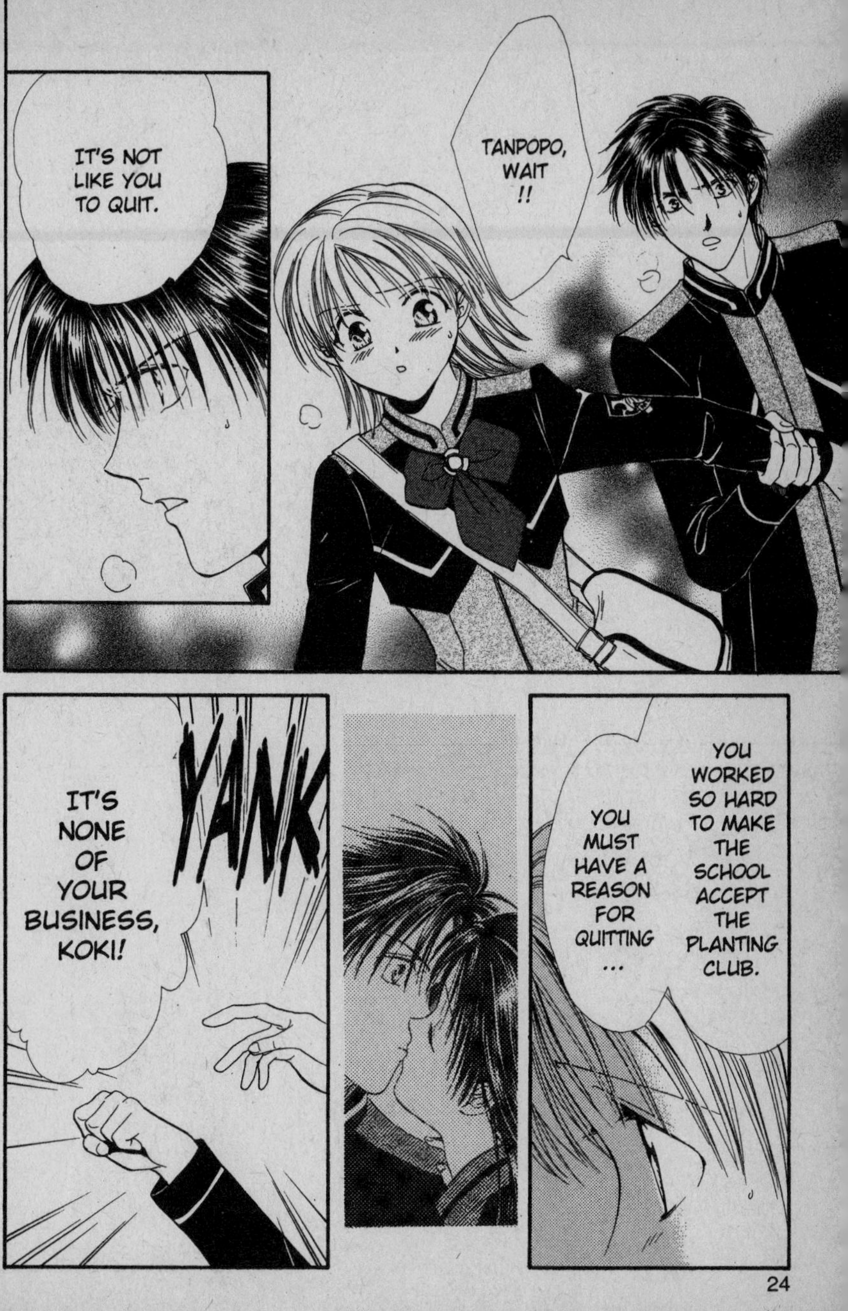
TANPOPO, WAIT !!
IT'S NOT LIKE YOU TO QUIT.
YOU WORKED SO HARD TO MAKE THE SCHOOL ACCEPT THE PLANTING CLUB.
YOU MUST HAVE A REASON FOR QUITTING ...
YANK
IT'S NONE OF YOUR BUSINESS, KOKI!

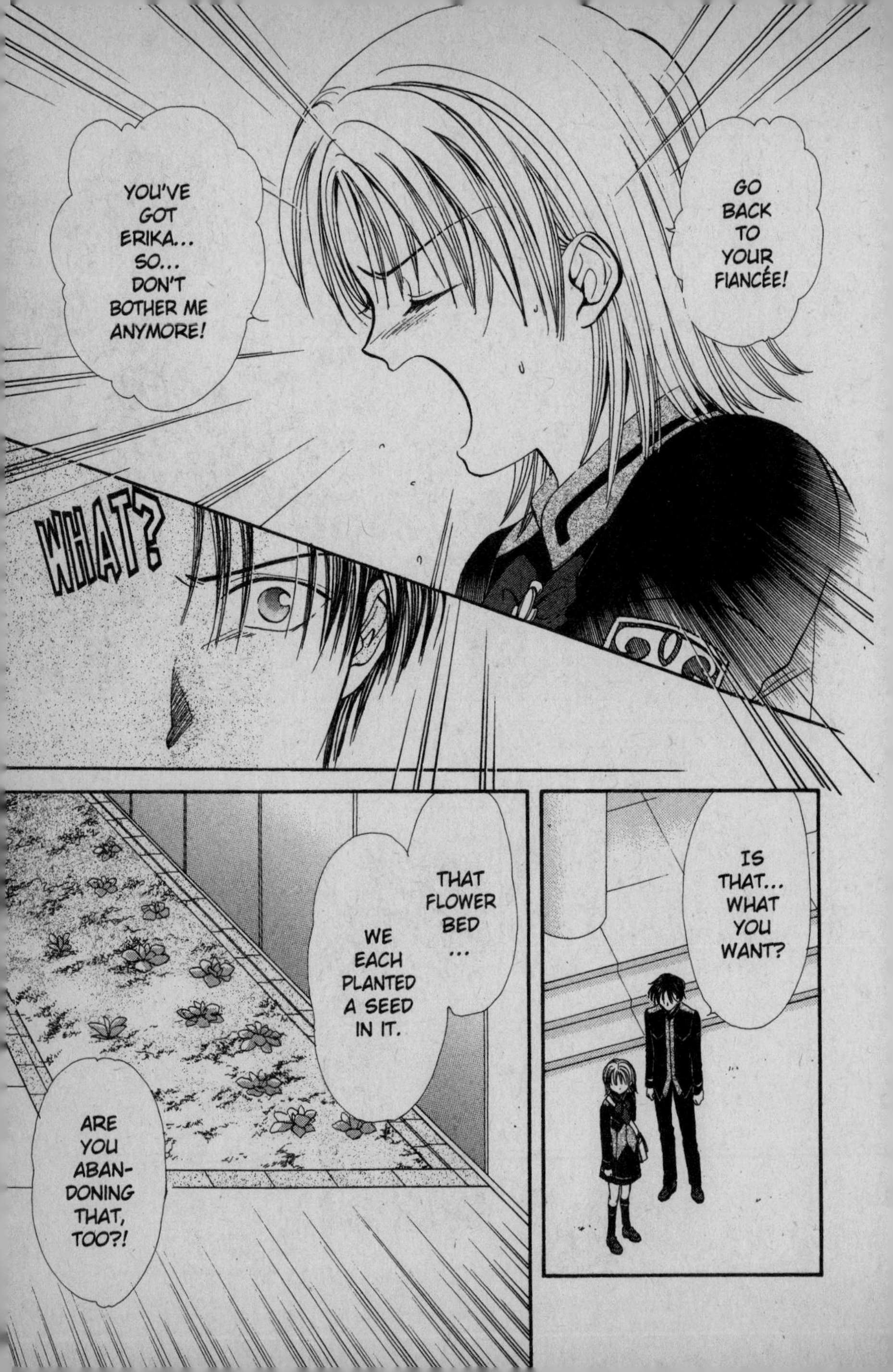
GO BACK TO YOUR FIANCÉE!
YOU'VE GOT ERIKA... SO... DON'T BOTHER ME ANYMORE!
WHAT?
IS THAT... WHAT YOU WANT?
...
THAT FLOWER BED ...
WE EACH PLANTED A SEED IN IT.
ARE YOU ABANDONING THAT, TOO?!

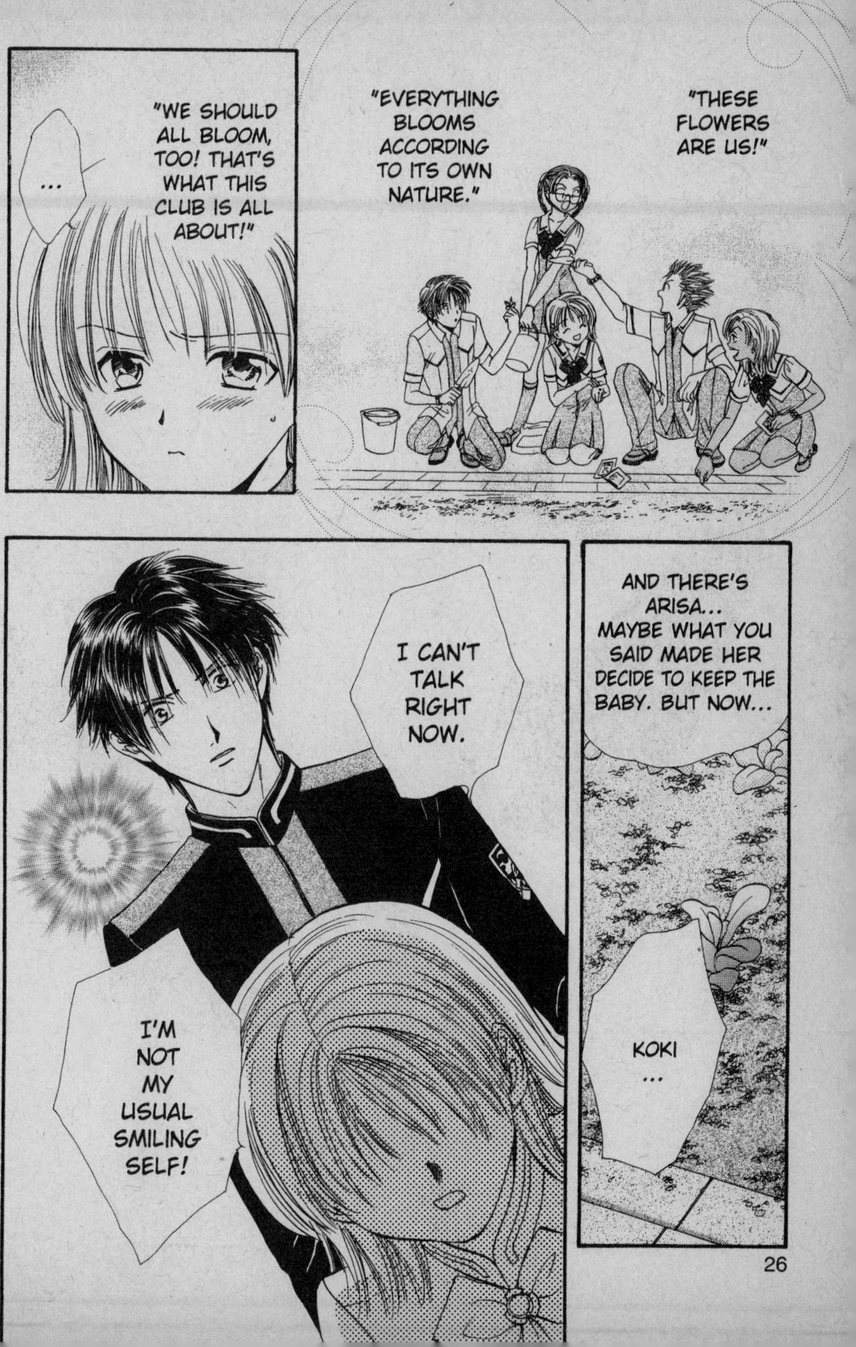
"THESE FLOWERS ARE US!"
"EVERYTHING BLOOMS ACCORDING TO ITS OWN NATURE."
"WE SHOULD ALL BLOOM, TOO! THAT'S WHAT THIS CLUB IS ALL ABOUT!"
...
AND THERE'S ARISA... MAYBE WHAT YOU SAID MADE HER DECIDE TO KEEP THE BABY. BUT NOW...
KOKI ...
I CAN'T TALK RIGHT NOW.
I'M NOT MY USUAL SMILING SELF!

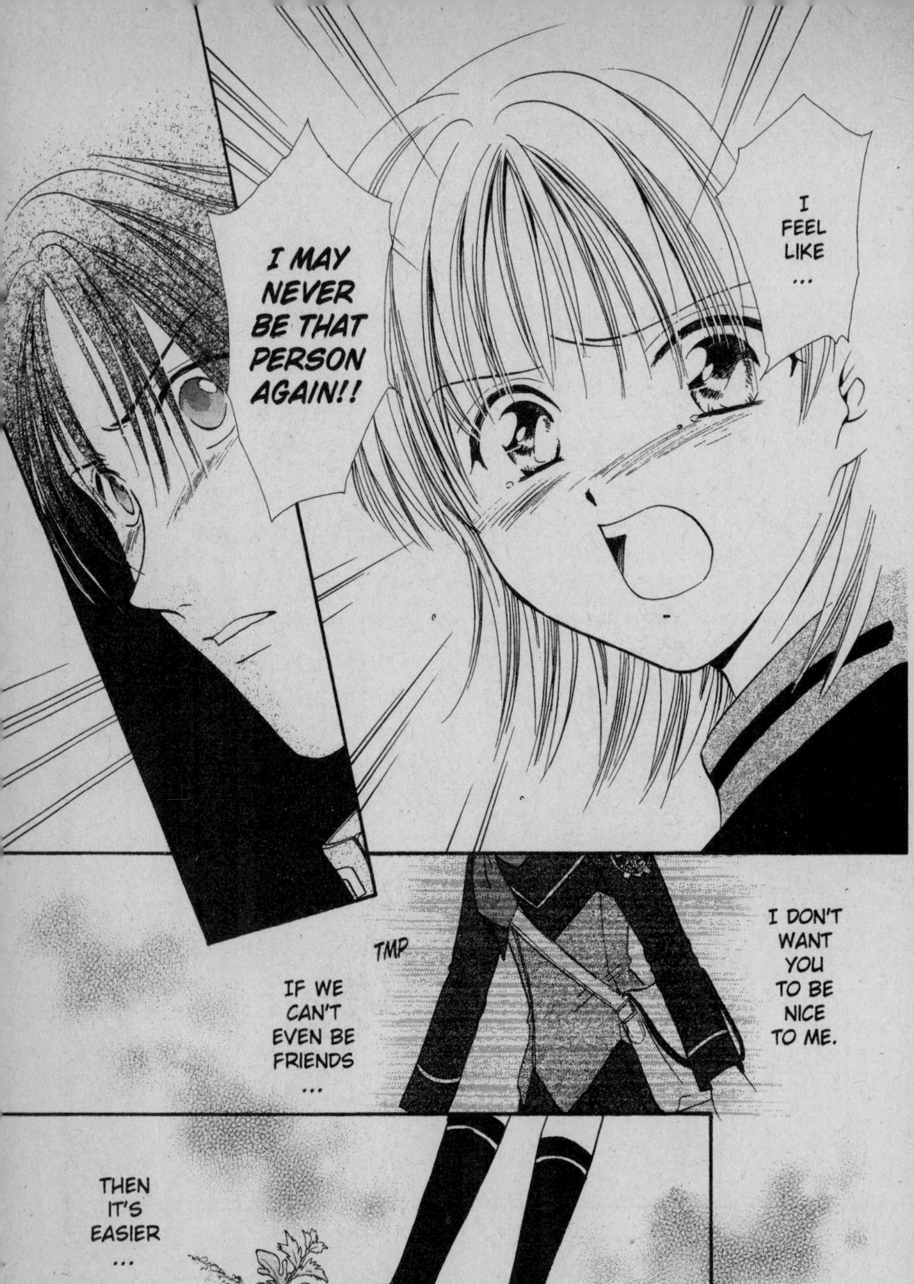
I FEEL LIKE ...
I MAY NEVER BE THAT PERSON AGAIN!!
I DON'T WANT YOU TO BE NICE TO ME.
TMP
IF WE CAN'T EVEN BE FRIENDS ...
THEN IT'S EASIER ...

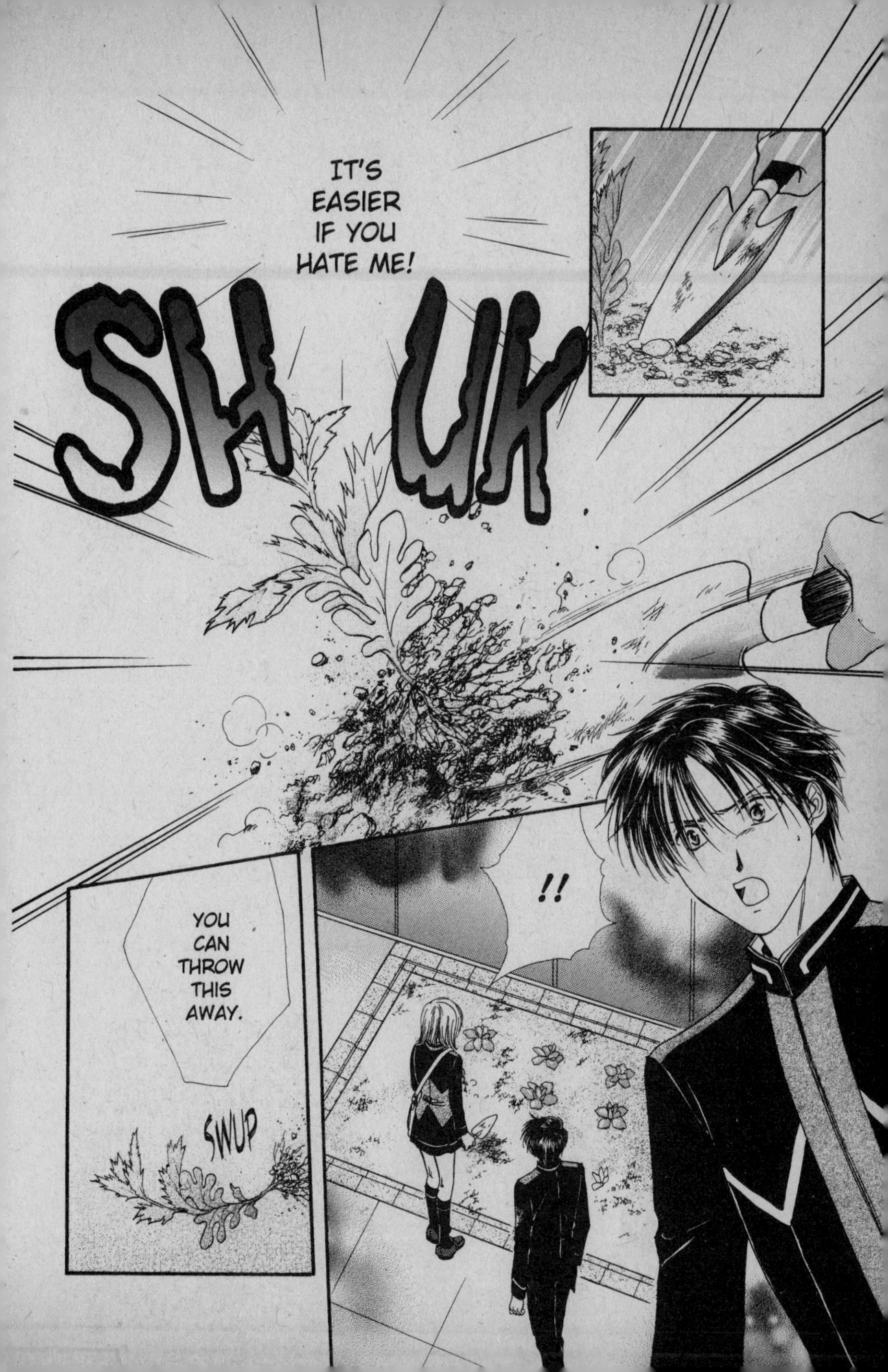
IT'S EASIER IF YOU HATE ME!
SH UK
!!
YOU CAN THROW THIS AWAY.
SWUP

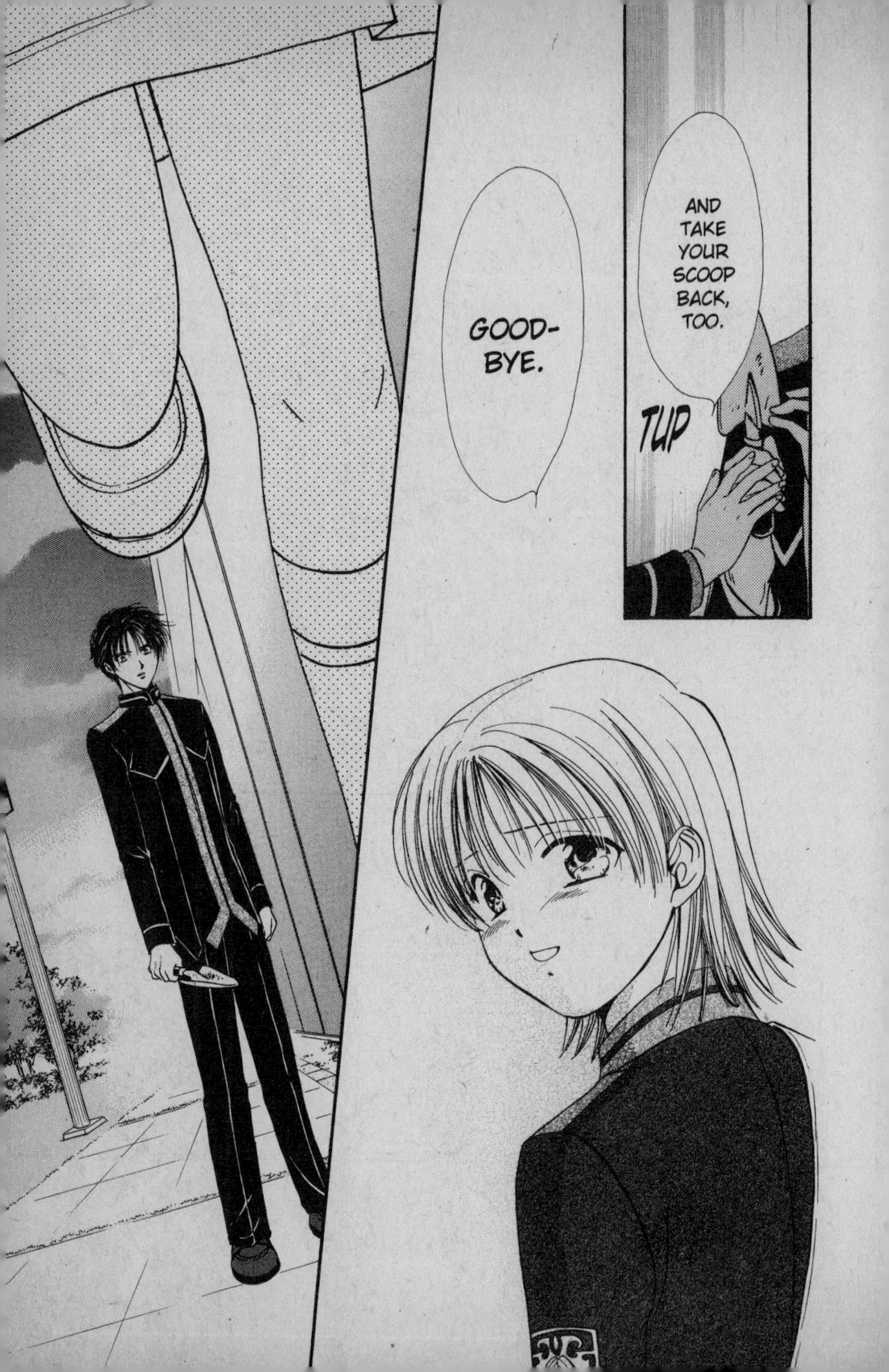
AND TAKE YOUR SCOOP BACK, TOO.
TUP
GOOD-BYE.

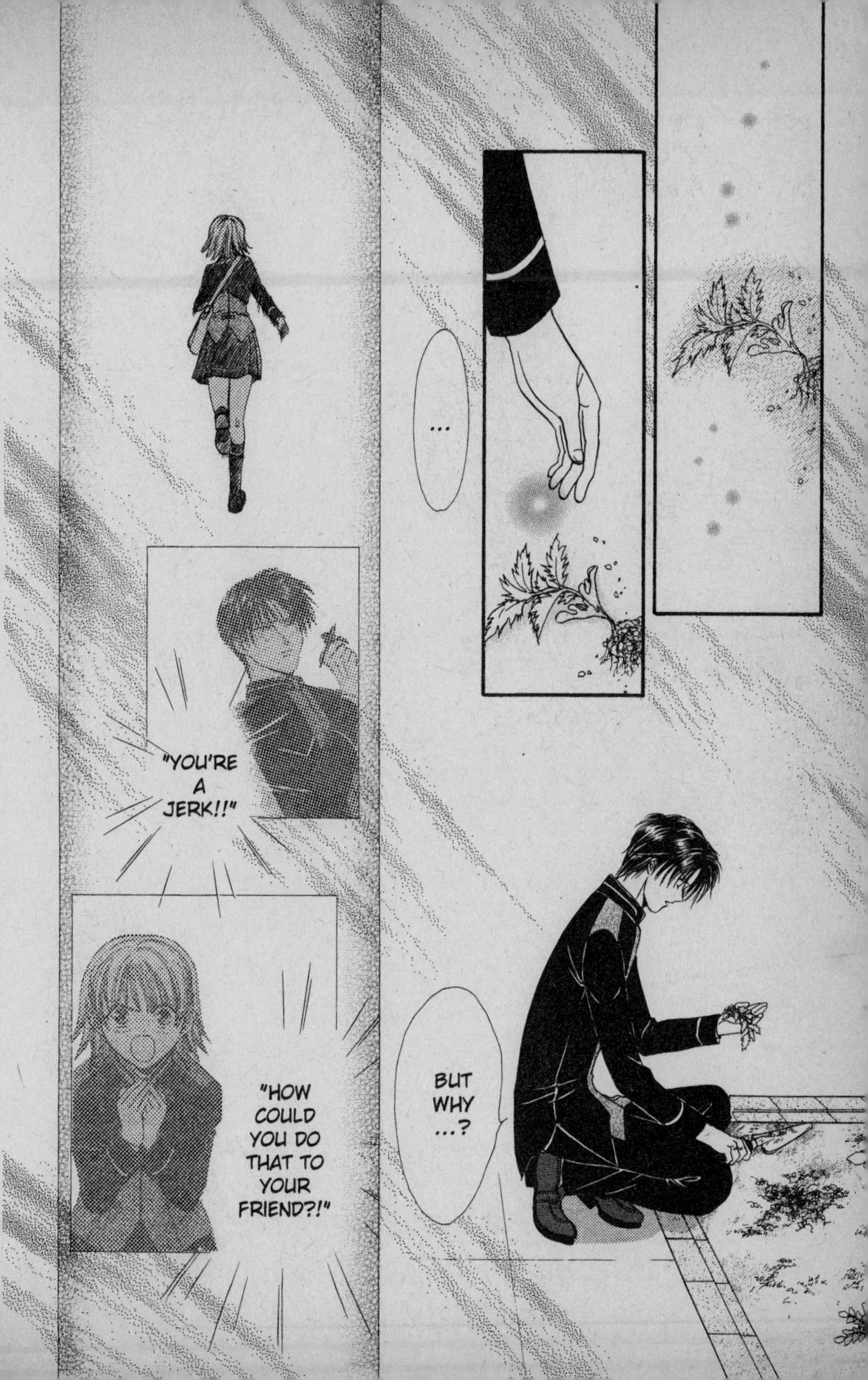
...
BUT WHY ...?
"YOU'RE A JERK!!"
"HOW COULD YOU DO THAT TO YOUR FRIEND?!"

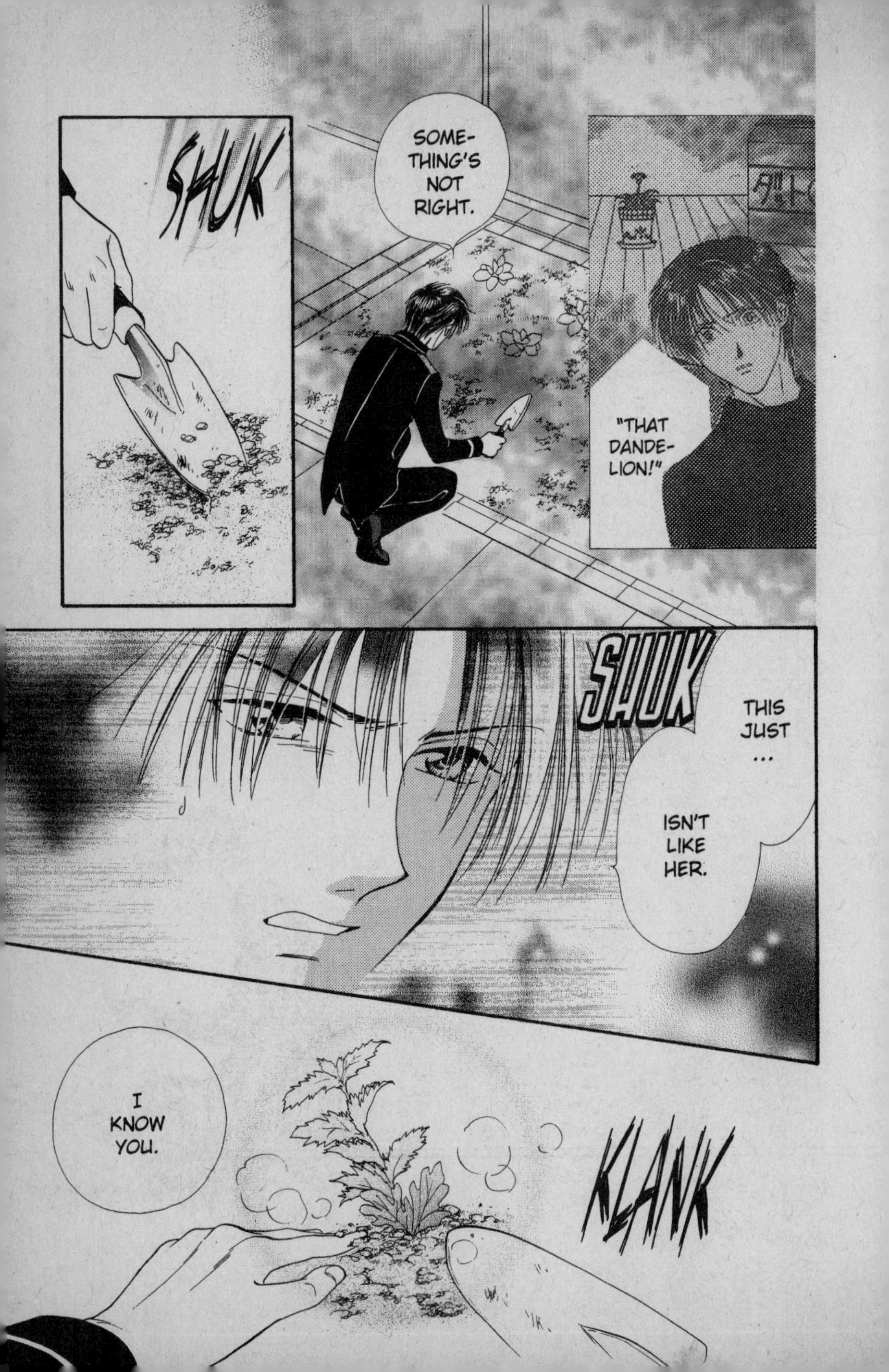
"THAT DANDELION!"
SOME-THING'S NOT RIGHT.
SHUK
SHUK
THIS JUST ...
ISN'T LIKE HER.
KLANK
I KNOW YOU.

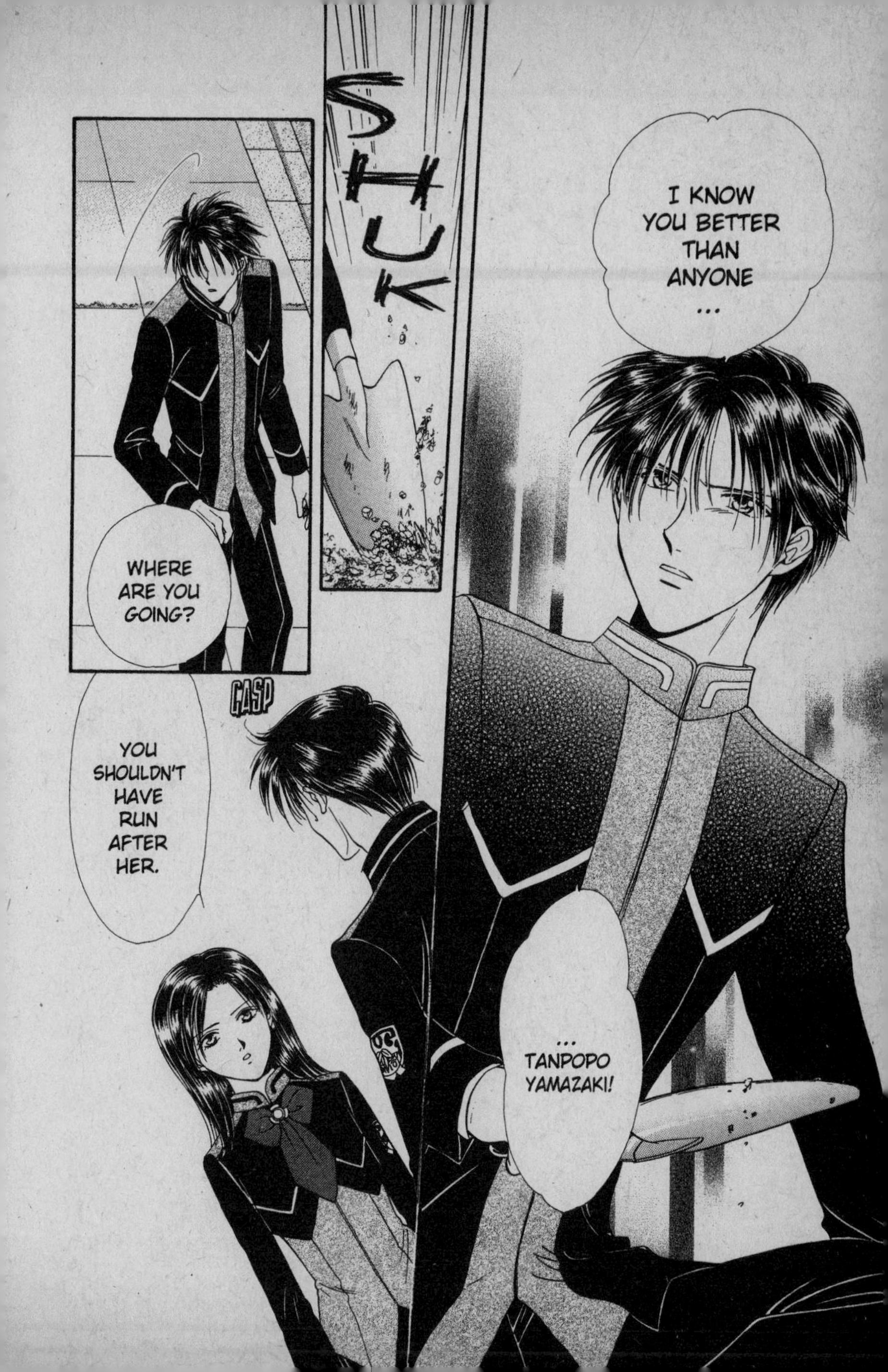
I KNOW YOU BETTER THAN ANYONE ...
... TANPOPO YAMAZAKI!
SHUK
WHERE ARE YOU GOING?
GASP
YOU SHOULDN'T HAVE RUN AFTER HER.

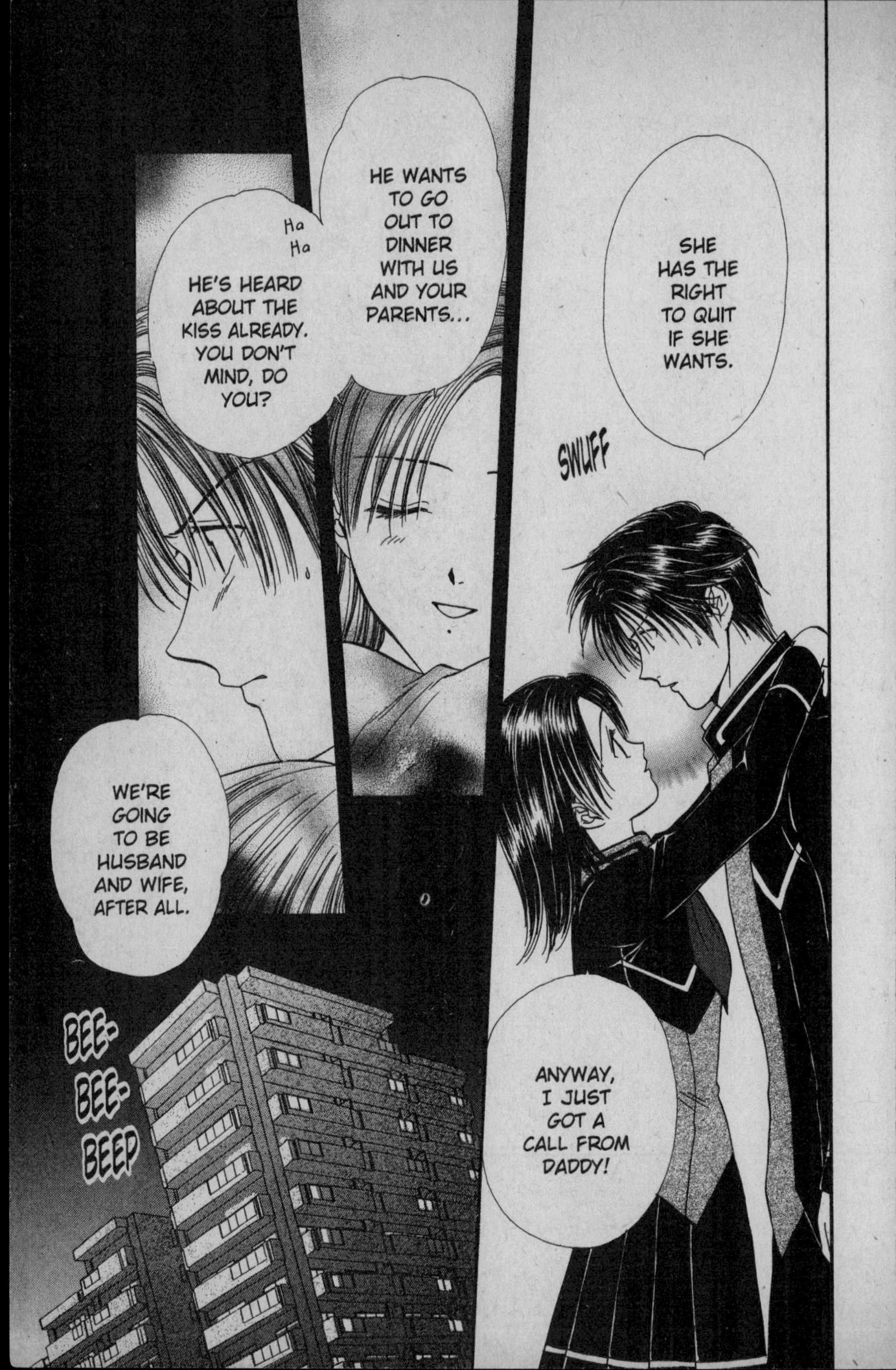
SHE HAS THE RIGHT TO QUIT IF SHE WANTS.
SWUFF
ANYWAY, I JUST GOT A CALL FROM DADDY!
HE WANTS TO GO OUT TO DINNER WITH US AND YOUR PARENTS...
Ha Ha
HE'S HEARD ABOUT THE KISS ALREADY. YOU DON'T MIND, DO YOU?
WE'RE GOING TO BE HUSBAND AND WIFE, AFTER ALL.
BEE- BEE- BEEP

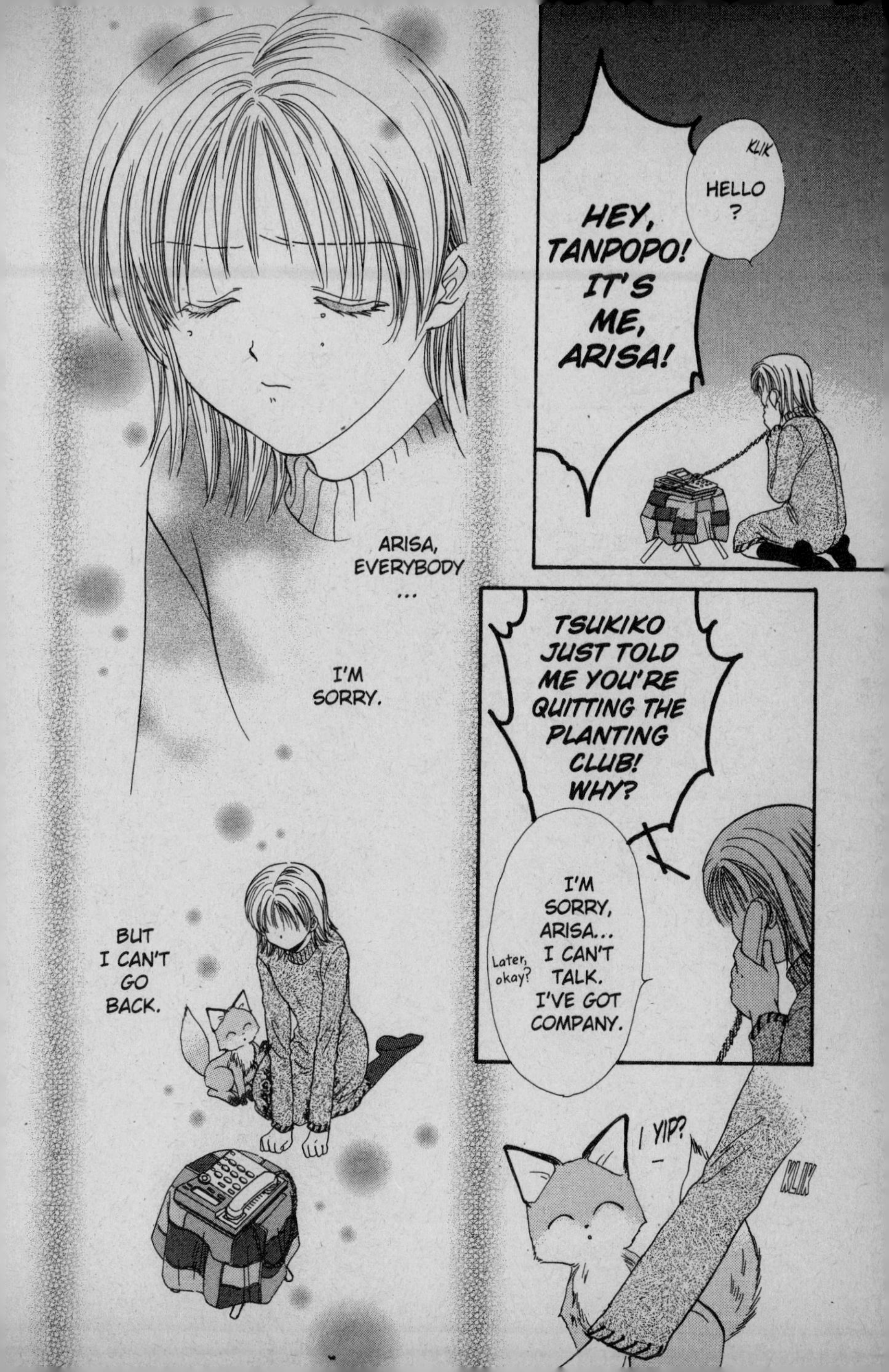

KLIK
HELLO ?
HEY, TANPOPO! IT'S ME, ARISA!
TSUKIKO JUST TOLD ME YOU'RE QUITTING THE PLANTING CLUB! WHY?
I'M SORRY, ARISA... I CAN'T TALK. I'VE GOT COMPANY.
Later, okay?
KLIK
YIP?
ARISA, EVERYBODY ...
I'M SORRY.
BUT I CAN'T GO BACK.

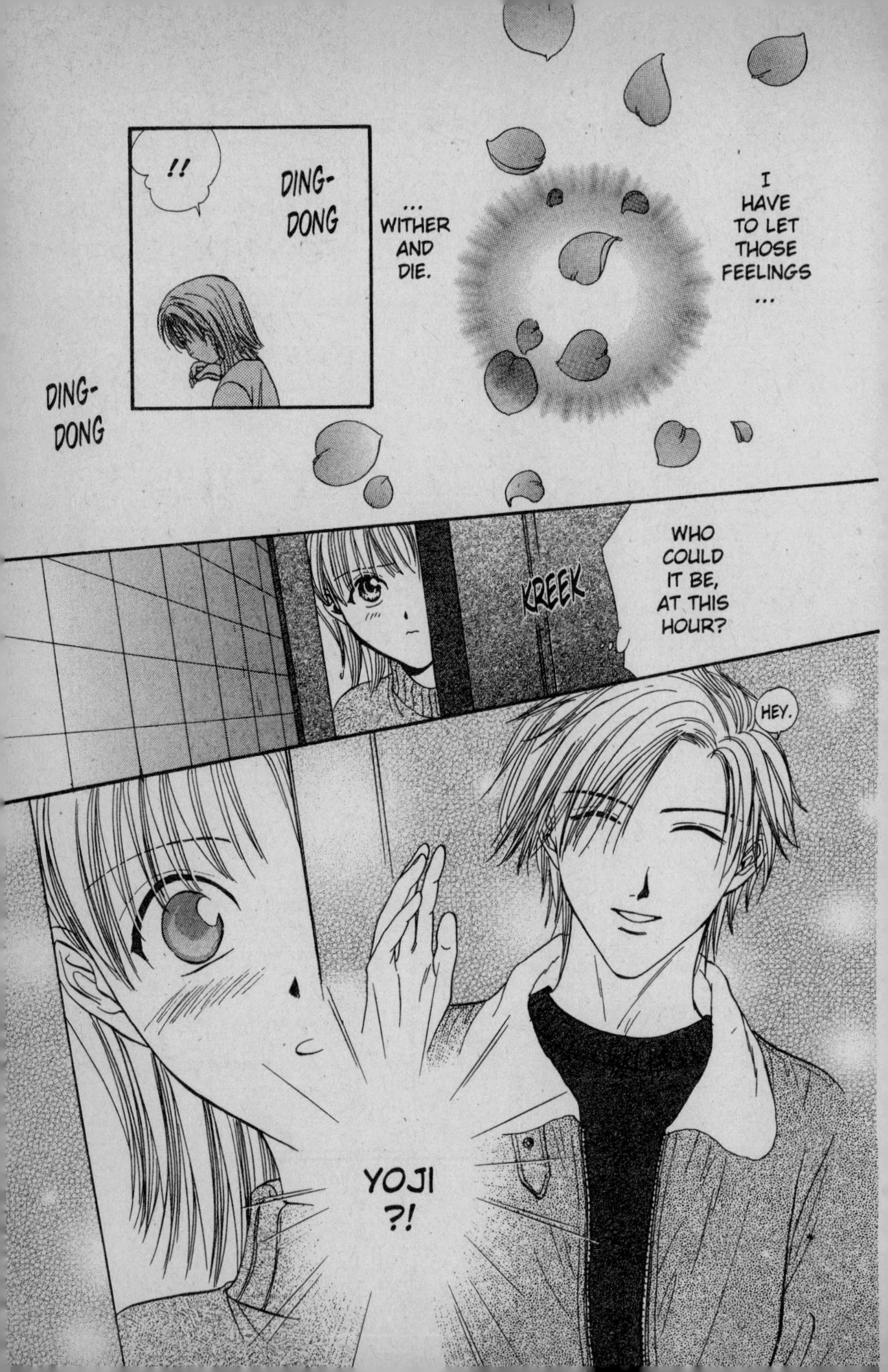
I HAVE TO LET THOSE FEELINGS...
...WITHER AND DIE.
DING-DONG
!!
DING-DONG
WHO COULD IT BE, AT THIS HOUR?
KREEK
HEY.
YOJI ?!

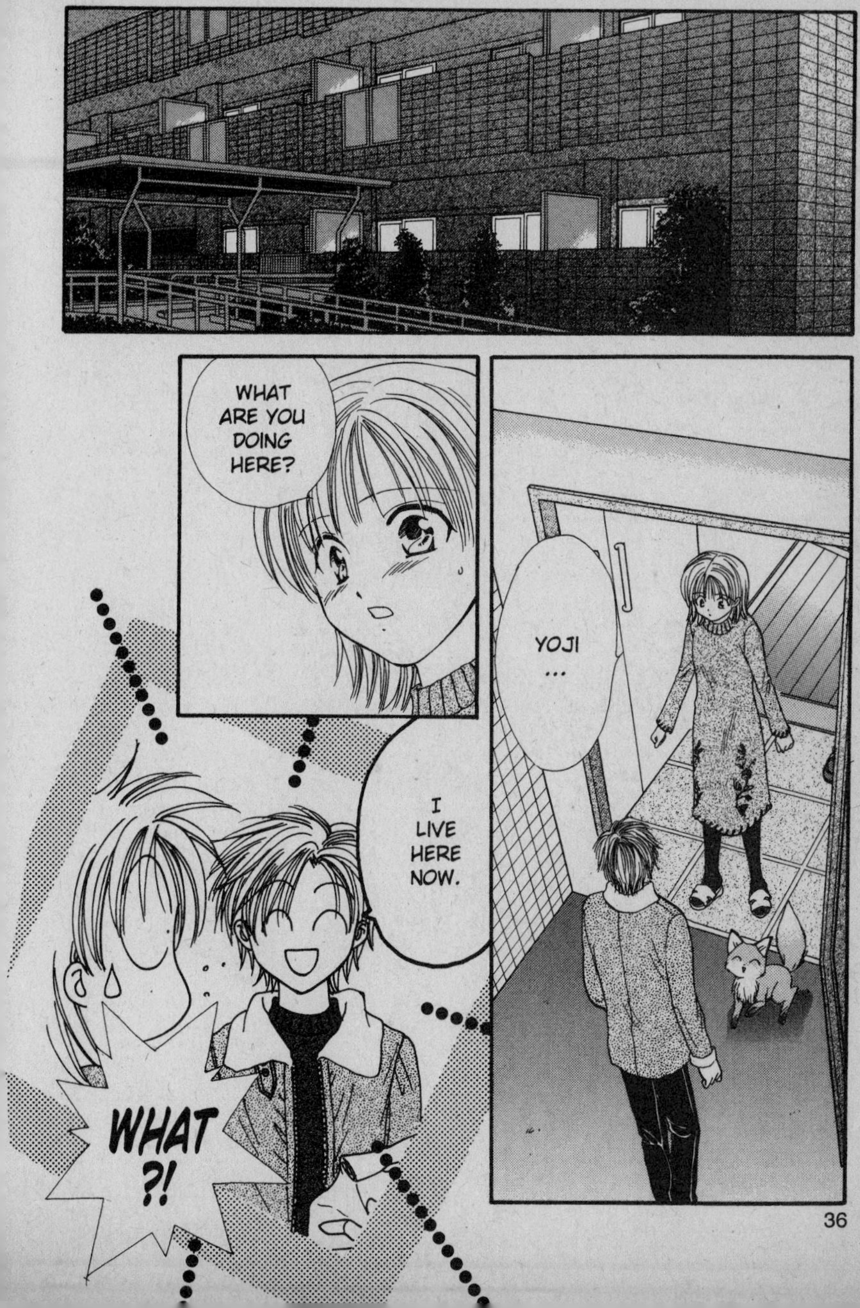
YOJI ...
WHAT ARE YOU DOING HERE?
I LIVE HERE NOW.
WHAT ?!

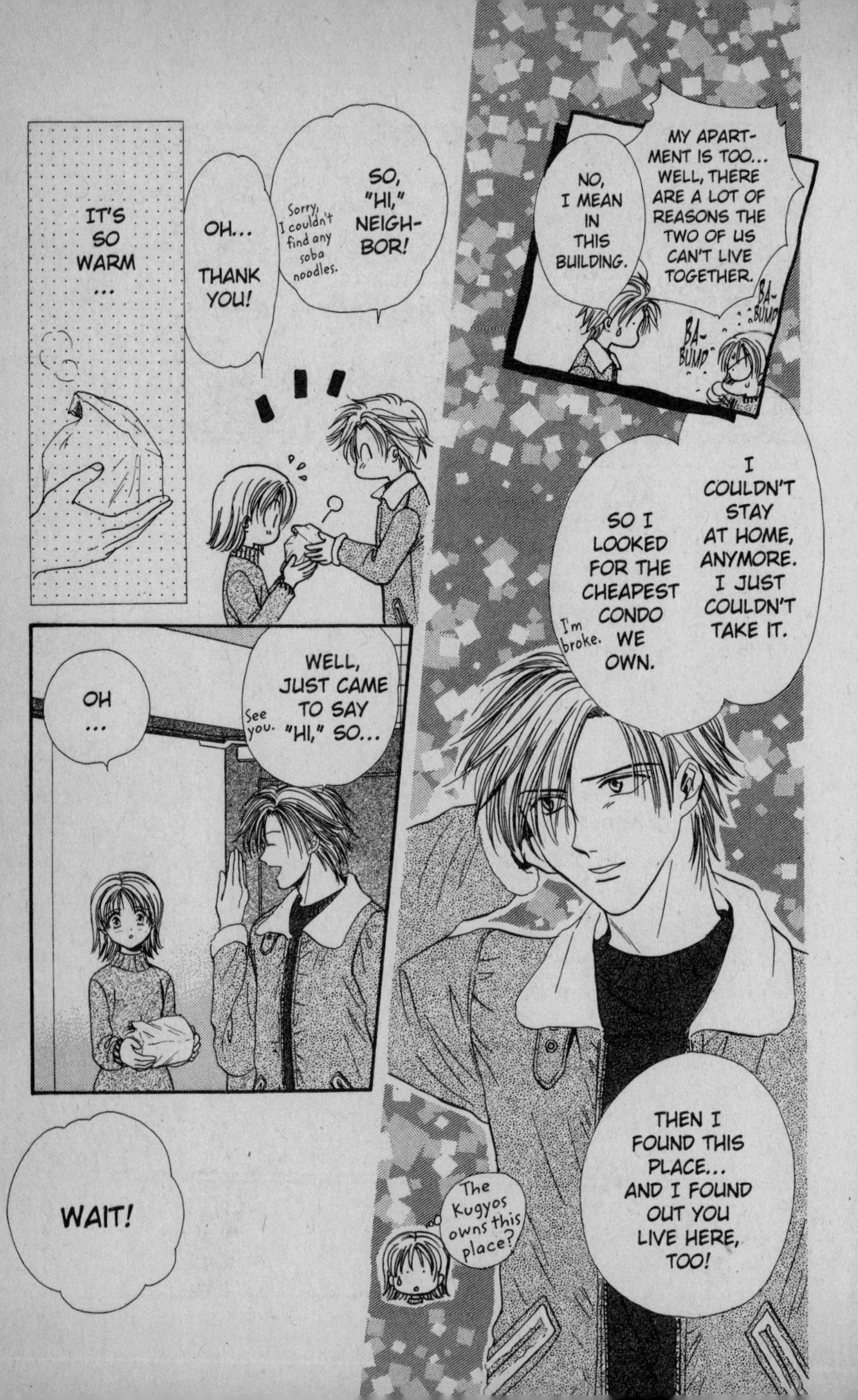
MY APARTMENT IS TOO... WELL, THERE ARE A LOT OF REASONS THE TWO OF US CAN'T LIVE TOGETHER.
NO, I MEAN IN THIS BUILDING.
BA-BUMP
BA-BUMP
I COULDN'T STAY AT HOME, ANYMORE. I JUST COULDN'T TAKE IT.
SO I LOOKED FOR THE CHEAPEST CONDO WE OWN.
I'm broke.
THEN I FOUND THIS PLACE... AND I FOUND OUT YOU LIVE HERE, TOO!
The Kugyos owns this place?
SO, "HI," NEIGHBOR!
Sorry, I couldn't find any soba noodles.
OH... THANK YOU!
IT'S SO WARM ...
WELL, JUST CAME TO SAY "HI," SO...
See you.
OH ...
WAIT!

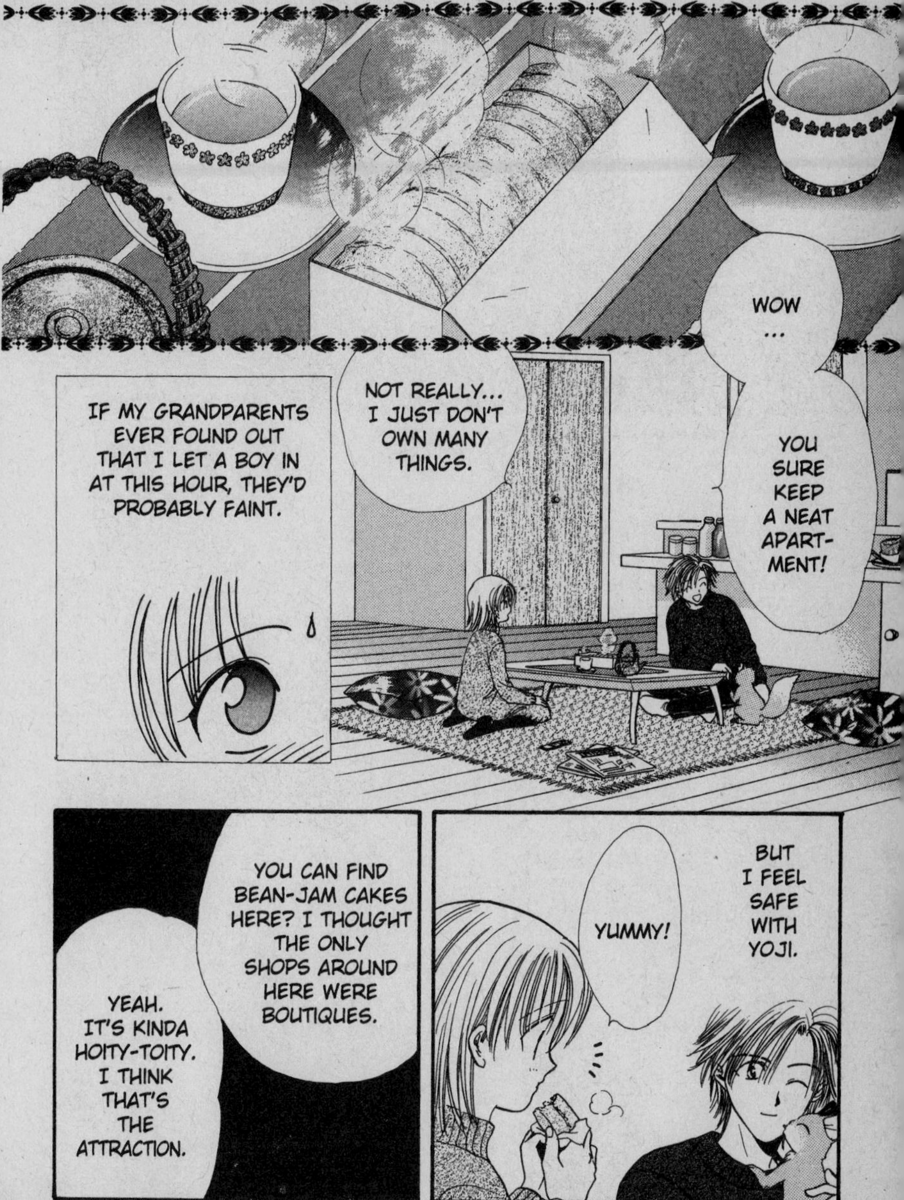
WOW ...
YOU SURE KEEP A NEAT APART-MENT!
NOT REALLY... I JUST DON'T OWN MANY THINGS.
IF MY GRANDPARENTS EVER FOUND OUT THAT I LET A BOY IN AT THIS HOUR, THEY'D PROBABLY FAINT.
BUT I FEEL SAFE WITH YOJI.
YUMMY!
YOU CAN FIND BEAN-JAM CAKES HERE? I THOUGHT THE ONLY SHOPS AROUND HERE WERE BOUTIQUES.
YEAH. IT'S KINDA HOITY-TOITY. I THINK THAT'S THE ATTRACTION.

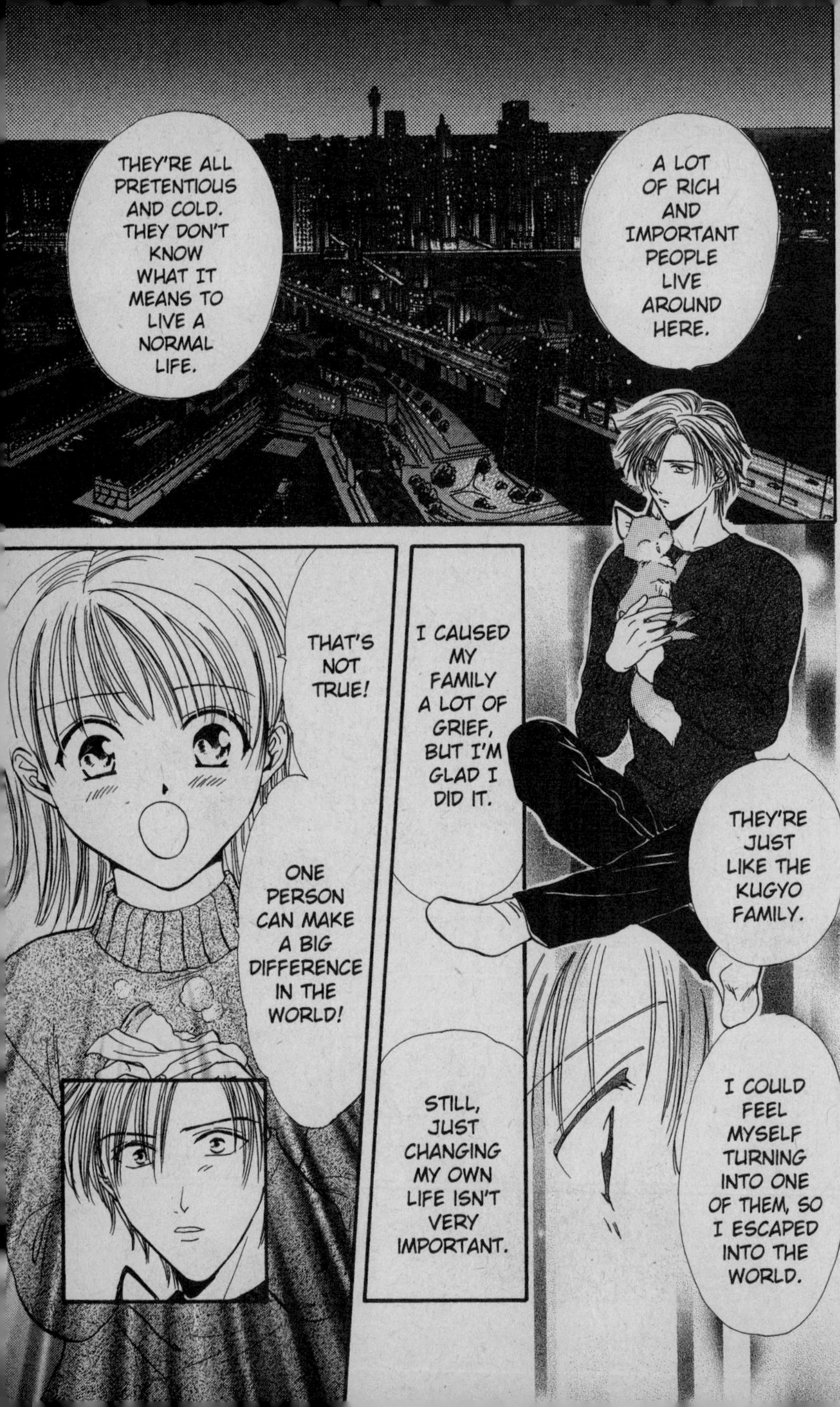
A LOT OF RICH AND IMPORTANT PEOPLE LIVE AROUND HERE.
THEY'RE ALL PRETENTIOUS AND COLD. THEY DON'T KNOW WHAT IT MEANS TO LIVE A NORMAL LIFE.
THEY'RE JUST LIKE THE KUGYO FAMILY.
I COULD FEEL MYSELF TURNING INTO ONE OF THEM, SO I ESCAPED INTO THE WORLD.
I CAUSED MY FAMILY A LOT OF GRIEF, BUT I'M GLAD I DID IT.
STILL, JUST CHANGING MY OWN LIFE ISN'T VERY IMPORTANT.
THAT'S NOT TRUE!
ONE PERSON CAN MAKE A BIG DIFFERENCE IN THE WORLD!

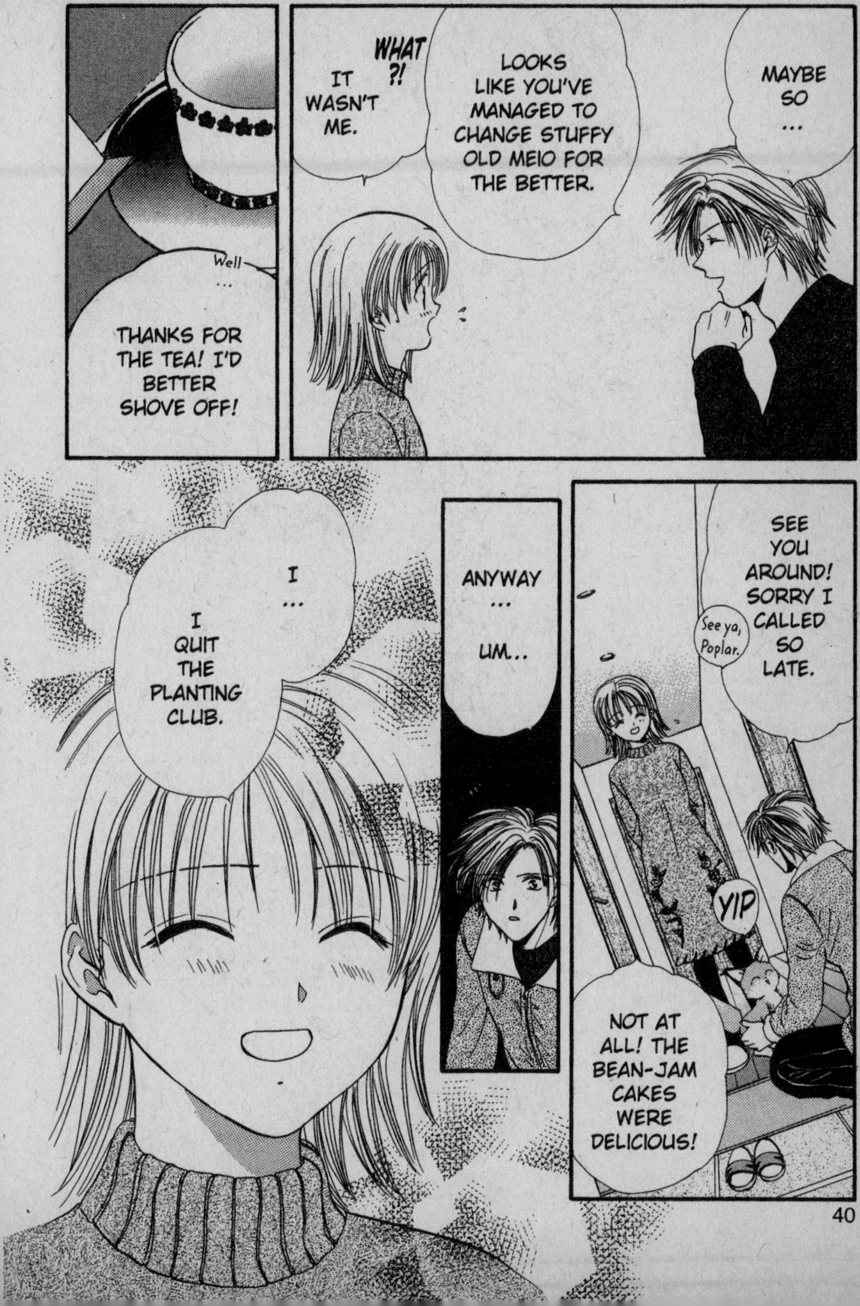
MAYBE SO ...
LOOKS LIKE YOU'VE MANAGED TO CHANGE STUFFY OLD MEIO FOR THE BETTER.
WHAT?!
IT WASN'T ME.
Well ...
THANKS FOR THE TEA! I'D BETTER SHOVE OFF!
SEE YOU AROUND! SORRY I CALLED SO LATE.
See ya, Poplar.
YIP
NOT AT ALL! THE BEAN-JAM CAKES WERE DELICIOUS!
ANYWAY ...
UM...
I ...
I QUIT THE PLANTING CLUB.

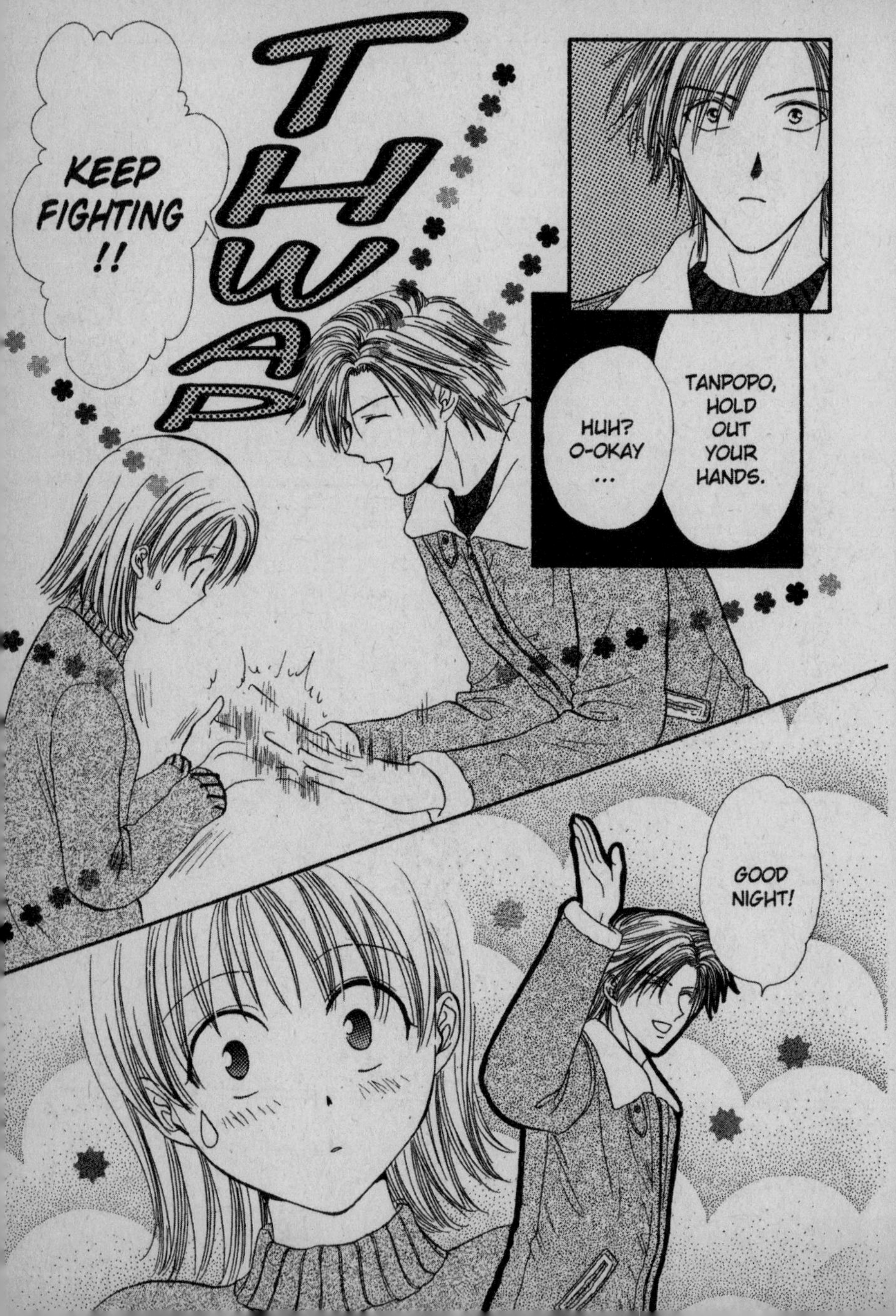
TANPOPO, HOLD OUT YOUR HANDS.
HUH? O-OKAY ...
THWAP
KEEP FIGHTING !!
GOOD NIGHT!

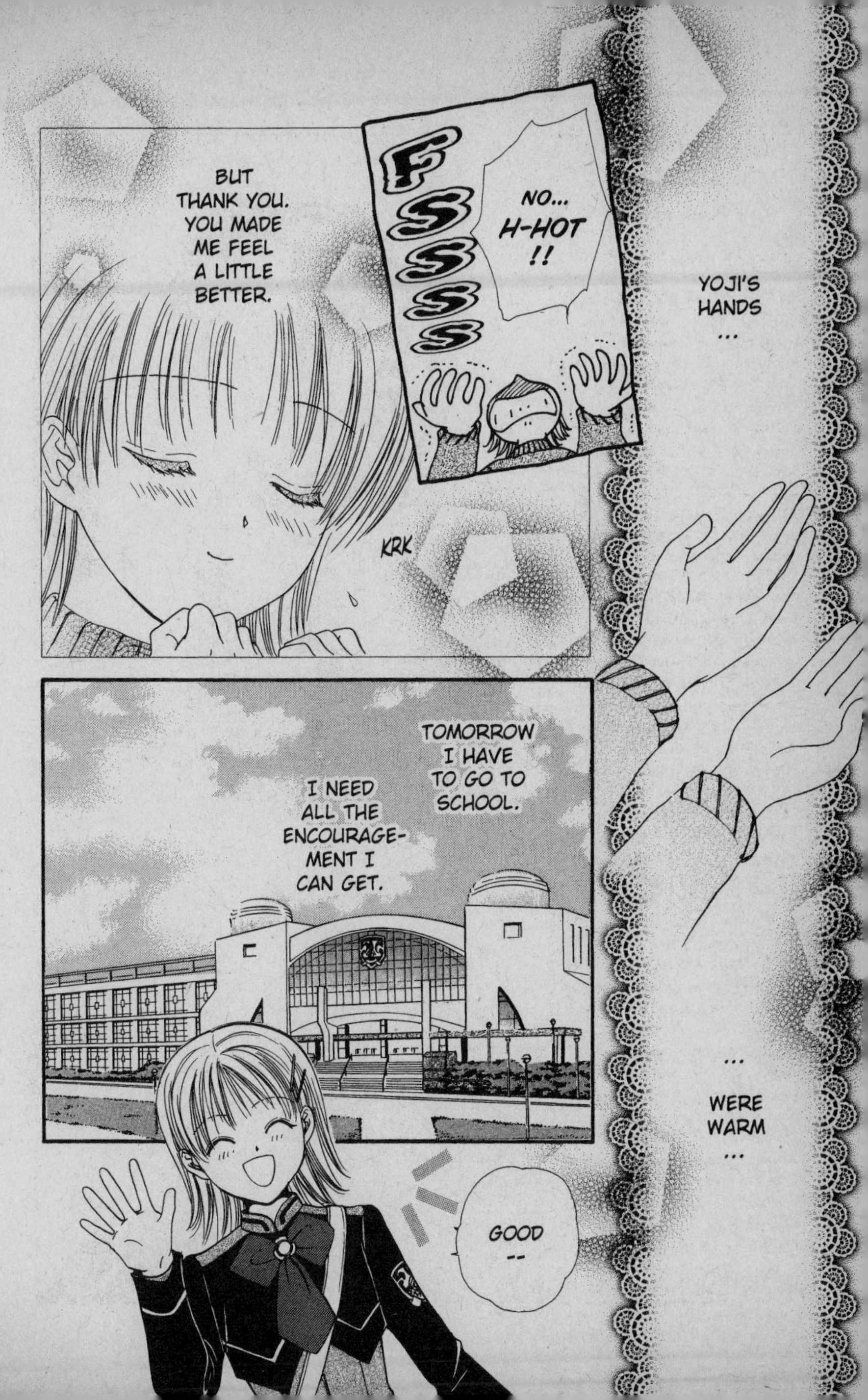
YOJI'S HANDS ...
... WERE WARM ...
FSSSS
NO... H-HOT !!
BUT THANK YOU. YOU MADE ME FEEL A LITTLE BETTER.
KRK
TOMORROW I HAVE TO GO TO SCHOOL.
I NEED ALL THE ENCOURAGE-MENT I CAN GET.
GOOD --

Why do I forget things about my own works when I'm the one who wrote them?
Well, it has nothing to do with age...
(I'm too young to be going senile. Supposedly.)
If my brain were a computer, it would be saying: memory full. Unnecessary data must be deleted in order to proceed...or something like that.
When I'm creating a new work, and there's new information inside my head, the old information has to be forgotten. Otherwise, my head would explode. So I let myself forget everything about the works that are finished. It can't be helped.
Well, I'm sure it's all just compressed and stored in a drawer somewhere in my head, anyway...
If you want to know about my old works, you'll have to ask the Watase of the past. The Watase of today has forgotten most of the details, so she's no help at all.
Even when I read a story again, I often think, "Why did I write this part this way? I don't have the slightest idea!" (^^;)
When I'm writing, I'm immersed in the world of the story, so it's like, "This is this way, so it has to turn out like this!" That's how it is, I guess...
But for readers who pick up **Fushigi Yûgi** or **Ayashi no Ceres** for the first time, they're reading in the present and a time warp occurs (amazingly, that's a span of more than ten years), so they might say, "The drawings are different!" (smile) That's the kind of thing that happens...
For the writer it's like going back in time, so the farther I've come, the more I can only think, "Ugh! Terrible!" about my past works. Actually, I try to find good things about them or laugh at them, which just goes to show how much I've forgotten.

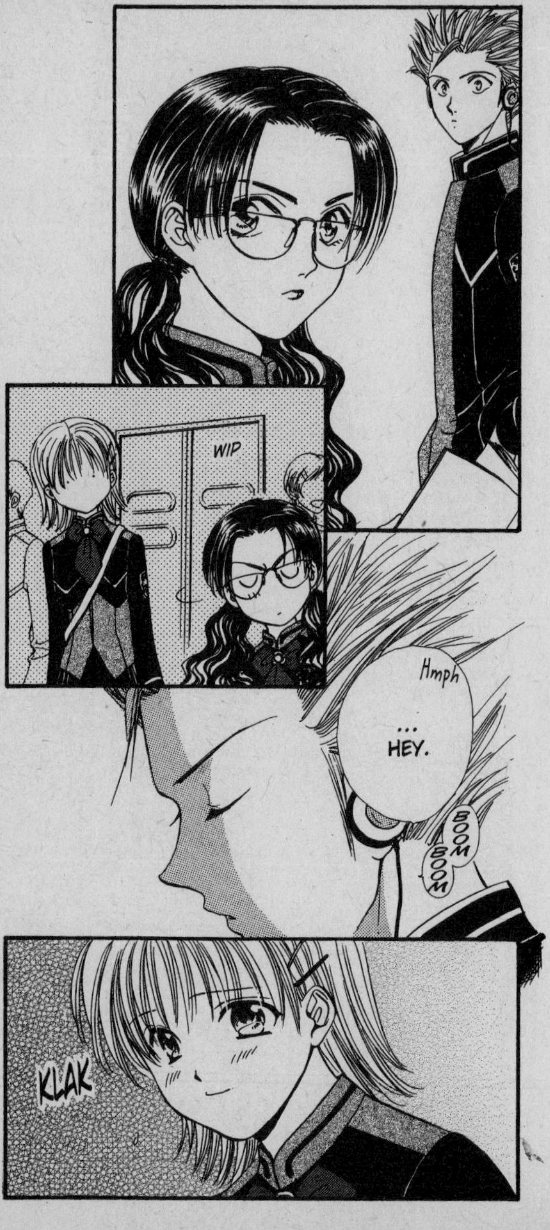
WIP
Hmph
... HEY.
BOOM BOOM
KLAK

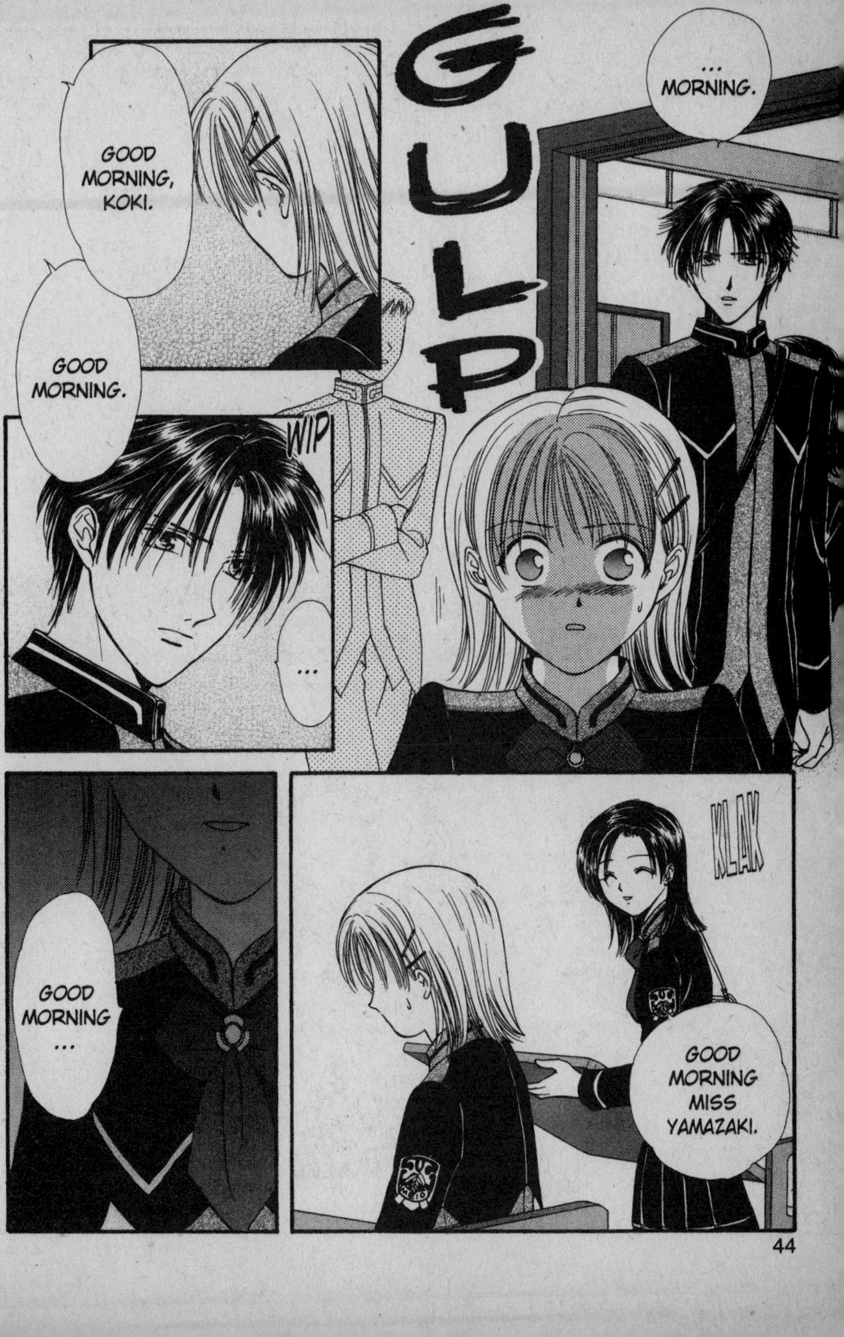
... MORNING.
GULP
GOOD MORNING, KOKI.
GOOD MORNING.
WIP
...
KLAK
GOOD MORNING MISS YAMAZAKI.
GOOD MORNING ...

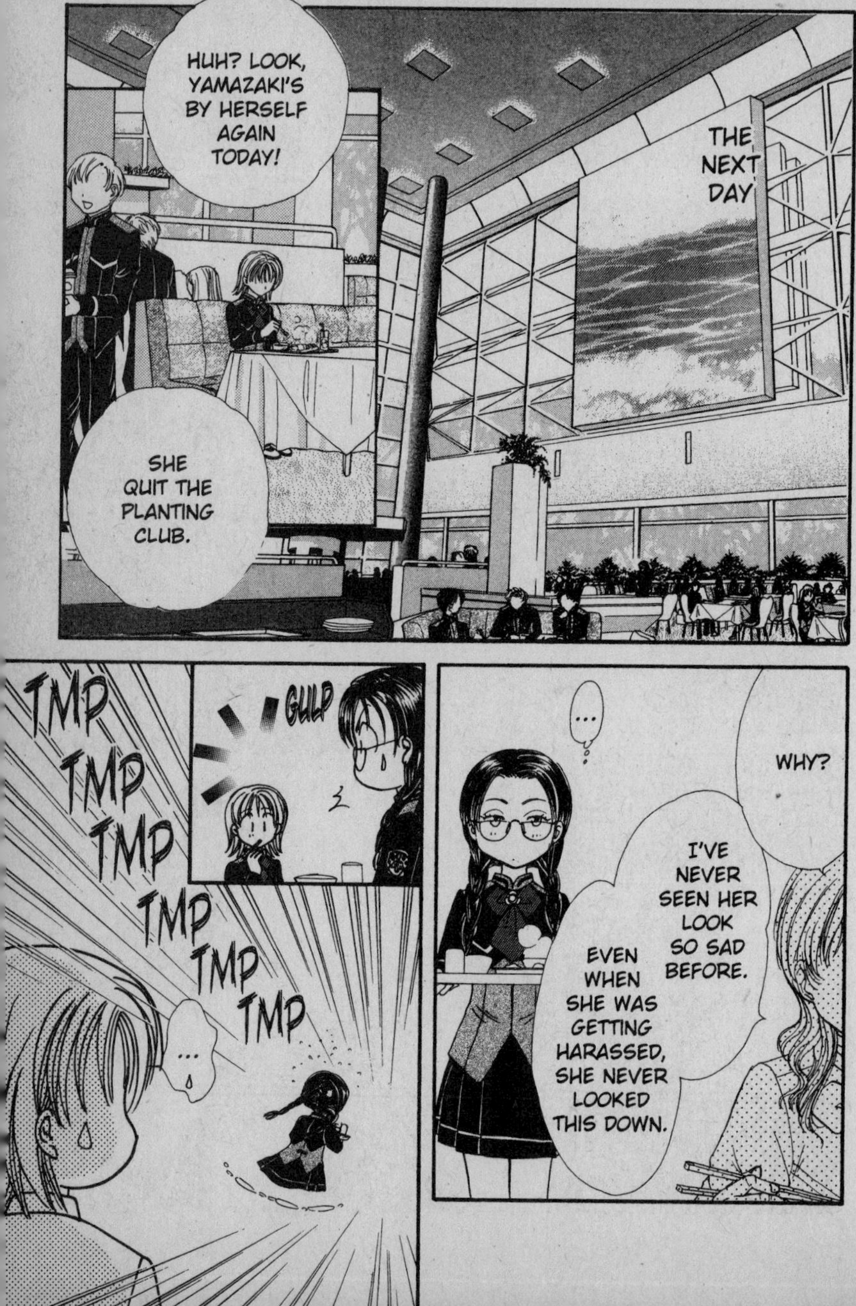
THE NEXT DAY
HUH? LOOK, YAMAZAKI'S BY HERSELF AGAIN TODAY!
SHE QUIT THE PLANTING CLUB.
WHY?
I'VE NEVER SEEN HER LOOK SO SAD BEFORE.
EVEN WHEN SHE WAS GETTING HARASSED, SHE NEVER LOOKED THIS DOWN.
...
GULP
TMP TMP TMP TMP TMP TMP
...

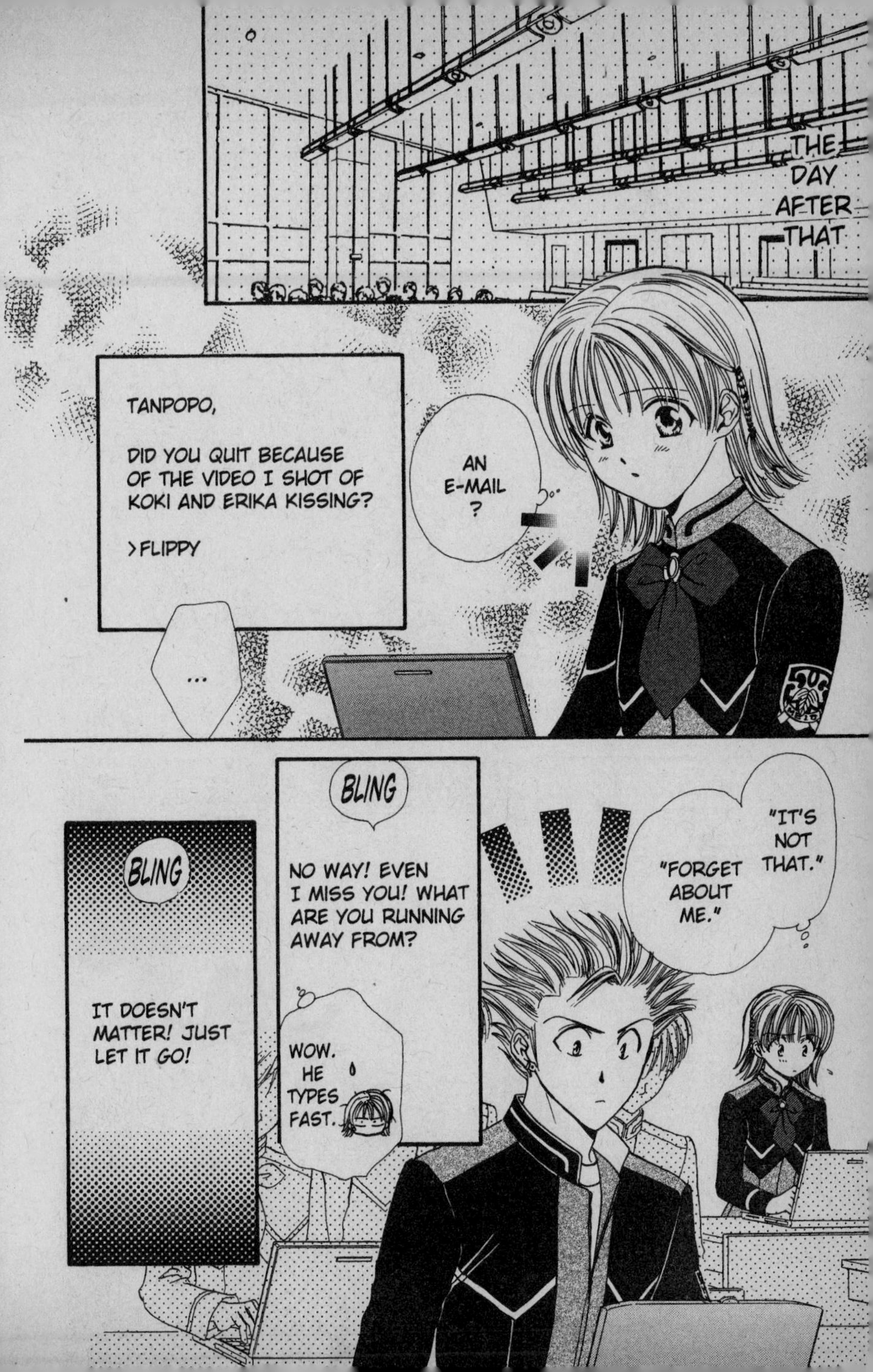
THE DAY AFTER THAT
AN E-MAIL ?
TANPOPO,
DID YOU QUIT BECAUSE OF THE VIDEO I SHOT OF KOKI AND ERIKA KISSING?
>FLIPPY
...
"IT'S NOT THAT."
"FORGET ABOUT ME."
BLING
NO WAY! EVEN I MISS YOU! WHAT ARE YOU RUNNING AWAY FROM?
WOW. HE TYPES FAST.
BLING
IT DOESN'T MATTER! JUST LET IT GO!

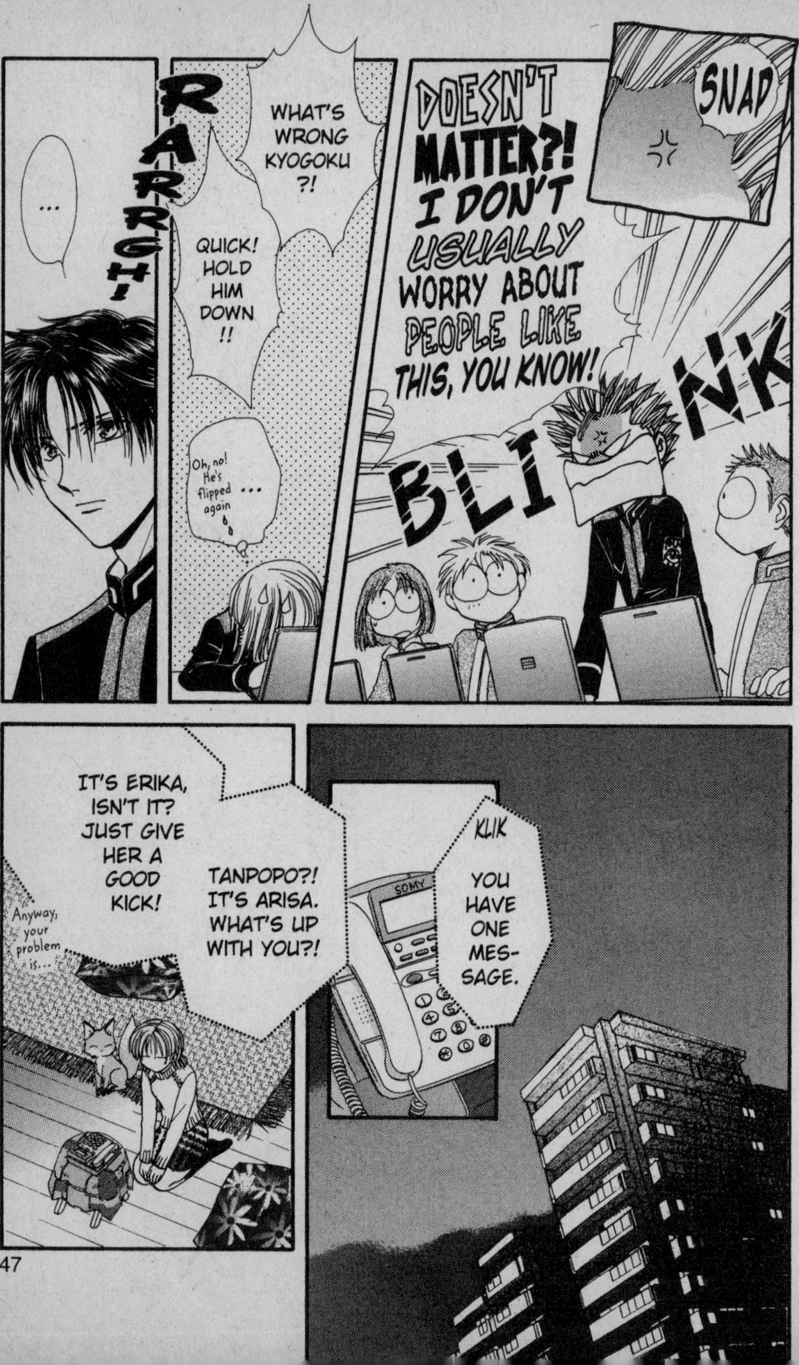
SNAP
DOESN'T MATTER?! I DON'T USUALLY WORRY ABOUT PEOPLE LIKE THIS, YOU KNOW!
BLINK
RARRGH!
WHAT'S WRONG KYOGOKU ?!
QUICK! HOLD HIM DOWN !!
Oh, no! He's flipped again ...
...
KLIK
YOU HAVE ONE MES-SAGE.
TANPOPO?! IT'S ARISA. WHAT'S UP WITH YOU?!
IT'S ERIKA, ISN'T IT? JUST GIVE HER A GOOD KICK!
Anyway, your problem is...

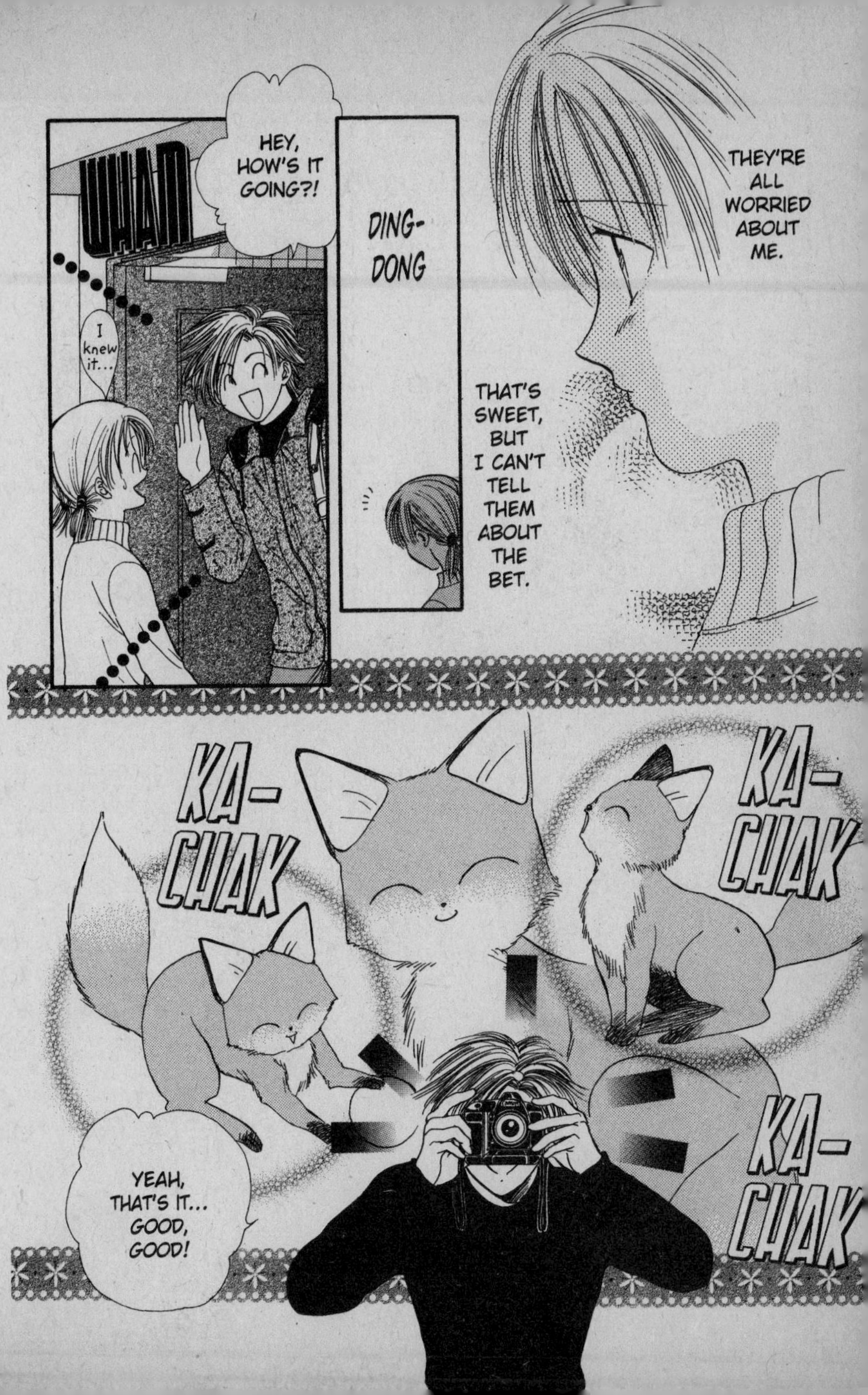
THEY'RE ALL WORRIED ABOUT ME.
THAT'S SWEET, BUT I CAN'T TELL THEM ABOUT THE BET.
DING-DONG
HEY, HOW'S IT GOING?!
WHAM
I knew it...
KA-CHAK
KA-CHAK
KA-CHAK
YEAH, THAT'S IT... GOOD, GOOD!

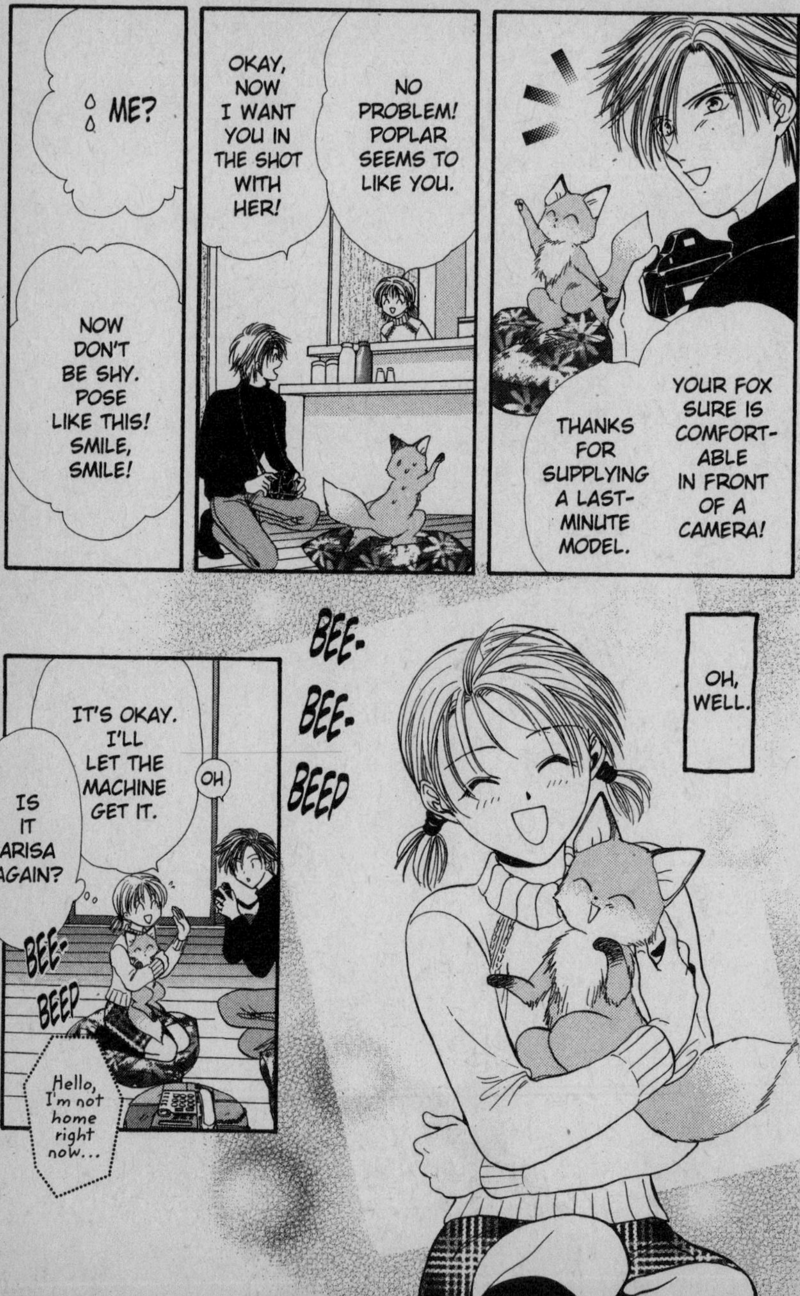
YOUR FOX SURE IS COMFORTABLE IN FRONT OF A CAMERA!
THANKS FOR SUPPLYING A LAST-MINUTE MODEL.
NO PROBLEM! POPLAR SEEMS TO LIKE YOU.
OKAY, NOW I WANT YOU IN THE SHOT WITH HER!
ME?
NOW DON'T BE SHY. POSE LIKE THIS! SMILE, SMILE!
OH, WELL.
BEE-BEE-BEEP
OH
IT'S OKAY. I'LL LET THE MACHINE GET IT.
IS IT ARISA AGAIN?
BEE-BEEP
Hello, I'm not home right now...

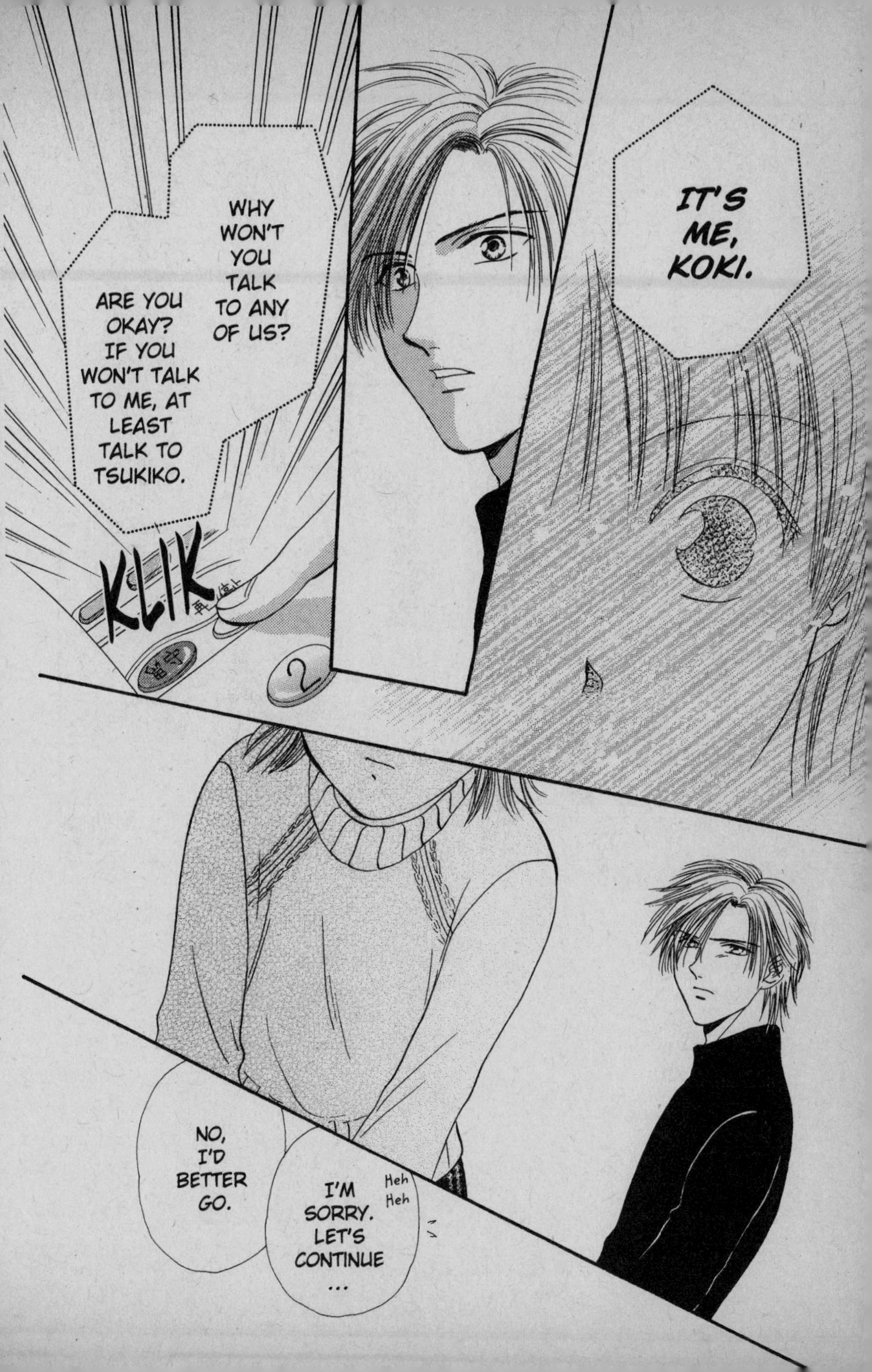
IT'S ME, KOKI.
WHY WON'T YOU TALK TO ANY OF US?
ARE YOU OKAY? IF YOU WON'T TALK TO ME, AT LEAST TALK TO TSUKIKO.
KLIK
Heh Heh
I'M SORRY. LET'S CONTINUE ...
NO, I'D BETTER GO.

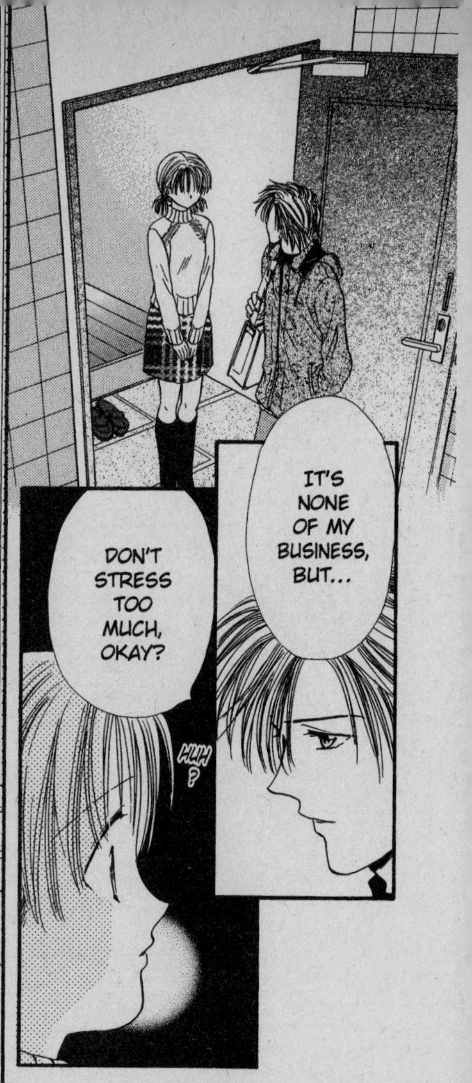
IT'S NONE OF MY BUSINESS, BUT...
DON'T STRESS TOO MUCH, OKAY?
HUH?

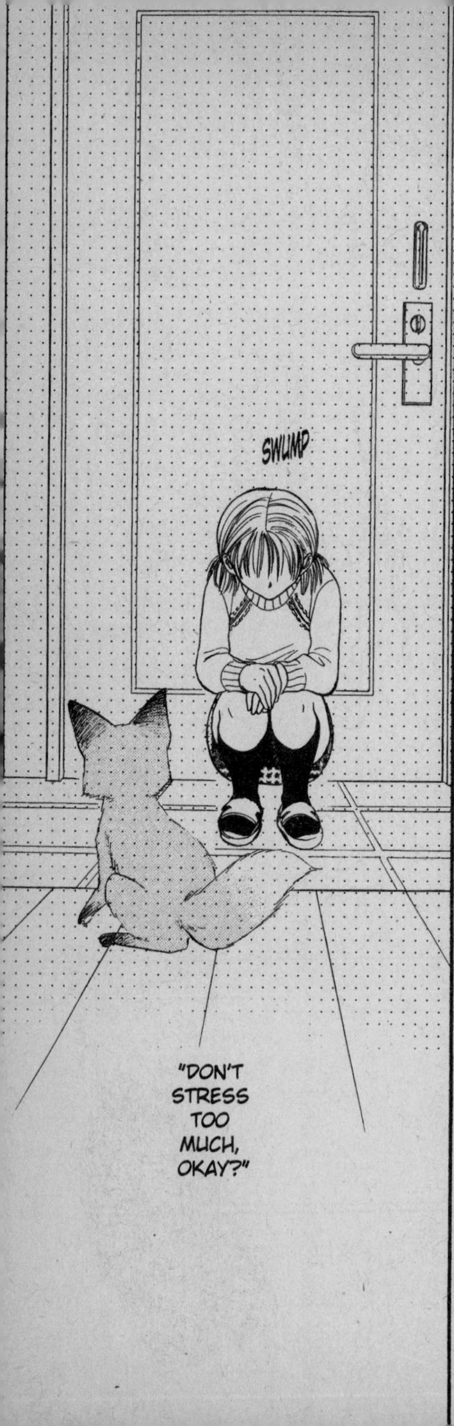
SWUMP
"DON'T STRESS TOO MUCH, OKAY?"

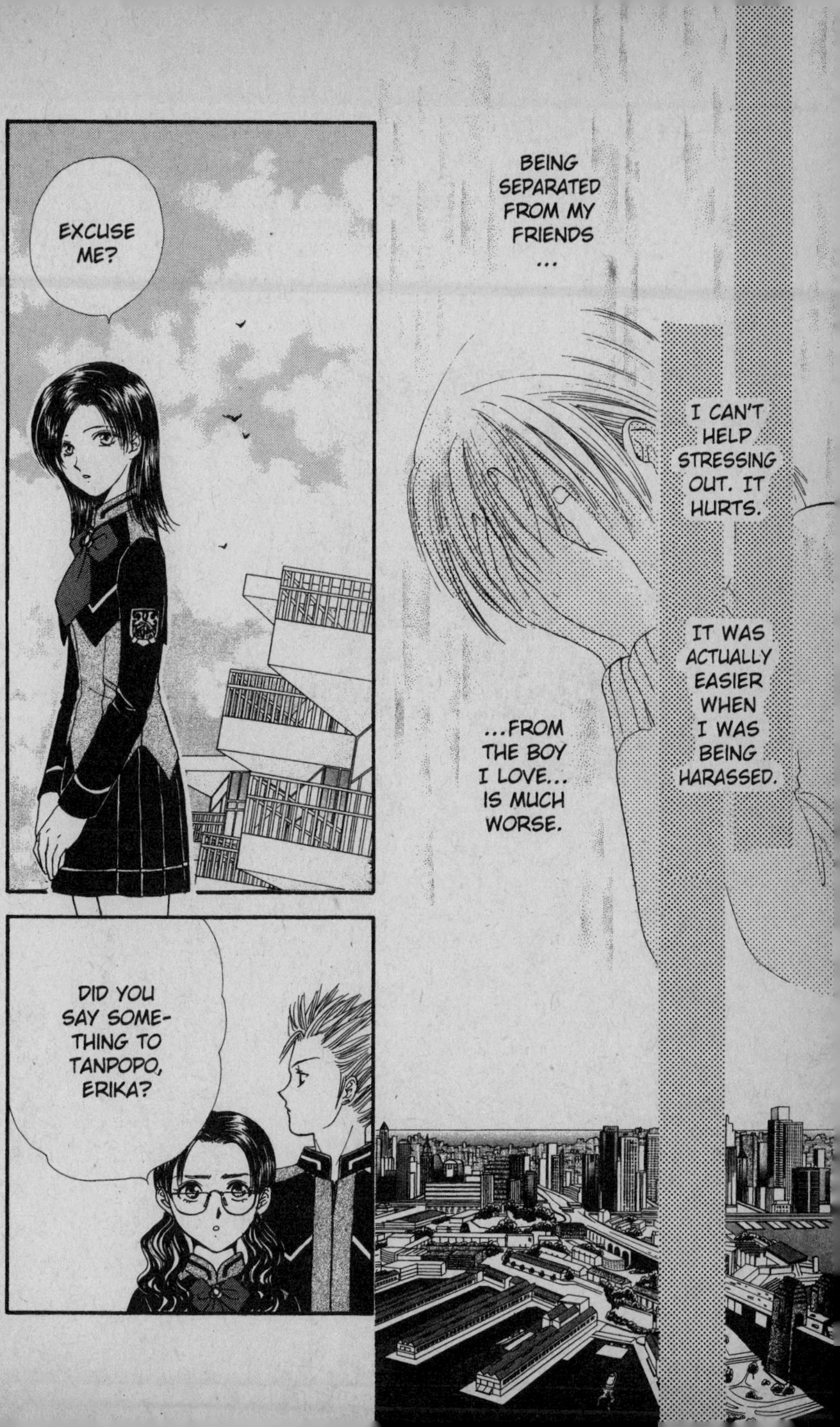
I CAN'T HELP STRESSING OUT. IT HURTS.
IT WAS ACTUALLY EASIER WHEN I WAS BEING HARASSED.
BEING SEPARATED FROM MY FRIENDS...
...FROM THE BOY I LOVE... IS MUCH WORSE.
EXCUSE ME?
DID YOU SAY SOME-THING TO TANPOPO, ERIKA?

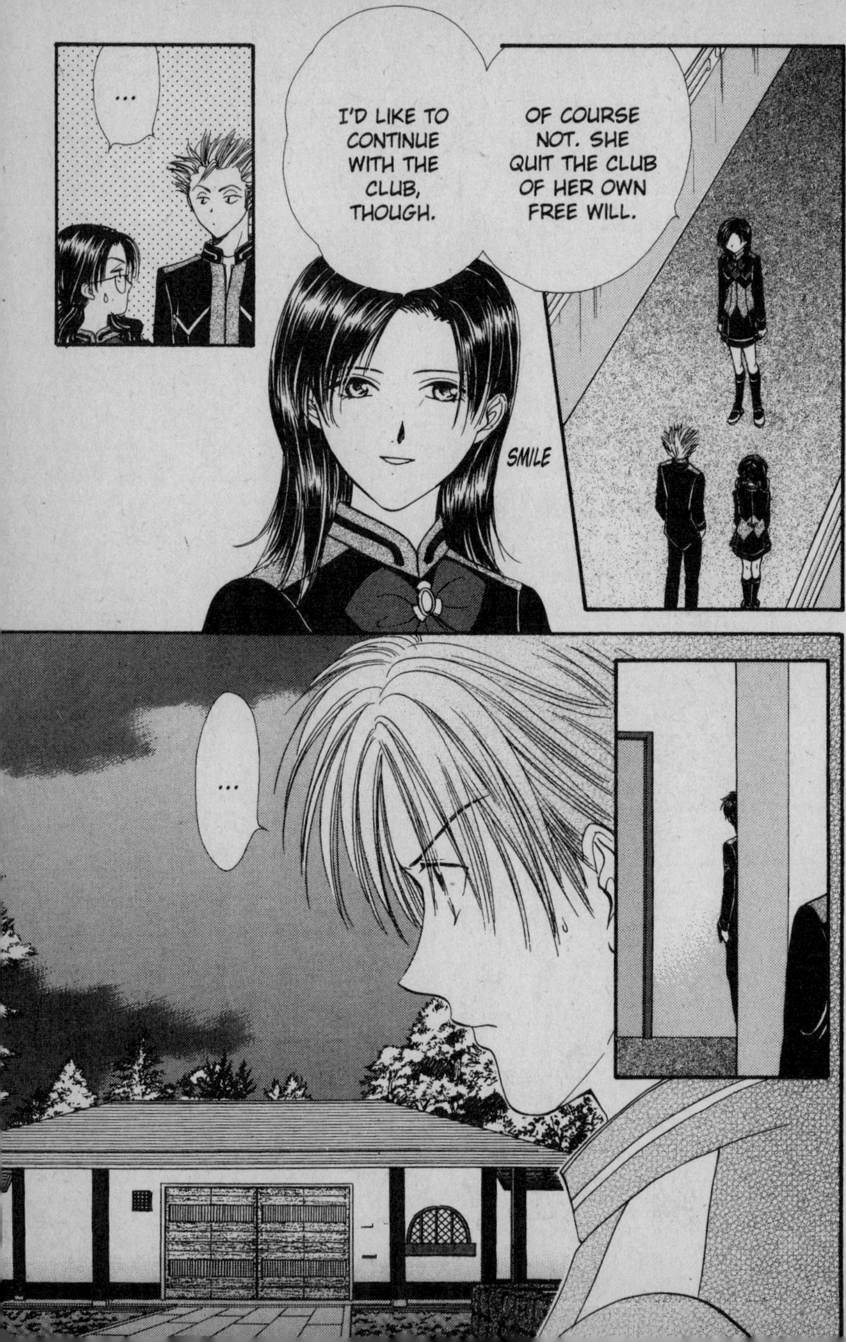
OF COURSE NOT. SHE QUIT THE CLUB OF HER OWN FREE WILL.
I'D LIKE TO CONTINUE WITH THE CLUB, THOUGH.
SMILE
...
...

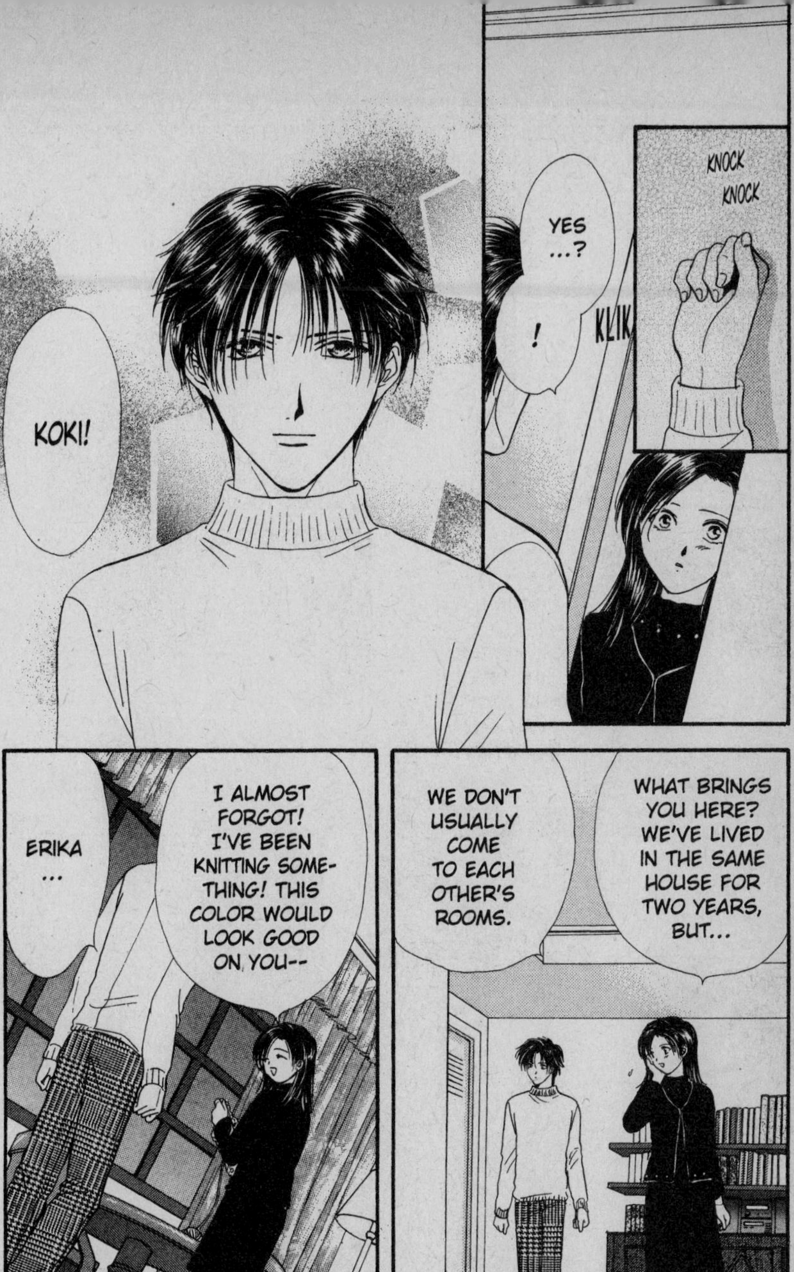
KNOCK
KNOCK
YES ...?
KLIK
!
KOKI!
WHAT BRINGS YOU HERE? WE'VE LIVED IN THE SAME HOUSE FOR TWO YEARS, BUT...
WE DON'T USUALLY COME TO EACH OTHER'S ROOMS.
I ALMOST FORGOT! I'VE BEEN KNITTING SOME-THING! THIS COLOR WOULD LOOK GOOD ON YOU--
ERIKA ...

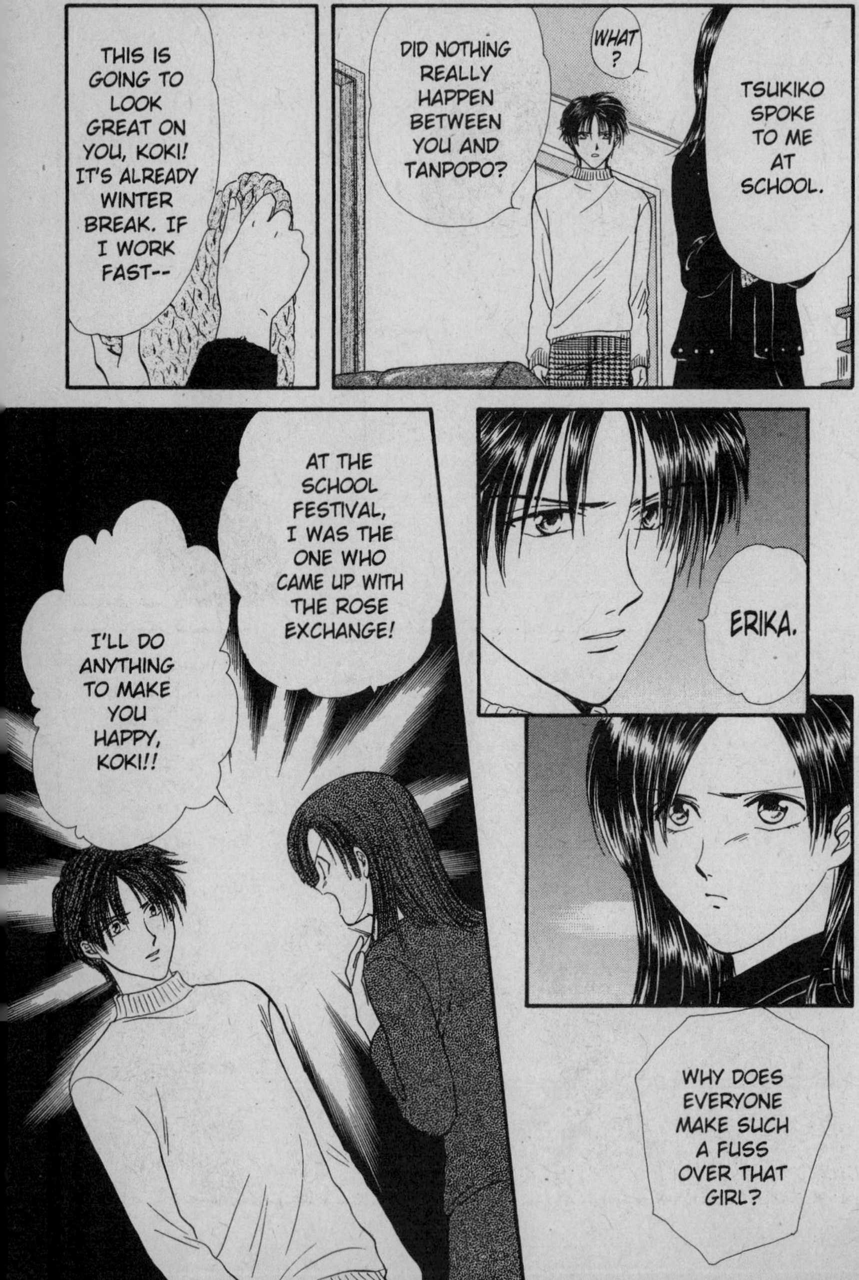
TSUKIKO SPOKE TO ME AT SCHOOL.
WHAT?
DID NOTHING REALLY HAPPEN BETWEEN YOU AND TANPOPO?
THIS IS GOING TO LOOK GREAT ON YOU, KOKI! IT'S ALREADY WINTER BREAK. IF I WORK FAST--
ERIKA.
WHY DOES EVERYONE MAKE SUCH A FUSS OVER THAT GIRL?
AT THE SCHOOL FESTIVAL, I WAS THE ONE WHO CAME UP WITH THE ROSE EXCHANGE!
I'LL DO ANYTHING TO MAKE YOU HAPPY, KOKI!!

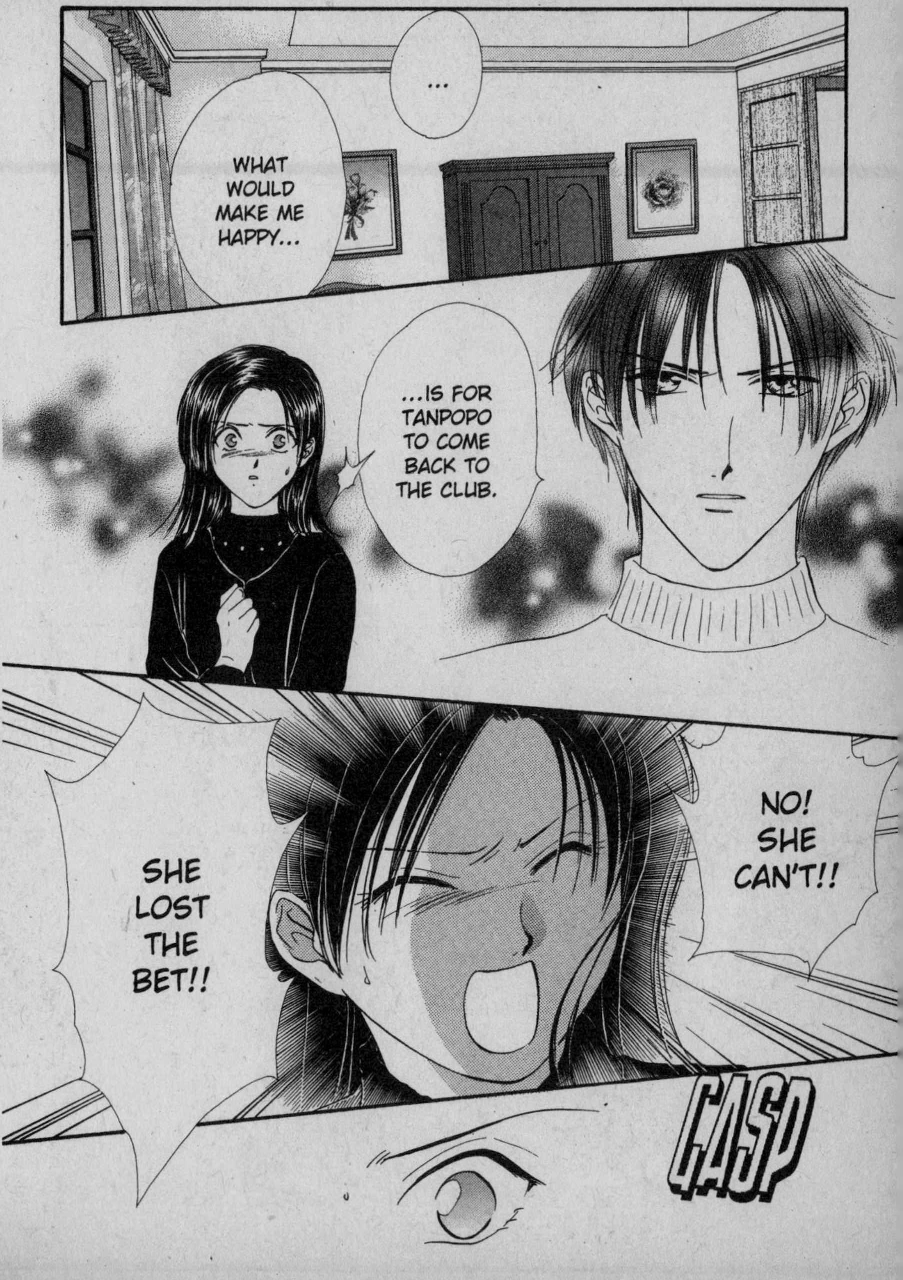
...
WHAT WOULD MAKE ME HAPPY...
...IS FOR TANPOPO TO COME BACK TO THE CLUB.
NO! SHE CAN'T!!
SHE LOST THE BET!!
GASP

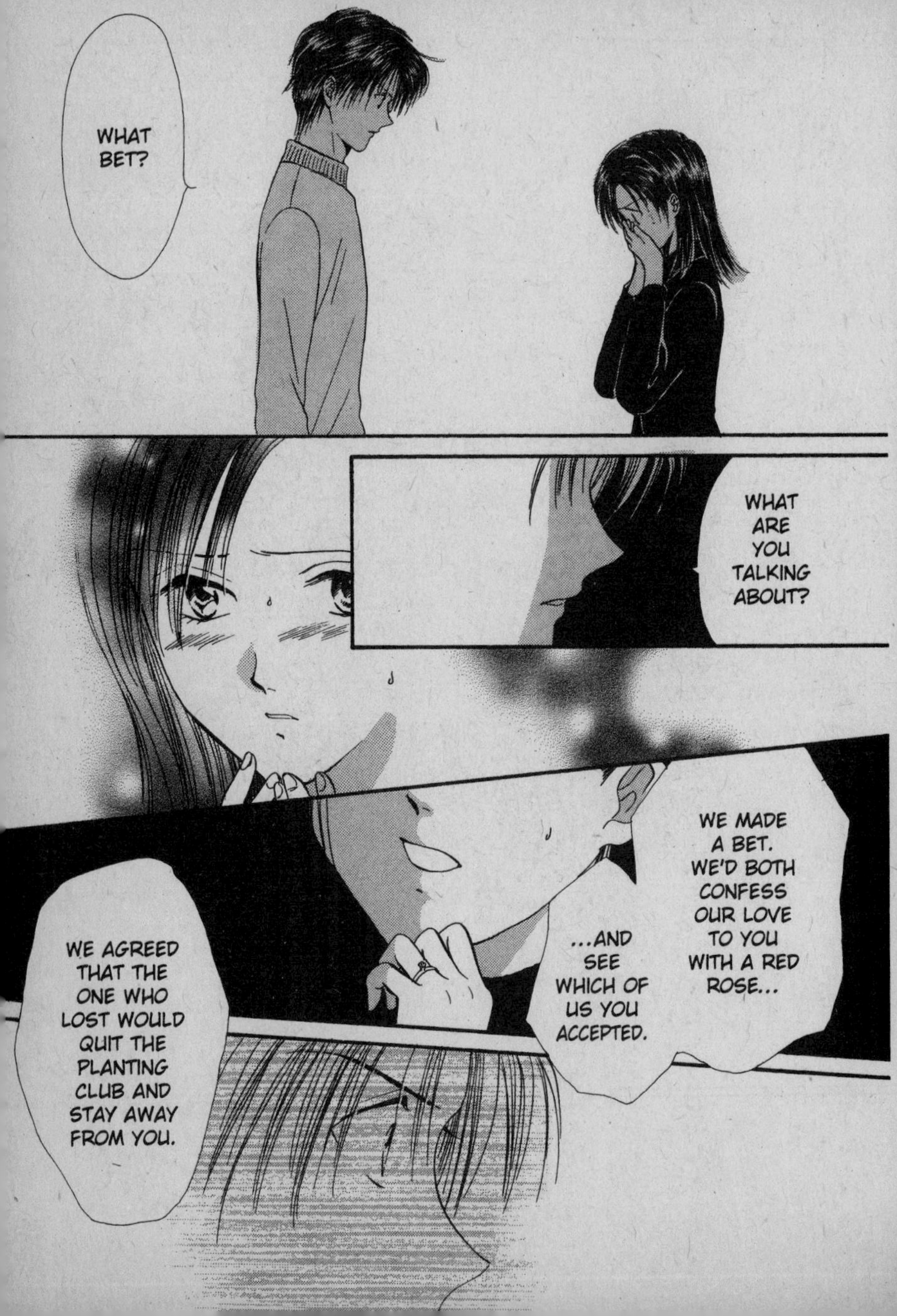
WHAT BET?
WHAT ARE YOU TALKING ABOUT?
WE MADE A BET. WE'D BOTH CONFESS OUR LOVE TO YOU WITH A RED ROSE...
...AND SEE WHICH OF US YOU ACCEPTED.
WE AGREED THAT THE ONE WHO LOST WOULD QUIT THE PLANTING CLUB AND STAY AWAY FROM YOU.

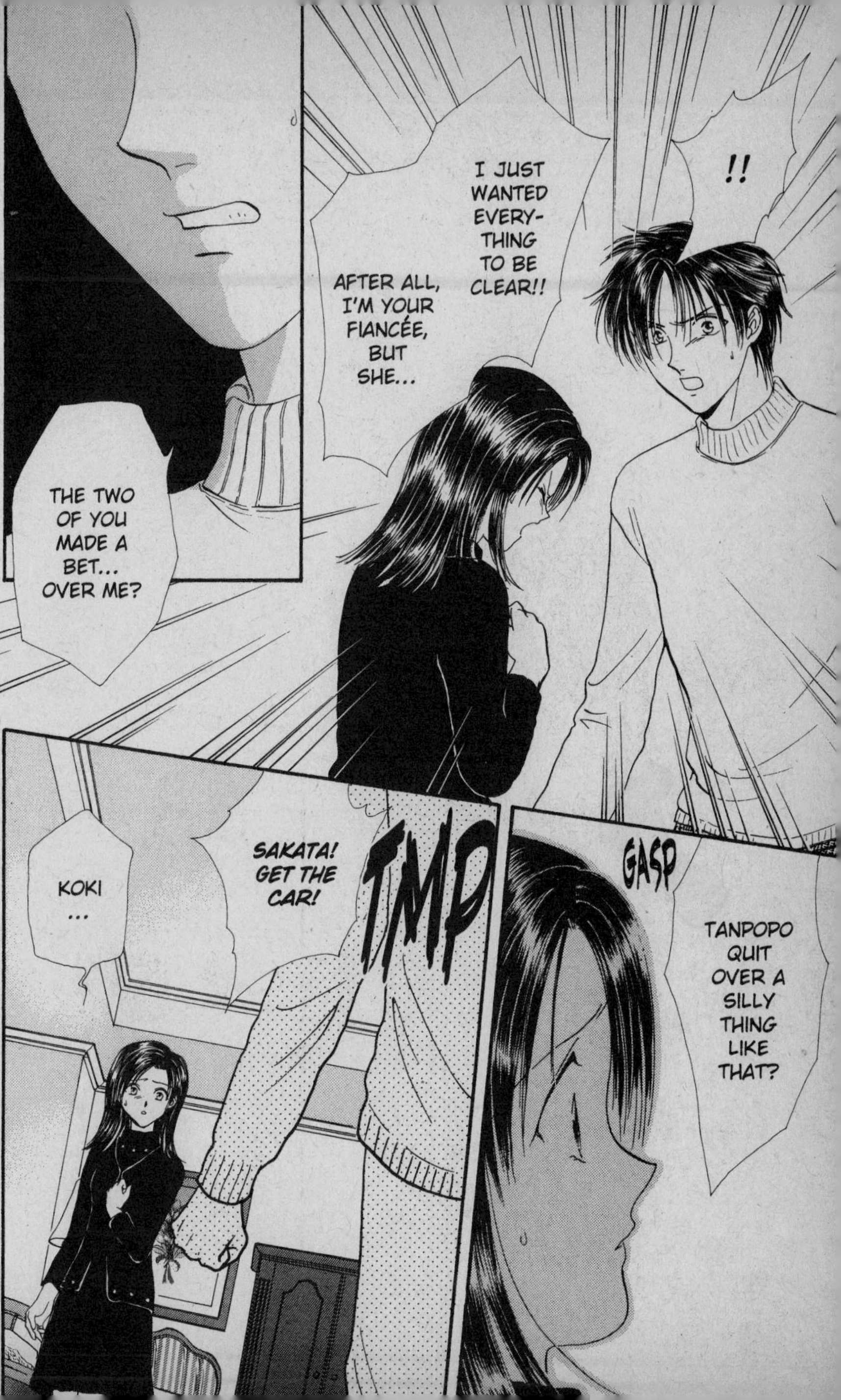
!!
I JUST WANTED EVERY-THING TO BE CLEAR!!
AFTER ALL, I'M YOUR FIANCÉE, BUT SHE...
THE TWO OF YOU MADE A BET... OVER ME?
GASP
TANPOPO QUIT OVER A SILLY THING LIKE THAT?
TMP
SAKATA! GET THE CAR!
KOKI ...

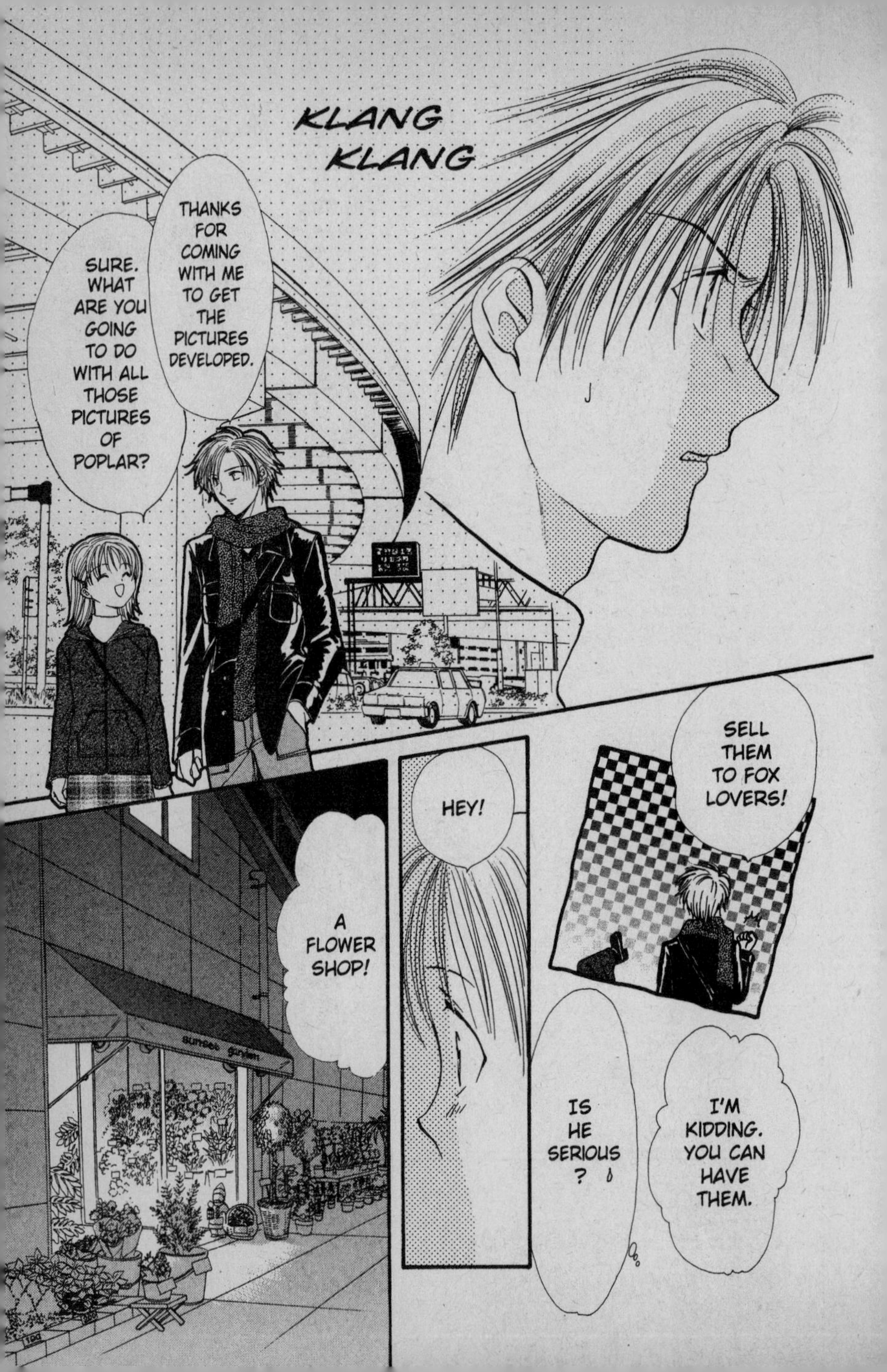
KLANG KLANG
THANKS FOR COMING WITH ME TO GET THE PICTURES DEVELOPED.
SURE. WHAT ARE YOU GOING TO DO WITH ALL THOSE PICTURES OF POPLAR?
SELL THEM TO FOX LOVERS!
I'M KIDDING. YOU CAN HAVE THEM.
IS HE SERIOUS?
HEY!
A FLOWER SHOP!
sunset garden

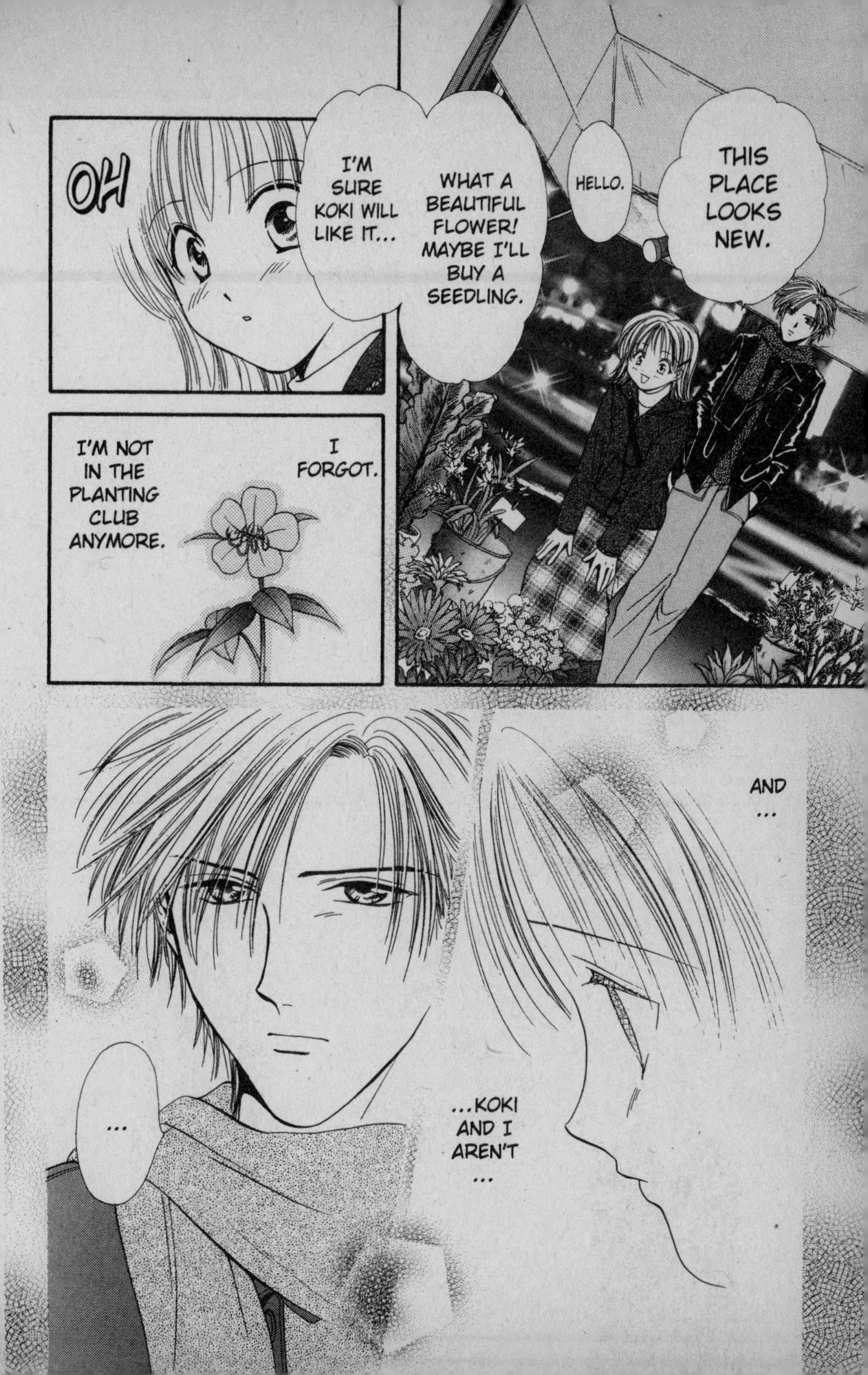
THIS PLACE LOOKS NEW.
HELLO.
WHAT A BEAUTIFUL FLOWER! MAYBE I'LL BUY A SEEDLING.
I'M SURE KOKI WILL LIKE IT...
OH
I FORGOT.
I'M NOT IN THE PLANTING CLUB ANYMORE.
AND ...
...KOKI AND I AREN'T ...
...

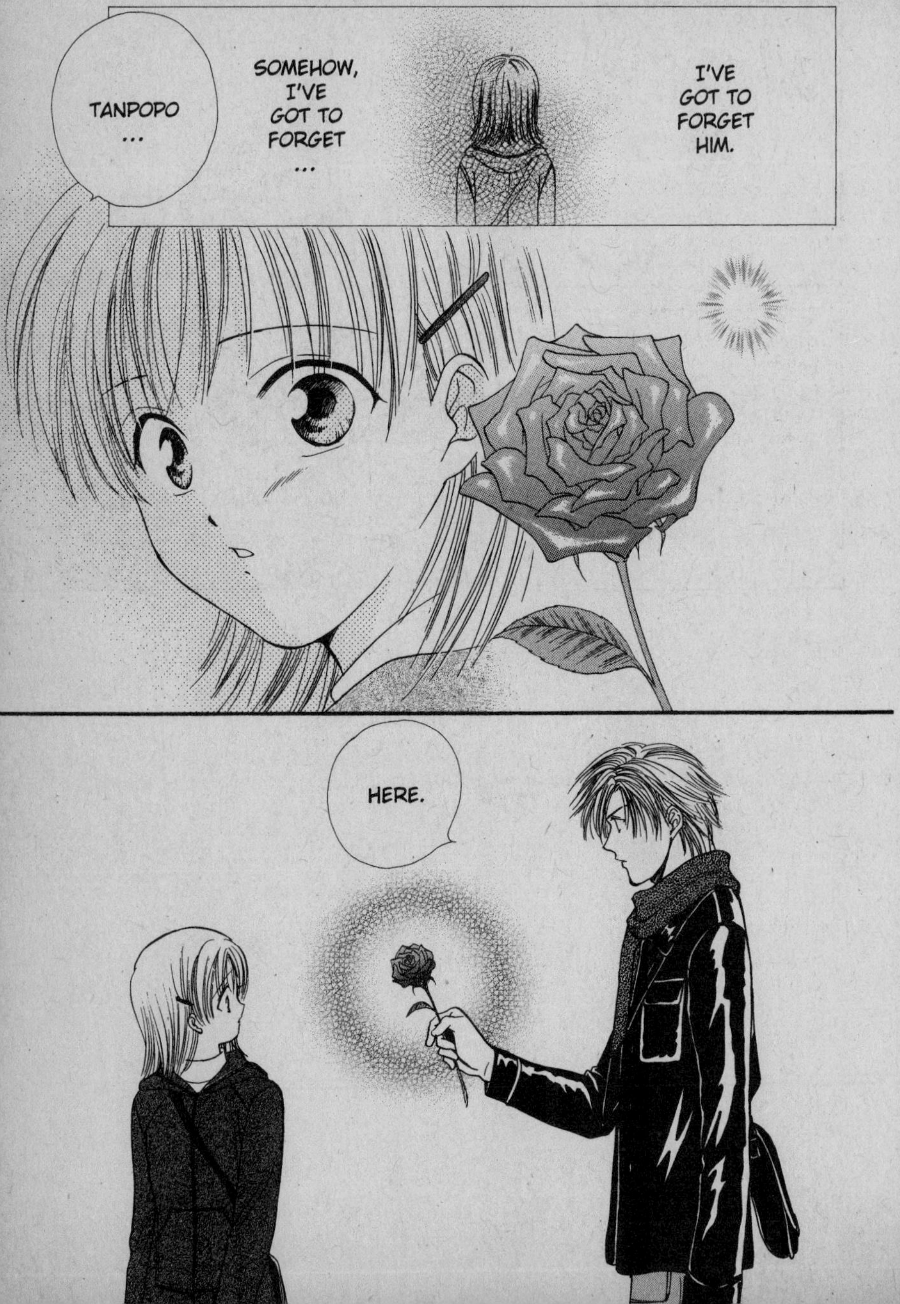
I'VE GOT TO FORGET HIM.
SOMEHOW, I'VE GOT TO FORGET ...
TANPOPO ...
HERE.

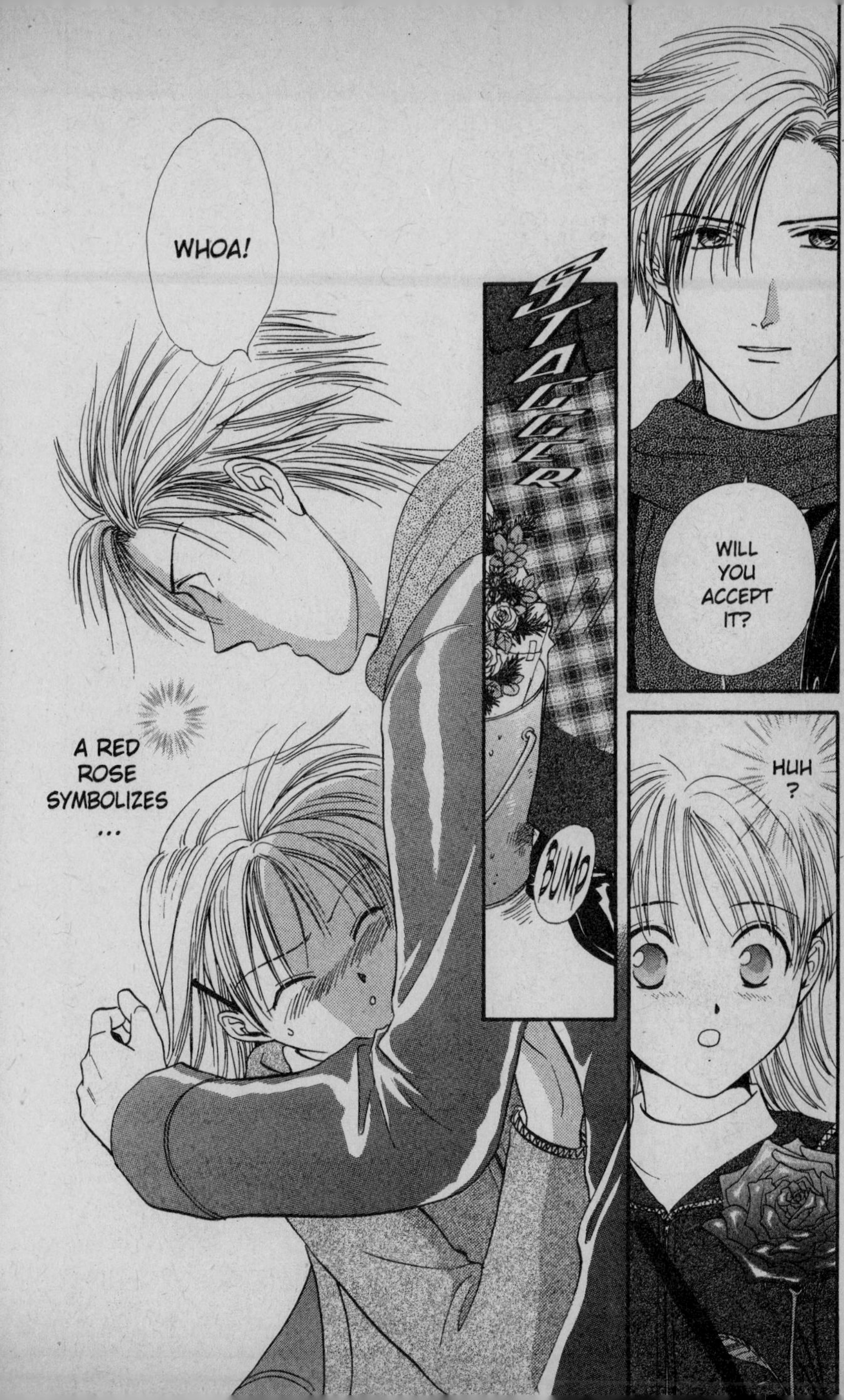
WILL YOU ACCEPT IT?
HUH?
STAGGER
BUMP
WHOA!
A RED ROSE SYMBOLIZES ...

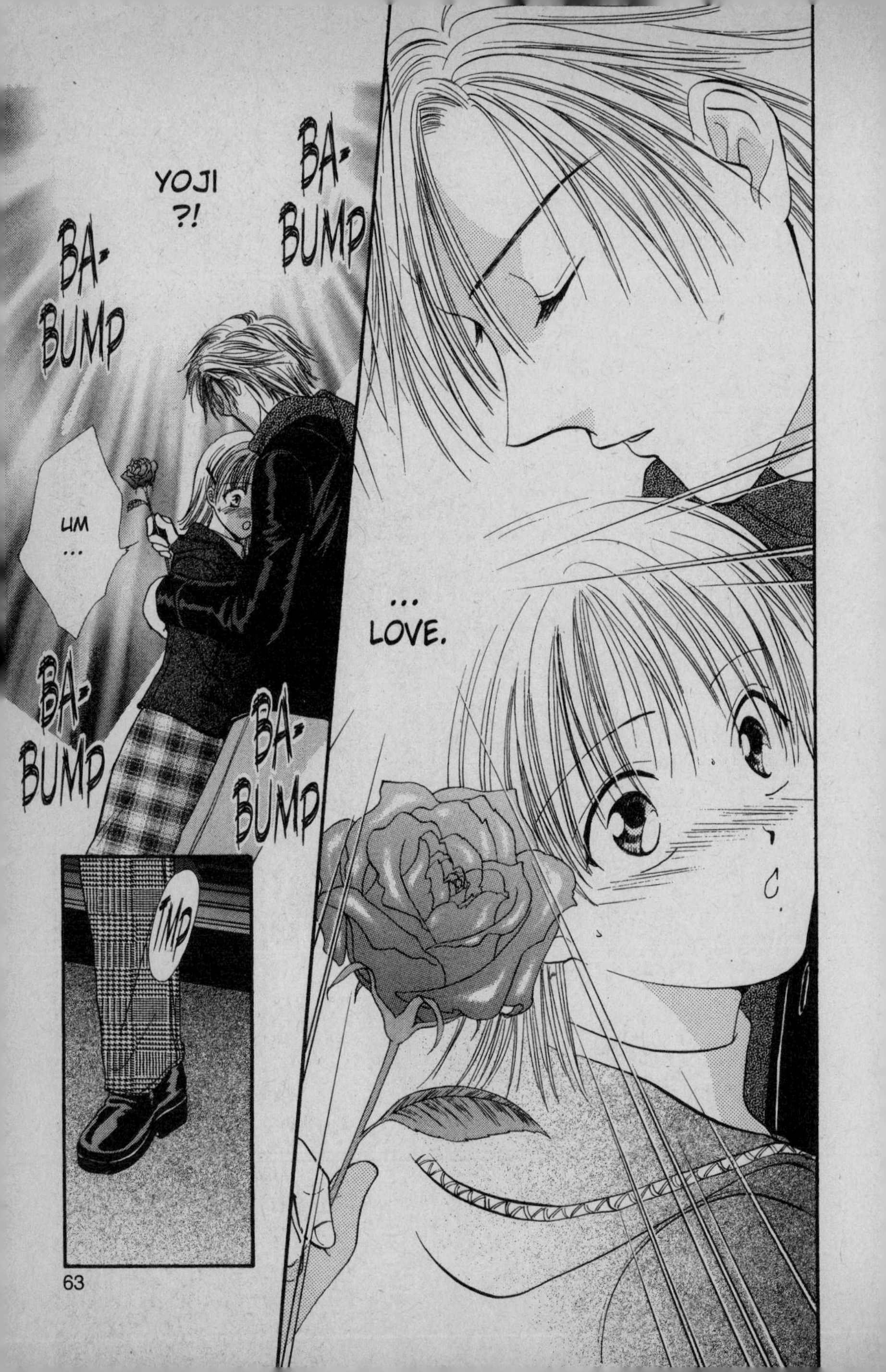
... LOVE.
BA-BUMP
YOJI ?!
BA-BUMP
UM ...
BA-BUMP
BA-BUMP
TMP

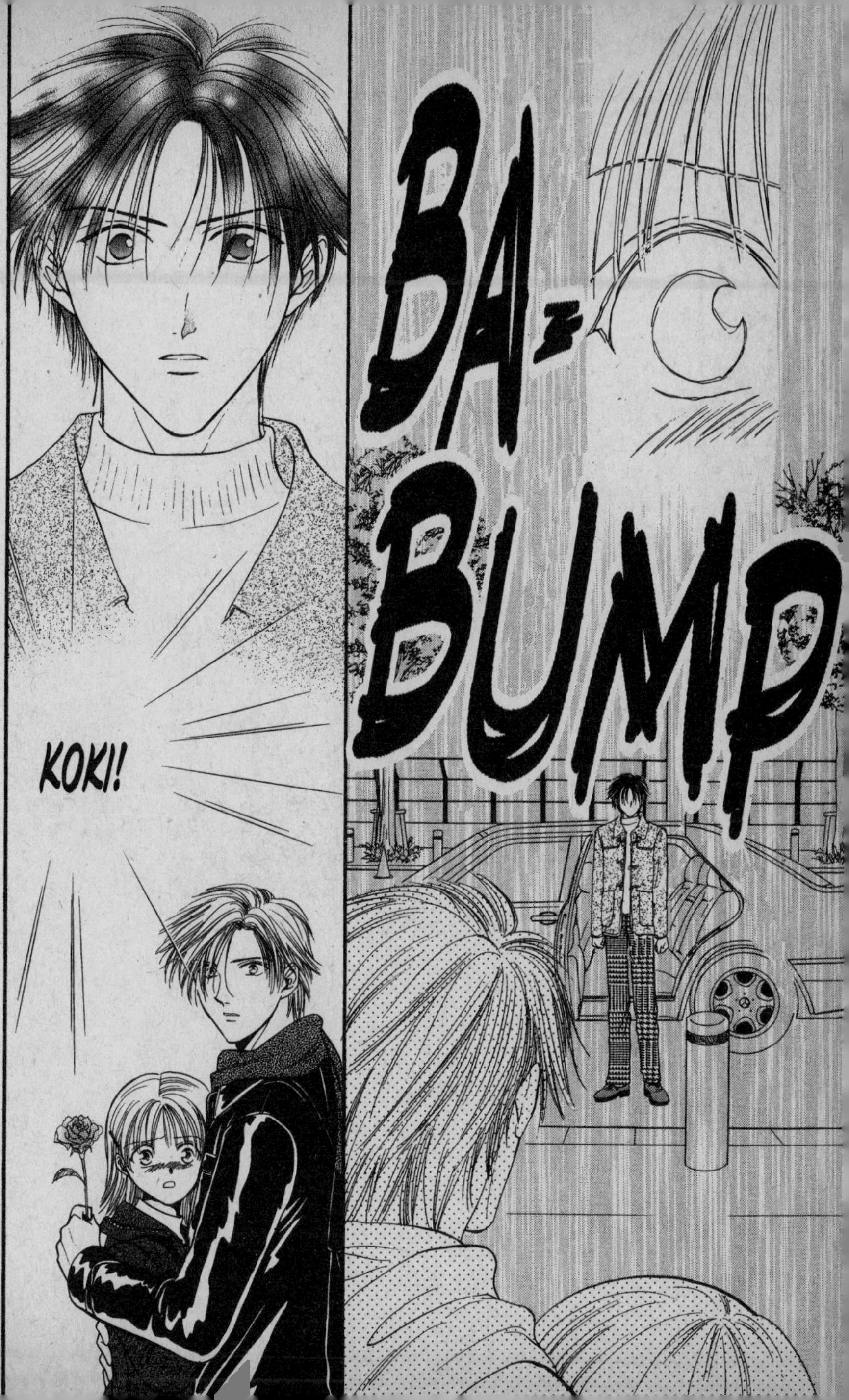
BA-BUMP
KOKI!

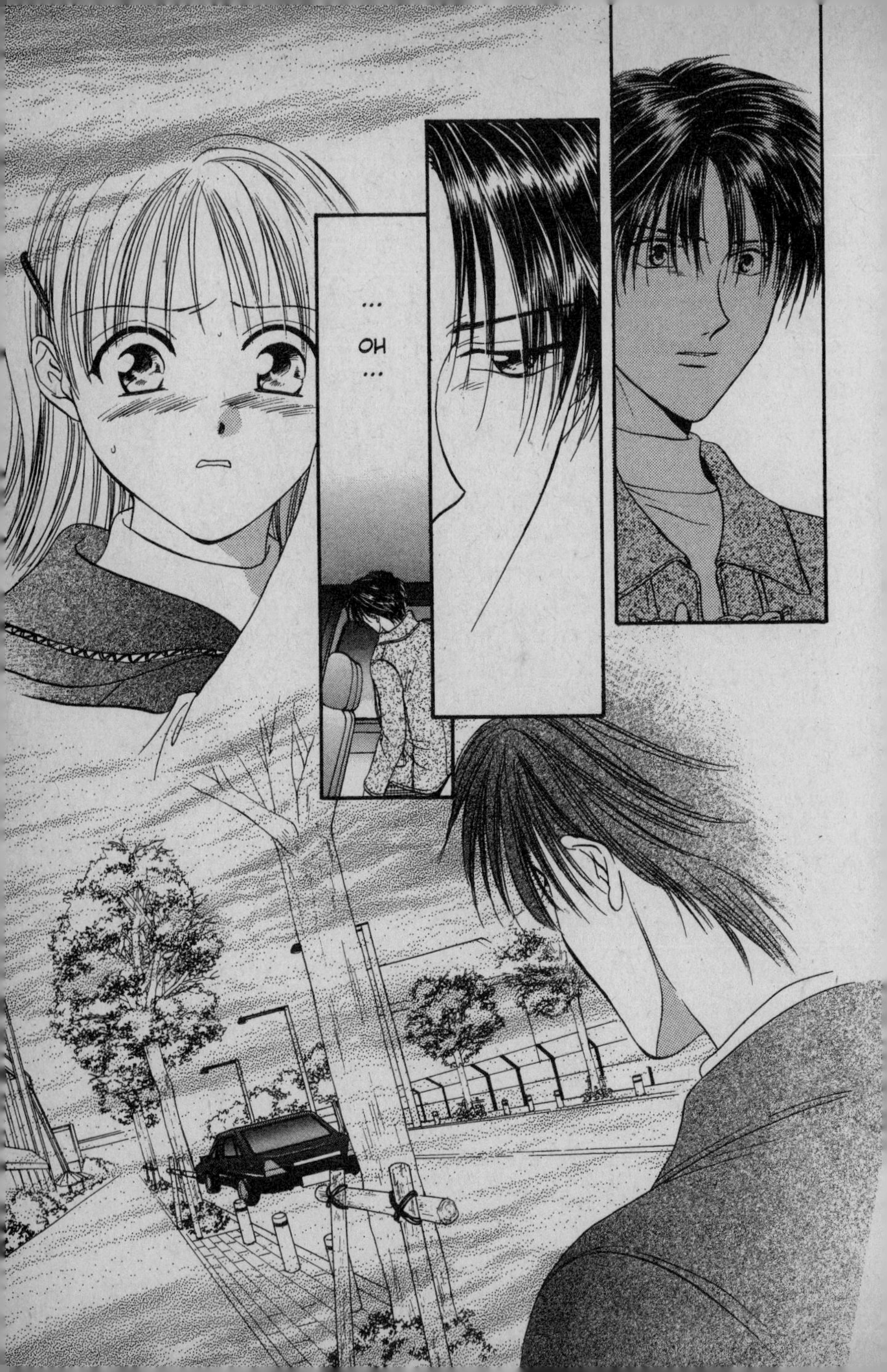
...
OH
...

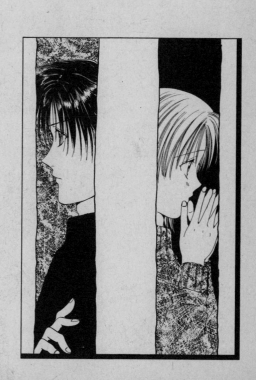

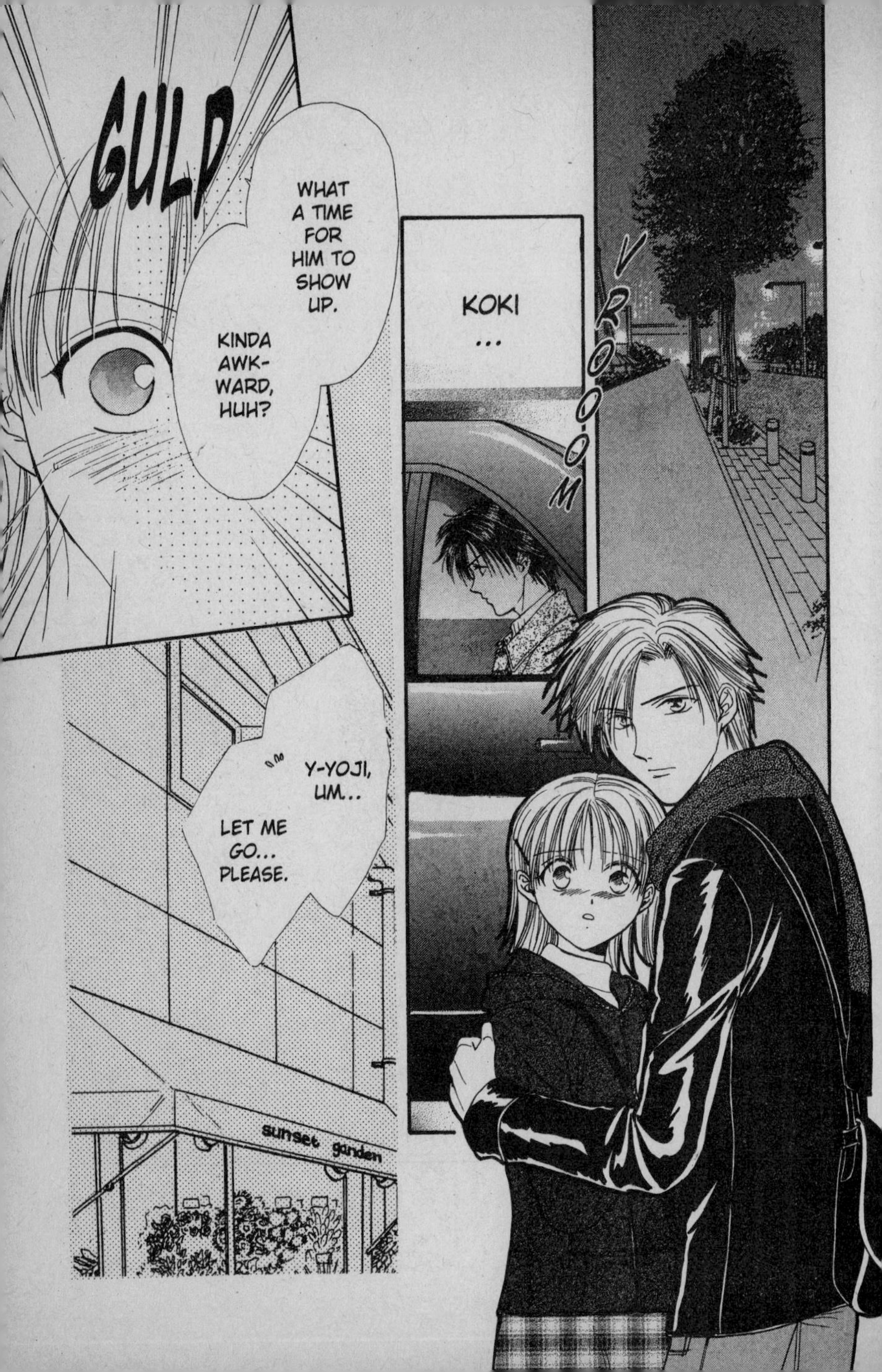
VROOOOOM
KOKI ...
GULP
WHAT A TIME FOR HIM TO SHOW UP.
KINDA AWK-WARD, HUH?
Y-YOJI, UM..
LET ME GO... PLEASE.
sunset garden

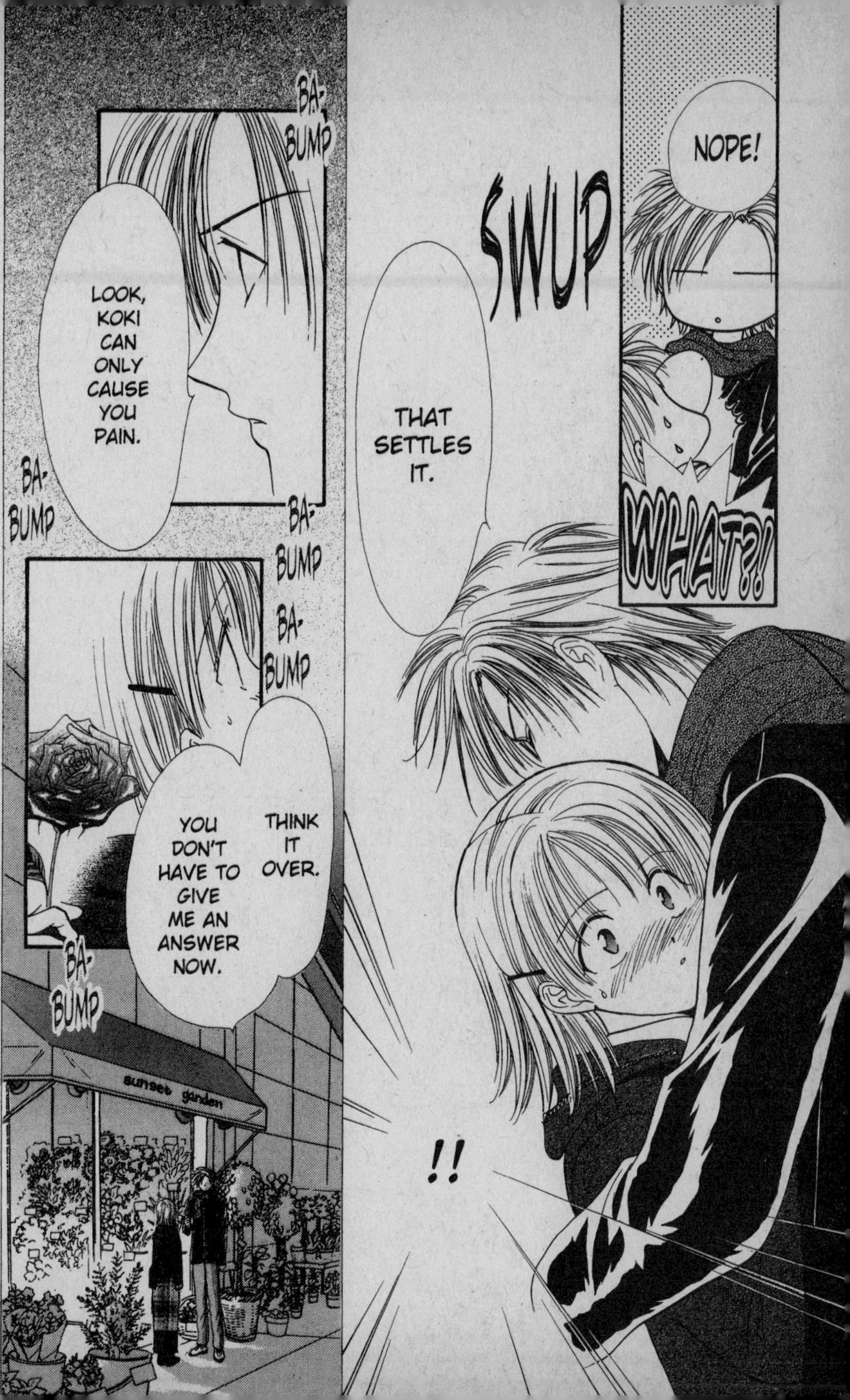
NOPE!
WHAT?!
SWUP
THAT SETTLES IT.
!!
BA-BUMP
LOOK, KOKI CAN ONLY CAUSE YOU PAIN.
BA-BUMP
BA-BUMP
BA-BUMP
BA-BUMP
THINK IT OVER.
YOU DON'T HAVE TO GIVE ME AN ANSWER NOW.
BA-BUMP
sunset garden

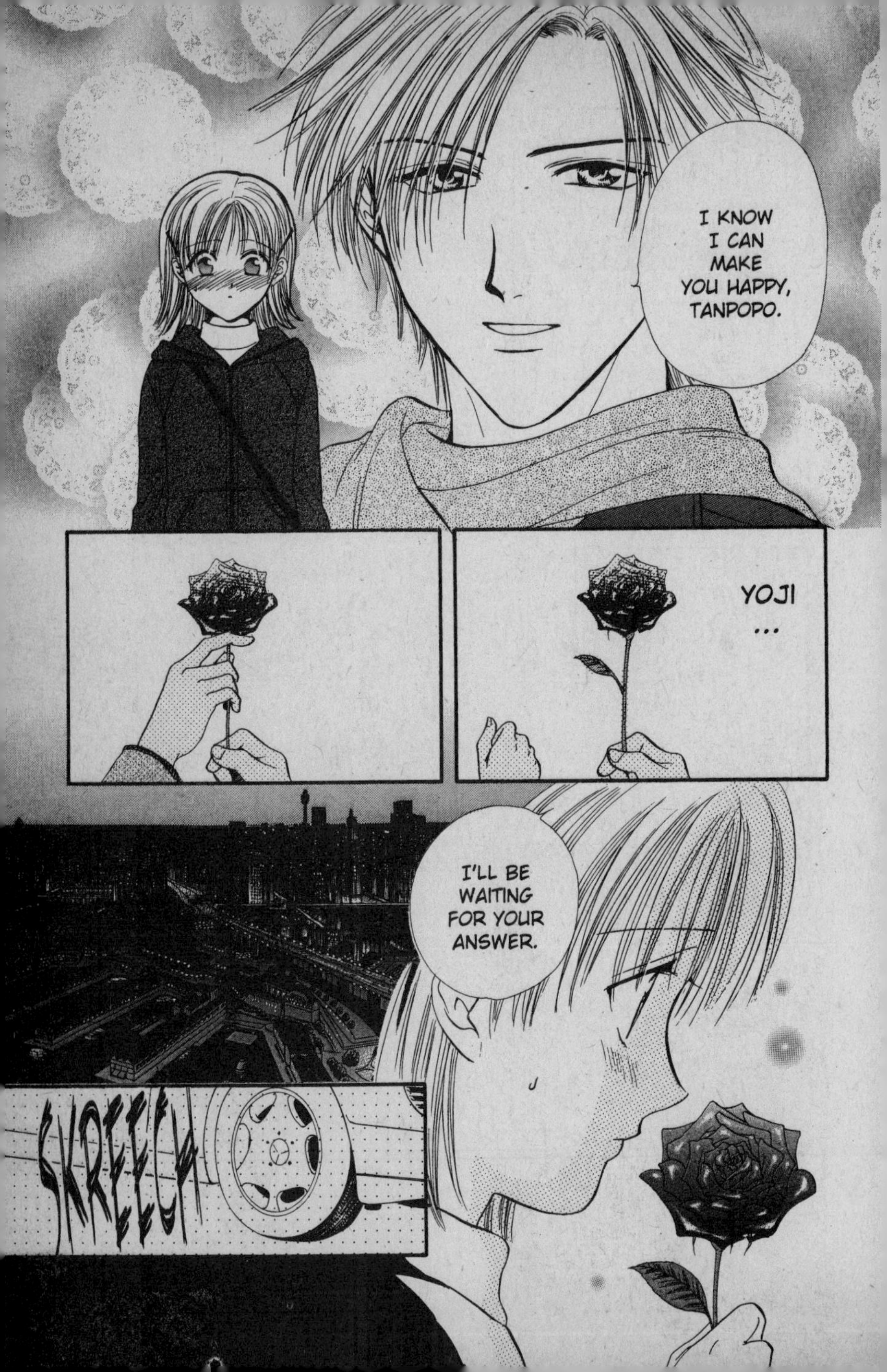
I KNOW I CAN MAKE YOU HAPPY, TANPOPO.
YOJI ...
I'LL BE WAITING FOR YOUR ANSWER.
SKREECH

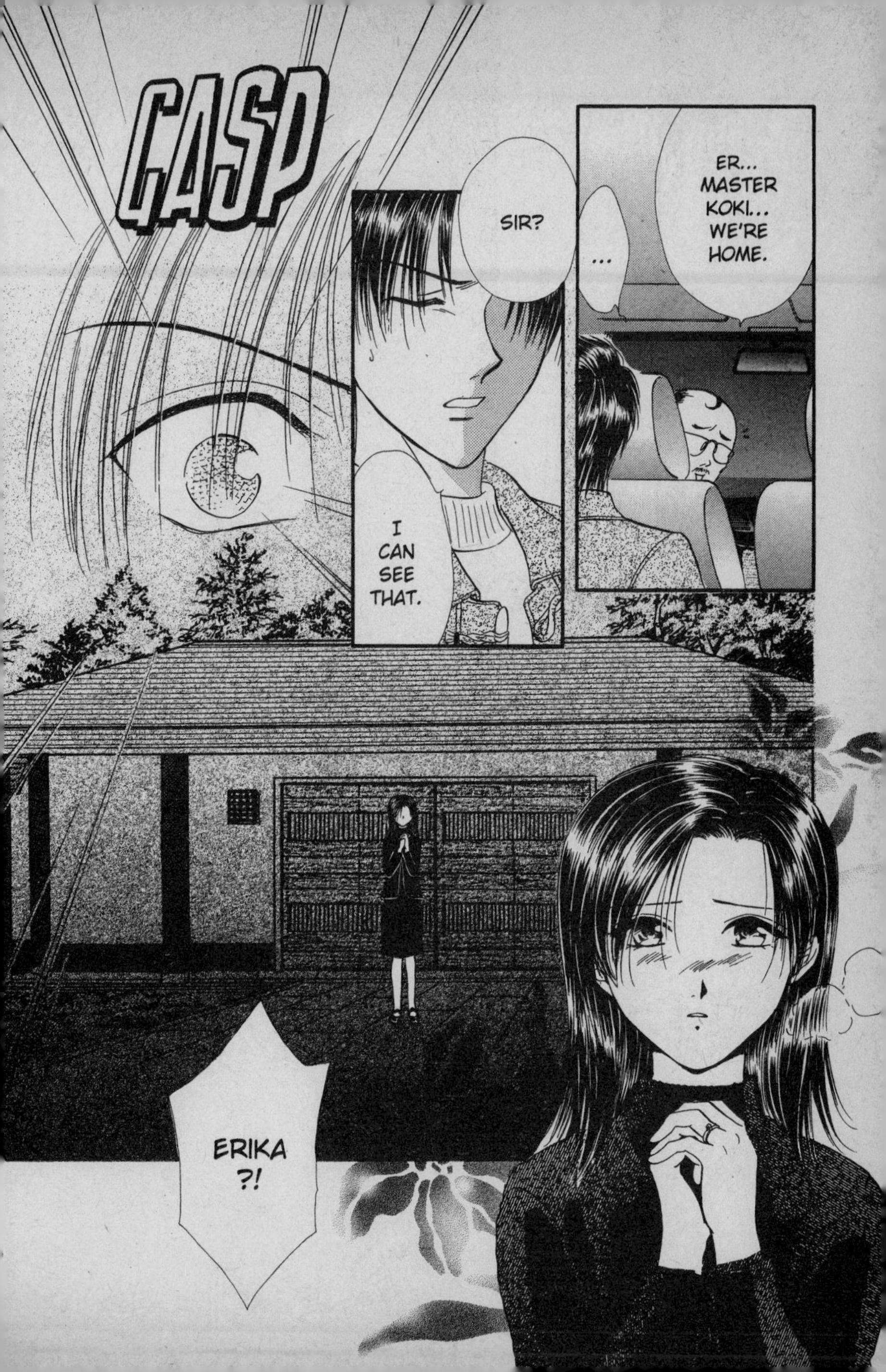
ER... MASTER KOKI... WE'RE HOME.
...
SIR?
I CAN SEE THAT.
GASP
ERIKA ?!

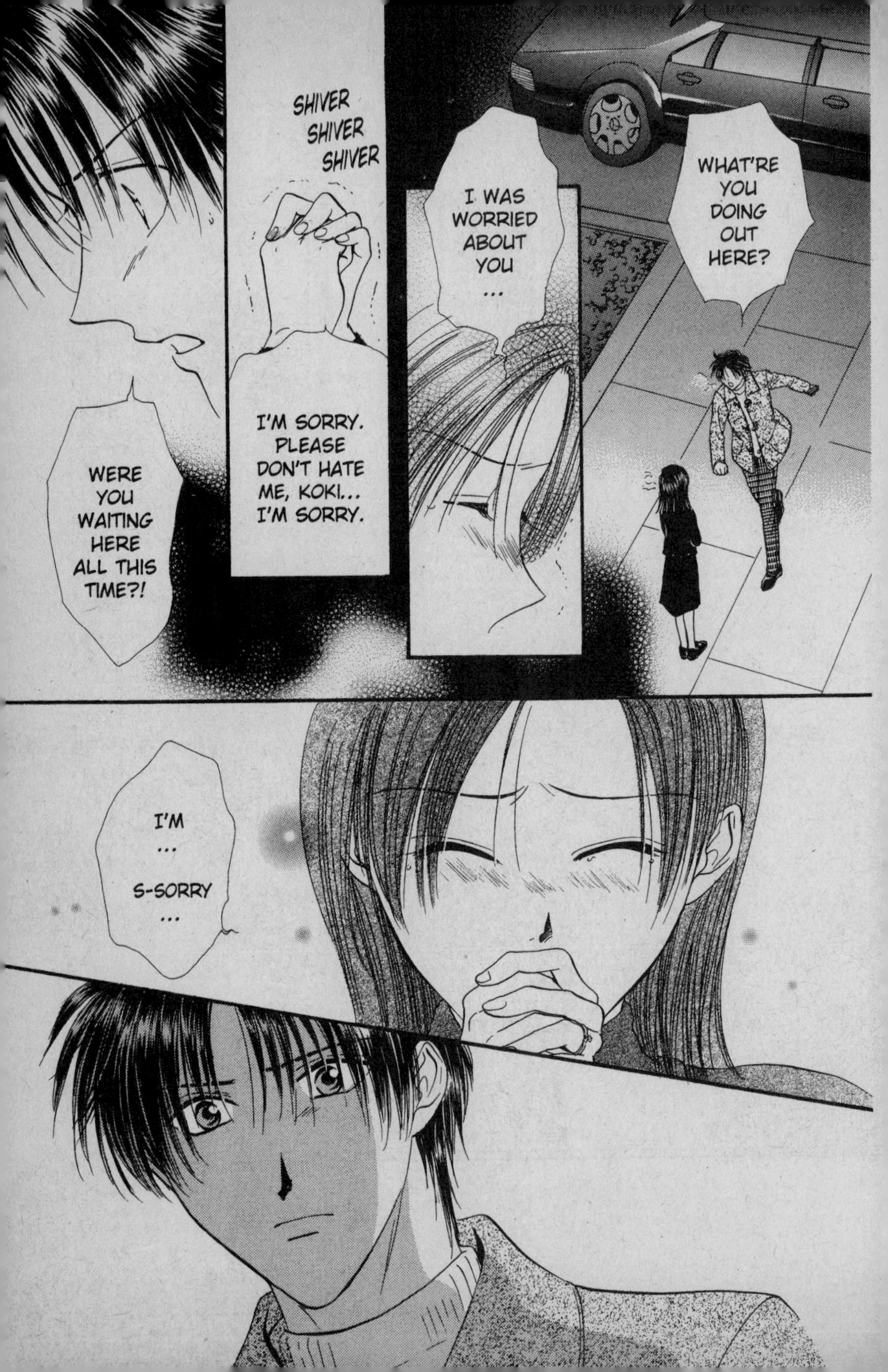
WHAT'RE YOU DOING OUT HERE?
I WAS WORRIED ABOUT YOU ...
SHIVER SHIVER SHIVER
I'M SORRY. PLEASE DON'T HATE ME, KOKI... I'M SORRY.
WERE YOU WAITING HERE ALL THIS TIME?!
I'M ... S-SORRY ...

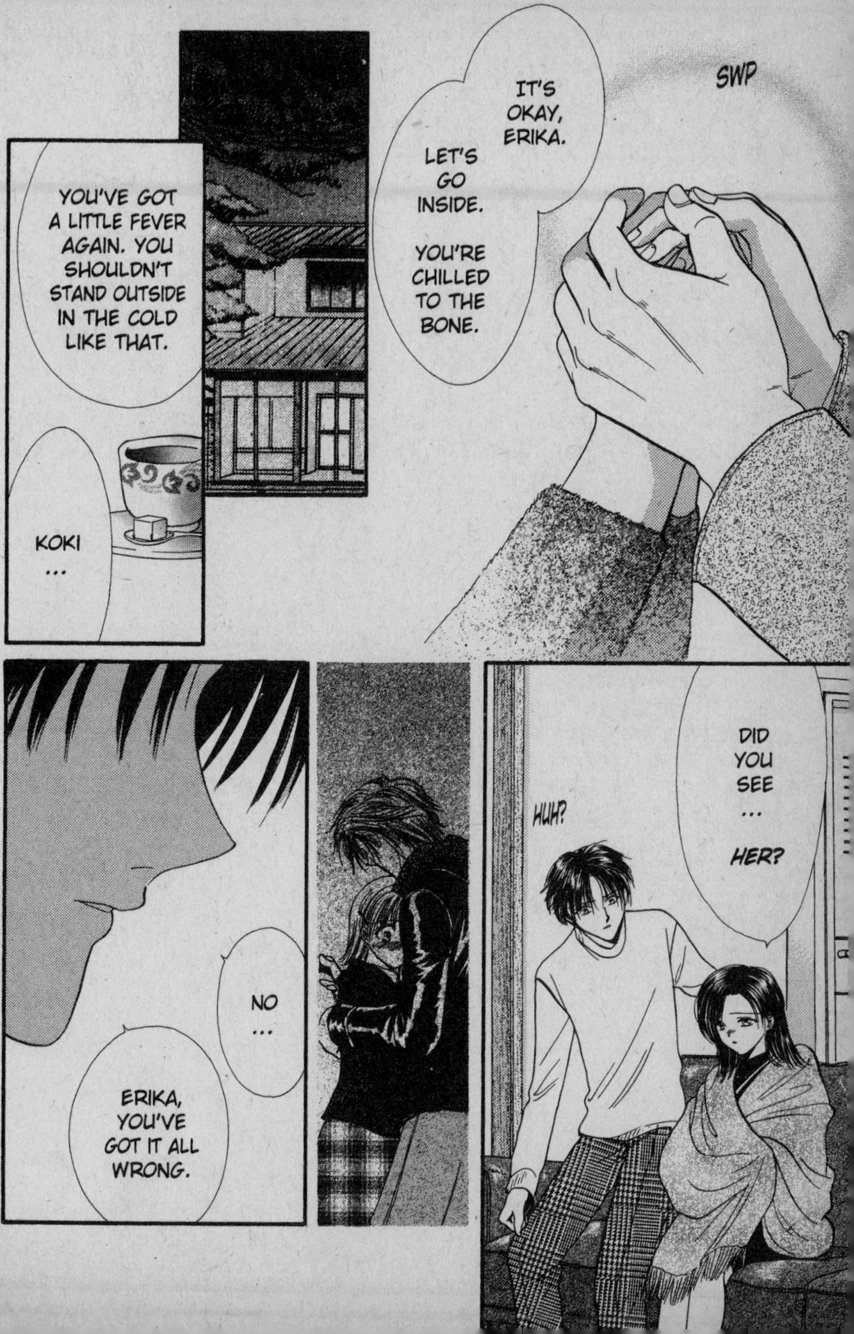
SWP
IT'S OKAY, ERIKA.
LET'S GO INSIDE.
YOU'RE CHILLED TO THE BONE.
YOU'VE GOT A LITTLE FEVER AGAIN. YOU SHOULDN'T STAND OUTSIDE IN THE COLD LIKE THAT.
KOKI ...
DID YOU SEE ... HER?
HUH?
NO ...
ERIKA, YOU'VE GOT IT ALL WRONG.

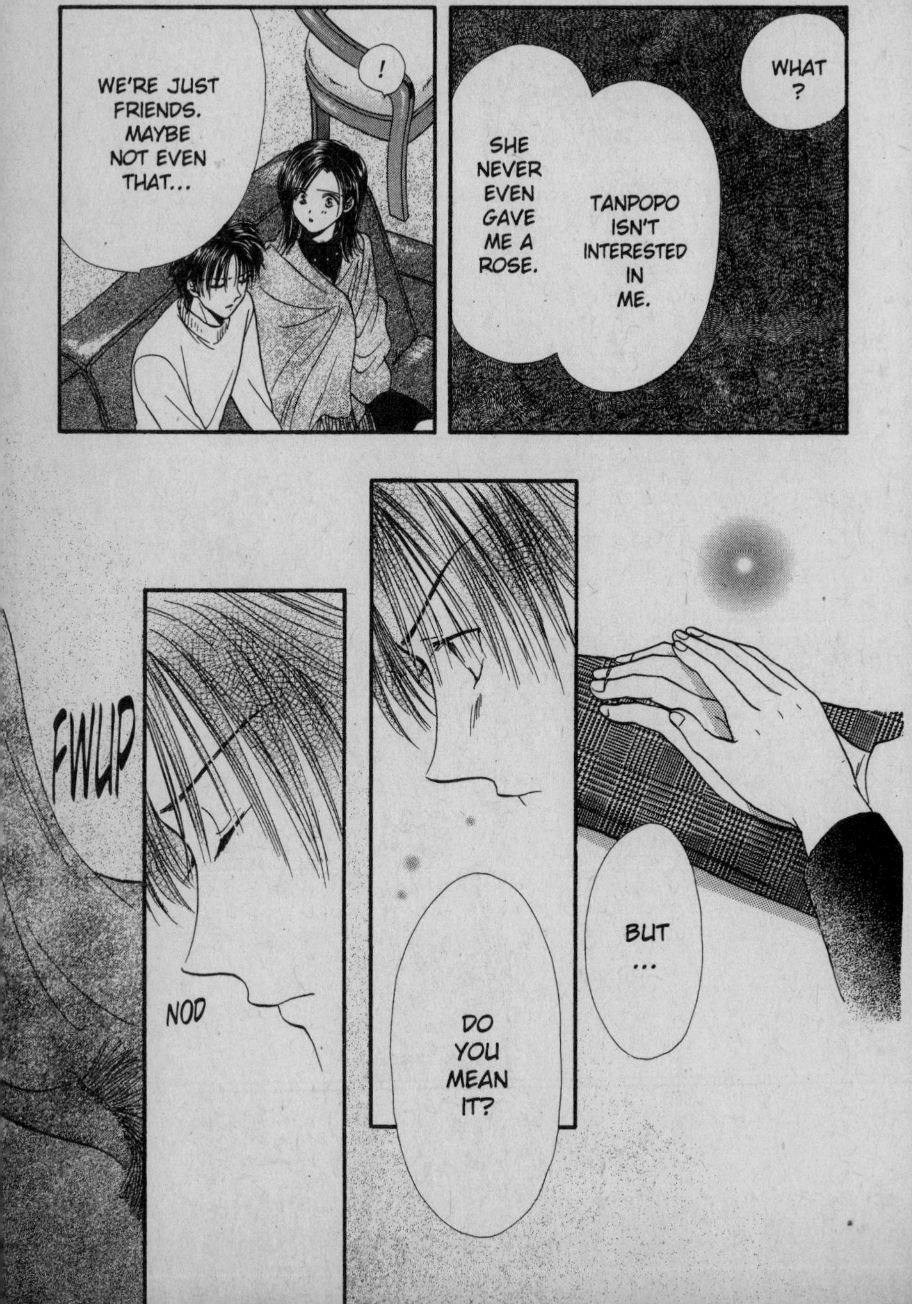
WHAT ?
TANPOPO ISN'T INTERESTED IN ME.
SHE NEVER EVEN GAVE ME A ROSE.
!
WE'RE JUST FRIENDS. MAYBE NOT EVEN THAT...
BUT ...
DO YOU MEAN IT?
FWUP
NOD

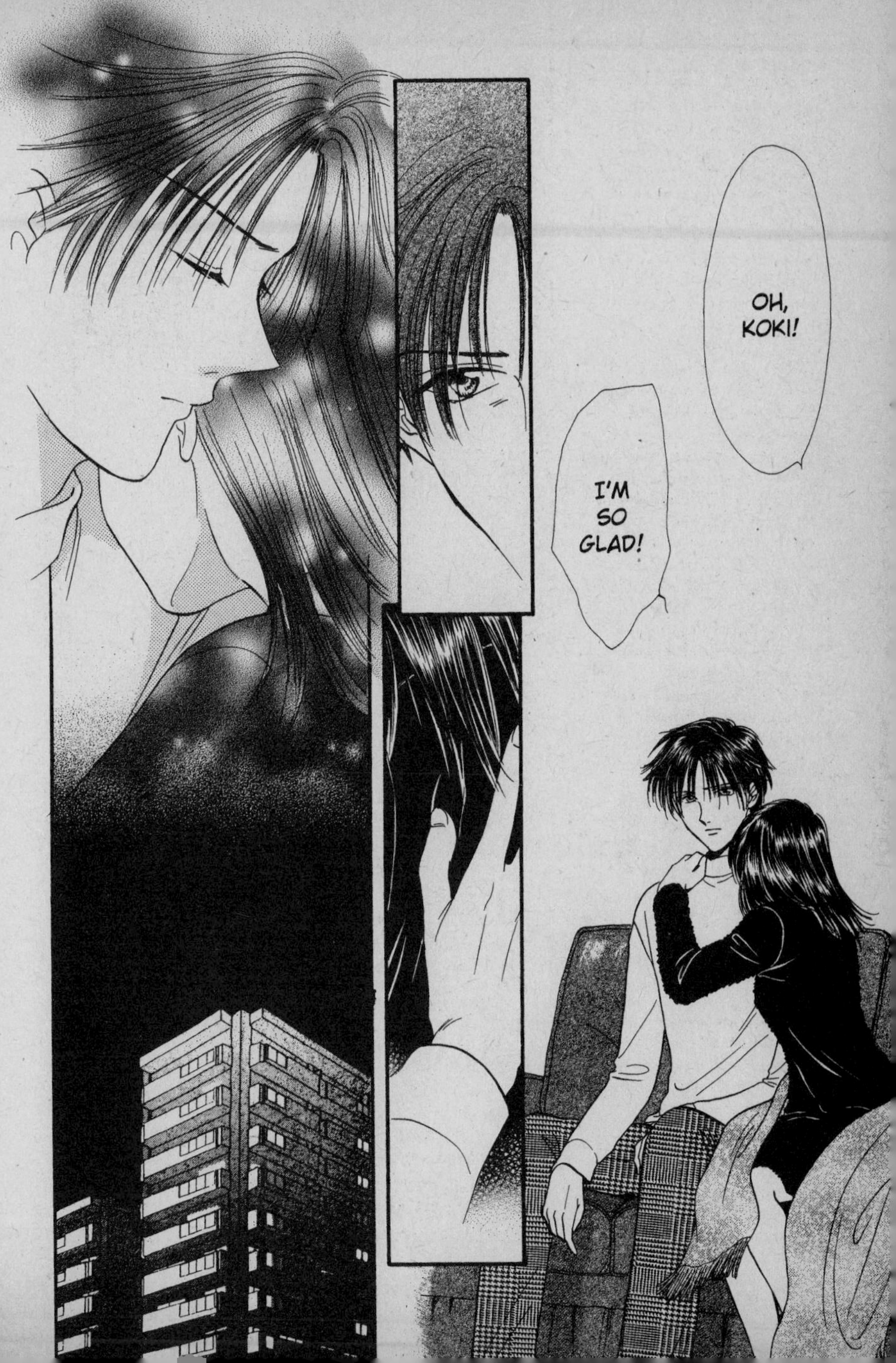
OH, KOKI!
I'M SO GLAD!

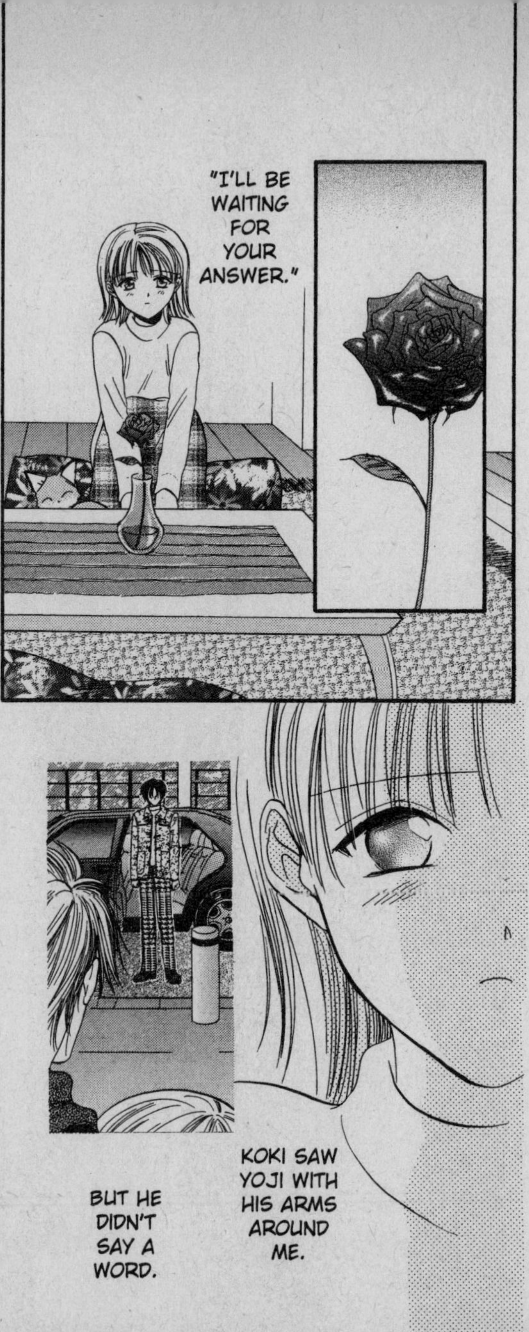
"I'LL BE WAITING FOR YOUR ANSWER."
KOKI SAW YOJI WITH HIS ARMS AROUND ME.
BUT HE DIDN'T SAY A WORD.

Continued...

By the way, "to forget" in this case doesn't mean "to abandon." It's more like "to put away for safekeeping." Because there's so much material, I just try to remember the important parts. Of course, I still like getting fan mail about my old works, but, for this reason, my responses are sometimes kind of weak. It's enough to make me wonder if my works really rate this kind of fan reaction, you know?

But then there's that old, old **Fushigi Yūgi**. The supplementary story from the archives, 7.8 **Eikoden**, will be made into an OVA (Original Video Animation) starting this summer. All four volumes are scheduled for release. The monthly magazine, **Shōjo Comic**, includes all kinds of anime-related news and merchandise. (The news is even on my friend's homepage.) Starting with the TV series that goes on sale in July, and the sale of reproductions of original prints, there are quite a few Fushigi Yūgi-related events, so if you know some **Fushigi Yūgi** fans, please do tell them about these.

Besides that, the **Ayashi no Ceres** novel, **Episode of Miku**, will go on sale in three consecutive volumes on 4/25, 6/1, and 7/1. It's the continuation of vol. 14 of the original series. If you know any fans, please tell them about this, too.

Also, **Fushigi Yūgi** and **Ayashi no Ceres** trading cards go on sale (the second time for **Fushigi Yūgi**). Please look for them at Animate stores and bookstores throughout Japan. The details are in **Shōjo Comic**. Surprisingly, when the (A lot of them) series is over, fans of **Fushigi Yūgi** or **Ayashi no Ceres** stop buying **Shojo Comic** or don't read my other works, so they don't find out about these things... That's too bad...

However, **Fushigi Yūgi** will keep on going and going. Really...

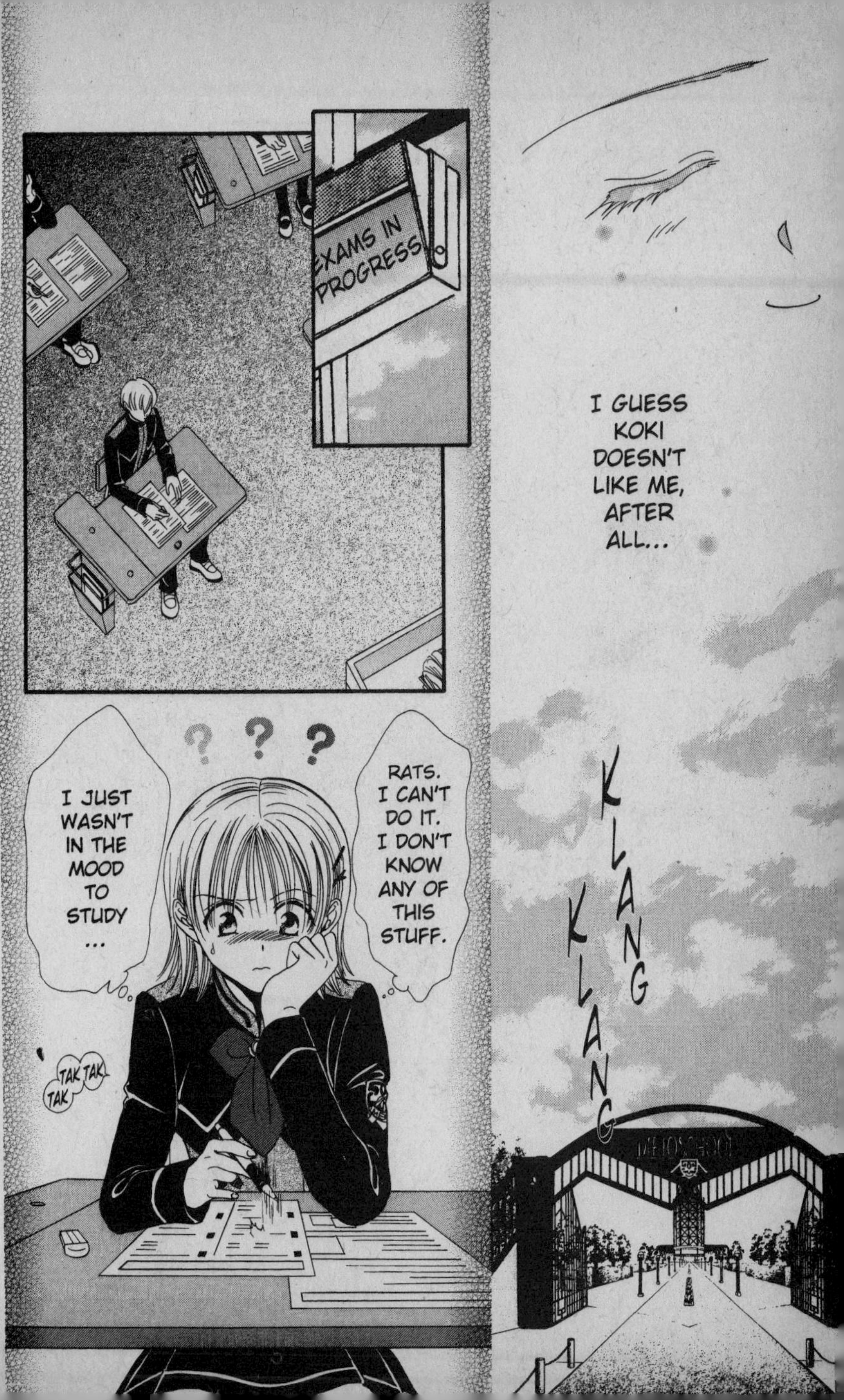
I GUESS KOKI DOESN'T LIKE ME, AFTER ALL...
KLANG
KLANG
EXAMS IN PROGRESS
RATS. I CAN'T DO IT. I DON'T KNOW ANY OF THIS STUFF.
I JUST WASN'T IN THE MOOD TO STUDY ...
TAK TAK TAK

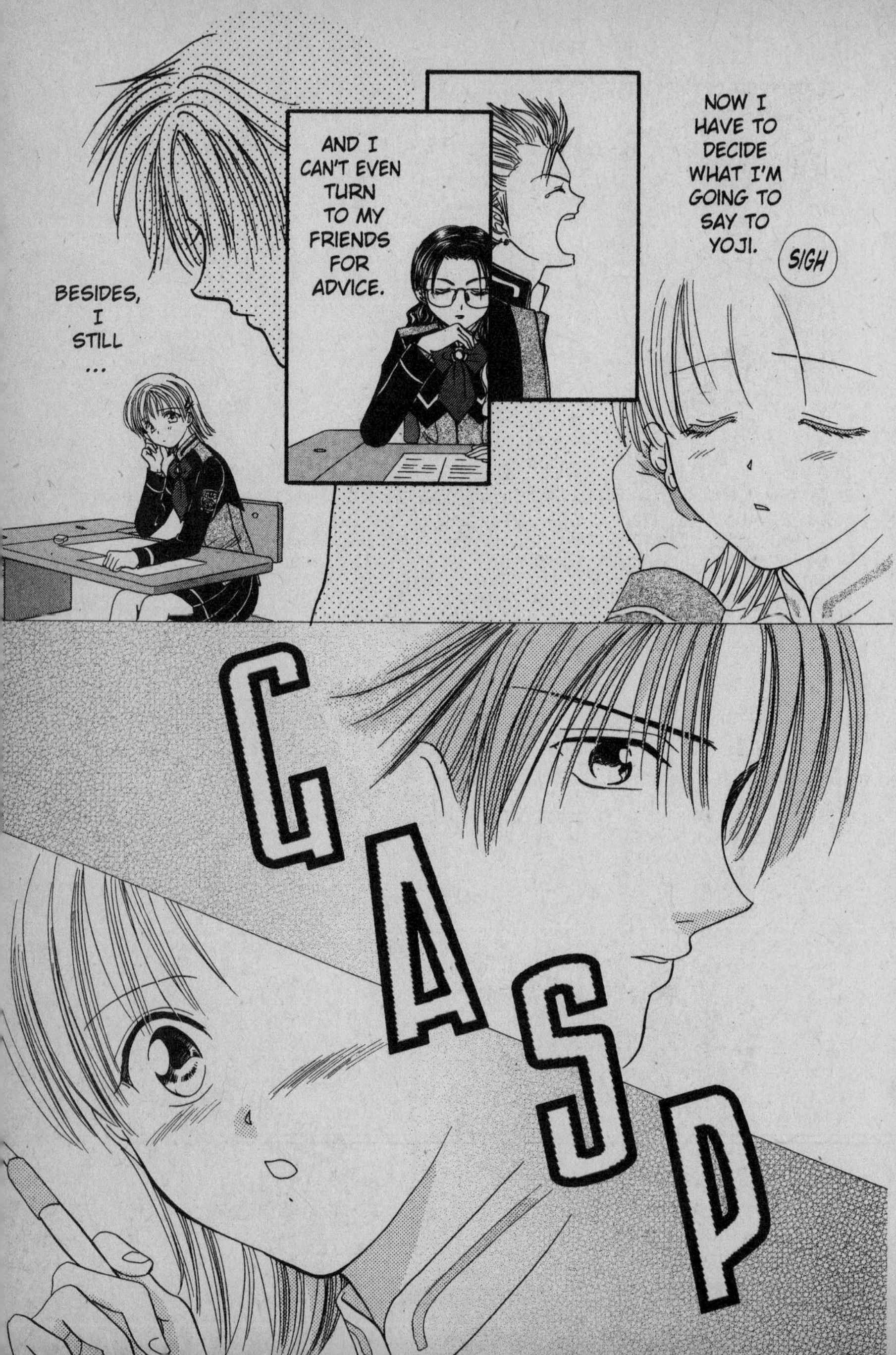
NOW I HAVE TO DECIDE WHAT I'M GOING TO SAY TO YOJI.
SIGH
AND I CAN'T EVEN TURN TO MY FRIENDS FOR ADVICE.
BESIDES, I STILL ...
GASP

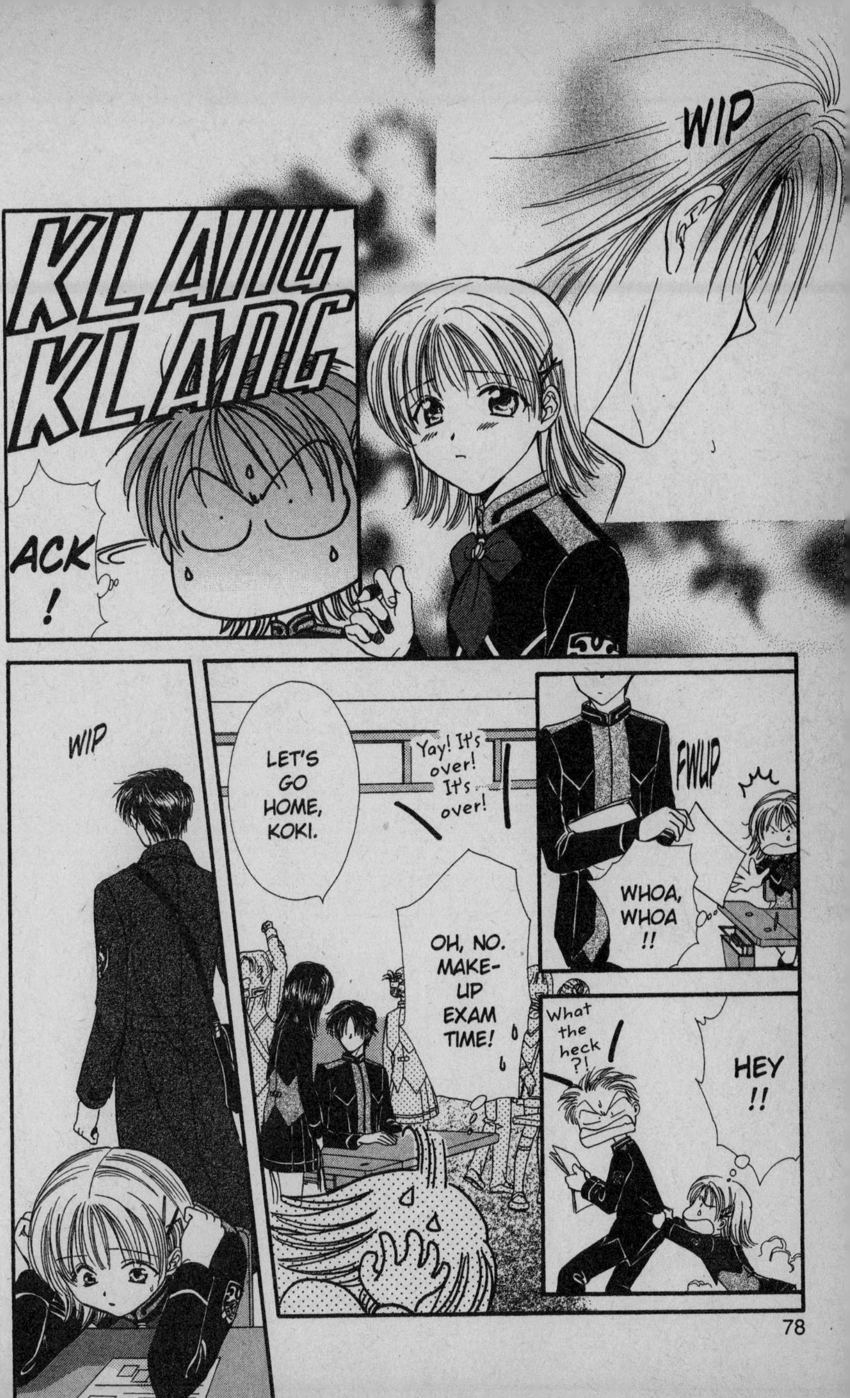
WIP
KLANG KLANG
ACK!
FWUP
WHOA, WHOA!!
HEY!!
What the heck?!
Yay! It's over! It's over!
LET'S GO HOME, KOKI.
OH, NO. MAKE-UP EXAM TIME!
WIP

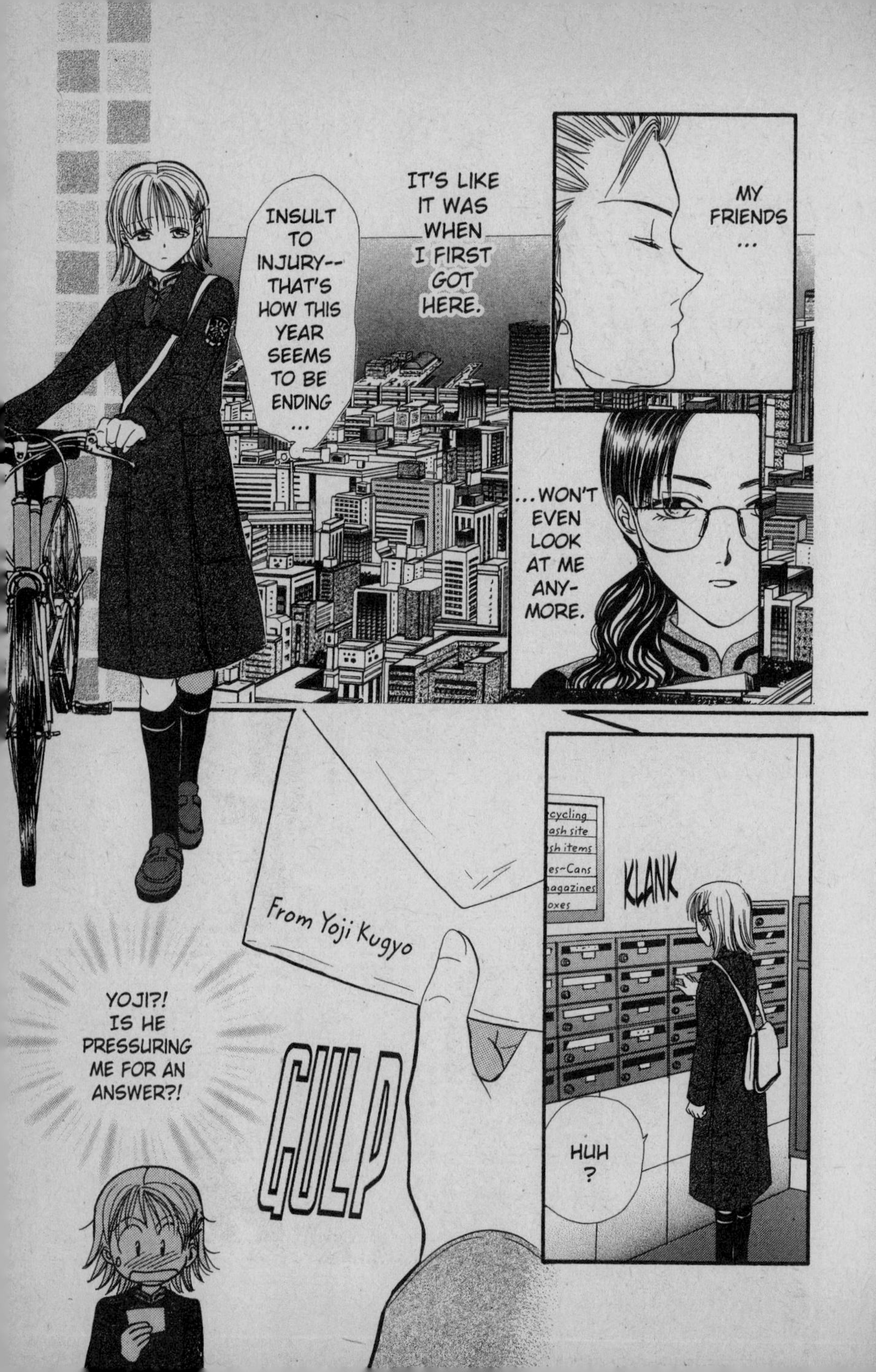
MY FRIENDS ...
...WON'T EVEN LOOK AT ME ANYMORE.
IT'S LIKE IT WAS WHEN I FIRST GOT HERE.
INSULT TO INJURY-- THAT'S HOW THIS YEAR SEEMS TO BE ENDING ...
KLANK
HUH ?
From Yoji Kugyo
GULP
YOJI?! IS HE PRESSURING ME FOR AN ANSWER?!

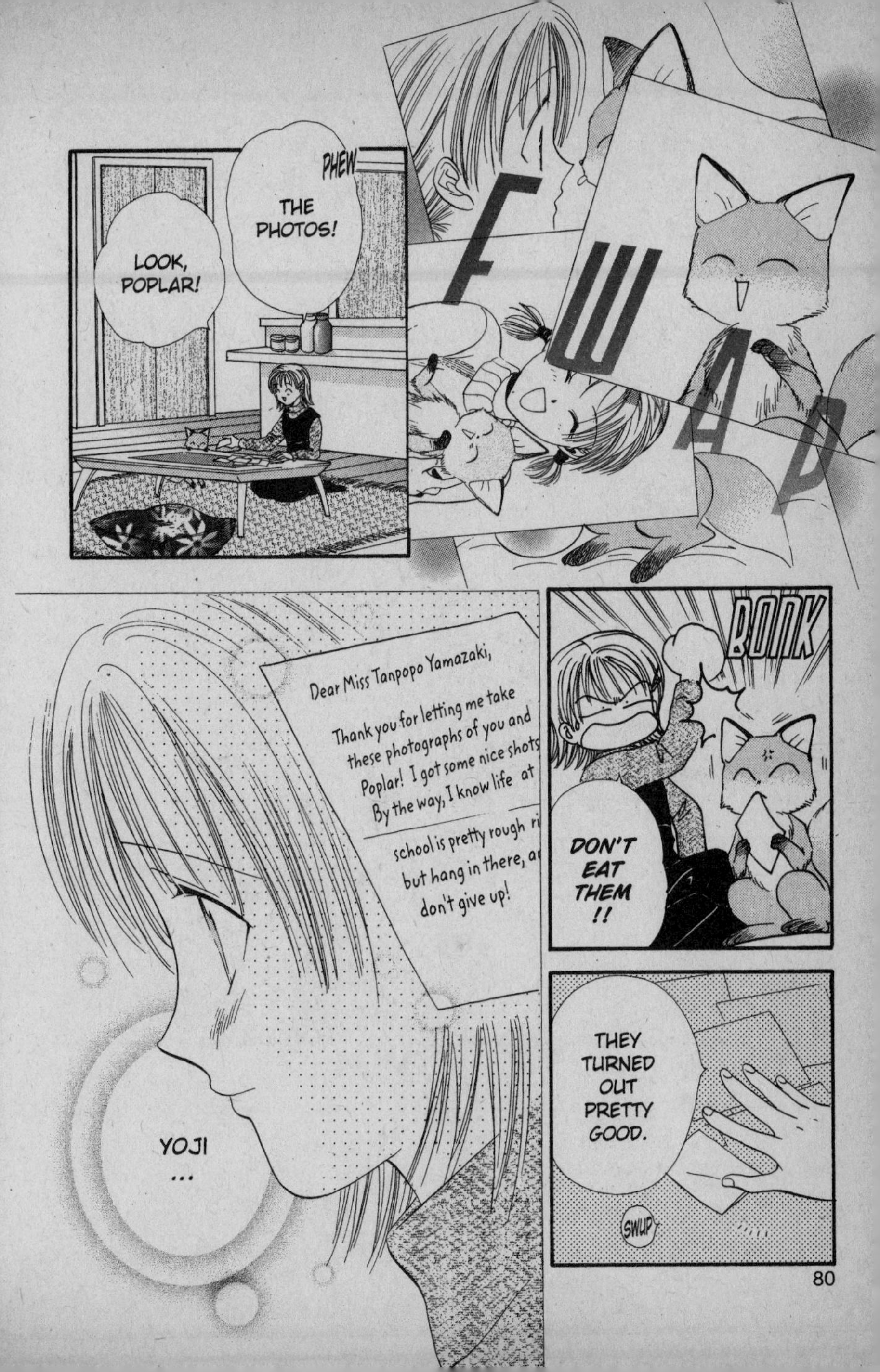
FWAP
PHEW
THE PHOTOS!
LOOK, POPLAR!
BONK
DON'T EAT THEM !!
THEY TURNED OUT PRETTY GOOD.
SWUP
Dear Miss Tanpopo Yamazaki,
Thank you for letting me take these photographs of you and Poplar! I got some nice shots By the way, I know life at
school is pretty rough ri but hang in there, a don't give up!
YOJI ...

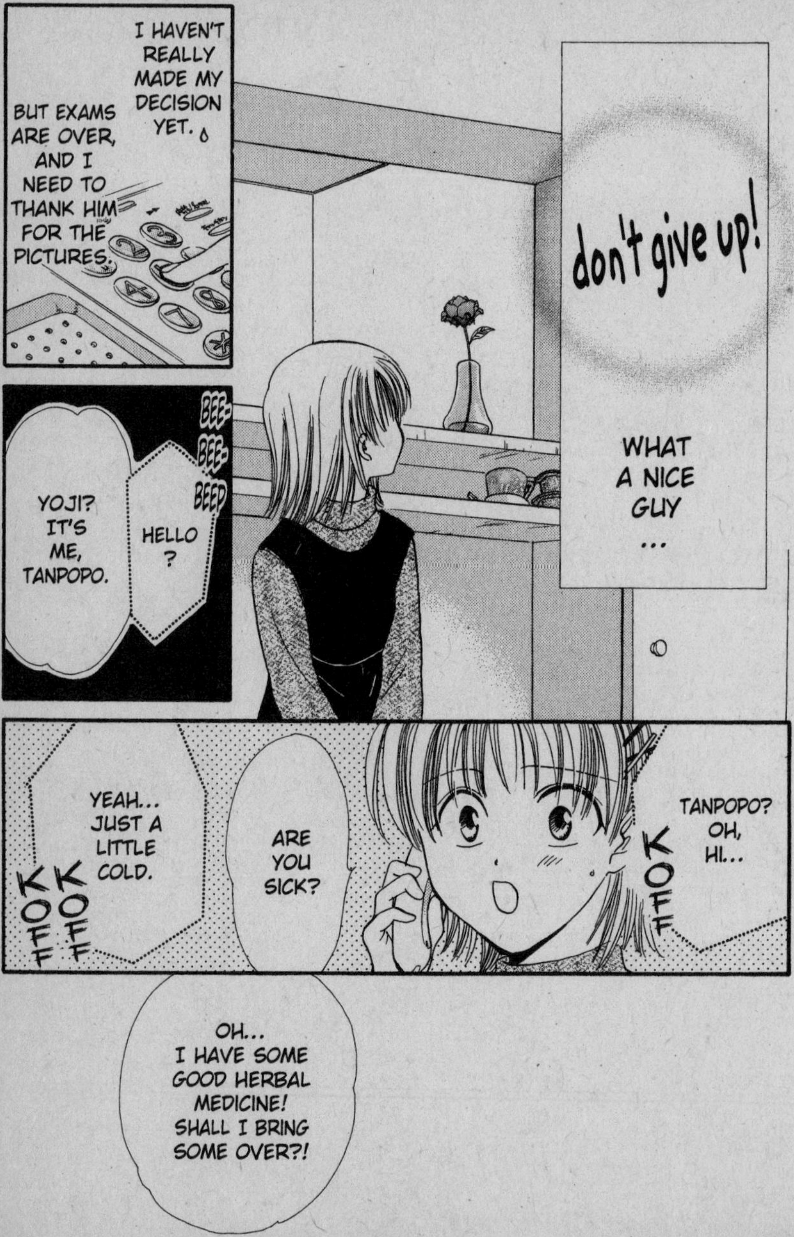
don't give up!
WHAT A NICE GUY ...
I HAVEN'T REALLY MADE MY DECISION YET.
BUT EXAMS ARE OVER, AND I NEED TO THANK HIM FOR THE PICTURES.
BEE-BEE-BEEP
HELLO?
YOJI? IT'S ME, TANPOPO.
KOFF
TANPOPO? OH, HI...
ARE YOU SICK?
YEAH... JUST A LITTLE COLD.
KOFF KOFF
OH... I HAVE SOME GOOD HERBAL MEDICINE! SHALL I BRING SOME OVER?!

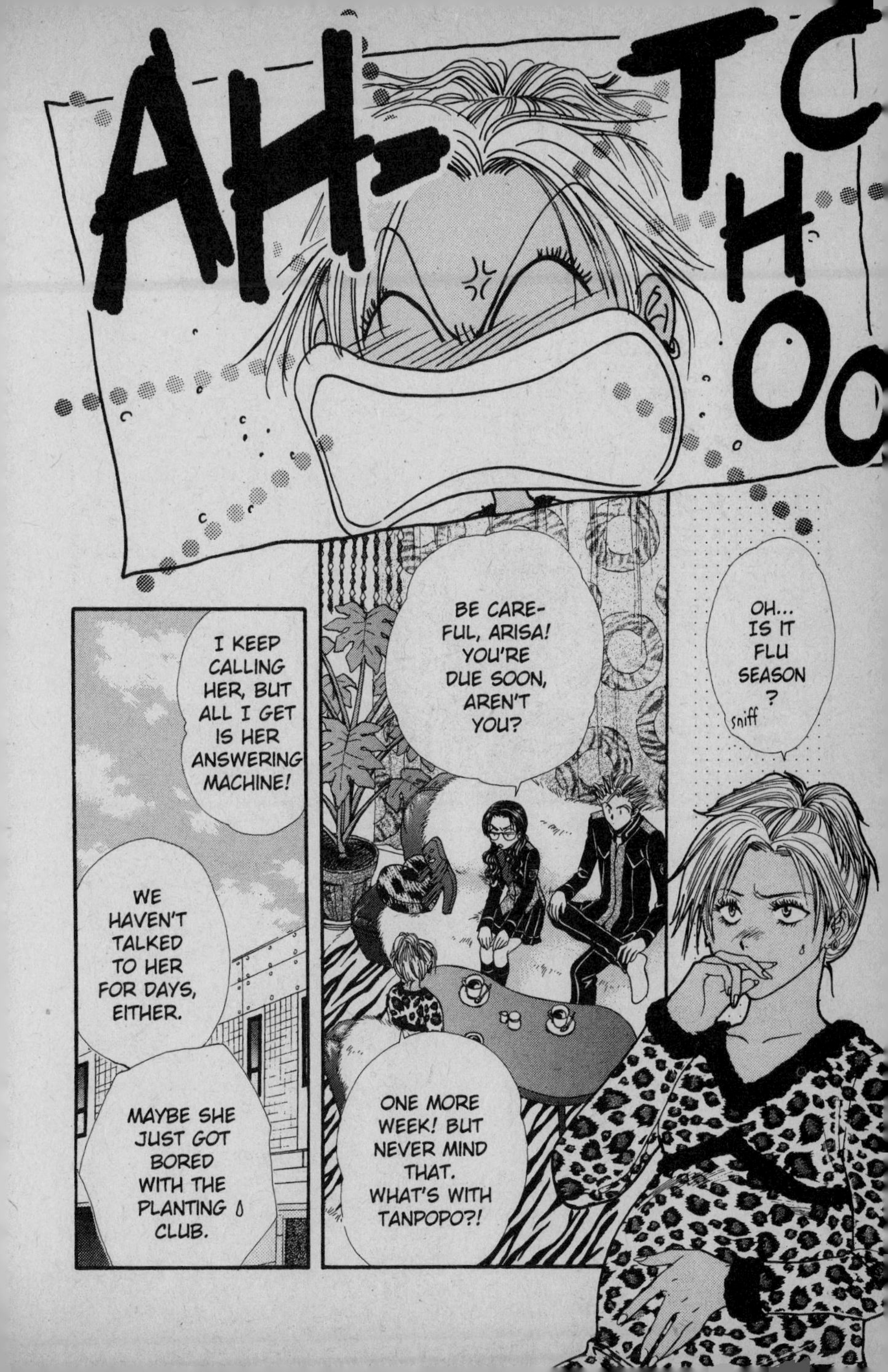
AH-TCHOO
OH... IS IT FLU SEASON?
sniff
BE CARE-FUL, ARISA! YOU'RE DUE SOON, AREN'T YOU?
ONE MORE WEEK! BUT NEVER MIND THAT. WHAT'S WITH TANPOPO?!
I KEEP CALLING HER, BUT ALL I GET IS HER ANSWERING MACHINE!
WE HAVEN'T TALKED TO HER FOR DAYS, EITHER.
MAYBE SHE JUST GOT BORED WITH THE PLANTING CLUB.

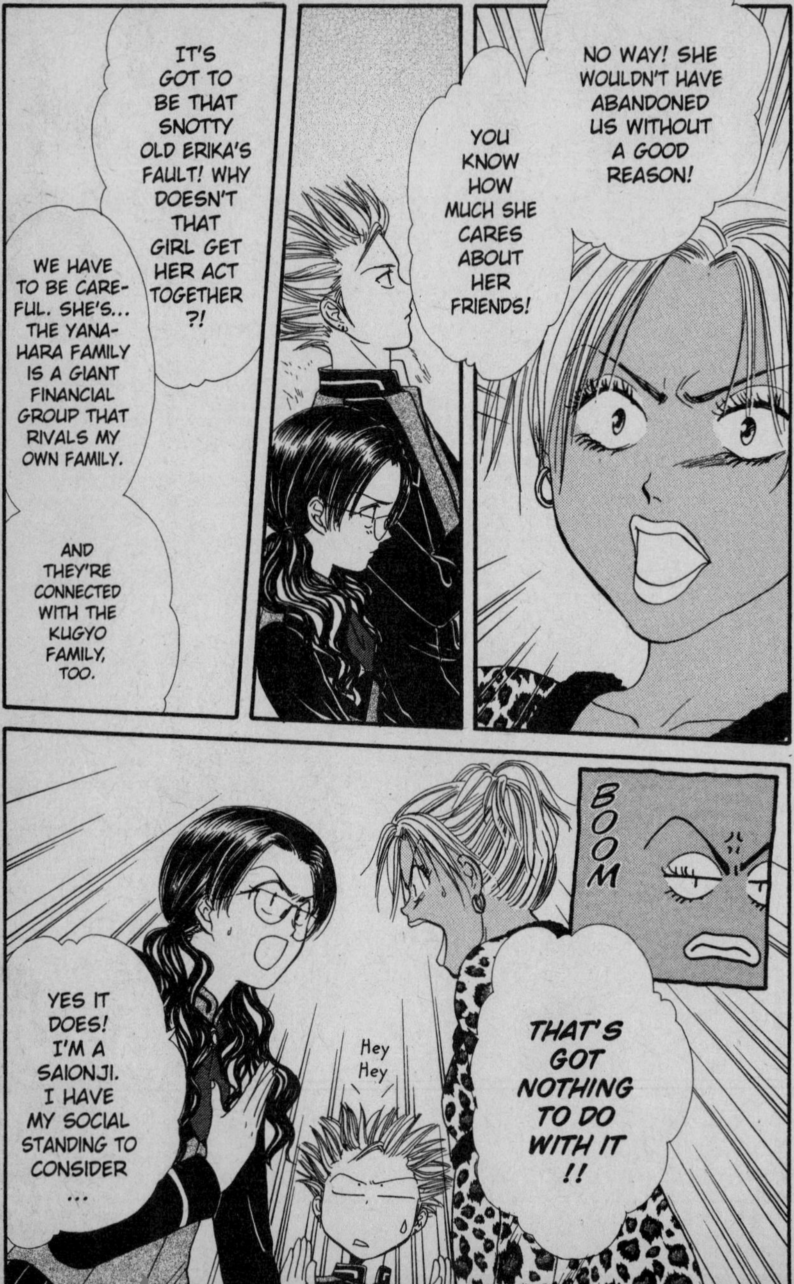
NO WAY! SHE WOULDN'T HAVE ABANDONED US WITHOUT A GOOD REASON!
YOU KNOW HOW MUCH SHE CARES ABOUT HER FRIENDS!
IT'S GOT TO BE THAT SNOTTY OLD ERIKA'S FAULT! WHY DOESN'T THAT GIRL GET HER ACT TOGETHER ?!
WE HAVE TO BE CARE-FUL. SHE'S... THE YANA-HARA FAMILY IS A GIANT FINANCIAL GROUP THAT RIVALS MY OWN FAMILY.
AND THEY'RE CONNECTED WITH THE KUGYO FAMILY, TOO.
BOOOM
THAT'S GOT NOTHING TO DO WITH IT !!
Hey Hey
YES IT DOES! I'M A SAIONJI. I HAVE MY SOCIAL STANDING TO CONSIDER ...

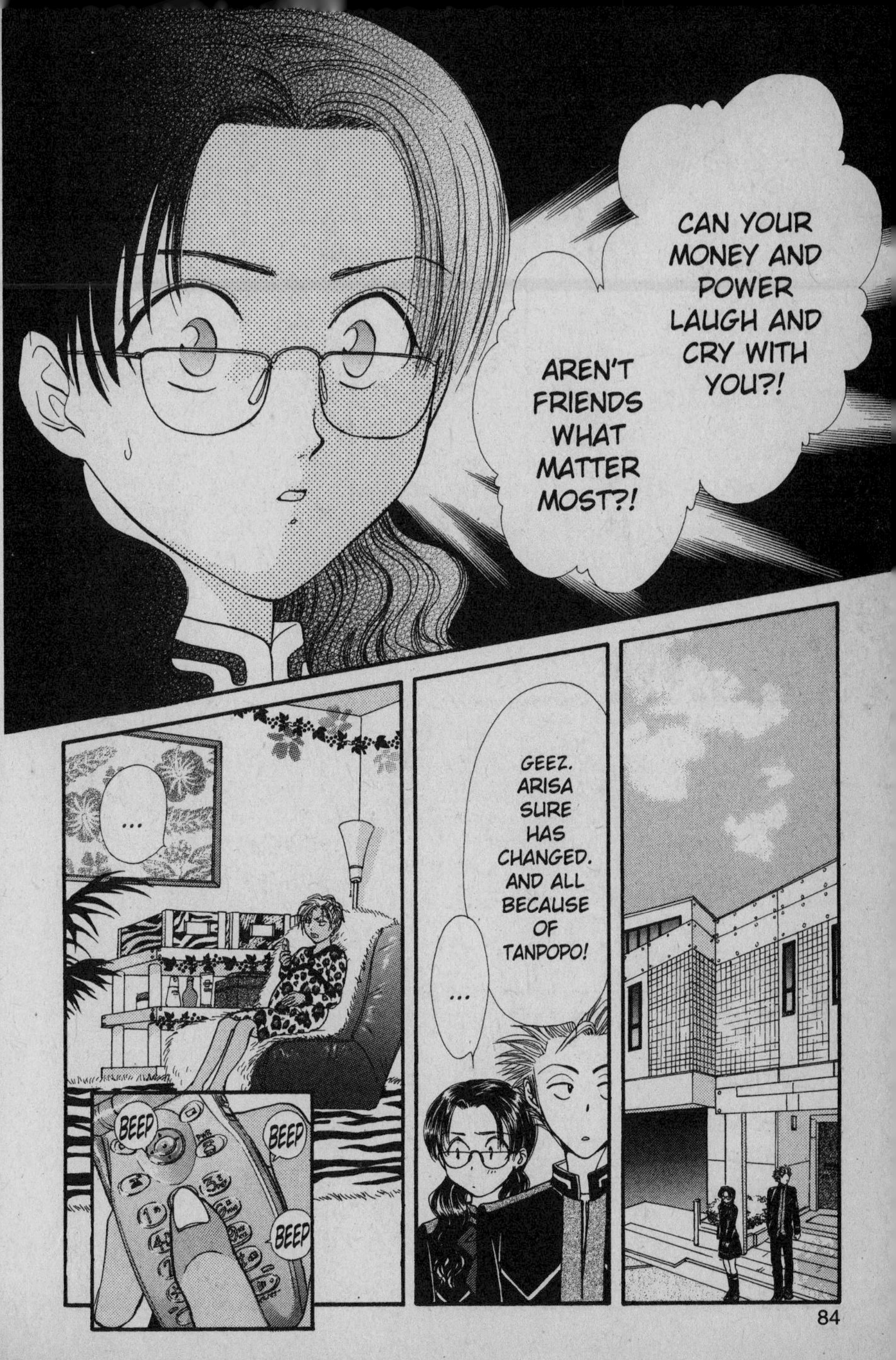
CAN YOUR MONEY AND POWER LAUGH AND CRY WITH YOU?!
AREN'T FRIENDS WHAT MATTER MOST?!
GEEZ. ARISA SURE HAS CHANGED. AND ALL BECAUSE OF TANPOPO!
...
...
BEEP
BEEP
BEEP

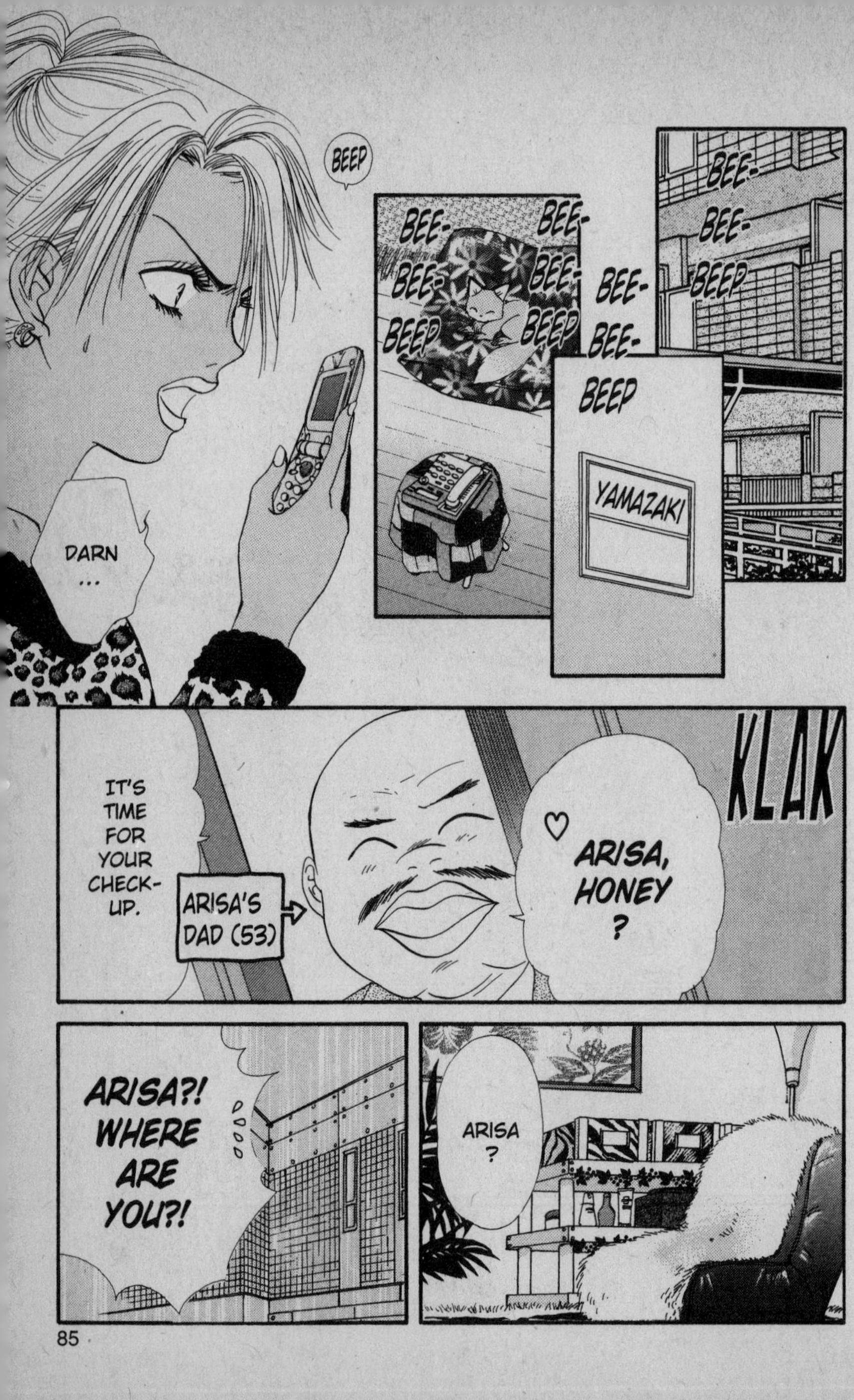
BEE-
BEE-
BEEP
BEE-
BEE-
BEEP
YAMAZAKI
BEE-
BEE-
BEEP
BEE-
BEE-
BEEP
BEEP
DARN ...
KLAK
ARISA, HONEY ?
ARISA'S DAD (53)
IT'S TIME FOR YOUR CHECK-UP.
ARISA ?
ARISA?! WHERE ARE YOU?!

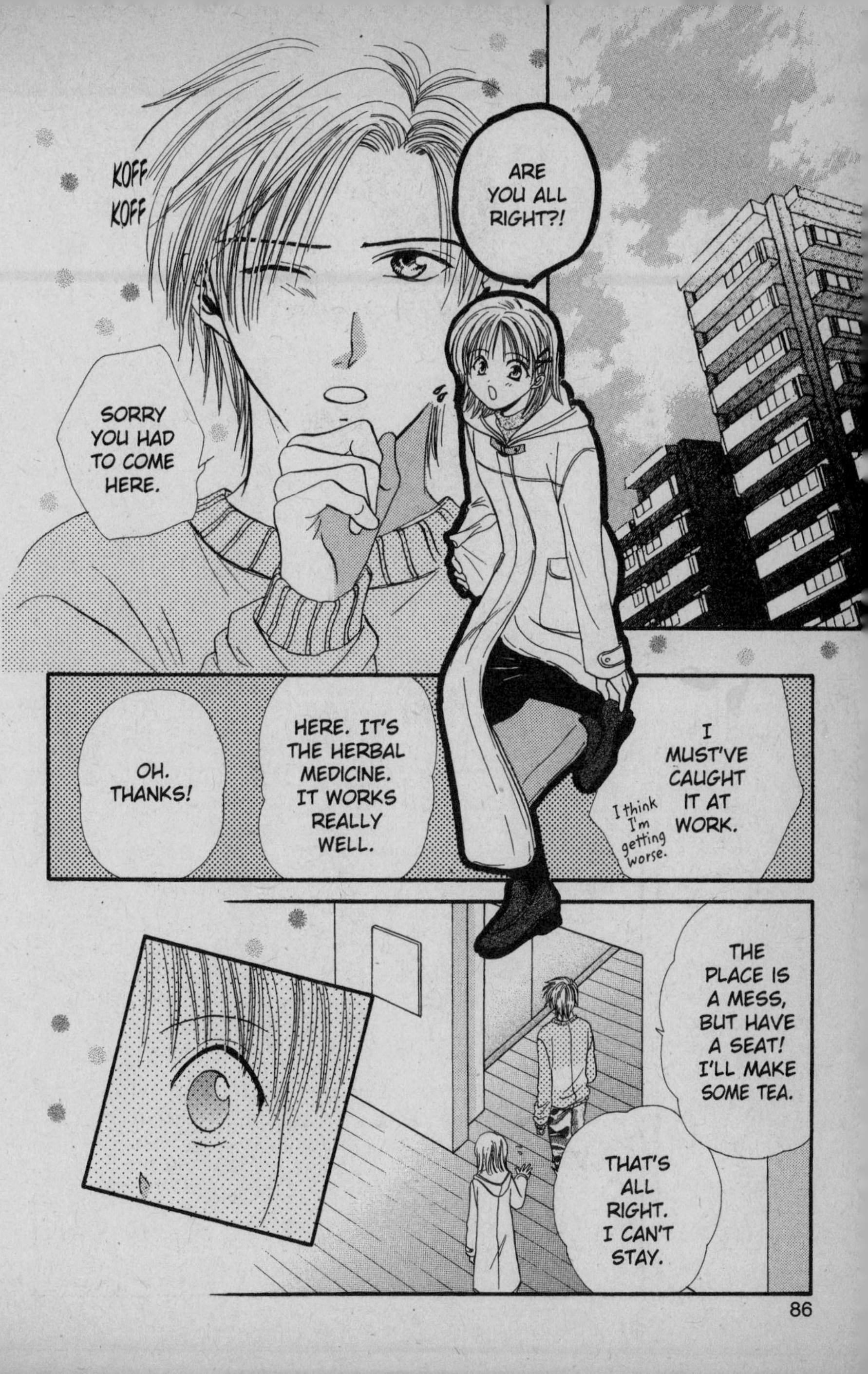
ARE YOU ALL RIGHT?!
KOFF KOFF
SORRY YOU HAD TO COME HERE.
I MUST'VE CAUGHT IT AT WORK.
I think I'm getting worse.
HERE. IT'S THE HERBAL MEDICINE. IT WORKS REALLY WELL.
OH. THANKS!
THE PLACE IS A MESS, BUT HAVE A SEAT! I'LL MAKE SOME TEA.
THAT'S ALL RIGHT. I CAN'T STAY.

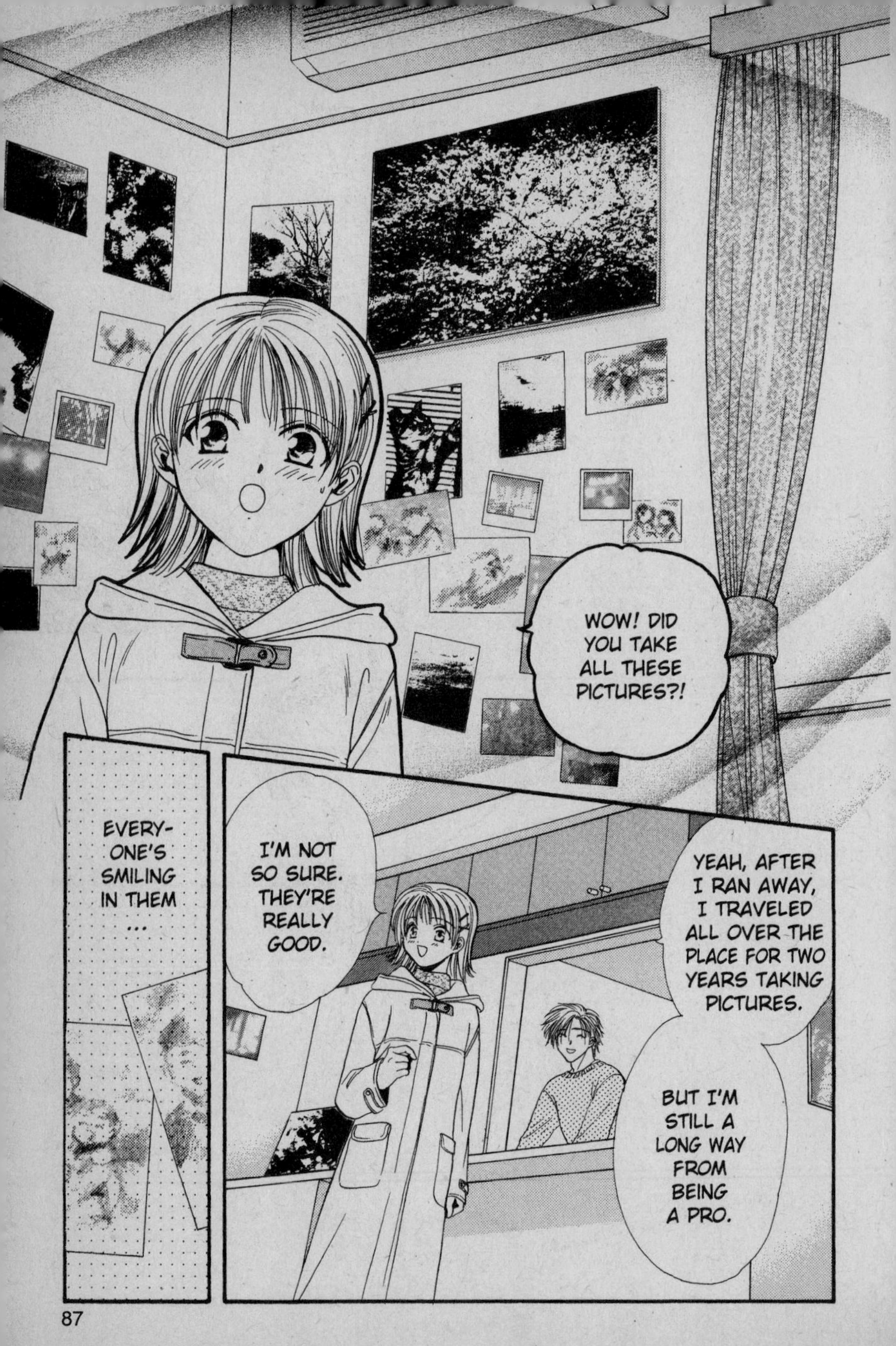
WOW! DID YOU TAKE ALL THESE PICTURES?!
YEAH, AFTER I RAN AWAY, I TRAVELED ALL OVER THE PLACE FOR TWO YEARS TAKING PICTURES.
BUT I'M STILL A LONG WAY FROM BEING A PRO.
I'M NOT SO SURE. THEY'RE REALLY GOOD.
EVERY-ONE'S SMILING IN THEM ...

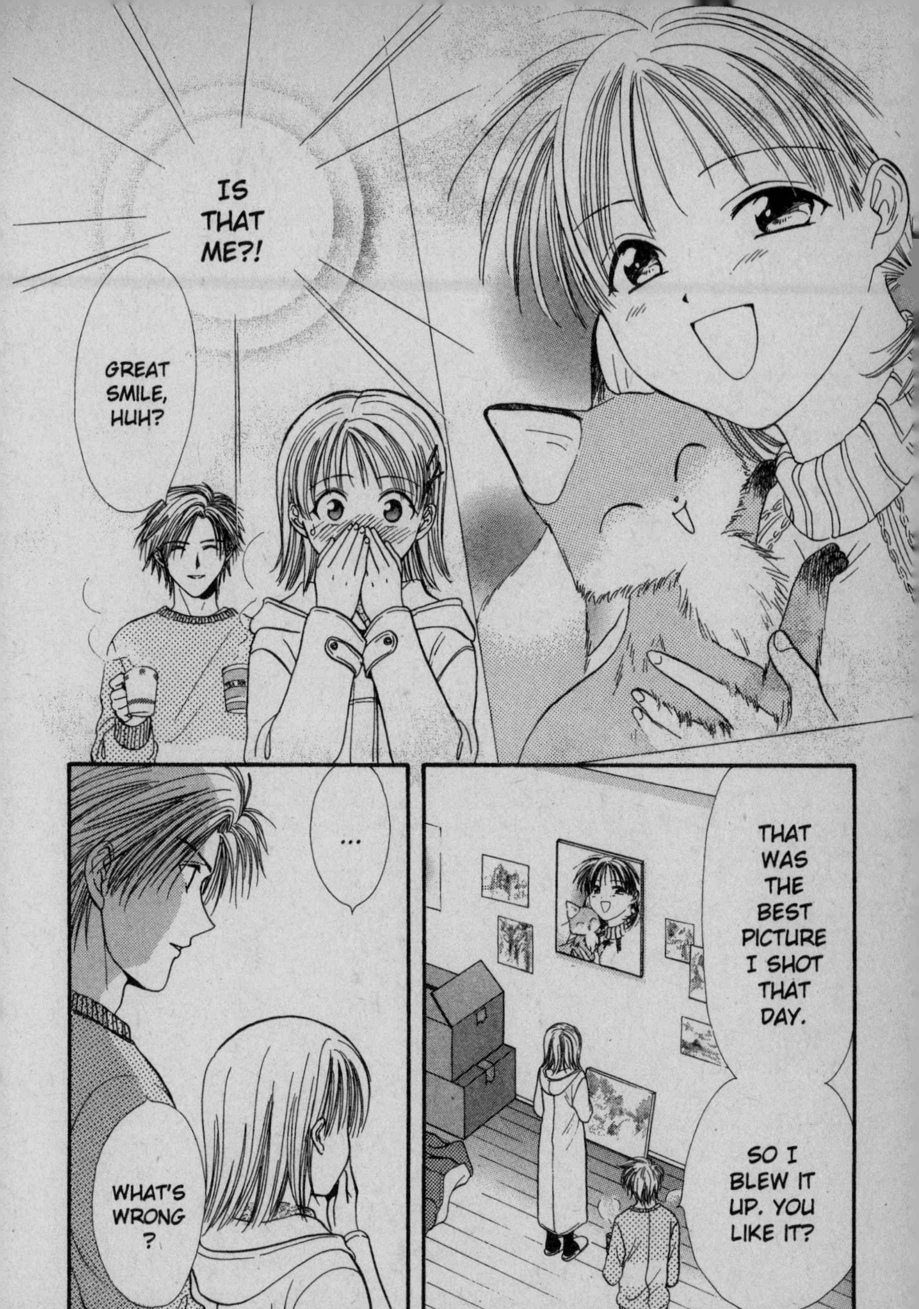
IS THAT ME?!
GREAT SMILE, HUH?
THAT WAS THE BEST PICTURE I SHOT THAT DAY.
SO I BLEW IT UP. YOU LIKE IT?
...
WHAT'S WRONG ?

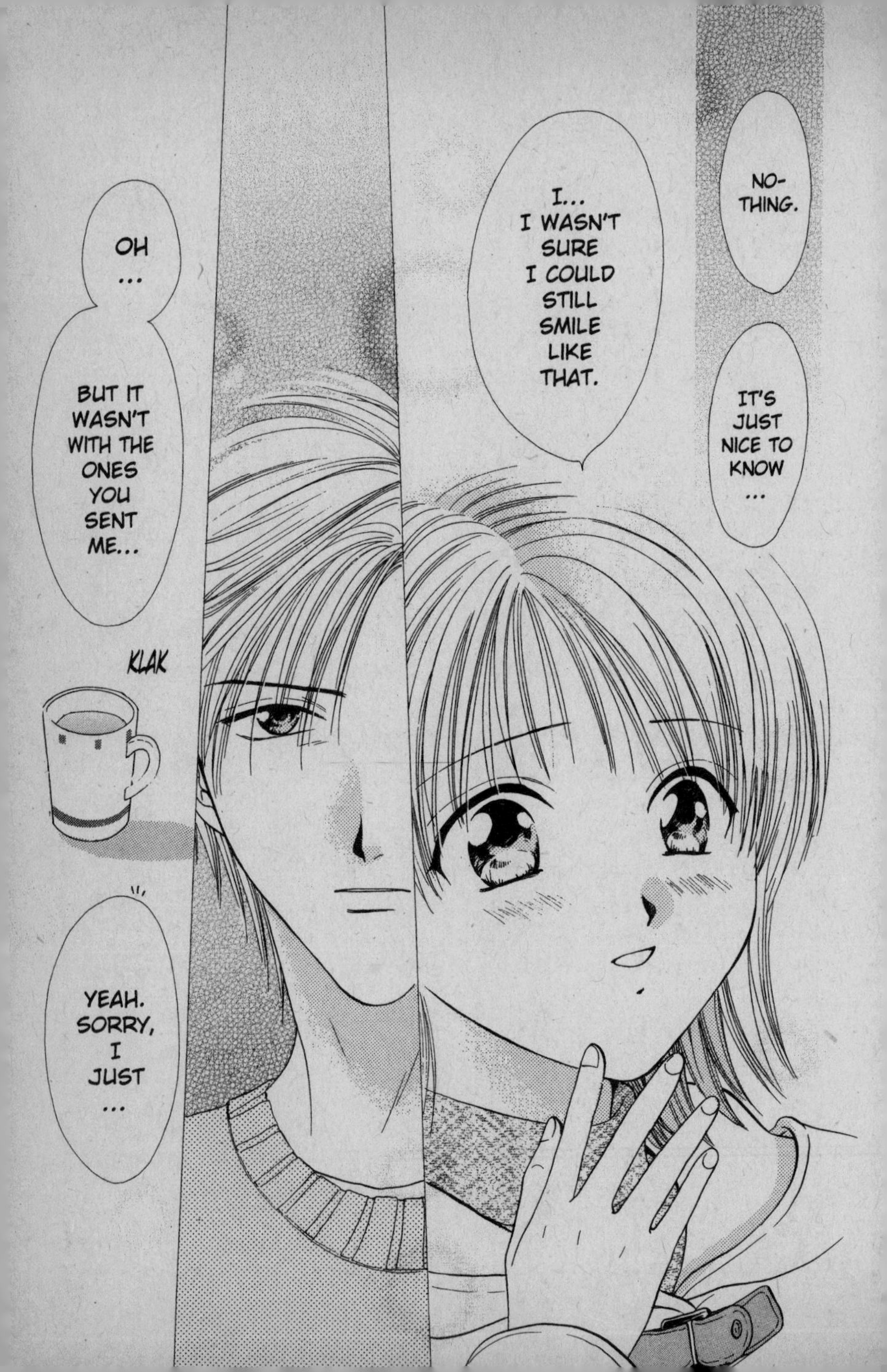
NO-THING.
IT'S JUST NICE TO KNOW ...
I... I WASN'T SURE I COULD STILL SMILE LIKE THAT.
OH ...
BUT IT WASN'T WITH THE ONES YOU SENT ME...
KLAK
YEAH. SORRY, I JUST ...

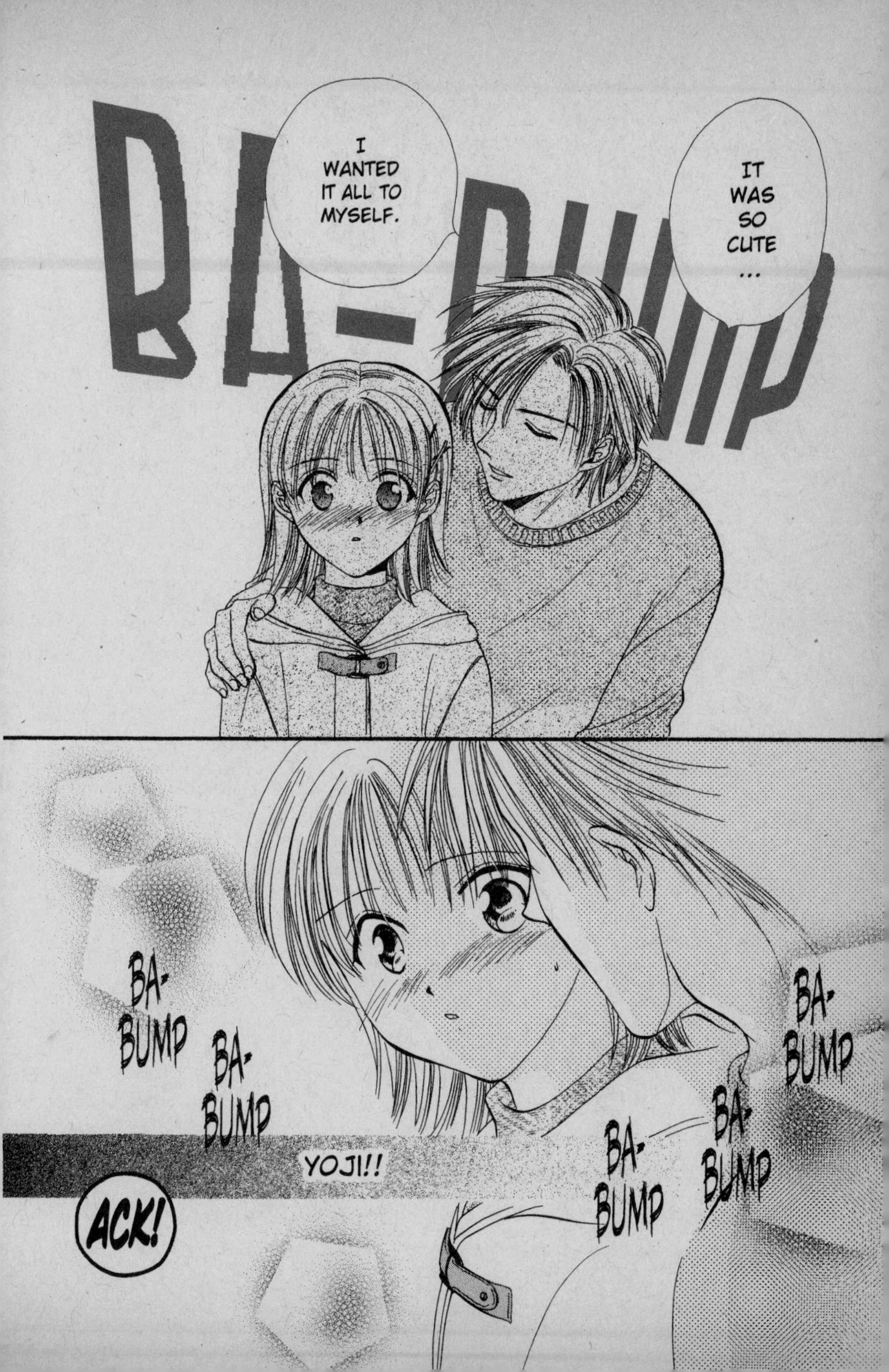
IT WAS SO CUTE ...
I WANTED IT ALL TO MYSELF.
BA-BUMP
BA-BUMP
BA-BUMP
BA-BUMP
BA-BUMP
BA-BUMP
YOJI!!
ACK!

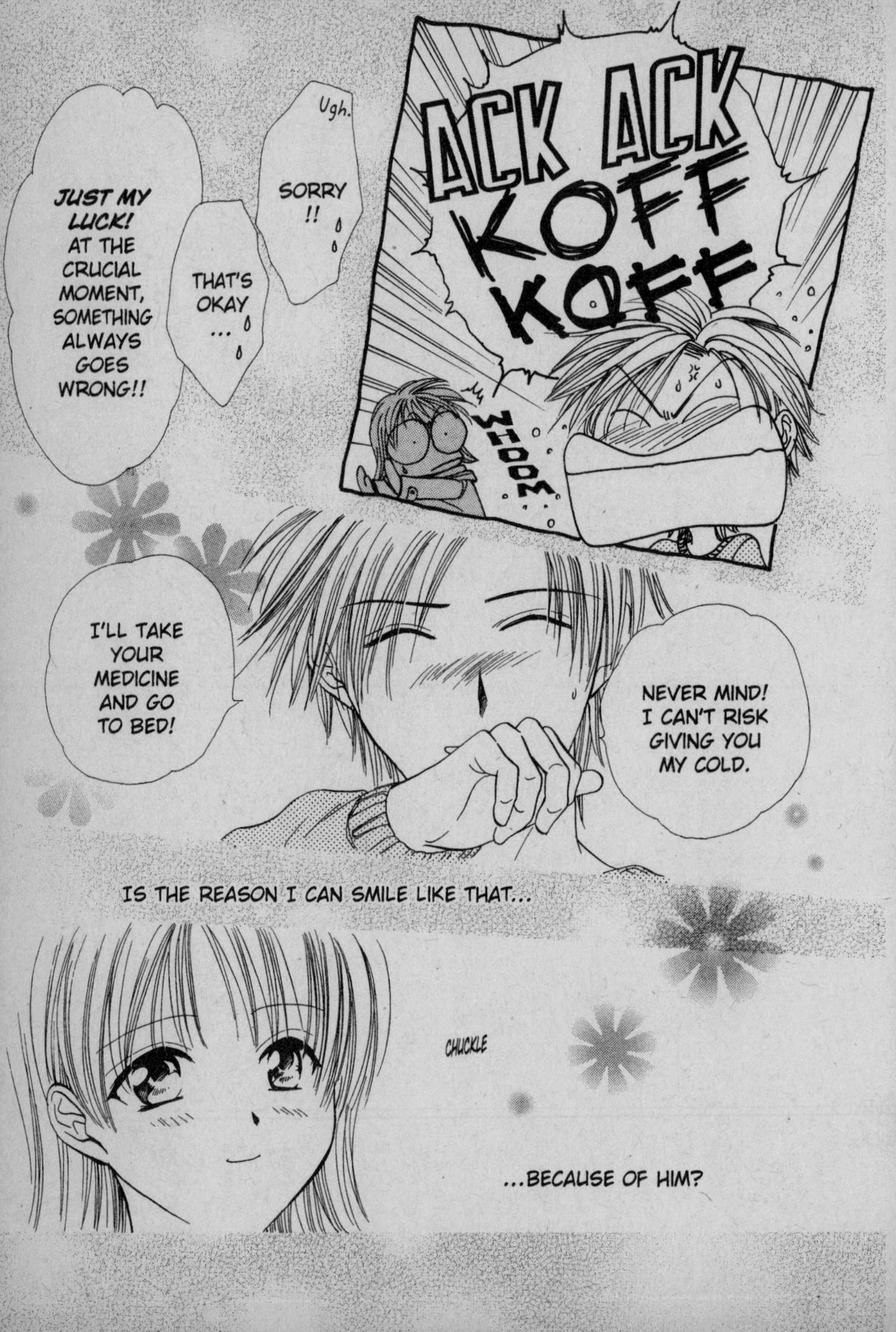
ACK ACK
KOFF KOFF
WHOOM
Ugh.
SORRY !!
THAT'S OKAY ...
JUST MY LUCK! AT THE CRUCIAL MOMENT, SOMETHING ALWAYS GOES WRONG!!
NEVER MIND! I CAN'T RISK GIVING YOU MY COLD.
I'LL TAKE YOUR MEDICINE AND GO TO BED!
IS THE REASON I CAN SMILE LIKE THAT...
CHUCKLE
...BECAUSE OF HIM?

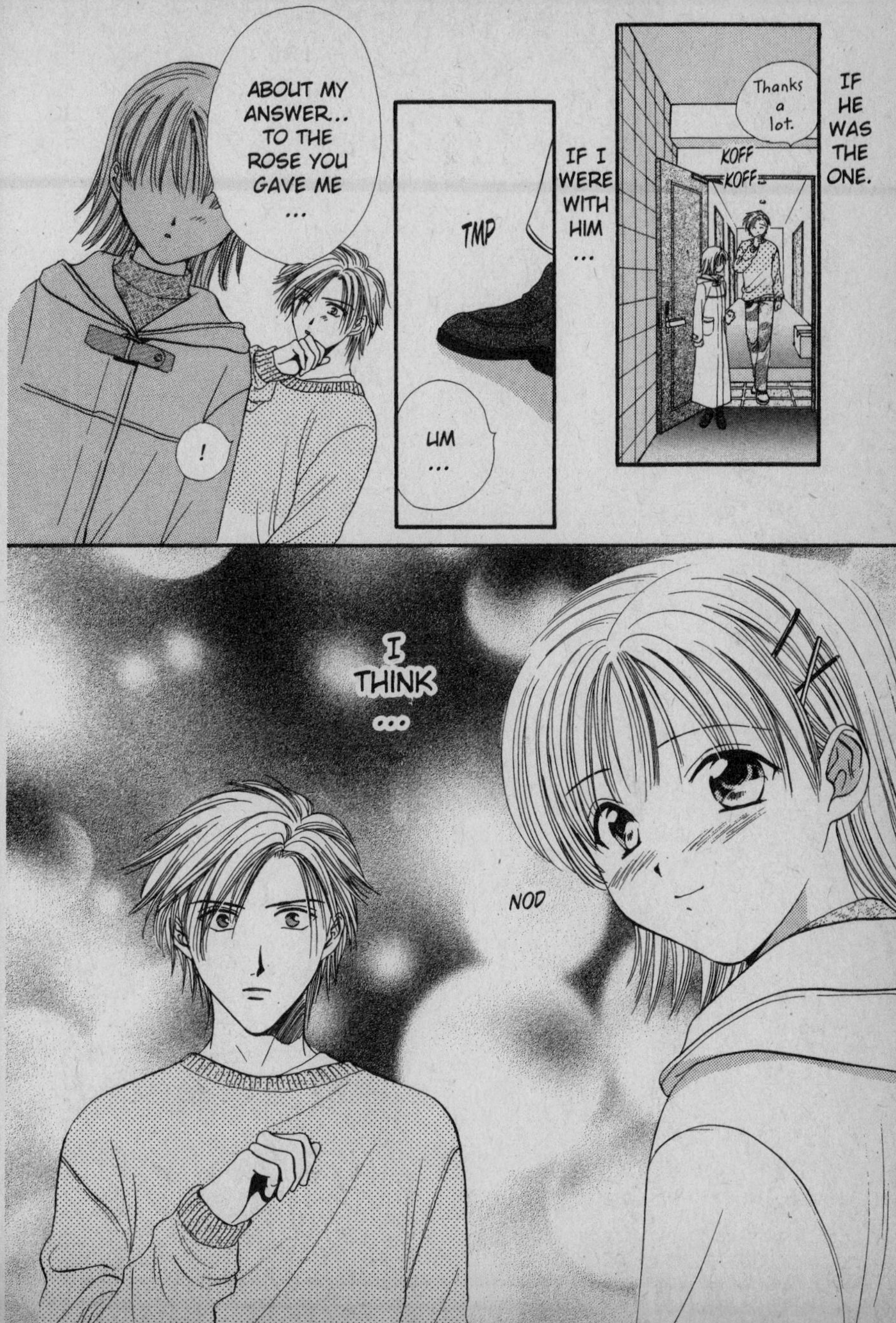
IF HE WAS THE ONE.
Thanks a lot.
KOFF KOFF
IF I WERE WITH HIM ...
TMP
UM ...
ABOUT MY ANSWER... TO THE ROSE YOU GAVE ME ...
!
I THINK ...
NOD

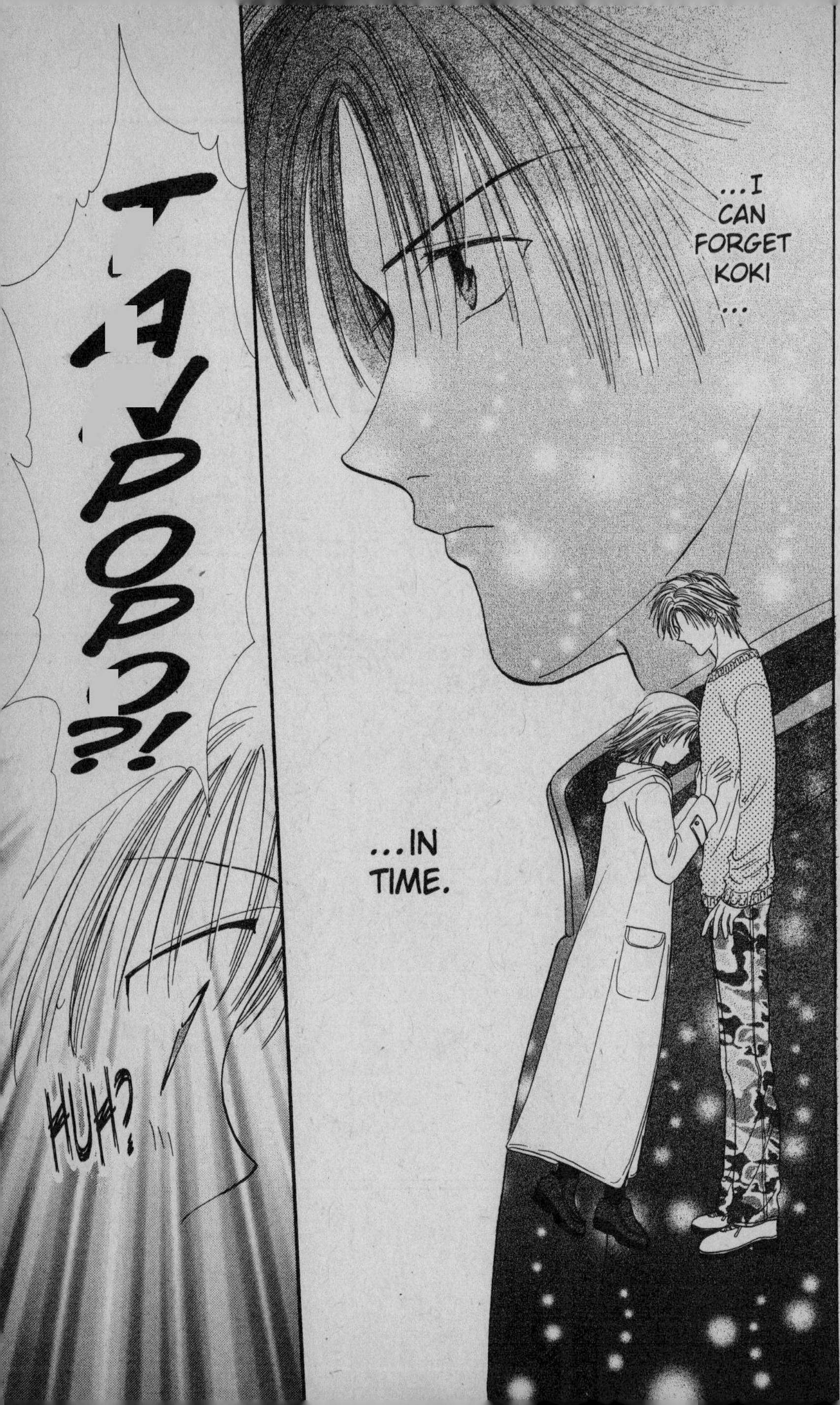
...I CAN FORGET KOKI ...
...IN TIME.
TANPOPO?!
HUH?

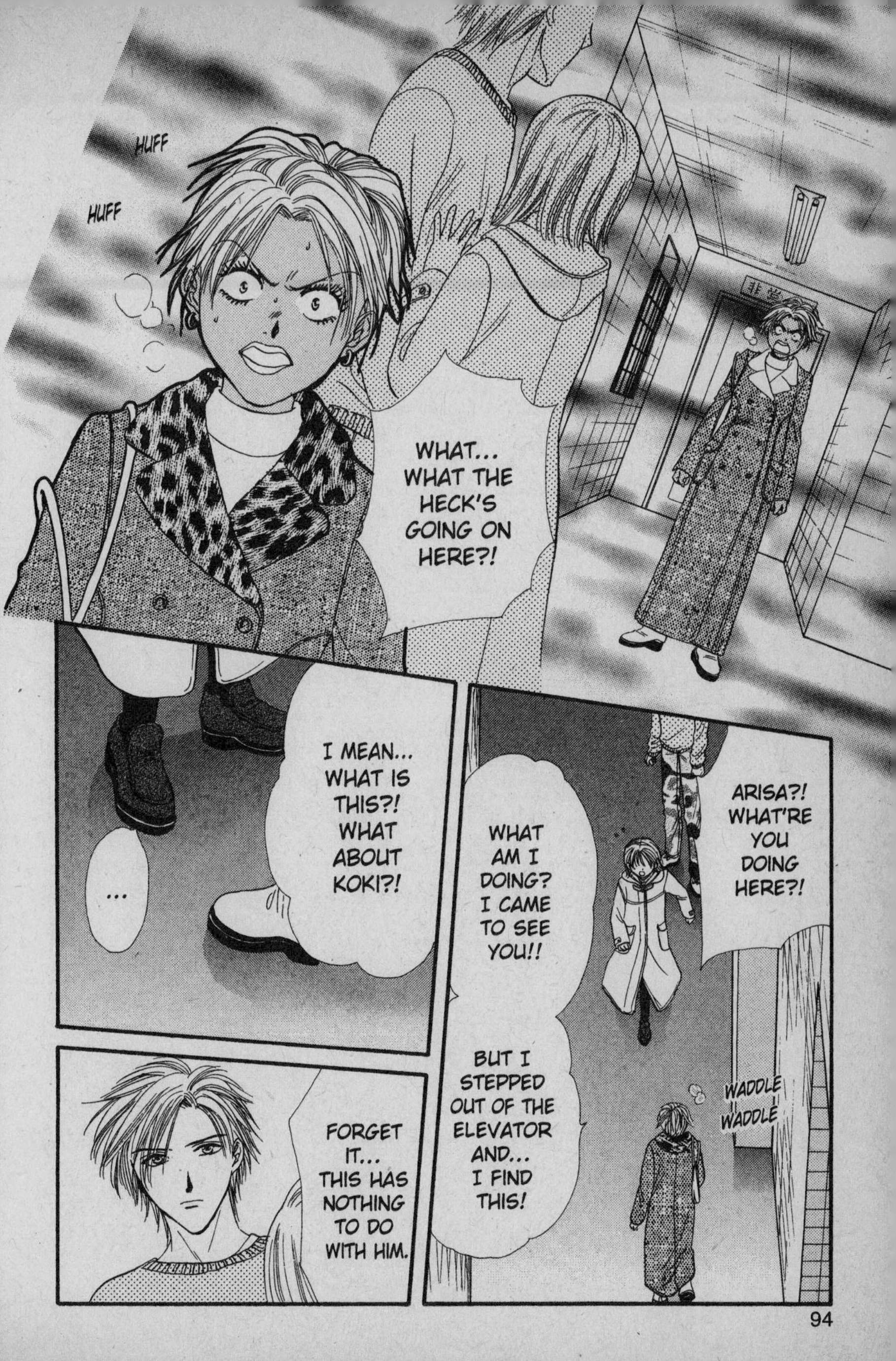
HUFF
HUFF
WHAT... WHAT THE HECK'S GOING ON HERE?!
ARISA?! WHAT'RE YOU DOING HERE?!
WHAT AM I DOING? I CAME TO SEE YOU!!
BUT I STEPPED OUT OF THE ELEVATOR AND... I FIND THIS!
WADDLE WADDLE
I MEAN... WHAT IS THIS?! WHAT ABOUT KOKI?!
...
FORGET IT... THIS HAS NOTHING TO DO WITH HIM.

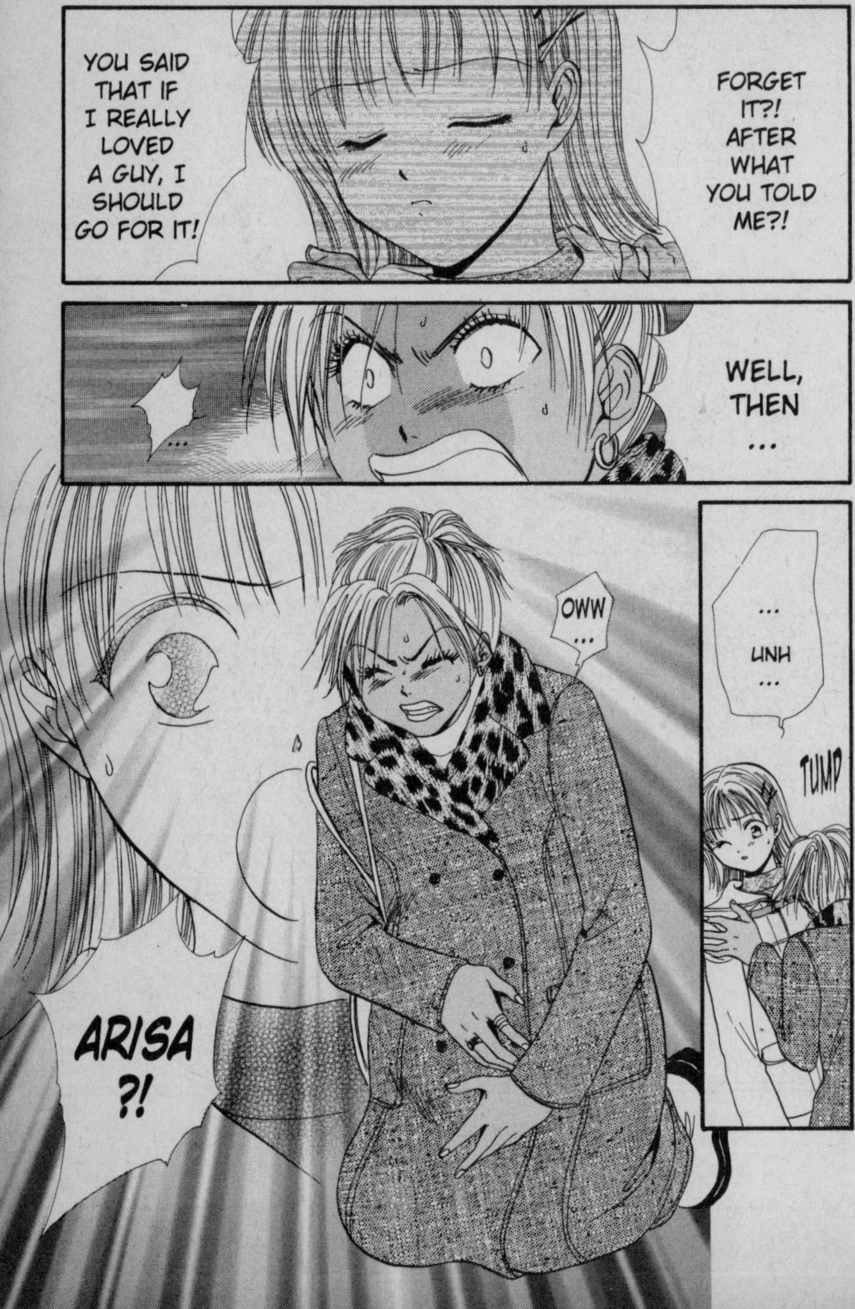
FORGET IT?! AFTER WHAT YOU TOLD ME?!
YOU SAID THAT IF I REALLY LOVED A GUY, I SHOULD GO FOR IT!
WELL, THEN ...
...
... UNH ...
TUMP
OWW ...
ARISA ?!

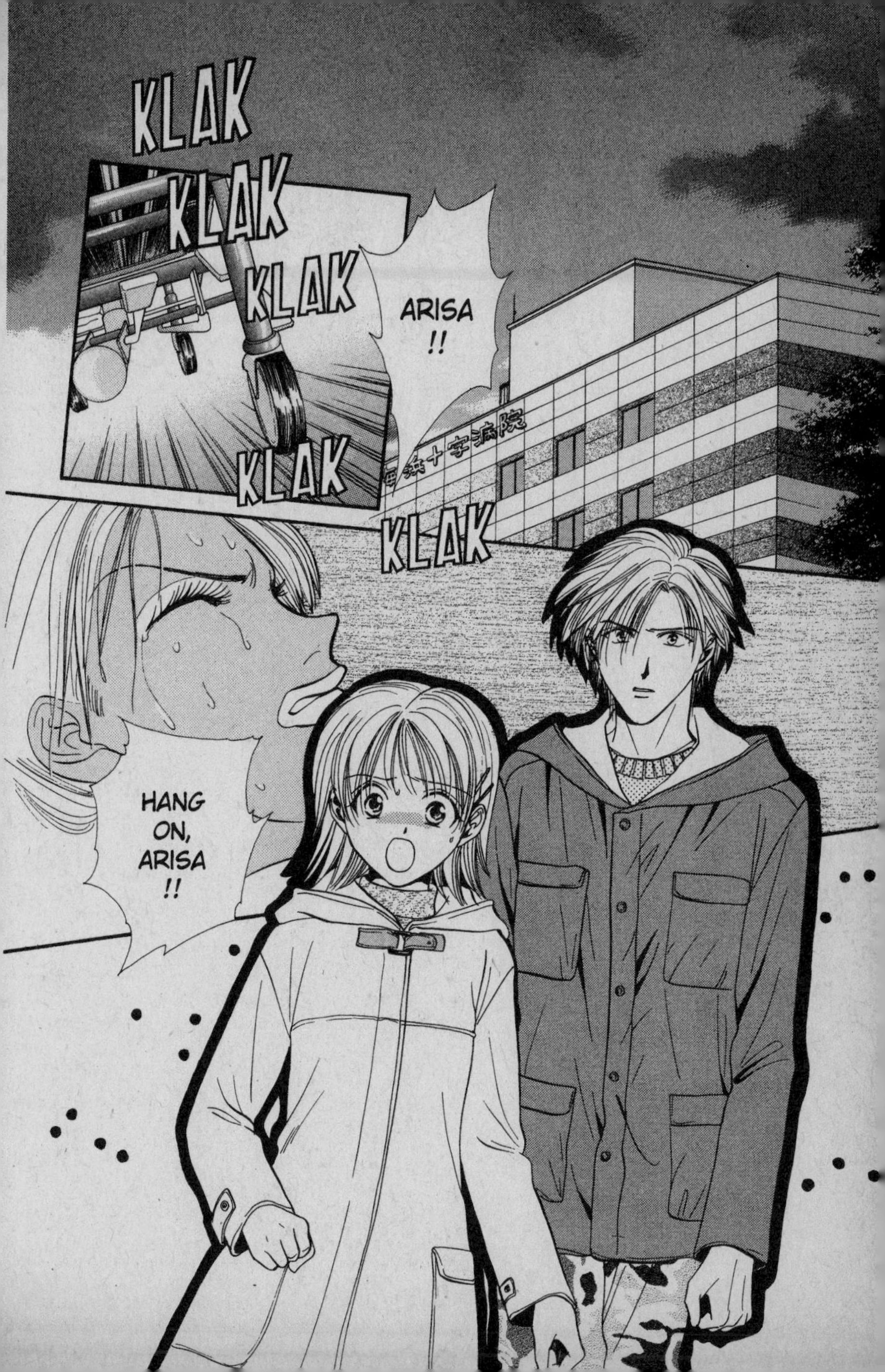
ARISA !!
KLAK
KLAK
KLAK
KLAK
KLAK
HANG ON, ARISA !!

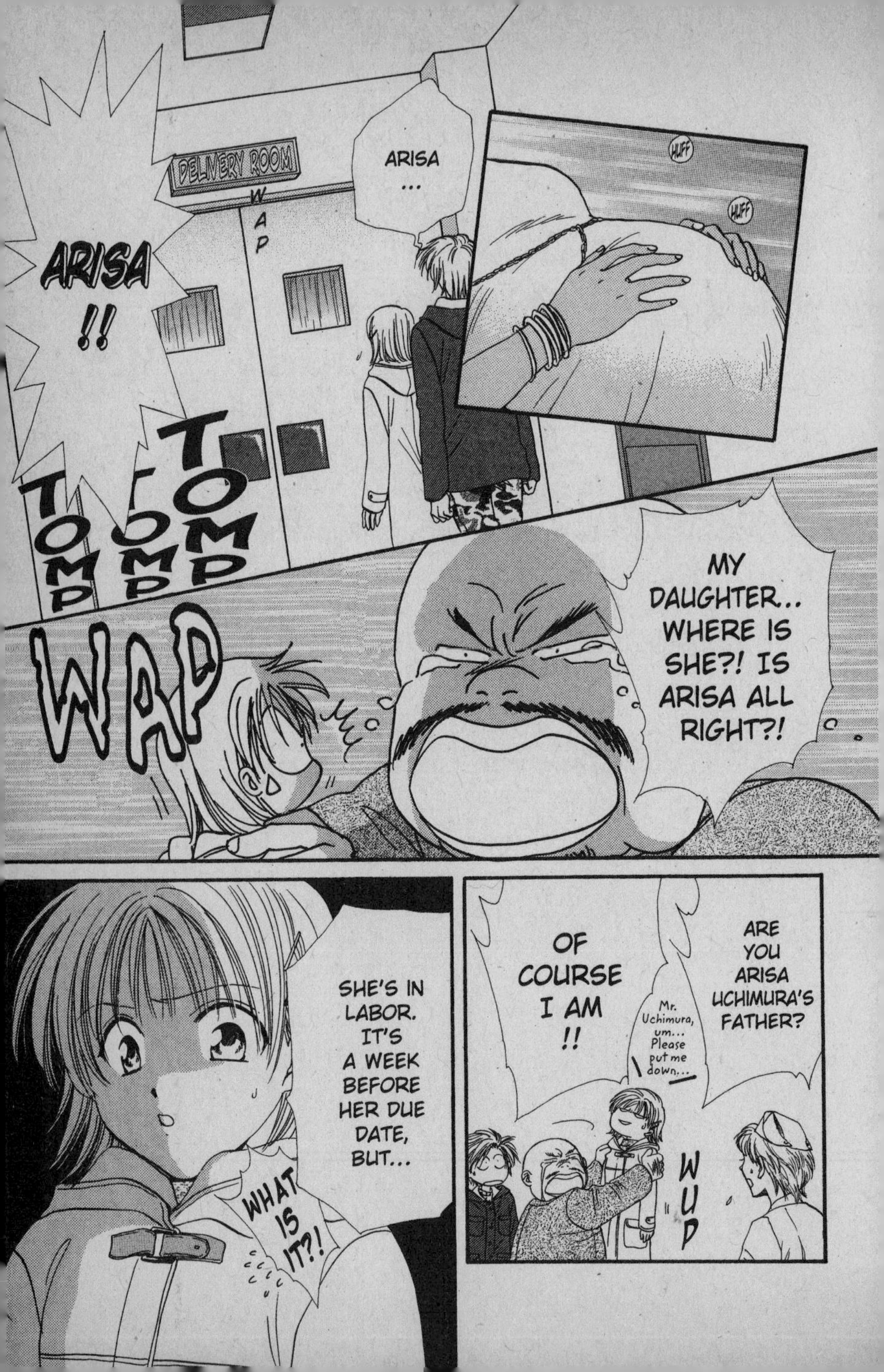
HUFF
HUFF
ARISA ...
ARISA !!
WAP
TOMP
TOMP
TOMP
MY DAUGHTER... WHERE IS SHE?! IS ARISA ALL RIGHT?!
WAP
ARE YOU ARISA UCHIMURA'S FATHER?
OF COURSE I AM !!
Mr. Uchimura, um... Please put me down...
WUP
SHE'S IN LABOR. IT'S A WEEK BEFORE HER DUE DATE, BUT...
WHAT IS IT?!

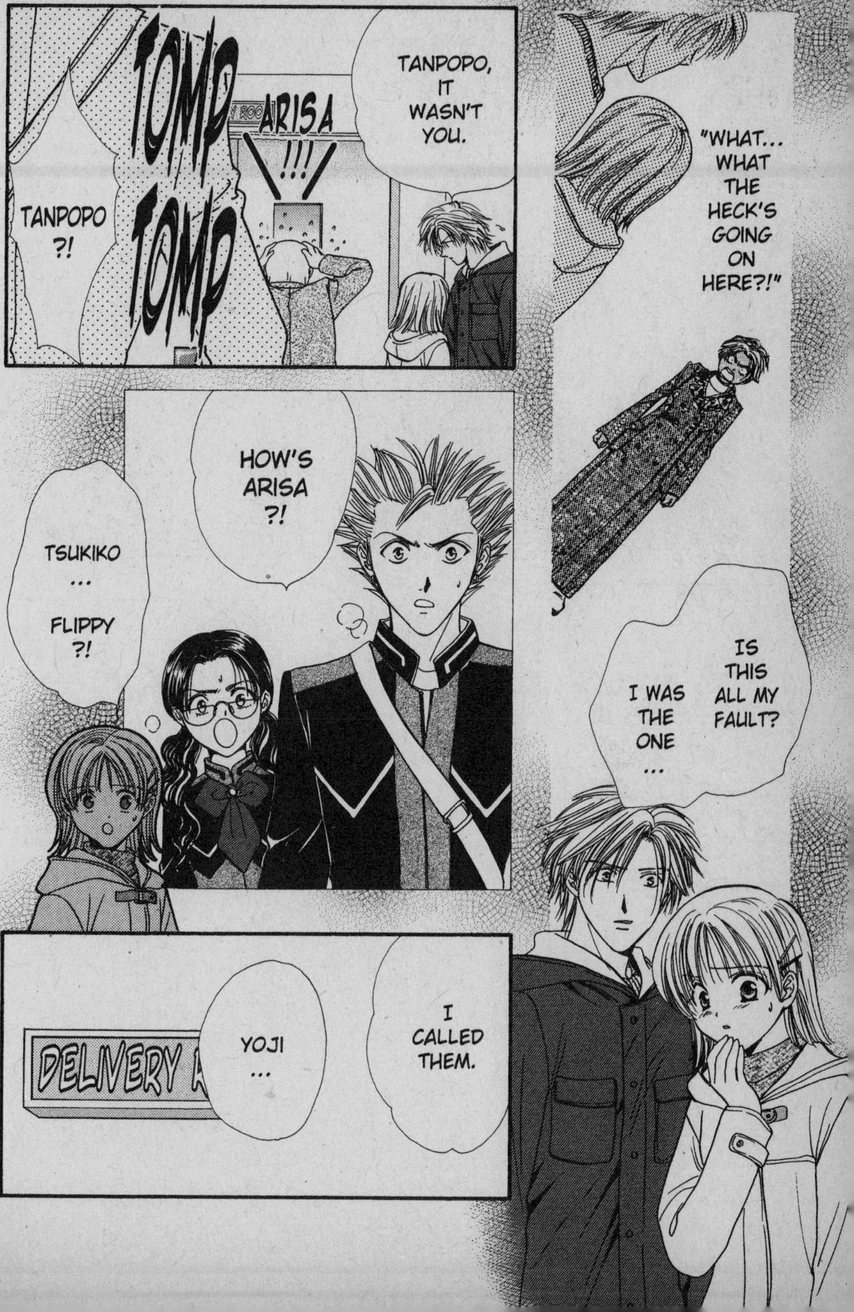
"WHAT... WHAT THE HECK'S GOING ON HERE?!"
I WAS THE ONE... IS THIS ALL MY FAULT?
TANPOPO, IT WASN'T YOU.
ARISA !!!
TOMP TOMP
TANPOPO ?!
HOW'S ARISA ?!
TSUKIKO ... FLIPPY ?!
I CALLED THEM.
YOJI ...
DELIVERY

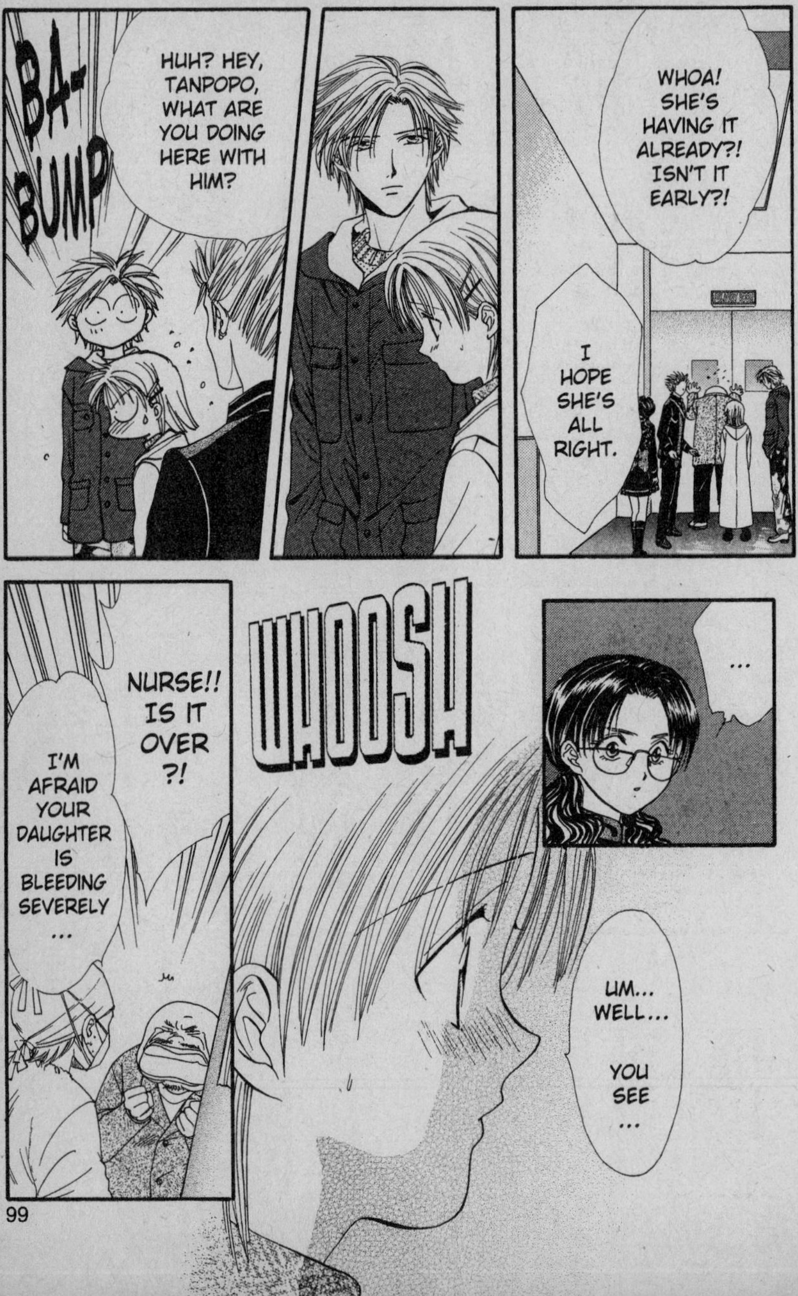
WHOA! SHE'S HAVING IT ALREADY?! ISN'T IT EARLY?!
I HOPE SHE'S ALL RIGHT.
BA-BUMP
HUH? HEY, TANPOPO, WHAT ARE YOU DOING HERE WITH HIM?
...
WHOOSH
UM... WELL... YOU SEE ...
NURSE!! IS IT OVER ?!
I'M AFRAID YOUR DAUGHTER IS BLEEDING SEVERELY ...

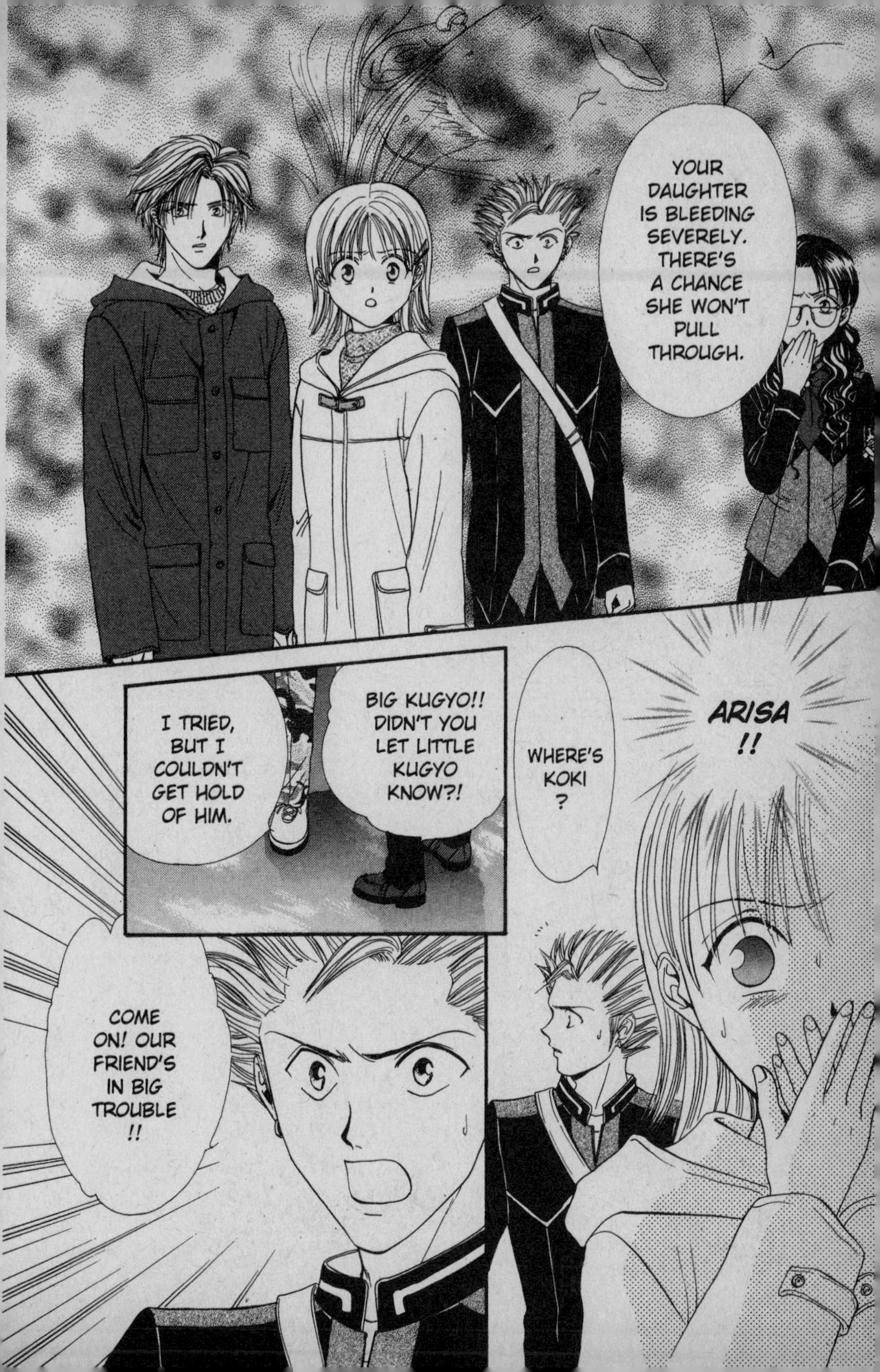
YOUR DAUGHTER IS BLEEDING SEVERELY. THERE'S A CHANCE SHE WON'T PULL THROUGH.
ARISA !!
WHERE'S KOKI ?
BIG KUGYO!! DIDN'T YOU LET LITTLE KUGYO KNOW?!
I TRIED, BUT I COULDN'T GET HOLD OF HIM.
COME ON! OUR FRIEND'S IN BIG TROUBLE !!

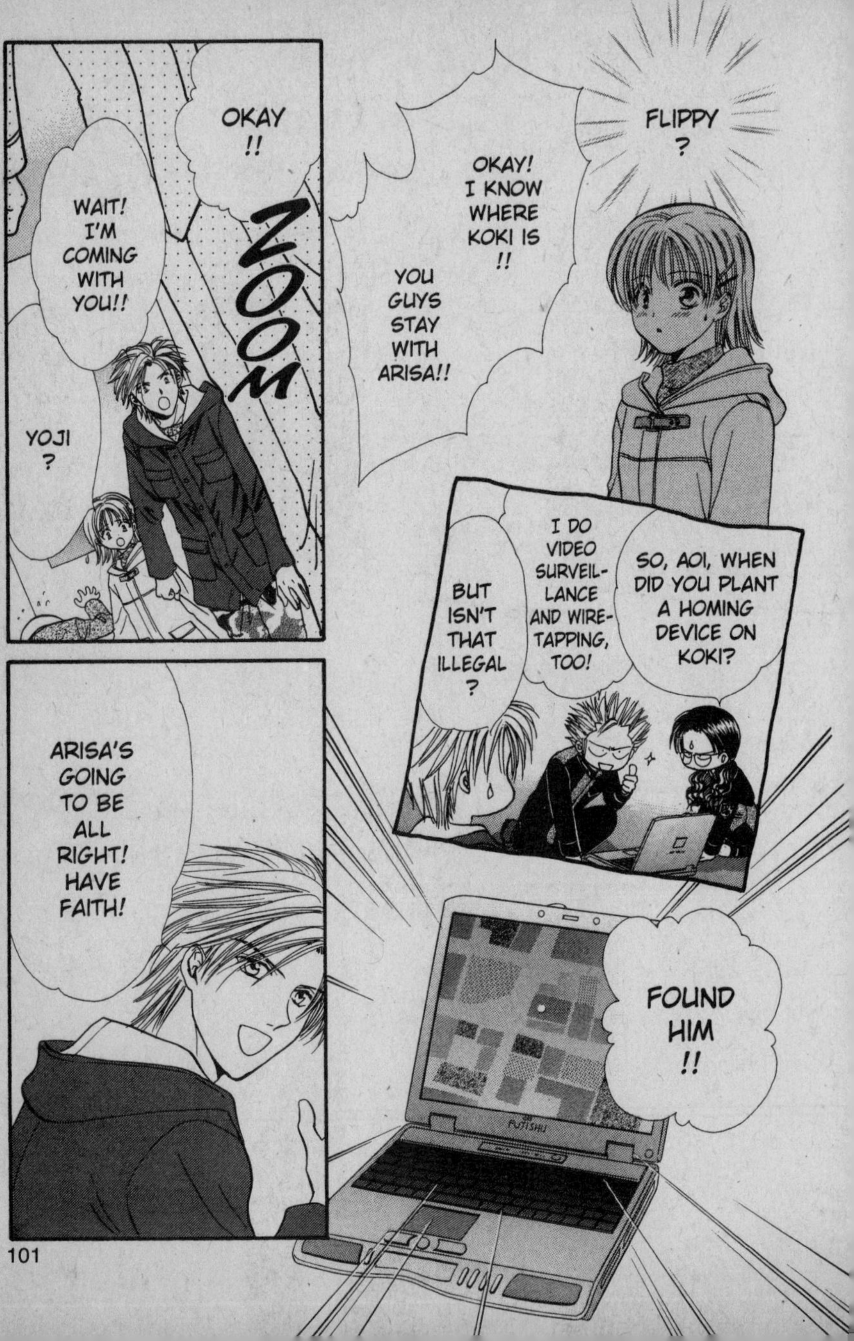
FLIPPY ?
OKAY! I KNOW WHERE KOKI IS !!
YOU GUYS STAY WITH ARISA!!
SO, AOI, WHEN DID YOU PLANT A HOMING DEVICE ON KOKI?
I DO VIDEO SURVEIL-LANCE AND WIRE-TAPPING, TOO!
BUT ISN'T THAT ILLEGAL ?
FOUND HIM !!
OKAY !!
WAIT! I'M COMING WITH YOU!!
ZOOM
YOJI ?
ARISA'S GOING TO BE ALL RIGHT! HAVE FAITH!

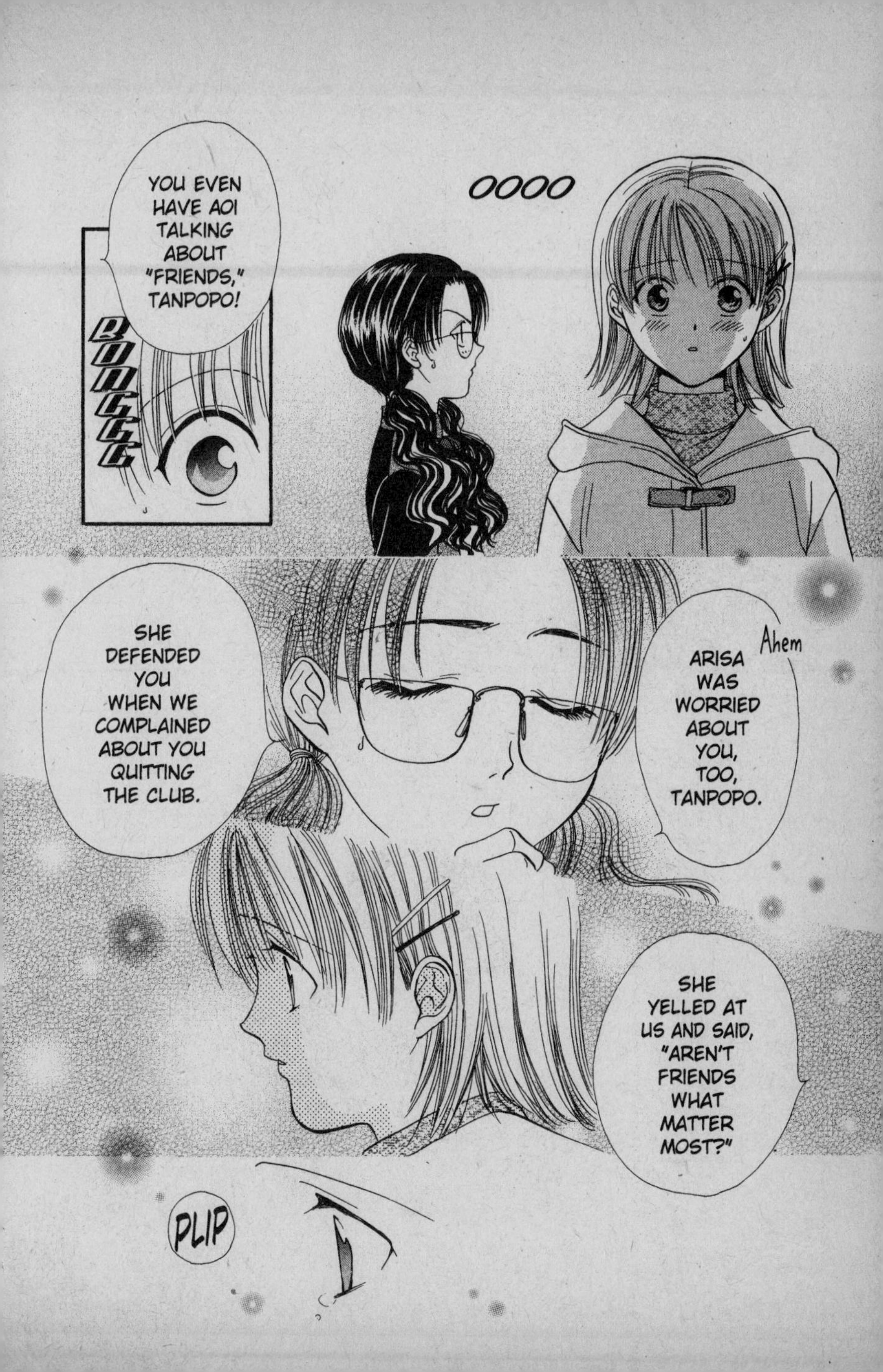
OOOO
YOU EVEN HAVE AOI TALKING ABOUT "FRIENDS," TANPOPO!
BOOGGG
Ahem
ARISA WAS WORRIED ABOUT YOU, TOO, TANPOPO.
SHE DEFENDED YOU WHEN WE COMPLAINED ABOUT YOU QUITTING THE CLUB.
SHE YELLED AT US AND SAID, "AREN'T FRIENDS WHAT MATTER MOST?"
PLIP

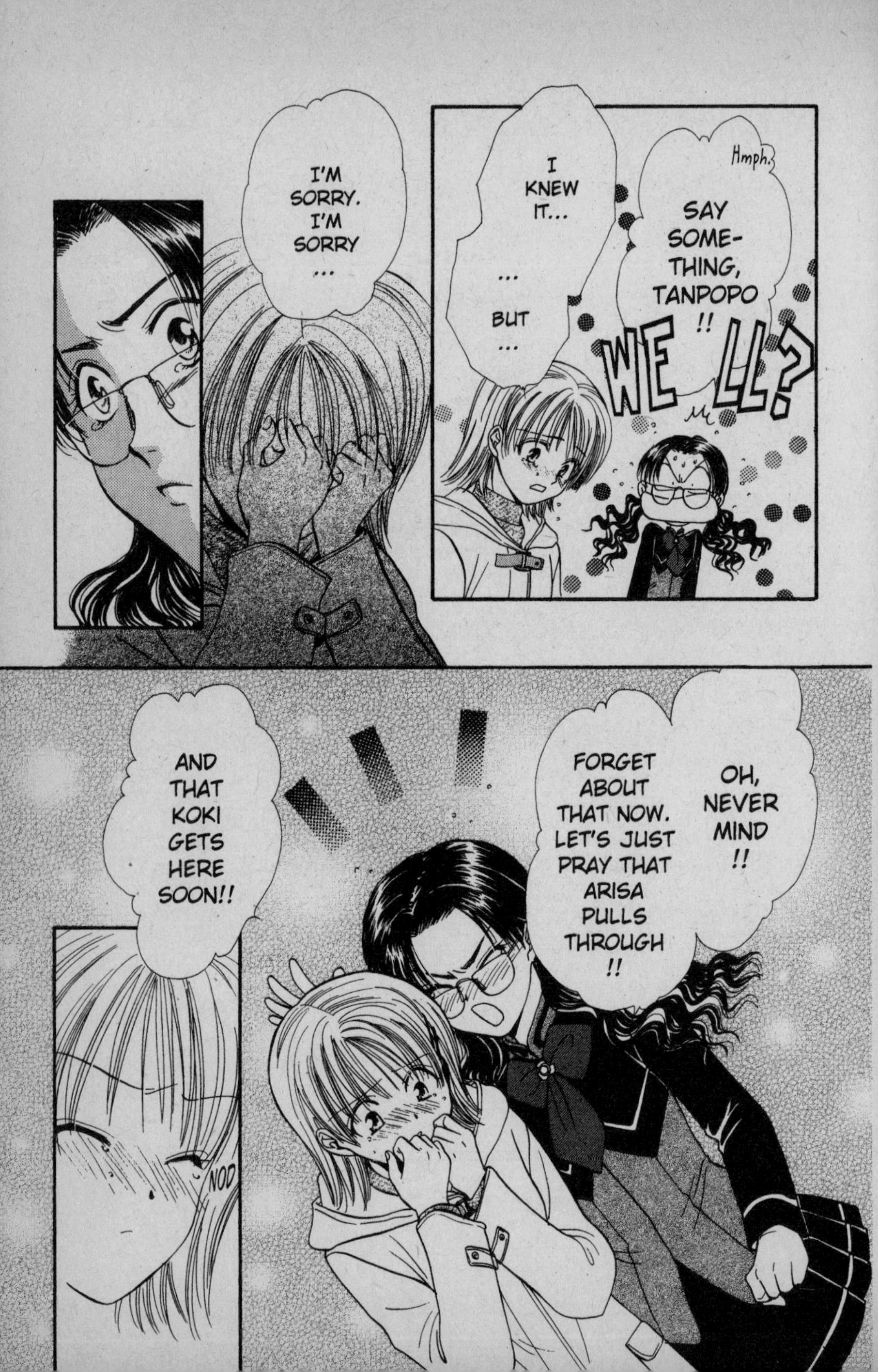
Hmph.
SAY SOME-THING, TANPOPO!!
WE LL?
I KNEW IT... ... BUT ...
I'M SORRY. I'M SORRY ...
OH, NEVER MIND!!
FORGET ABOUT THAT NOW. LET'S JUST PRAY THAT ARISA PULLS THROUGH!!
AND THAT KOKI GETS HERE SOON!!
NOD

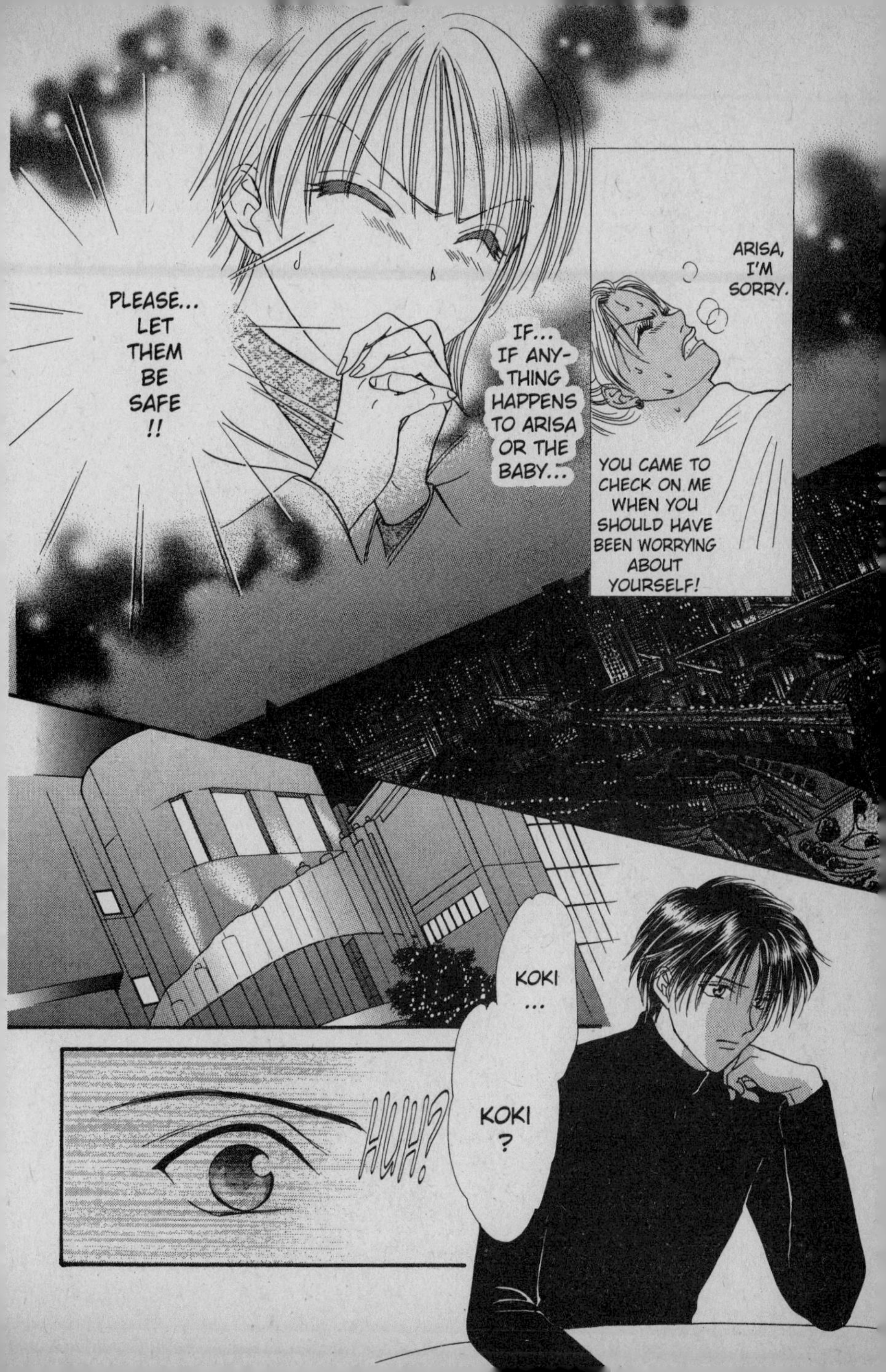
ARISA, I'M SORRY.
YOU CAME TO CHECK ON ME WHEN YOU SHOULD HAVE BEEN WORRYING ABOUT YOURSELF!
IF... IF ANY-THING HAPPENS TO ARISA OR THE BABY...
PLEASE... LET THEM BE SAFE !!
KOKI ...
KOKI ?
HUH!?

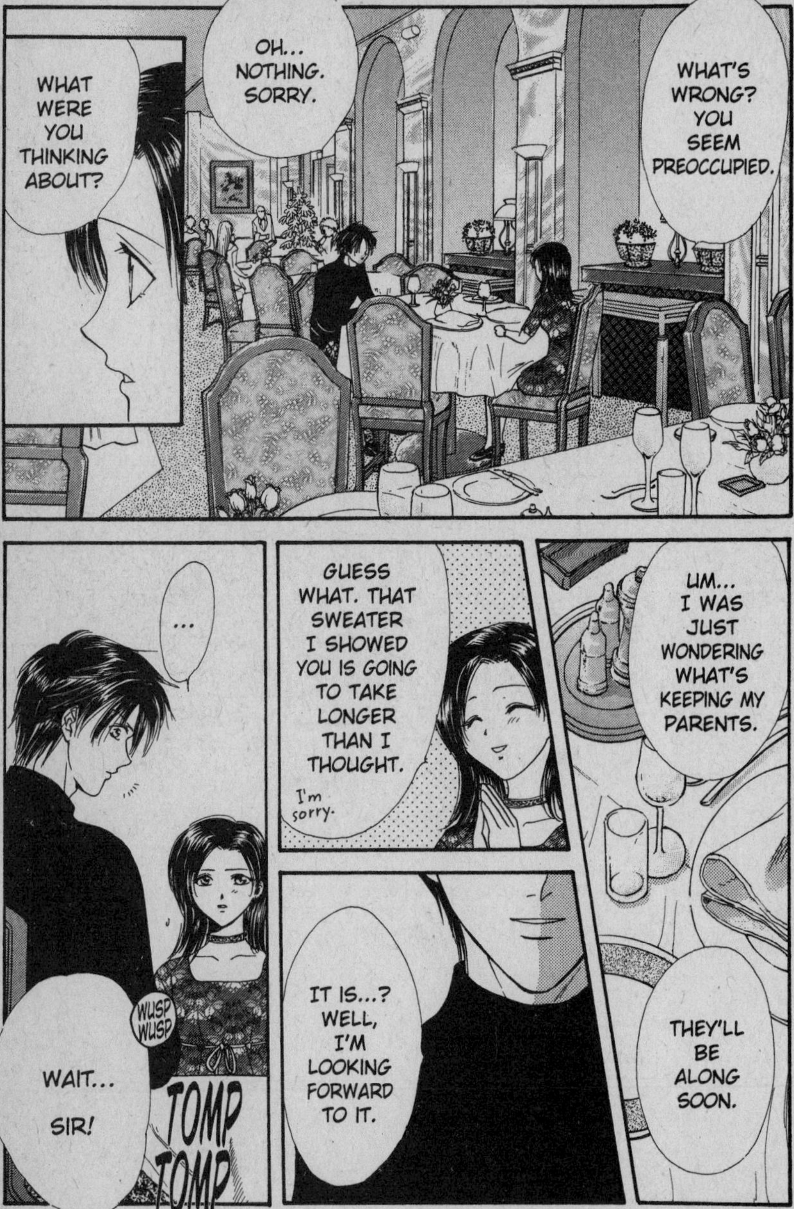
WHAT'S WRONG? YOU SEEM PREOCCUPIED.
OH... NOTHING. SORRY.
WHAT WERE YOU THINKING ABOUT?
UM... I WAS JUST WONDERING WHAT'S KEEPING MY PARENTS.
THEY'LL BE ALONG SOON.
GUESS WHAT. THAT SWEATER I SHOWED YOU IS GOING TO TAKE LONGER THAN I THOUGHT.
I'm sorry.
IT IS...? WELL, I'M LOOKING FORWARD TO IT.
...
WUSP WUSP
WAIT... SIR!
TOMP TOMP

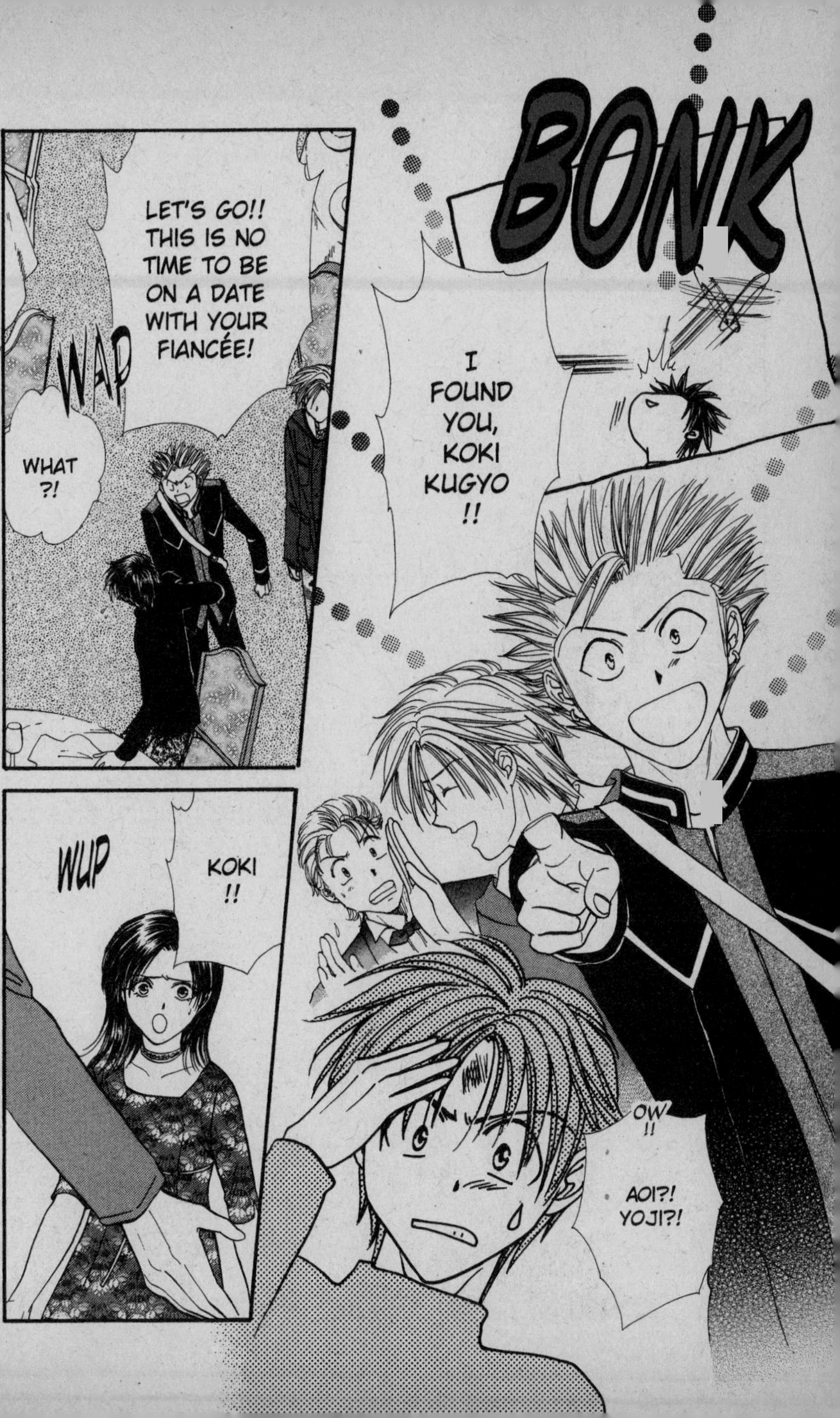
BONK
I FOUND YOU, KOKI KUGYO !!
OW !!
AOI?! YOJI?!
LET'S GO!! THIS IS NO TIME TO BE ON A DATE WITH YOUR FIANCÉE!
WAP
WHAT ?!
WUP
KOKI !!

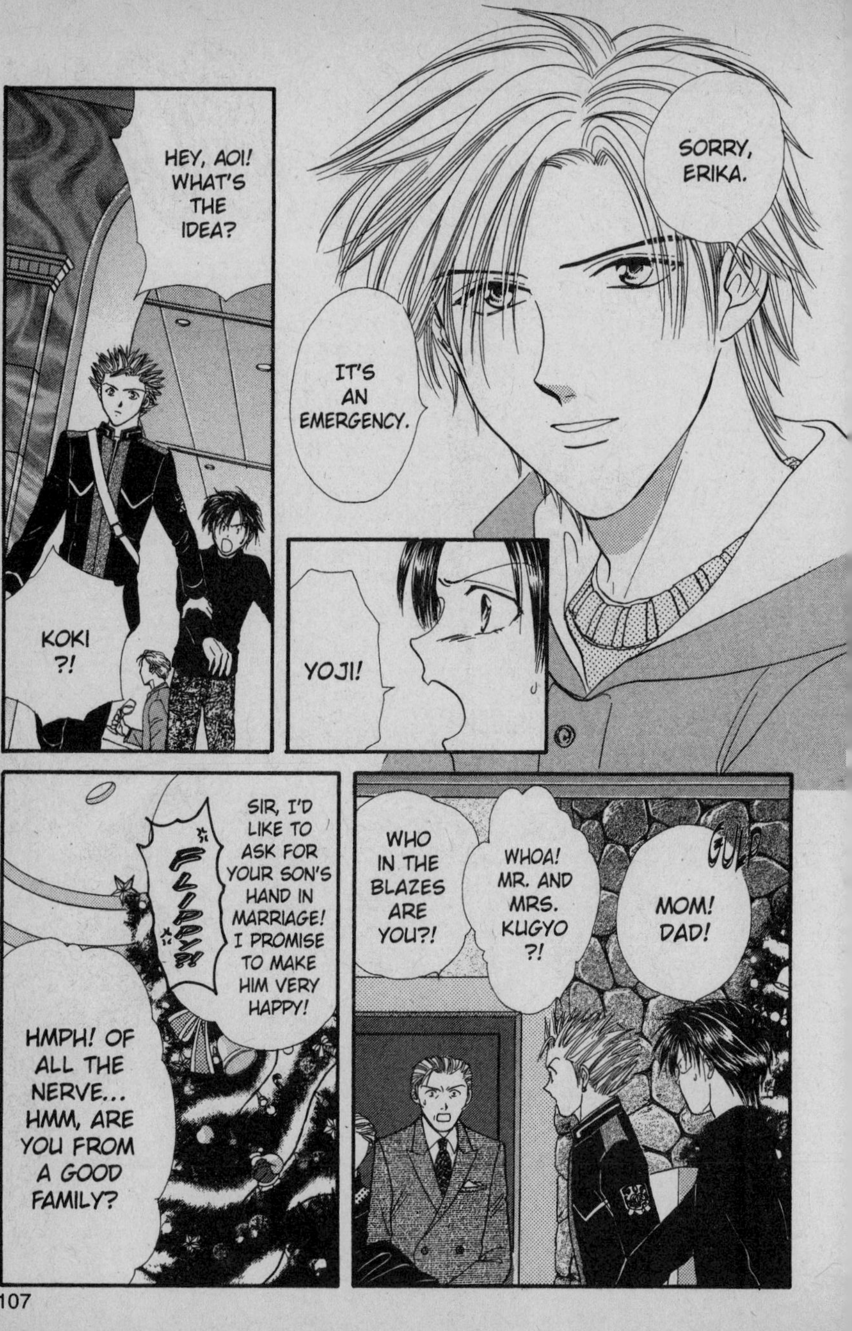
SORRY, ERIKA.
IT'S AN EMERGENCY.
YOJI!
HEY, AOI! WHAT'S THE IDEA?
KOKI ?!
GULP
MOM! DAD!
WHOA! MR. AND MRS. KUGYO ?!
WHO IN THE BLAZES ARE YOU?!
SIR, I'D LIKE TO ASK FOR YOUR SON'S HAND IN MARRIAGE! I PROMISE TO MAKE HIM VERY HAPPY!
FLIPPY?!
HMPH! OF ALL THE NERVE... HMM, ARE YOU FROM A GOOD FAMILY?

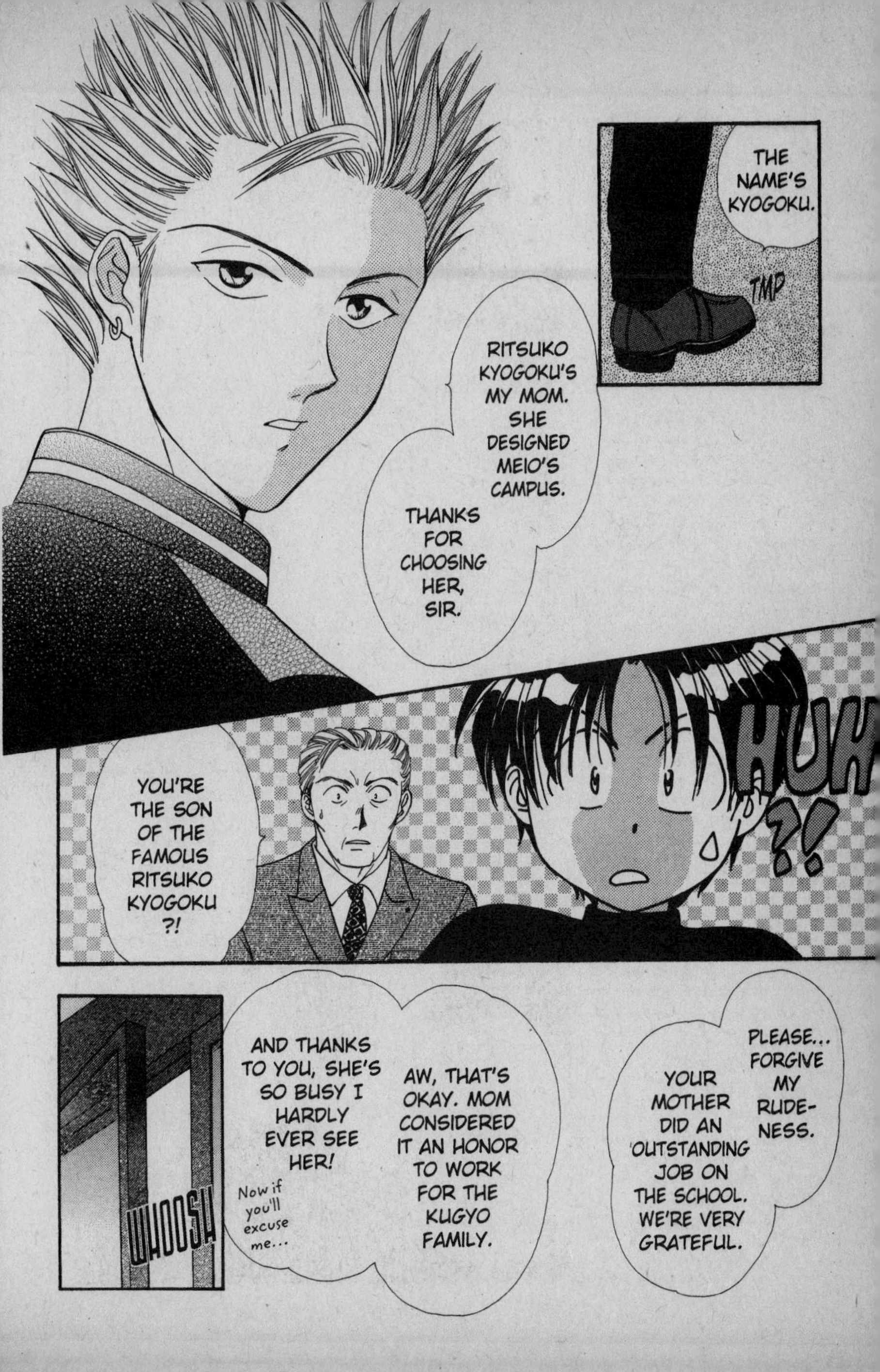
THE NAME'S KYOGOKU.
TMP
RITSUKO KYOGOKU'S MY MOM. SHE DESIGNED MEIO'S CAMPUS.
THANKS FOR CHOOSING HER, SIR.
HUH ?!
YOU'RE THE SON OF THE FAMOUS RITSUKO KYOGOKU ?!
PLEASE... FORGIVE MY RUDE-NESS.
YOUR MOTHER DID AN OUTSTANDING JOB ON THE SCHOOL. WE'RE VERY GRATEFUL.
AW, THAT'S OKAY. MOM CONSIDERED IT AN HONOR TO WORK FOR THE KUGYO FAMILY.
AND THANKS TO YOU, SHE'S SO BUSY I HARDLY EVER SEE HER!
Now if you'll excuse me...
WHOOSH

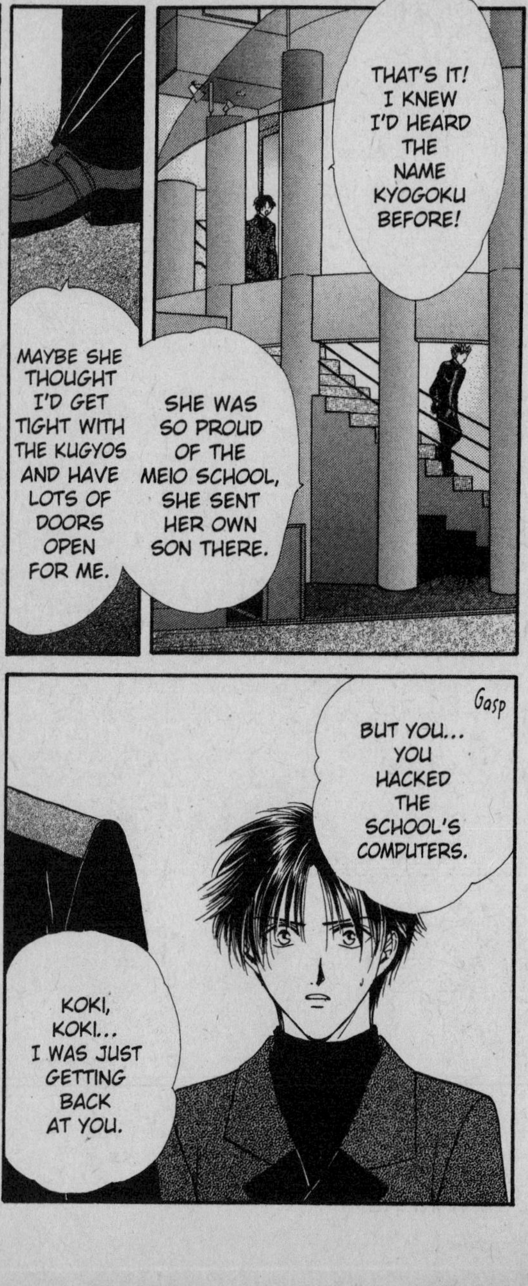
THAT'S IT! I KNEW I'D HEARD THE NAME KYOGOKU BEFORE!
SHE WAS SO PROUD OF THE MEIO SCHOOL, SHE SENT HER OWN SON THERE.
MAYBE SHE THOUGHT I'D GET TIGHT WITH THE KUGYOS AND HAVE LOTS OF DOORS OPEN FOR ME.
Gasp
BUT YOU... YOU HACKED THE SCHOOL'S COMPUTERS.
KOKI, KOKI... I WAS JUST GETTING BACK AT YOU.

Now then, here's another question:

"I want to be a manga writer." (Assuming this is okay.) "Please make me your assistant!" (smile)

(From a 12-year-old fan)

Well...As a rule, these are the conditions for becoming my assistant: **You must be over 18.** That's because you have to sleep over at my house sometimes, and many writers live in Tokyo. See, you have to come to Tokyo and live by yourself, which isn't easy.

Those of you who think, "I just have to do it!" will need to hone your skills, convince your parents to let you move to Tokyo, (smile), get up the nerve, and go for it!

Next, for the ones who think "I just have to work for Watase!" You shouldn't think that way, but if you do, master doing backgrounds, effects and tones starting with those in **Imadoki!** and **Ayashi no Ceres**, so I won't have to go to the trouble of training you from scratch. (smile)

Well, no, don't just study my work. Look at work by all kinds of manga artists (good ones), and then study and practice. Anyway, make sure you have a broad background. Another important point: **a good personality is a plus!** Even if your skill is a little lacking, you'll be hired if you have a good personality.

No matter how skilled you are, if you can't get along with others... Well, anyway, people with unpleasant personalities aren't in demand. That's true no matter what you do.

And--this is crucial--you must never ruin a manuscript with too much painting, whiteout or erasing. Neatness and speed are **good!**

This is crucial to a manga artist.

For some writers, you might even have to cook, so cooking skills might be a plus.

All this and more is required of a professional manga artist. (Not cooking, though.)

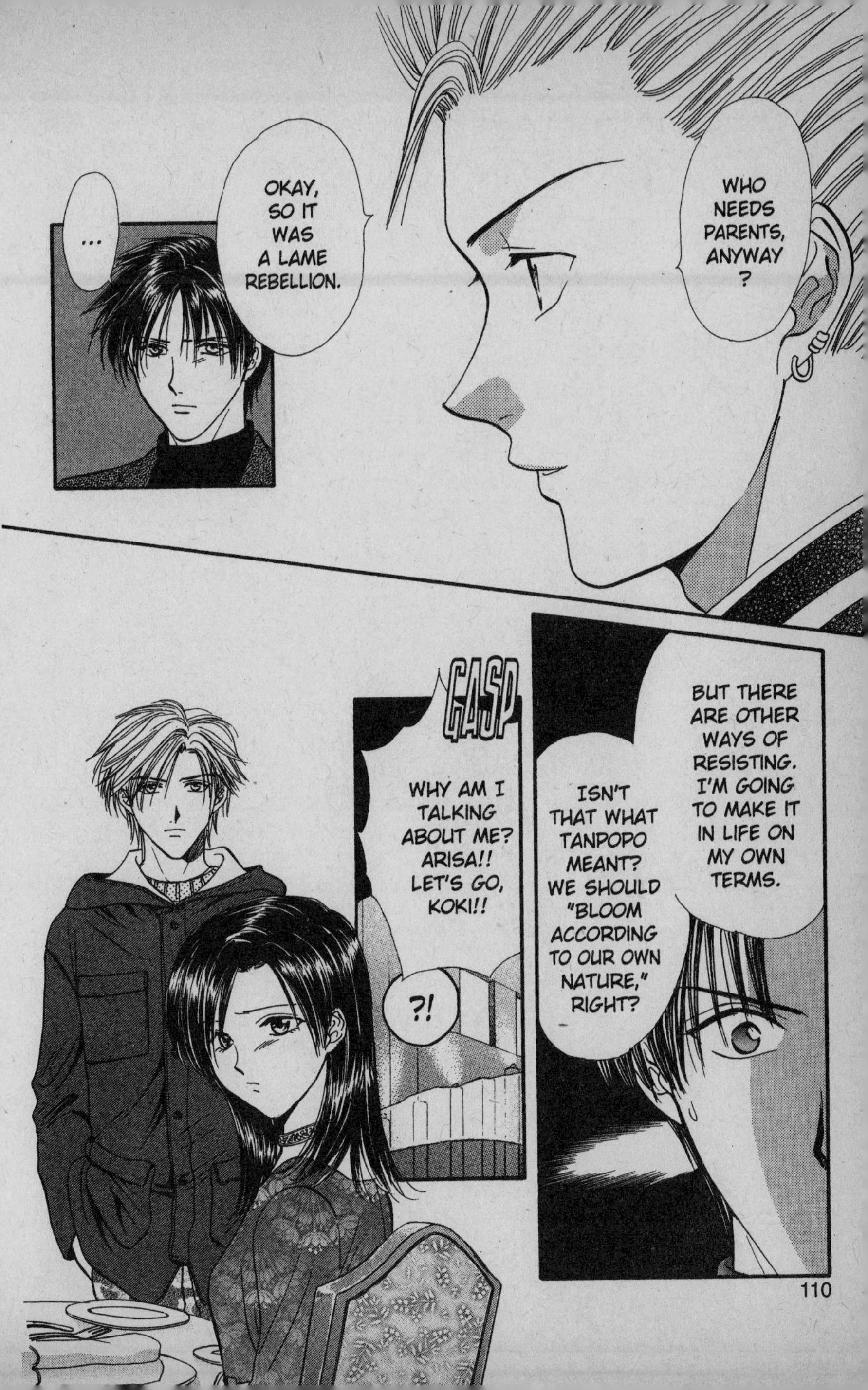
WHO NEEDS PARENTS, ANYWAY ?
OKAY, SO IT WAS A LAME REBELLION.
...
BUT THERE ARE OTHER WAYS OF RESISTING. I'M GOING TO MAKE IT IN LIFE ON MY OWN TERMS.
ISN'T THAT WHAT TANPOPO MEANT? WE SHOULD "BLOOM ACCORDING TO OUR OWN NATURE," RIGHT?
GASP
WHY AM I TALKING ABOUT ME? ARISA!! LET'S GO, KOKI!!
?!

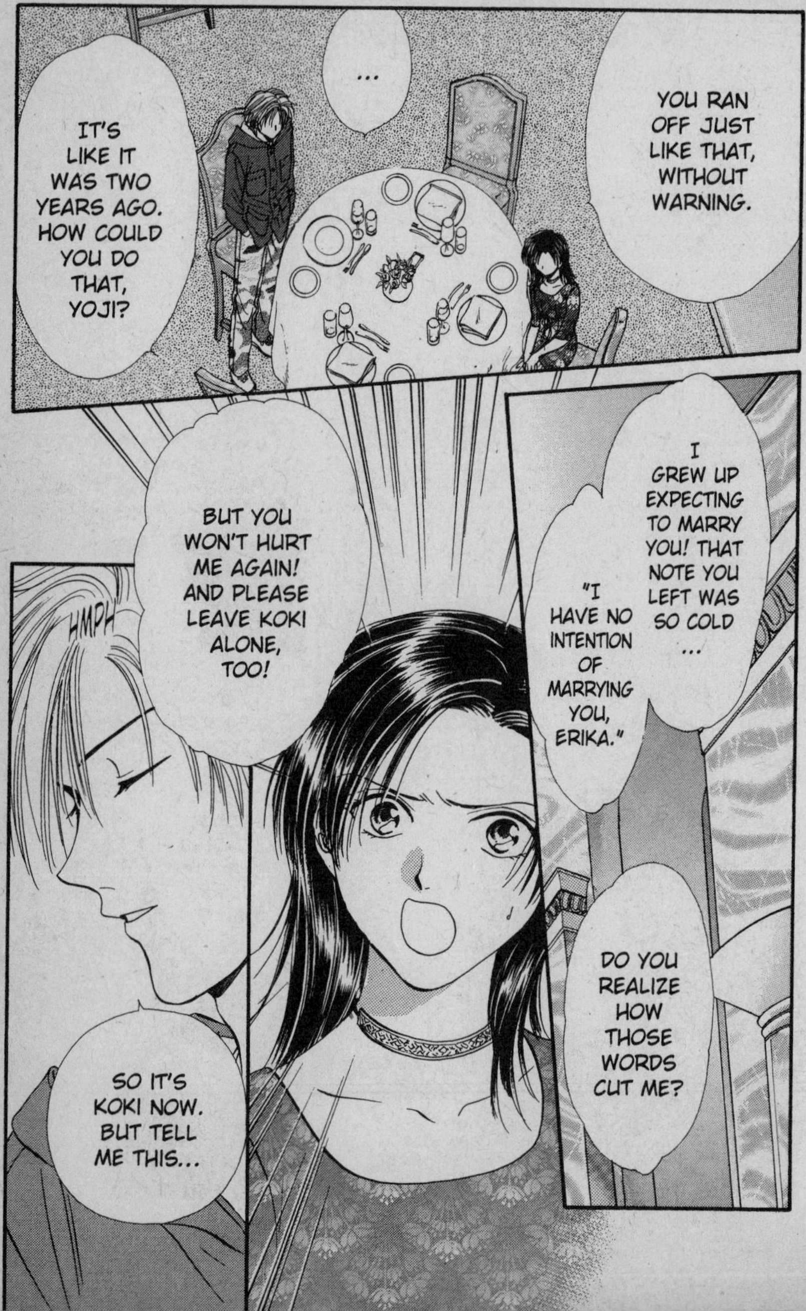
YOU RAN OFF JUST LIKE THAT, WITHOUT WARNING.
...
IT'S LIKE IT WAS TWO YEARS AGO. HOW COULD YOU DO THAT, YOJI?
I GREW UP EXPECTING TO MARRY YOU! THAT NOTE YOU LEFT WAS SO COLD ...
"I HAVE NO INTENTION OF MARRYING YOU, ERIKA."
DO YOU REALIZE HOW THOSE WORDS CUT ME?
BUT YOU WON'T HURT ME AGAIN! AND PLEASE LEAVE KOKI ALONE, TOO!
HMPH
SO IT'S KOKI NOW. BUT TELL ME THIS...

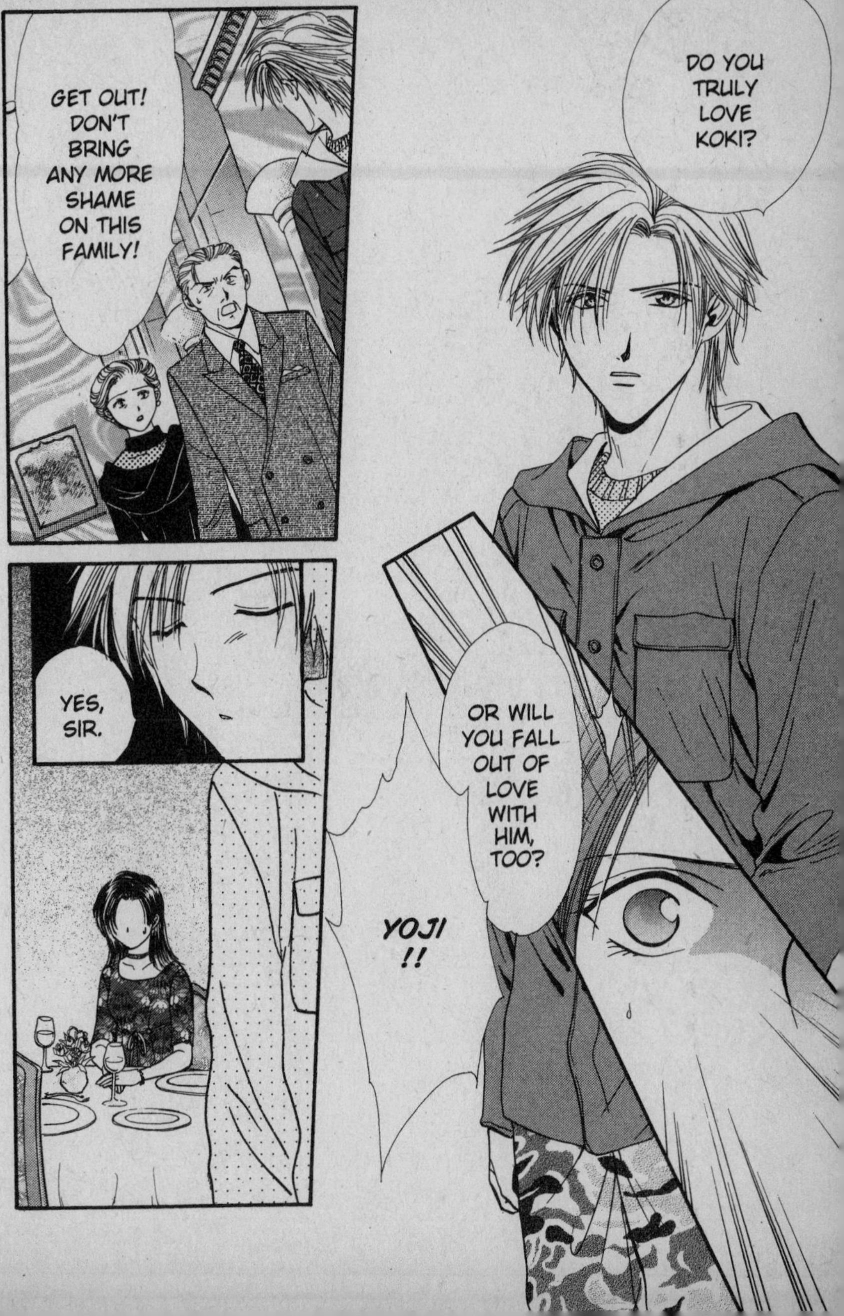
DO YOU TRULY LOVE KOKI?
OR WILL YOU FALL OUT OF LOVE WITH HIM, TOO?
YOJI !!
GET OUT! DON'T BRING ANY MORE SHAME ON THIS FAMILY!
YES, SIR.

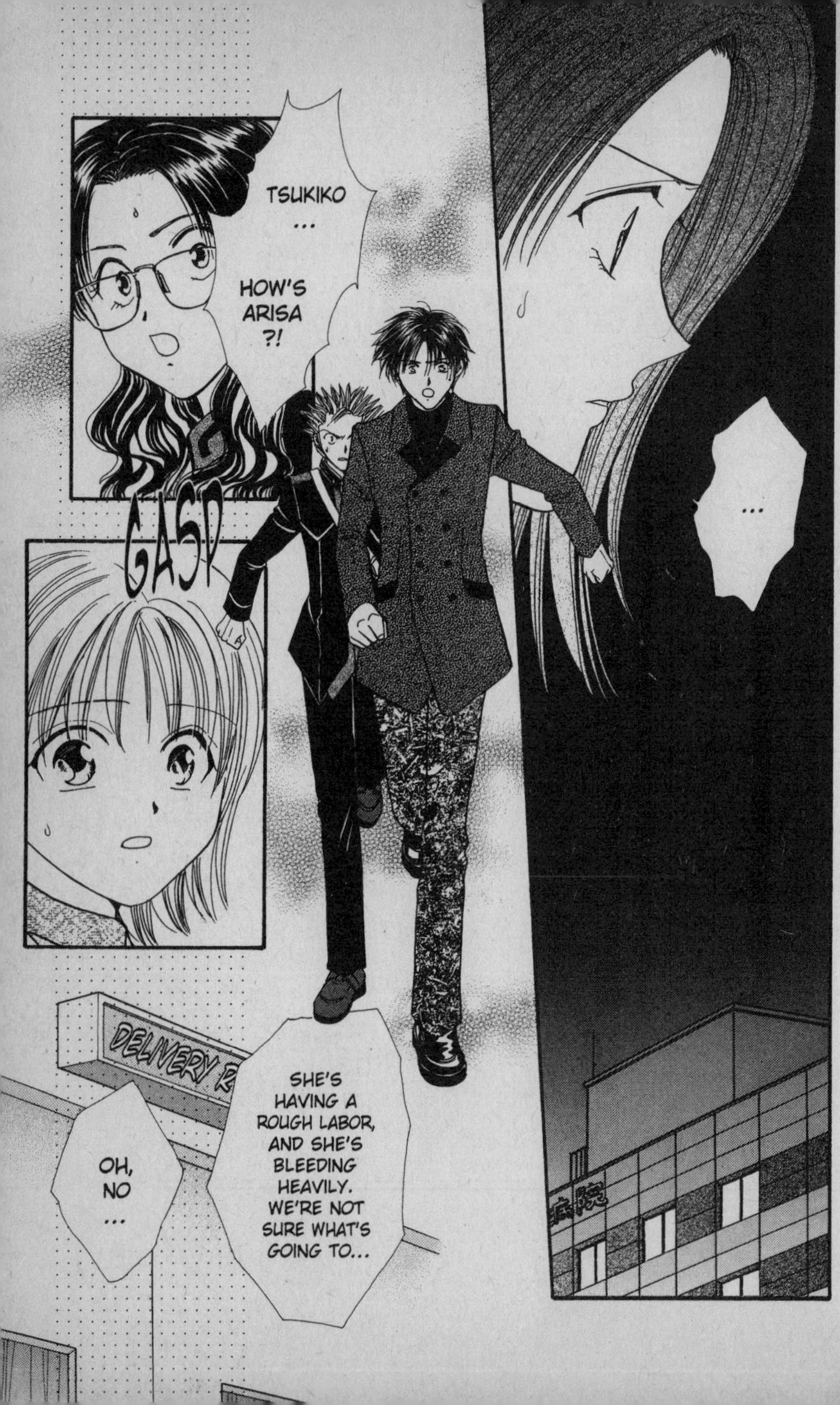
...
TSUKIKO ...
HOW'S ARISA ?!
GASP
SHE'S HAVING A ROUGH LABOR, AND SHE'S BLEEDING HEAVILY. WE'RE NOT SURE WHAT'S GOING TO...
OH, NO ...
DELIVERY R

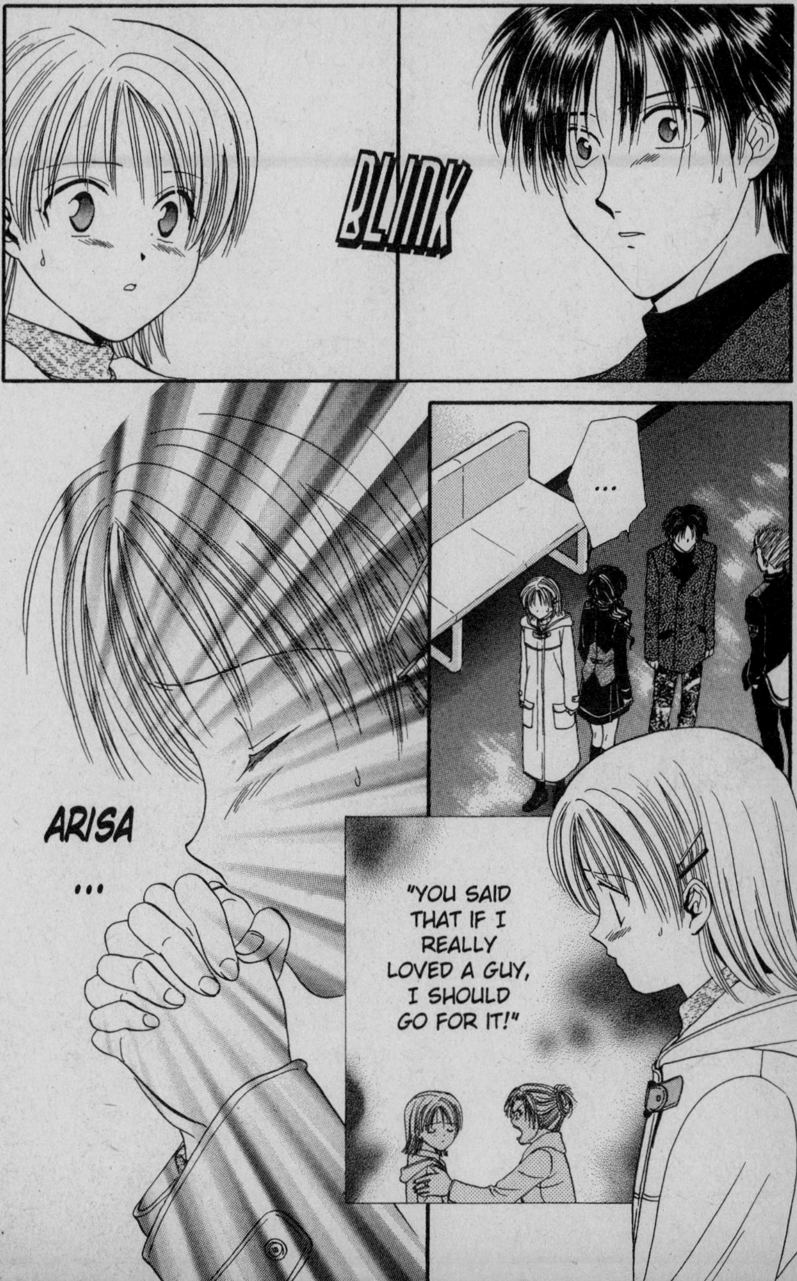
BLINK
...
"YOU SAID THAT IF I REALLY LOVED A GUY, I SHOULD GO FOR IT!"
ARISA ...

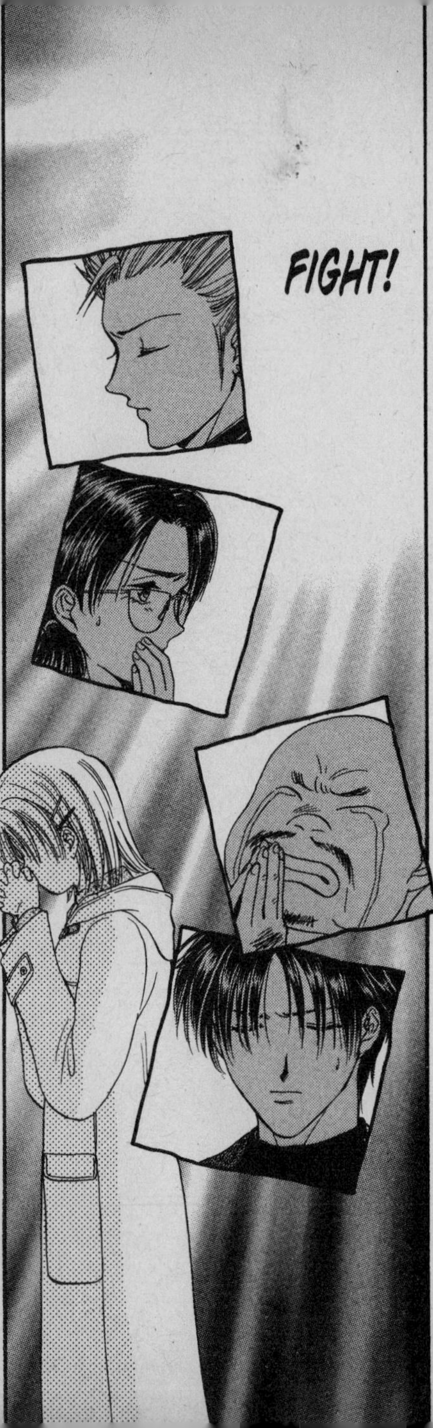
FIGHT!

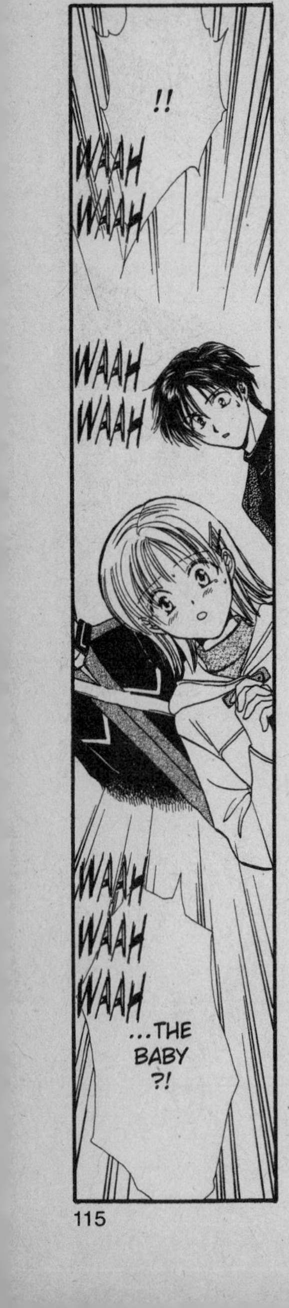
!!
WAAH WAAH
WAAH WAAH
WAAH WAAH WAAH
...THE BABY ?!

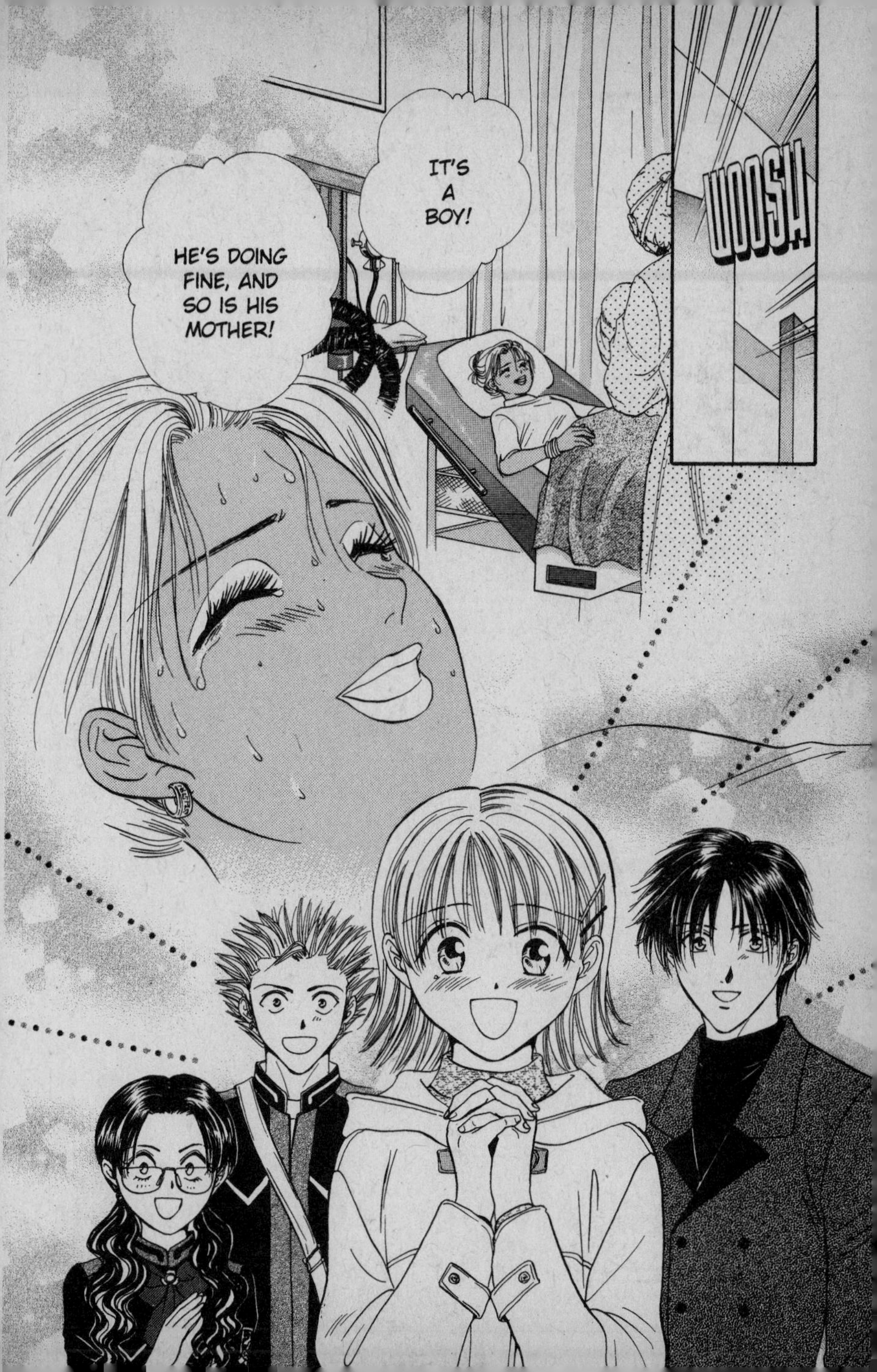
WOOSH
IT'S A BOY!
HE'S DOING FINE, AND SO IS HIS MOTHER!

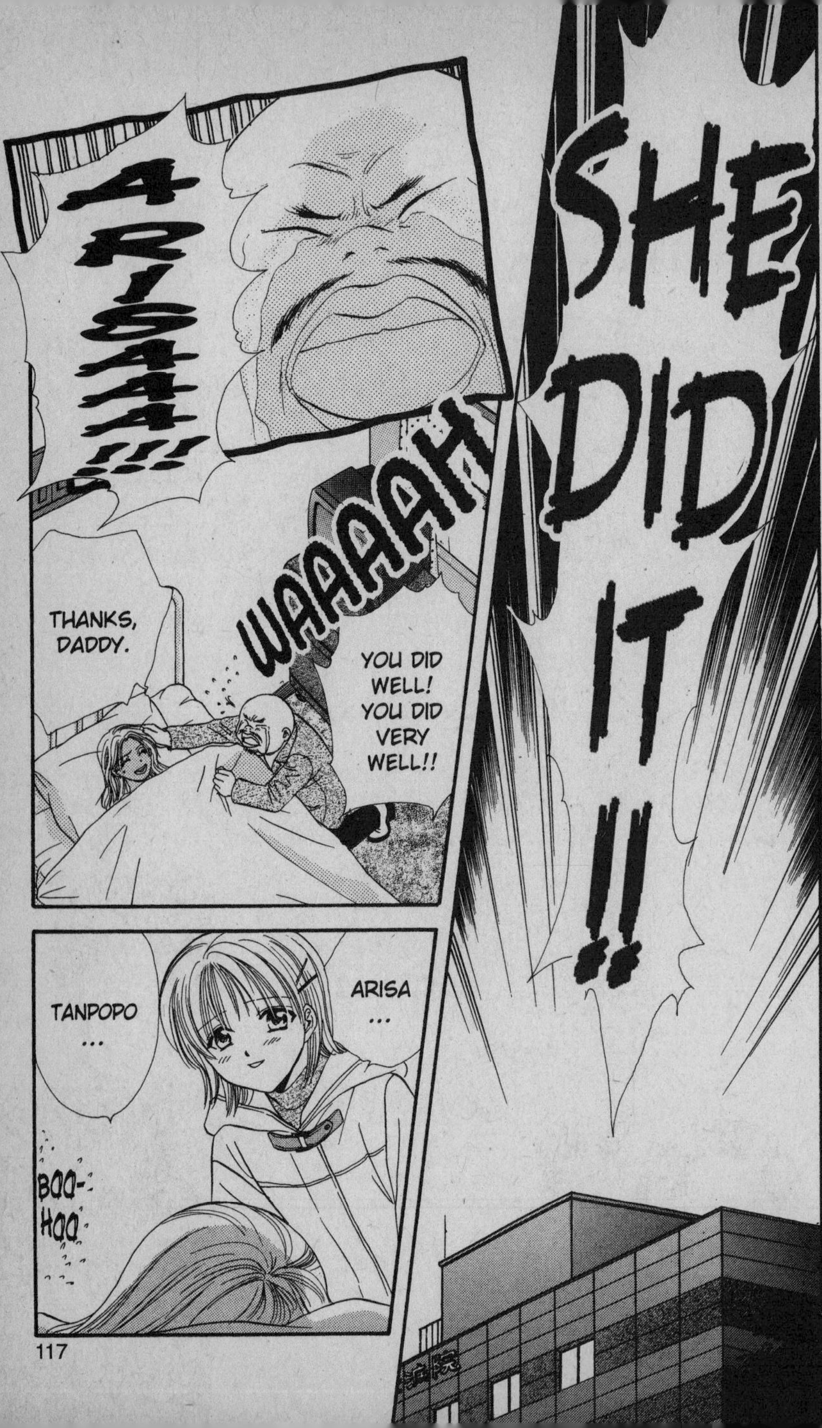
SHE DID IT!!
ARISAAA!!!
WAAAAH
YOU DID WELL! YOU DID VERY WELL!!
THANKS, DADDY.
ARISA ...
TANPOPO ...
BOO-HOO

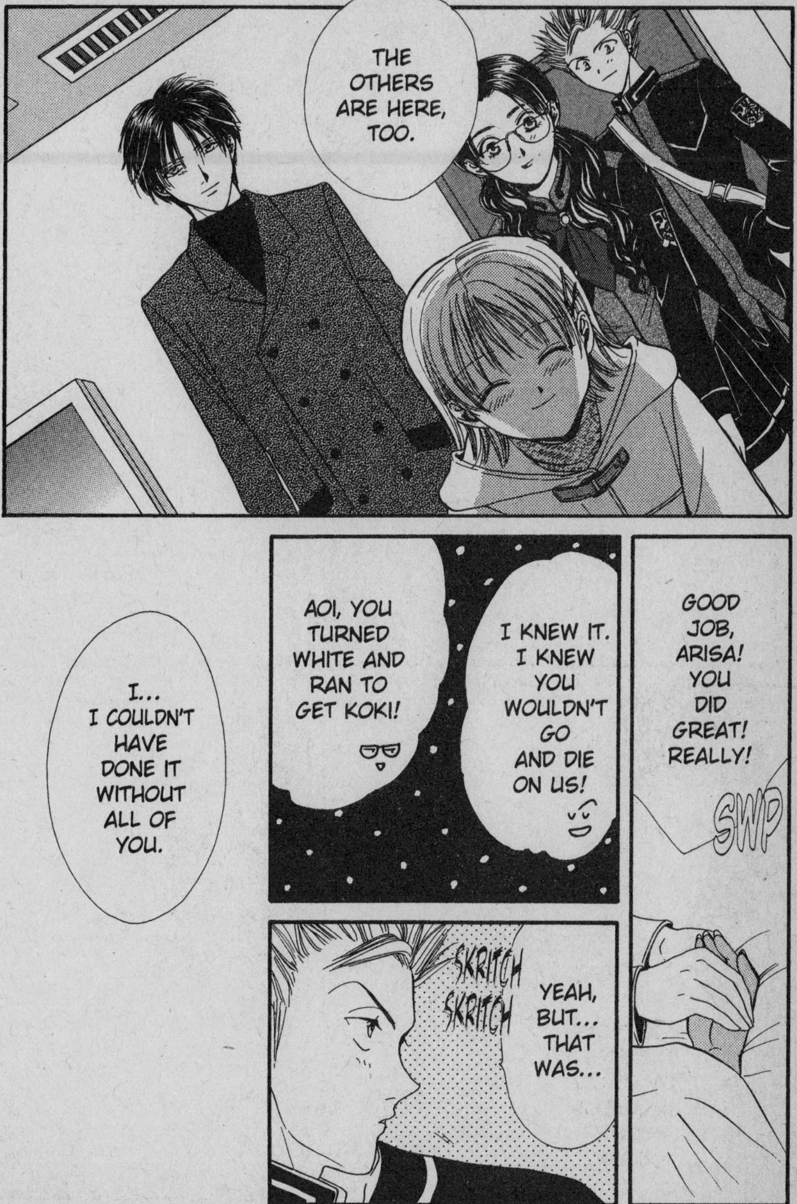
THE OTHERS ARE HERE, TOO.
GOOD JOB, ARISA! YOU DID GREAT! REALLY!
SWP
I KNEW IT. I KNEW YOU WOULDN'T GO AND DIE ON US!
AOI, YOU TURNED WHITE AND RAN TO GET KOKI!
I... I COULDN'T HAVE DONE IT WITHOUT ALL OF YOU.
SKRITCH SKRITCH
YEAH, BUT... THAT WAS...

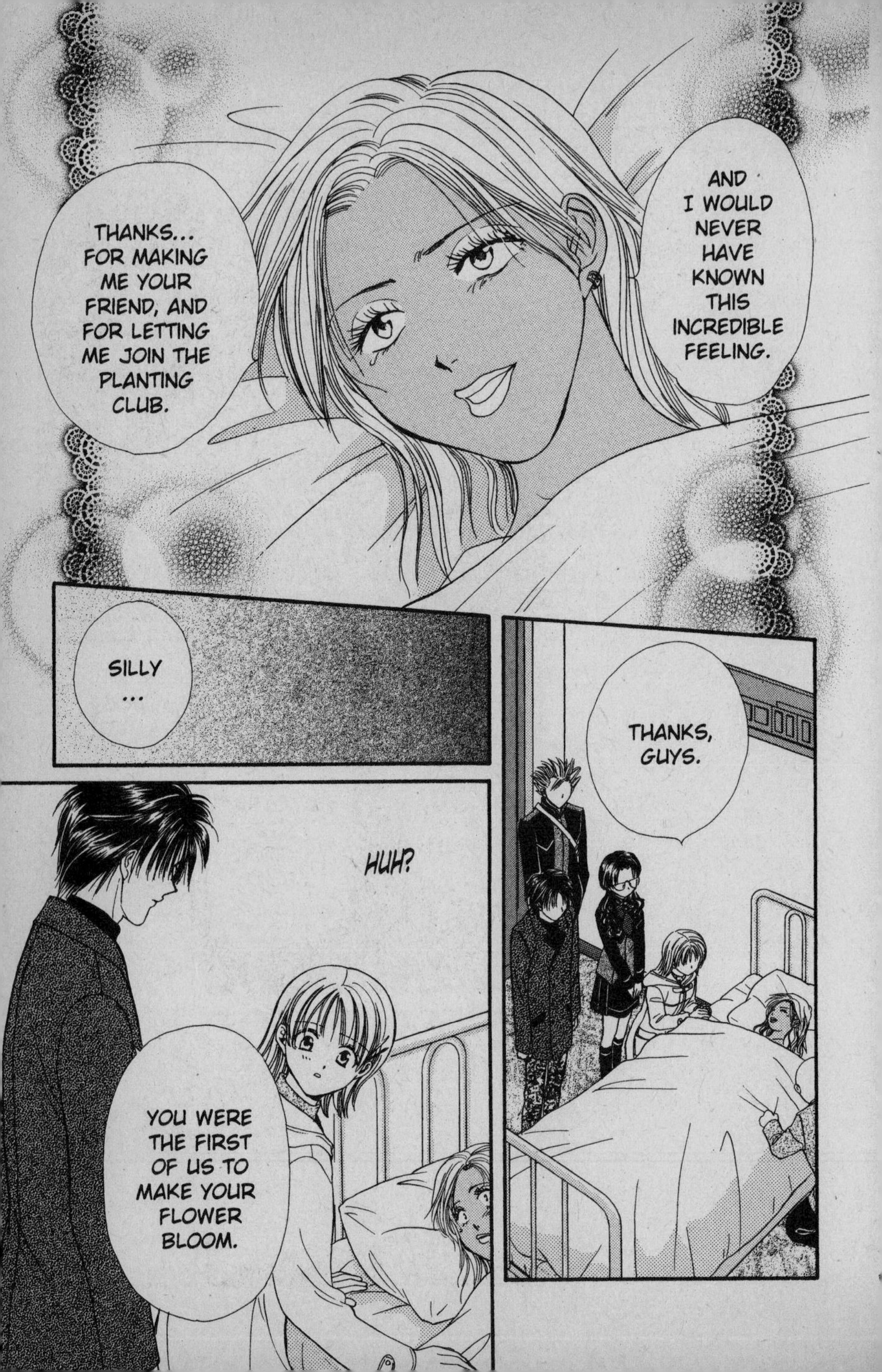
AND I WOULD NEVER HAVE KNOWN THIS INCREDIBLE FEELING.
THANKS... FOR MAKING ME YOUR FRIEND, AND FOR LETTING ME JOIN THE PLANTING CLUB.
THANKS, GUYS.
SILLY ...
HUH?
YOU WERE THE FIRST OF US TO MAKE YOUR FLOWER BLOOM.

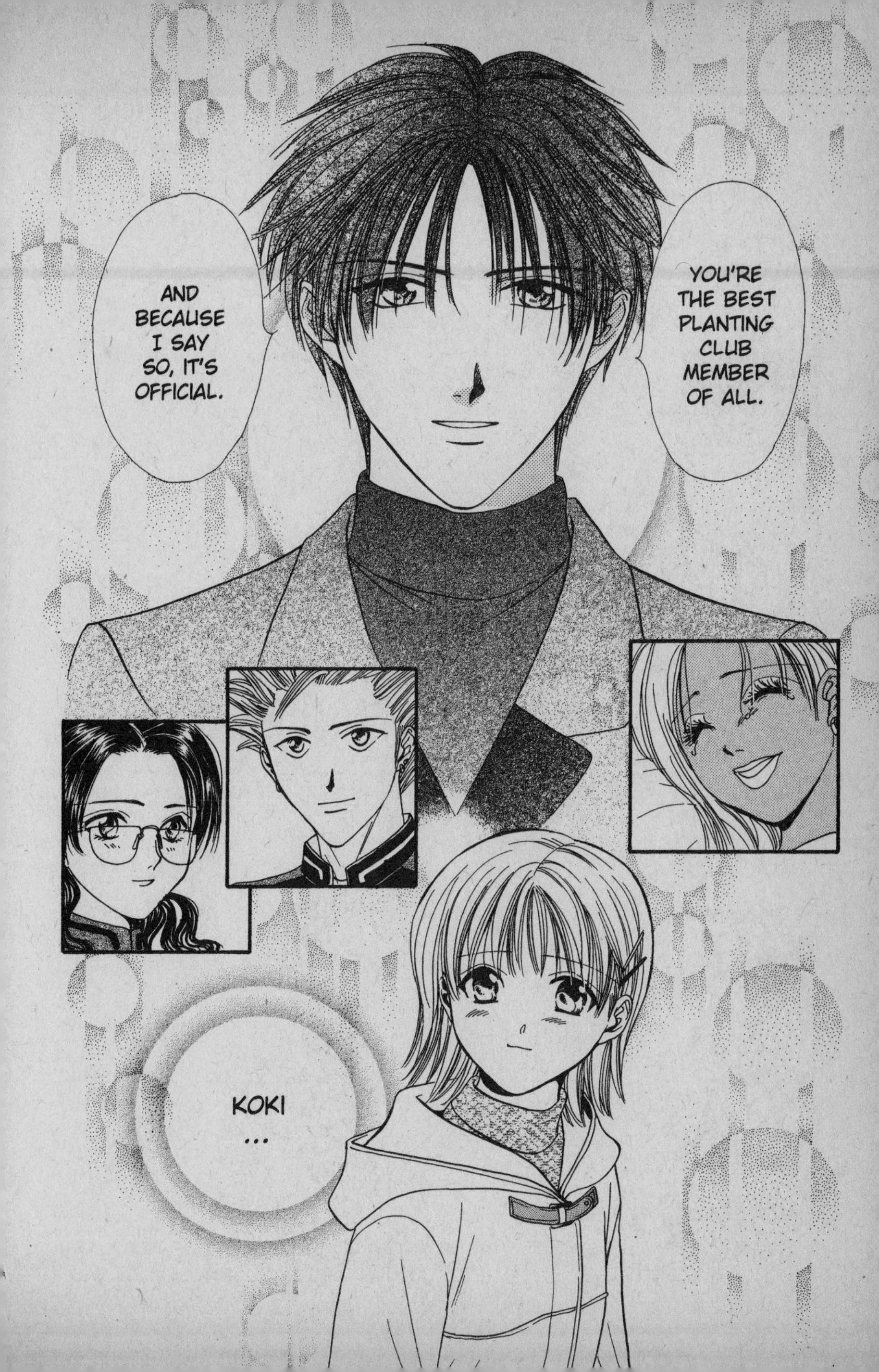
YOU'RE THE BEST PLANTING CLUB MEMBER OF ALL.
AND BECAUSE I SAY SO, IT'S OFFICIAL.
KOKI ...

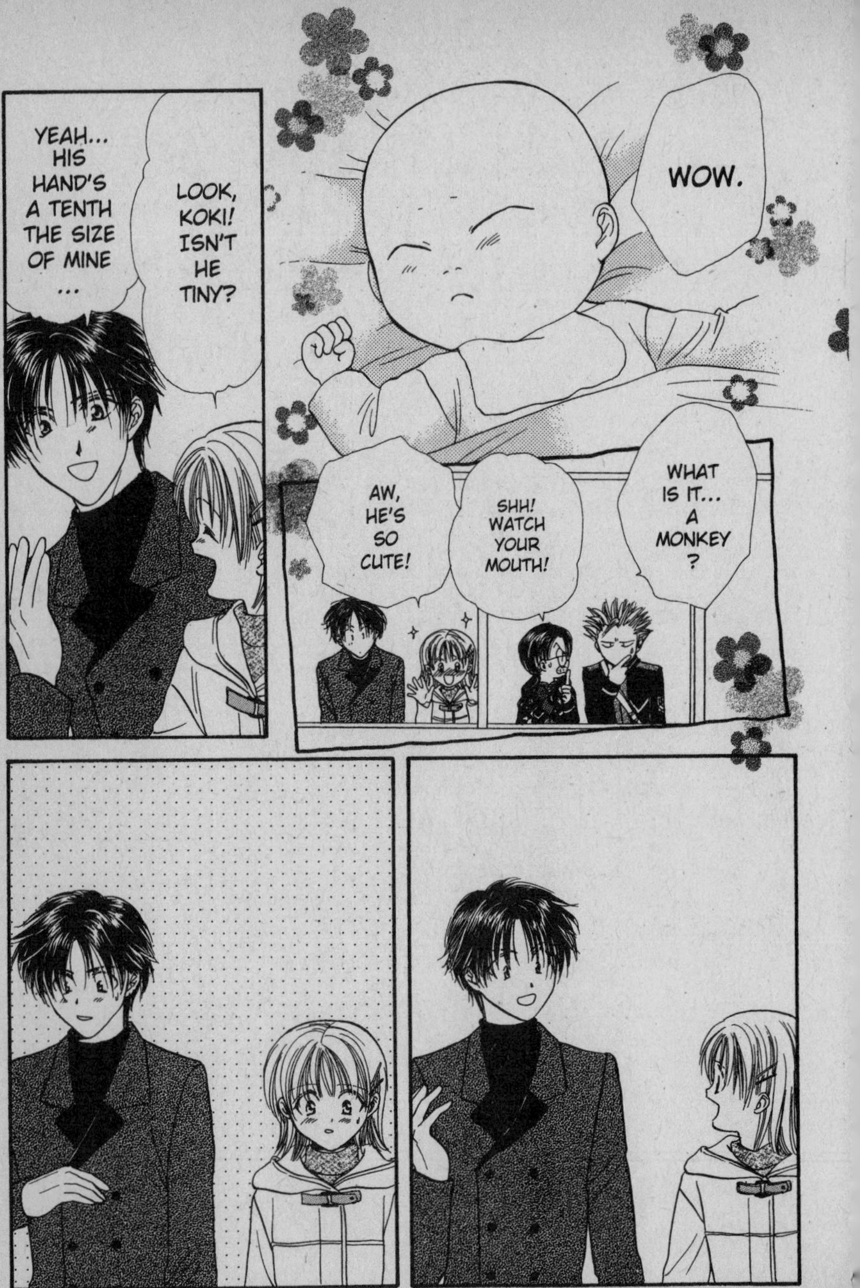
WOW.
WHAT IS IT... A MONKEY?
SHH! WATCH YOUR MOUTH!
AW, HE'S SO CUTE!
LOOK, KOKI! ISN'T HE TINY?
YEAH... HIS HAND'S A TENTH THE SIZE OF MINE ...

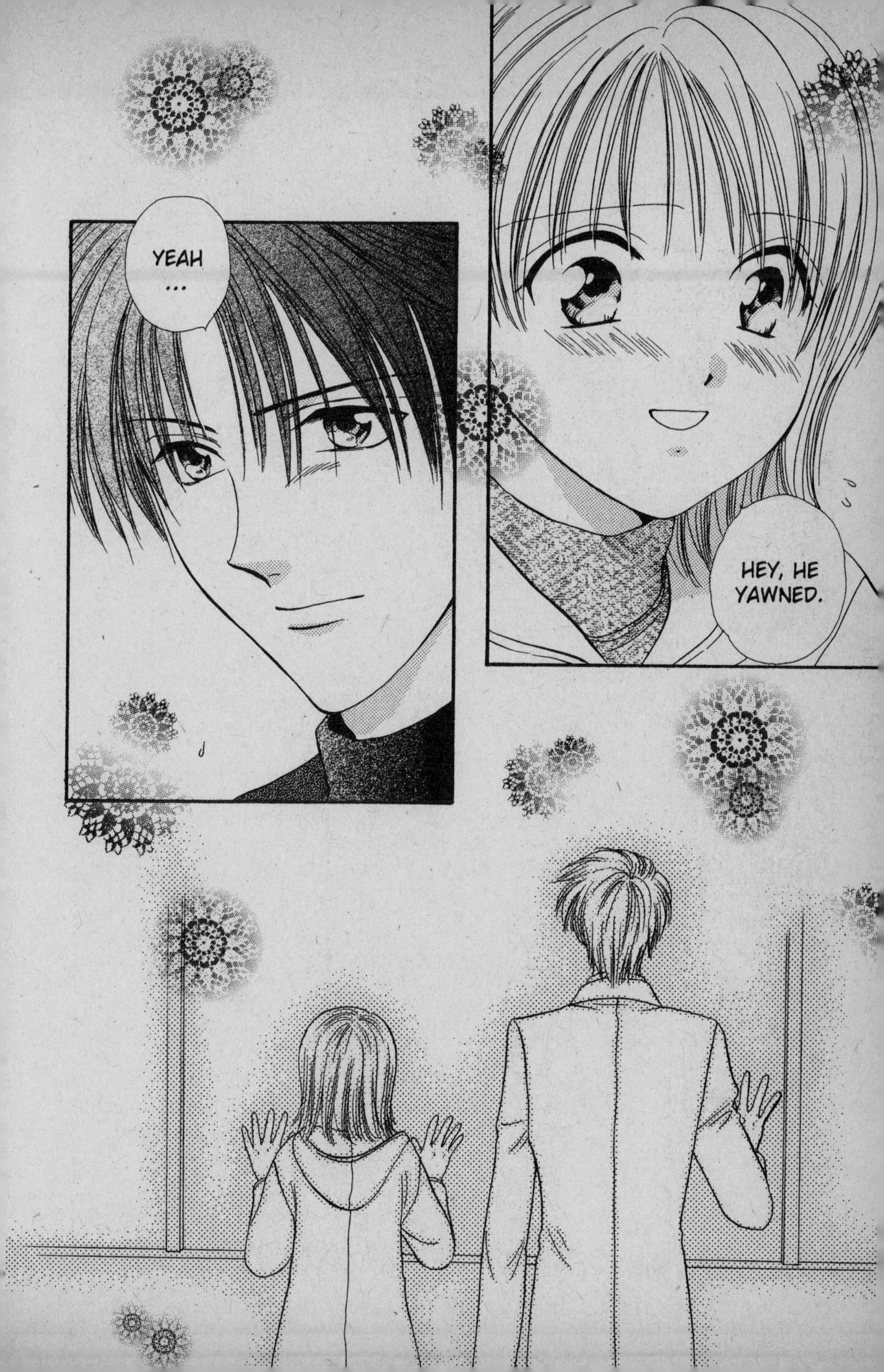
HEY, HE YAWNED.
YEAH ...

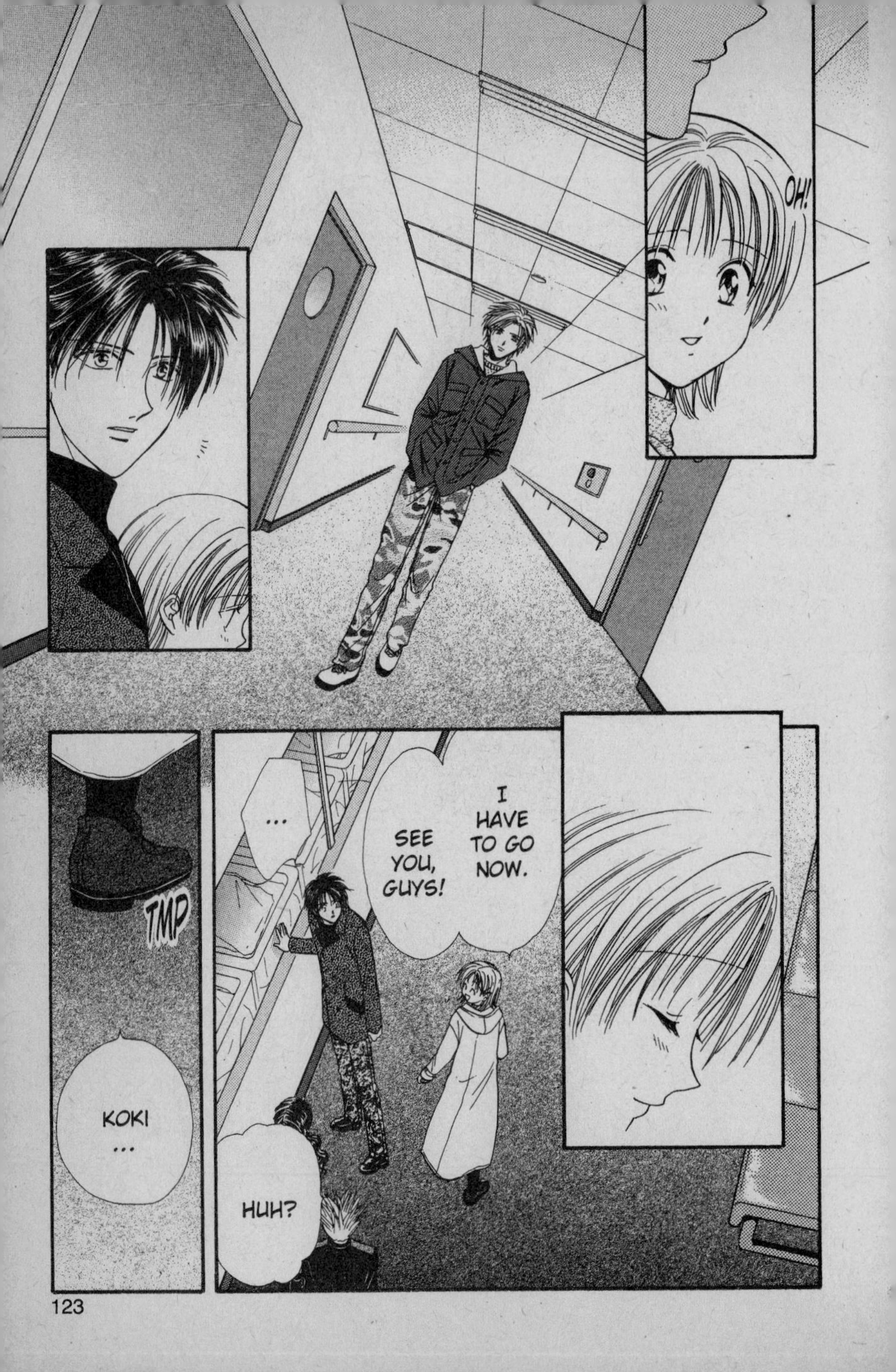
OH!
I HAVE TO GO NOW.
SEE YOU, GUYS!
...
HUH?
TMP
KOKI ...

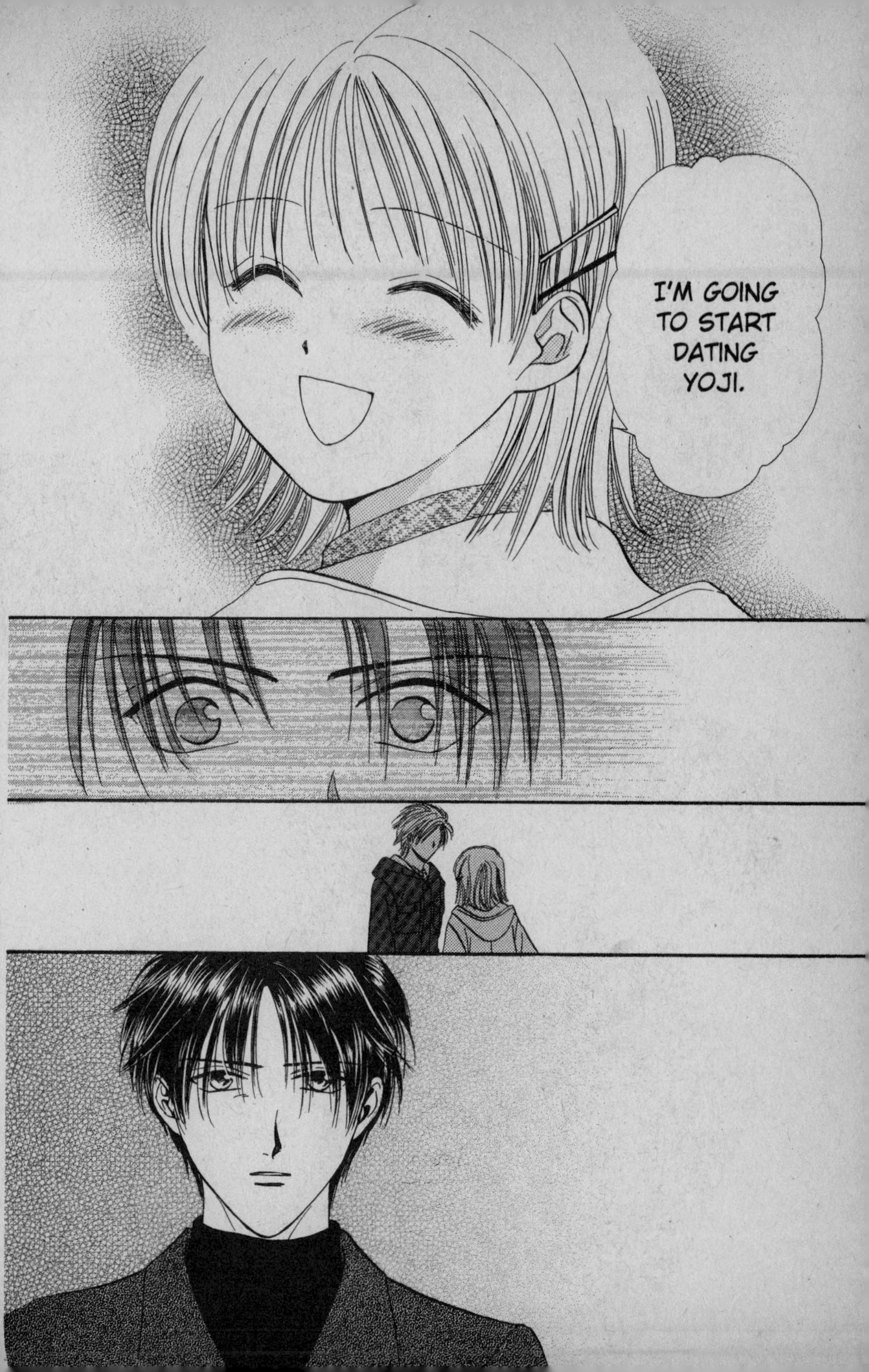
I'M GOING TO START DATING YOJI.

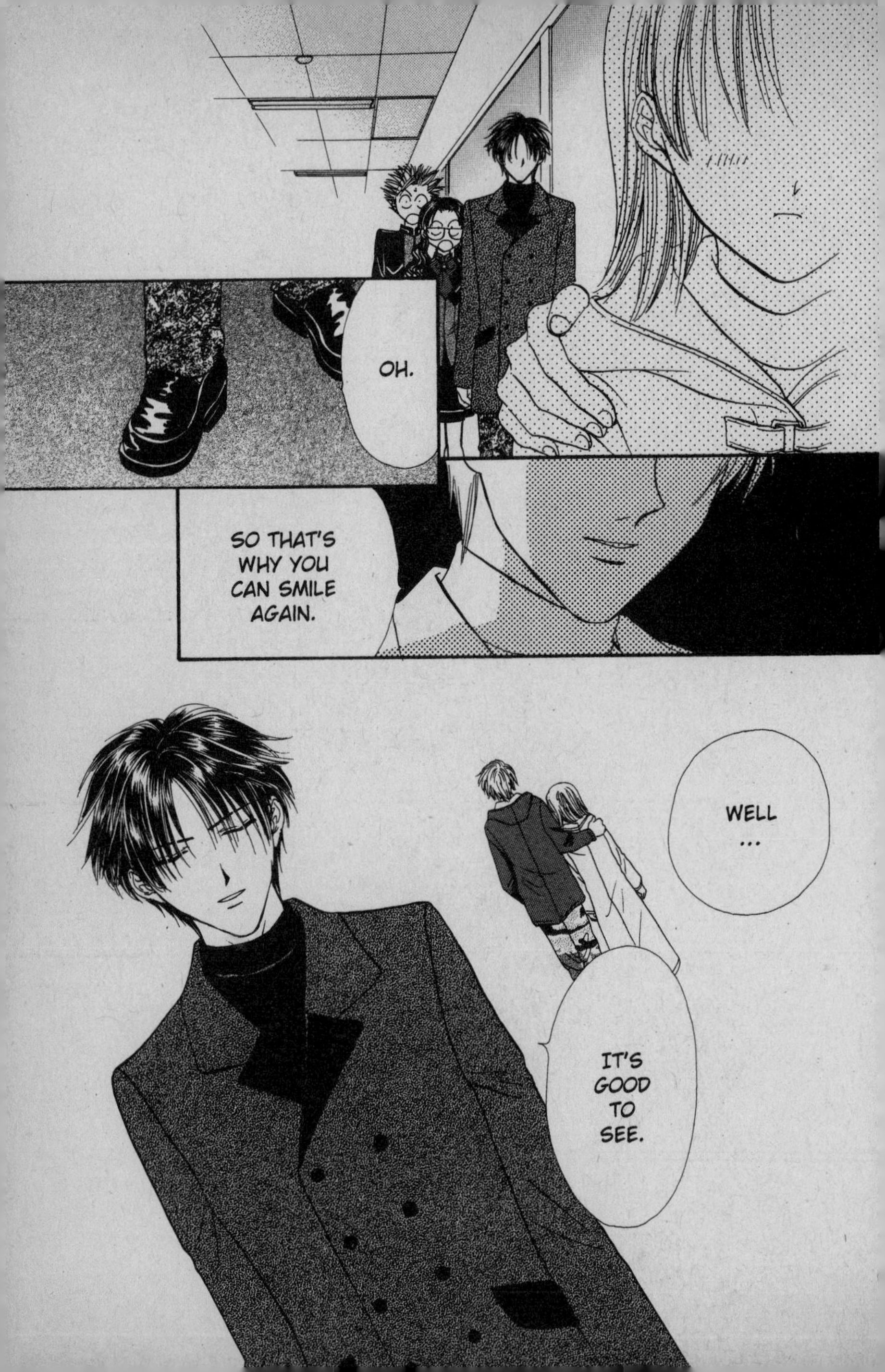
OH.
SO THAT'S WHY YOU CAN SMILE AGAIN.
WELL ...
IT'S GOOD TO SEE.

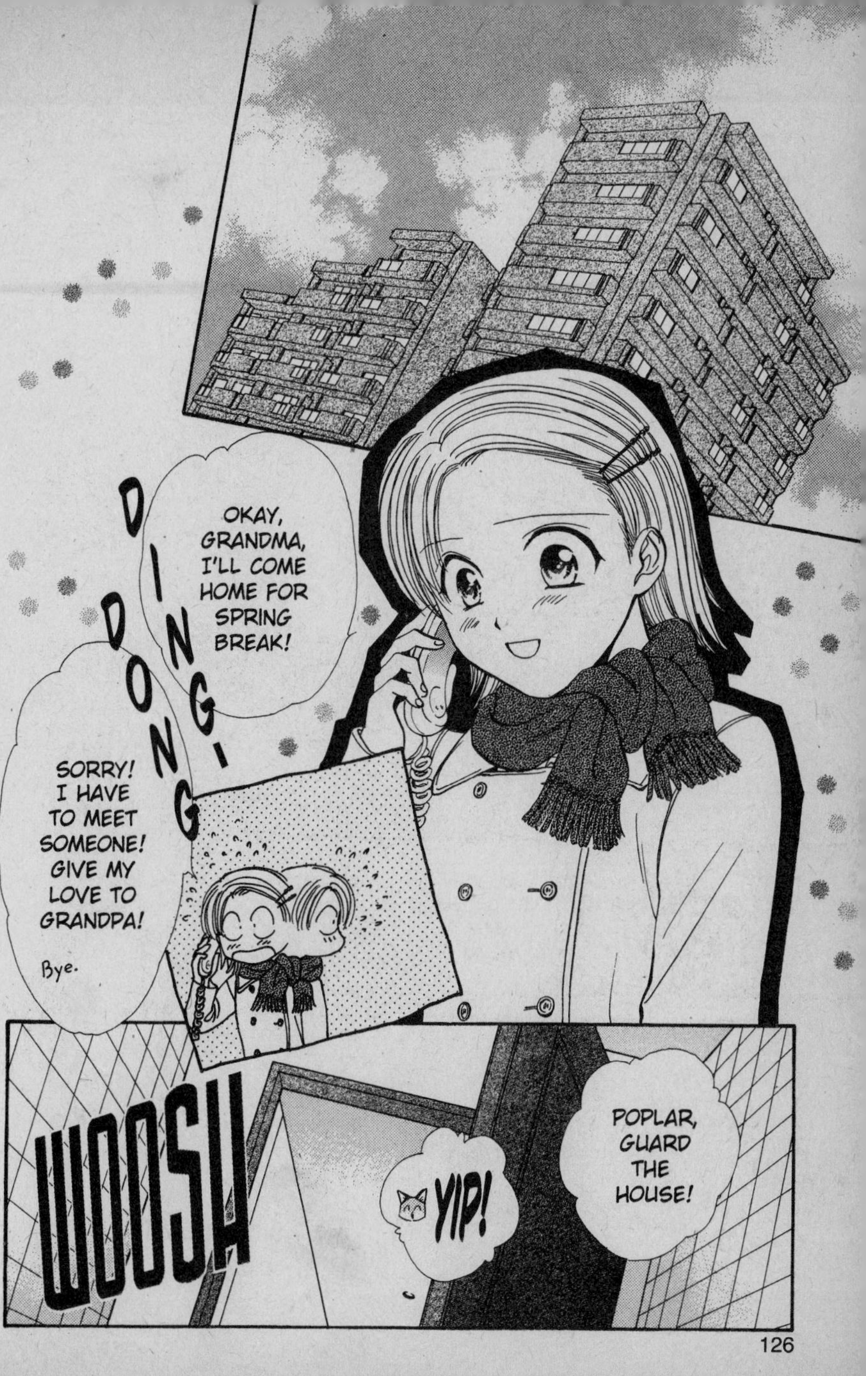
OKAY, GRANDMA, I'LL COME HOME FOR SPRING BREAK!
DING DONG!
SORRY! I HAVE TO MEET SOMEONE! GIVE MY LOVE TO GRANDPA!
Bye.
POPLAR, GUARD THE HOUSE!
YIP!
WOOSH

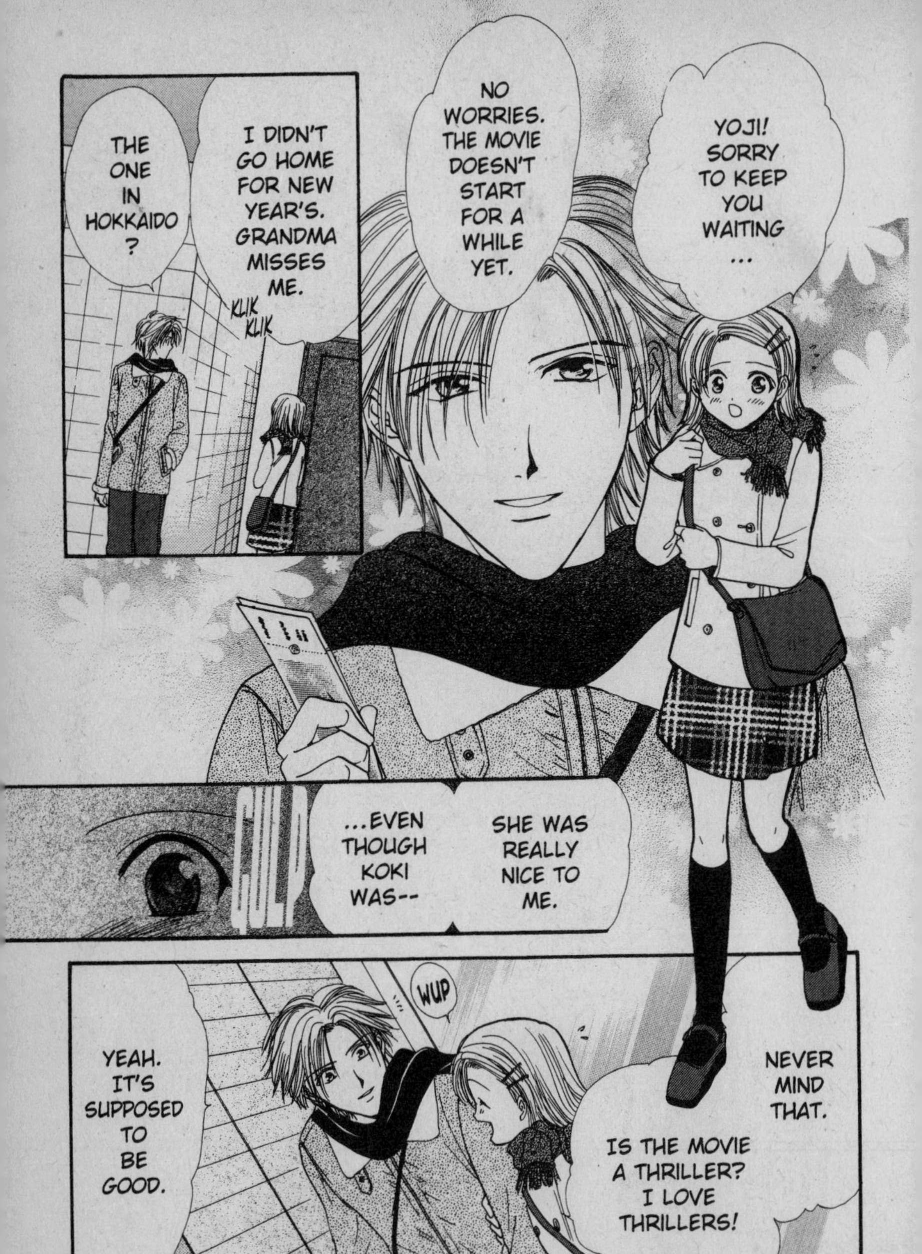
YOJI! SORRY TO KEEP YOU WAITING ...
NO WORRIES. THE MOVIE DOESN'T START FOR A WHILE YET.
I DIDN'T GO HOME FOR NEW YEAR'S. GRANDMA MISSES ME.
THE ONE IN HOKKAIDO ?
KLIK KLIK
SHE WAS REALLY NICE TO ME.
...EVEN THOUGH KOKI WAS--
GULP
NEVER MIND THAT.
IS THE MOVIE A THRILLER? I LOVE THRILLERS!
WUP
YEAH. IT'S SUPPOSED TO BE GOOD.

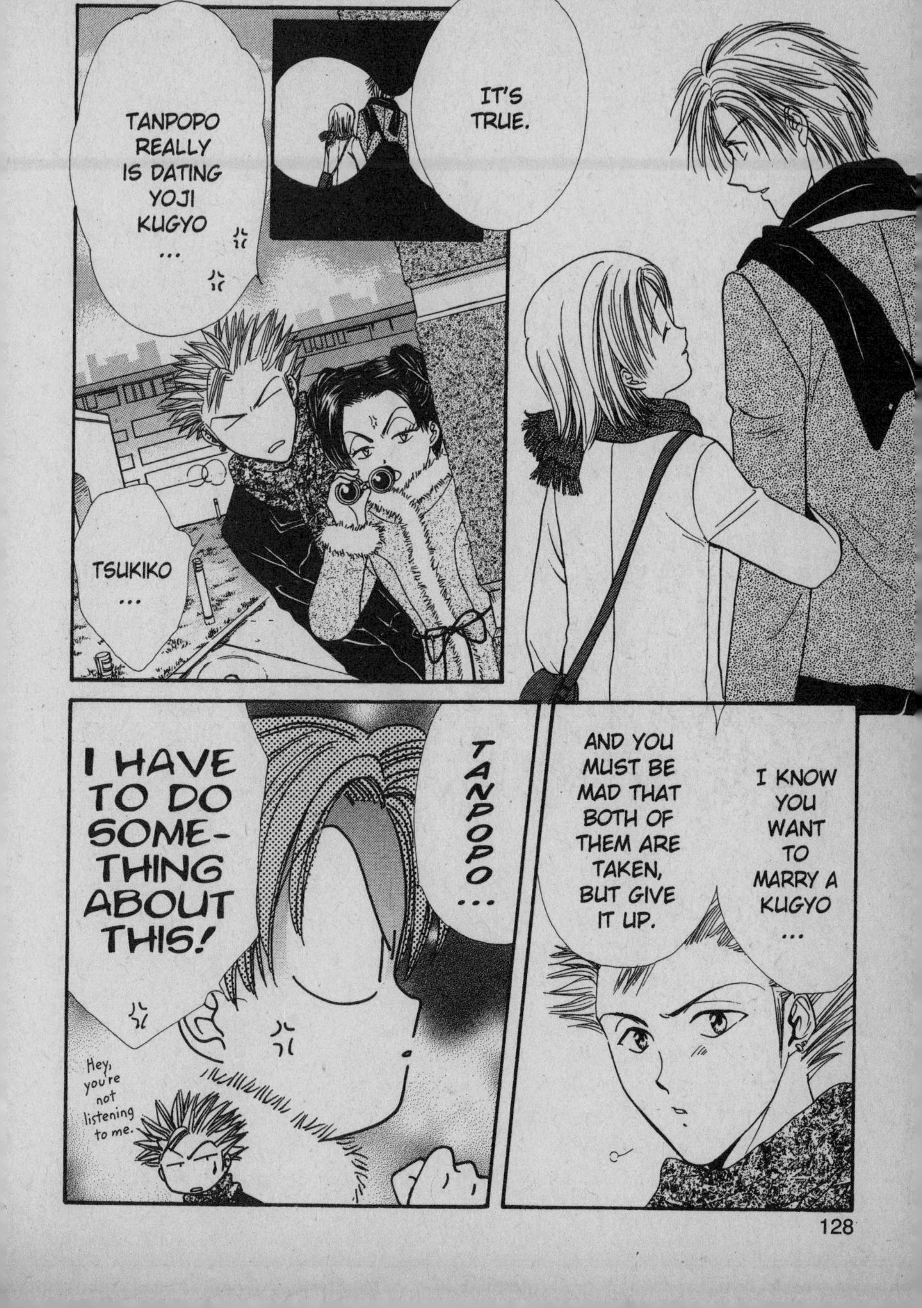
IT'S TRUE.
TANPOPO REALLY IS DATING YOJI KUGYO ...
TSUKIKO ...
I KNOW YOU WANT TO MARRY A KUGYO ...
AND YOU MUST BE MAD THAT BOTH OF THEM ARE TAKEN, BUT GIVE IT UP.
TANPOPO ...
I HAVE TO DO SOME-THING ABOUT THIS!
Hey, you're not listening to me.

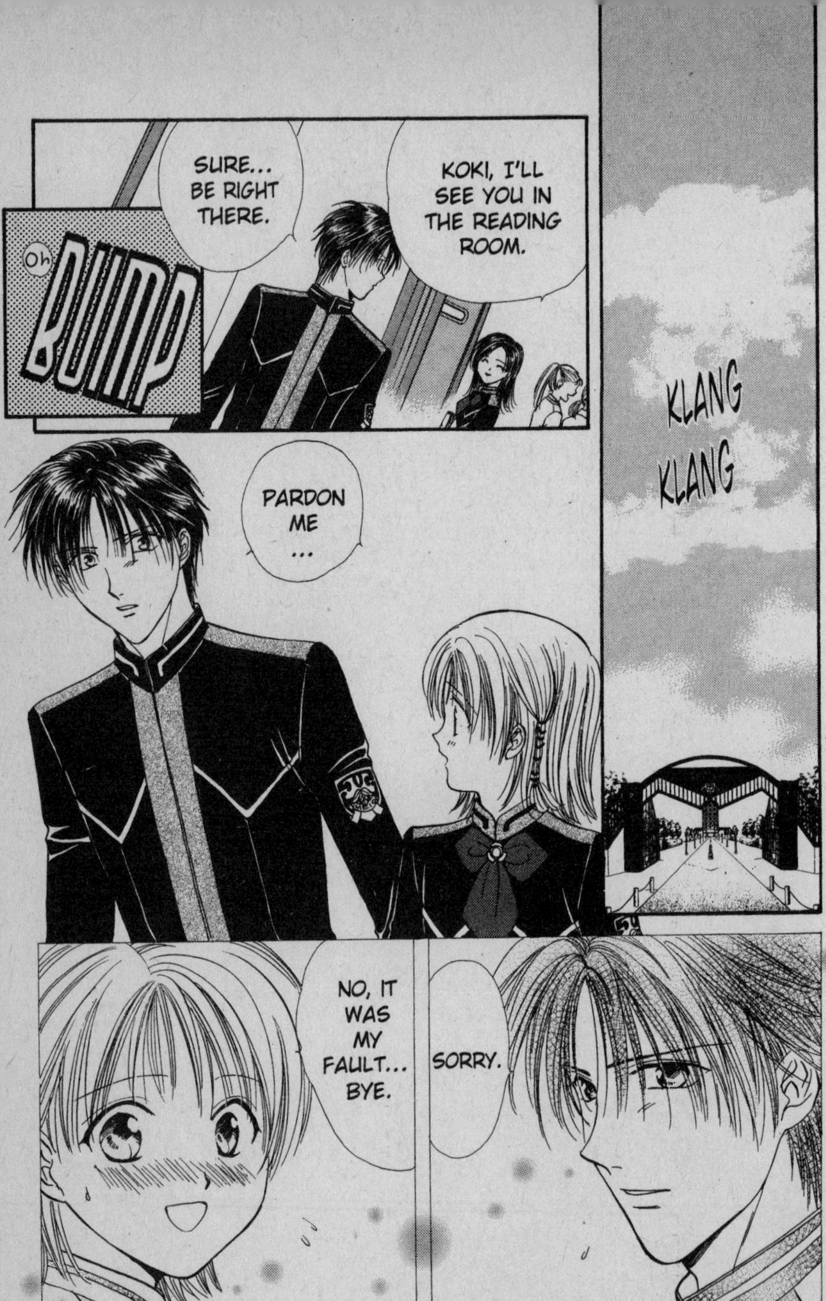
KLANG
KLANG
KOKI, I'LL SEE YOU IN THE READING ROOM.
SURE... BE RIGHT THERE.
Oh
BUMP
PARDON ME ...
SORRY.
NO, IT WAS MY FAULT... BYE.

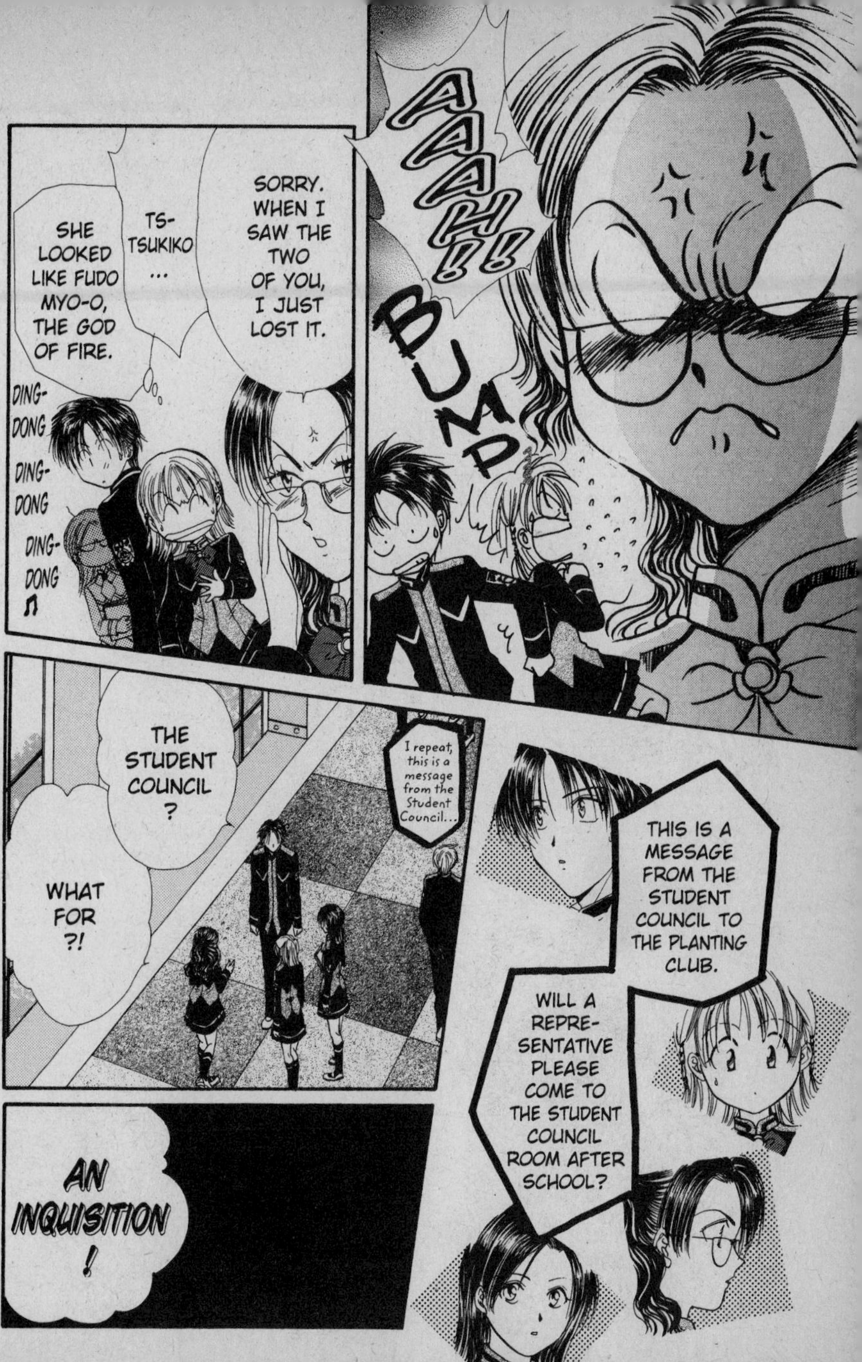
AAAAH!!
BUMP
SORRY. WHEN I SAW THE TWO OF YOU, I JUST LOST IT.
TS-TSUKIKO ...
SHE LOOKED LIKE FUDO MYO-O, THE GOD OF FIRE.
DING-DONG
DING-DONG
DING-DONG ♫
THIS IS A MESSAGE FROM THE STUDENT COUNCIL TO THE PLANTING CLUB.
WILL A REPRESENTATIVE PLEASE COME TO THE STUDENT COUNCIL ROOM AFTER SCHOOL?
I repeat, this is a message from the Student Council...
THE STUDENT COUNCIL ?
WHAT FOR ?!
AN INQUISITION !

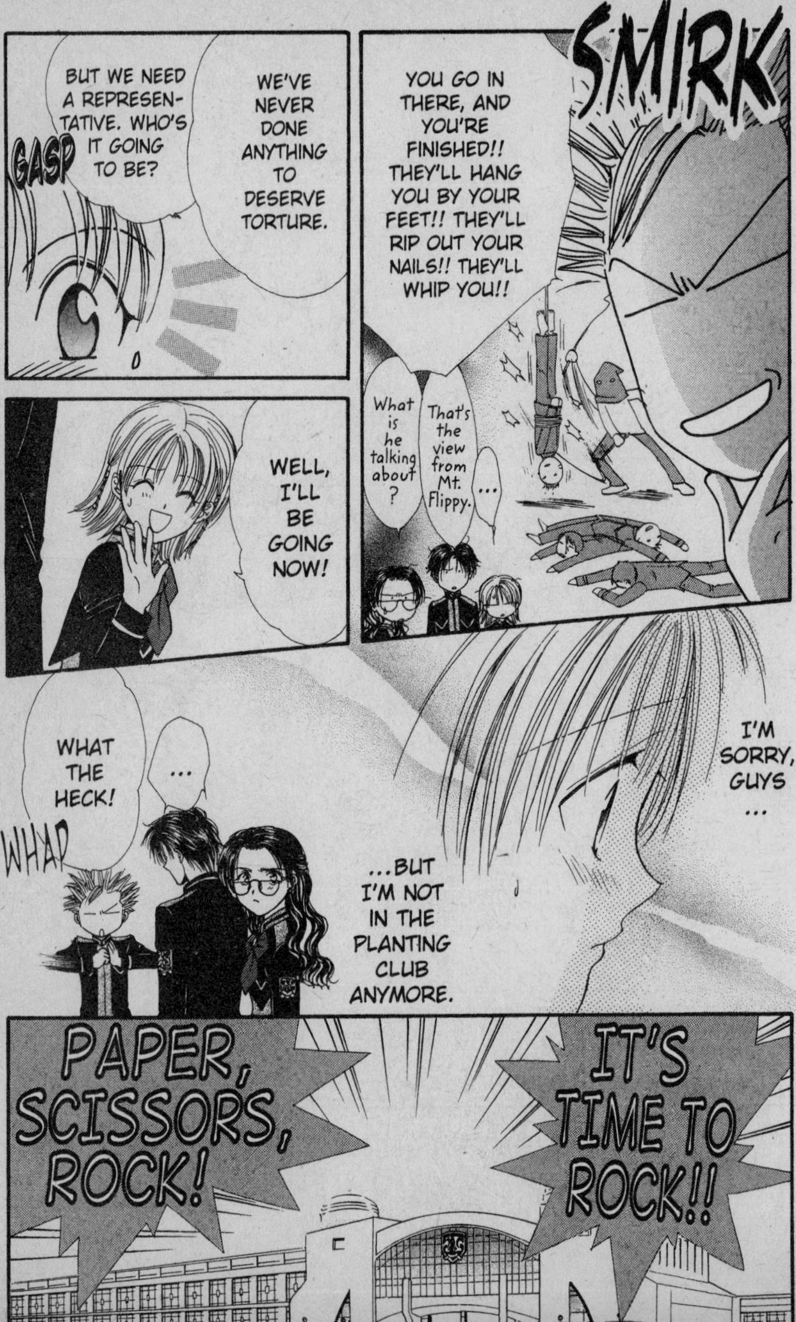
SMIRK
YOU GO IN THERE, AND YOU'RE FINISHED!! THEY'LL HANG YOU BY YOUR FEET!! THEY'LL RIP OUT YOUR NAILS!! THEY'LL WHIP YOU!!
...
That's the view from Mt. Flippy.
What is he talking about?
WE'VE NEVER DONE ANYTHING TO DESERVE TORTURE.
BUT WE NEED A REPRESEN-TATIVE. WHO'S IT GOING TO BE?
GASP
WELL, I'LL BE GOING NOW!
I'M SORRY, GUYS ...
...BUT I'M NOT IN THE PLANTING CLUB ANYMORE.
...
WHAT THE HECK!
WHAP
IT'S TIME TO ROCK!!
PAPER, SCISSORS, ROCK!

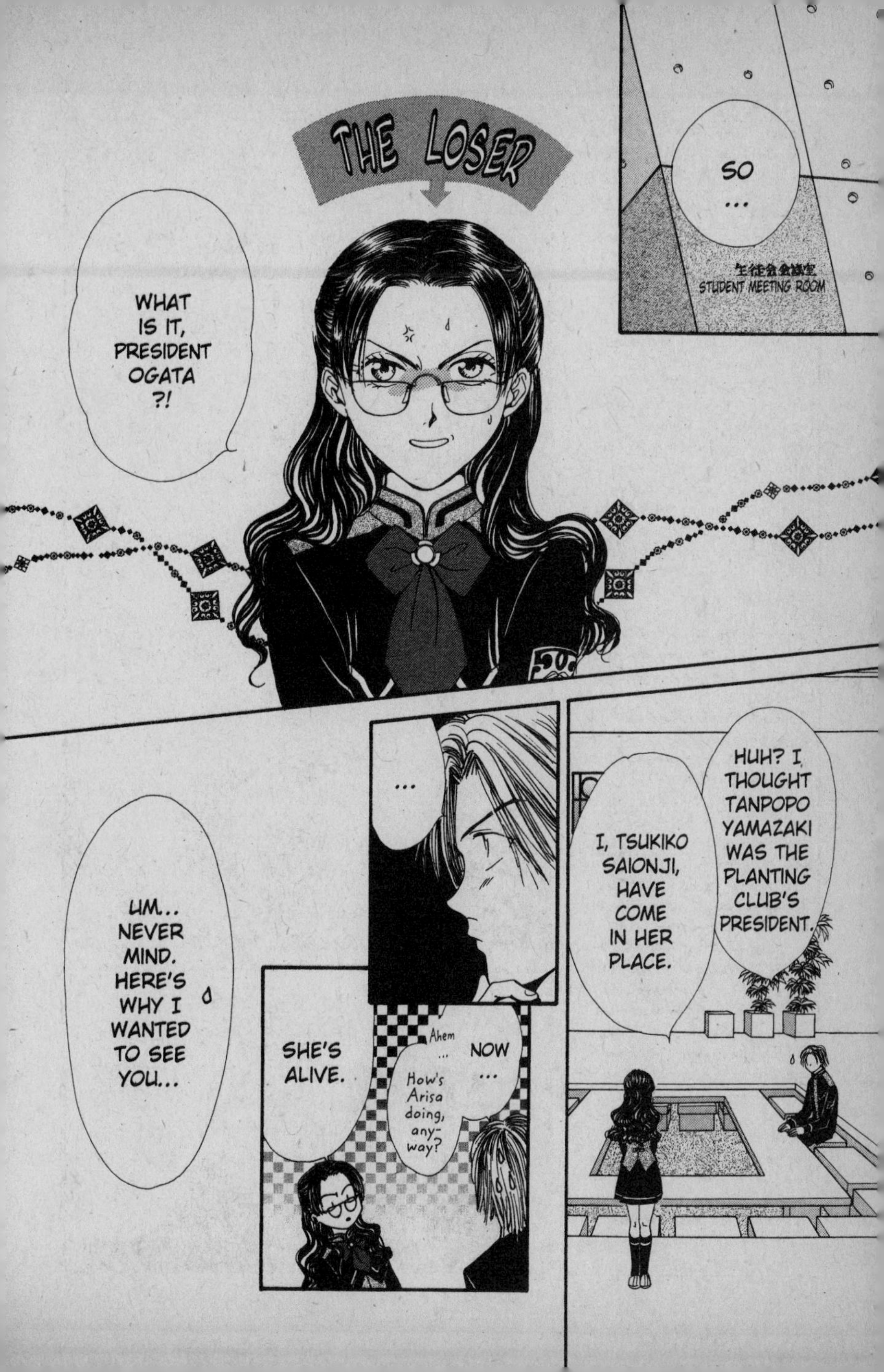
SO ...
生徒会会議室
STUDENT MEETING ROOM
THE LOSER
WHAT IS IT, PRESIDENT OGATA ?!
HUH? I THOUGHT TANPOPO YAMAZAKI WAS THE PLANTING CLUB'S PRESIDENT.
I, TSUKIKO SAIONJI, HAVE COME IN HER PLACE.
...
NOW ...
Ahem ... How's Arisa doing, anyway?
SHE'S ALIVE.
UM... NEVER MIND. HERE'S WHY I WANTED TO SEE YOU...

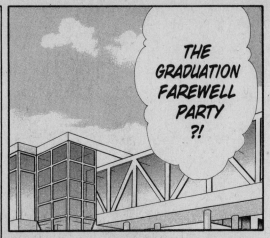

THE GRADUATION FAREWELL PARTY ?!
THE STUDENT COUNCIL IS SPONSORING IT, BUT THEY WANT THE PLANTING CLUB TO HANDLE IT...
...BECAUSE WE DID SUCH A GOOD JOB AT LAST YEAR'S SCHOOL FESTIVAL.
THE STUDENT COUNCIL WANTS US TO DO IT?! RIGHTEOUS !!
IT'S A BIG RESPONSIBILITY ...

It's hard work to be an assistant and learn from the pros firsthand, but if you want to become a pro yourself, this is probably the best thing to do.

Different writers have different schedules, methods and workloads (in other words, you can't sleep, eat or go home) so things can be tough. Think you can take it? Actually, you might learn to think of yourself as a professional (if you've got the grit).

An animator once told me that mentors and teachers used to be very strict in the old days. Even when manga artists (the real veterans) talk about their early days, they say it was normal for students' work to be thrown away, stomped on or harshly criticized.

But some re-did the work even while thinking, "You jerk," and they doggedly stuck with it. You can really see the difference in these people, who are now professionals. They have staying power.

I hear that if you're strict with young people nowadays, or if they get a little tired, they quit right away. I think, with an attitude like that, they can never be professionals. Even if they got the chance to be an assistant, they wouldn't last!

But if your teacher isn't, say, a decent person, it's probably better that you find another teacher quick. (smile) But this work isn't so easy. Nothing that counts in this world is easy. Anyway, I'm working so hard, I'm shortening my own life. (smile)

I read somewhere that one artist said, "A professional has to worry every day about popularity and sales, and be exhausted both physically and mentally, but an assistant has things much easier." Well, work, after all, is hard for everybody. For all I've said, I have no experience as an assistant (bitter smile), and that's been one thing I've regretted...

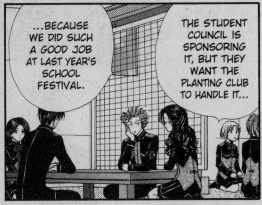

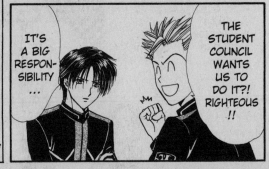

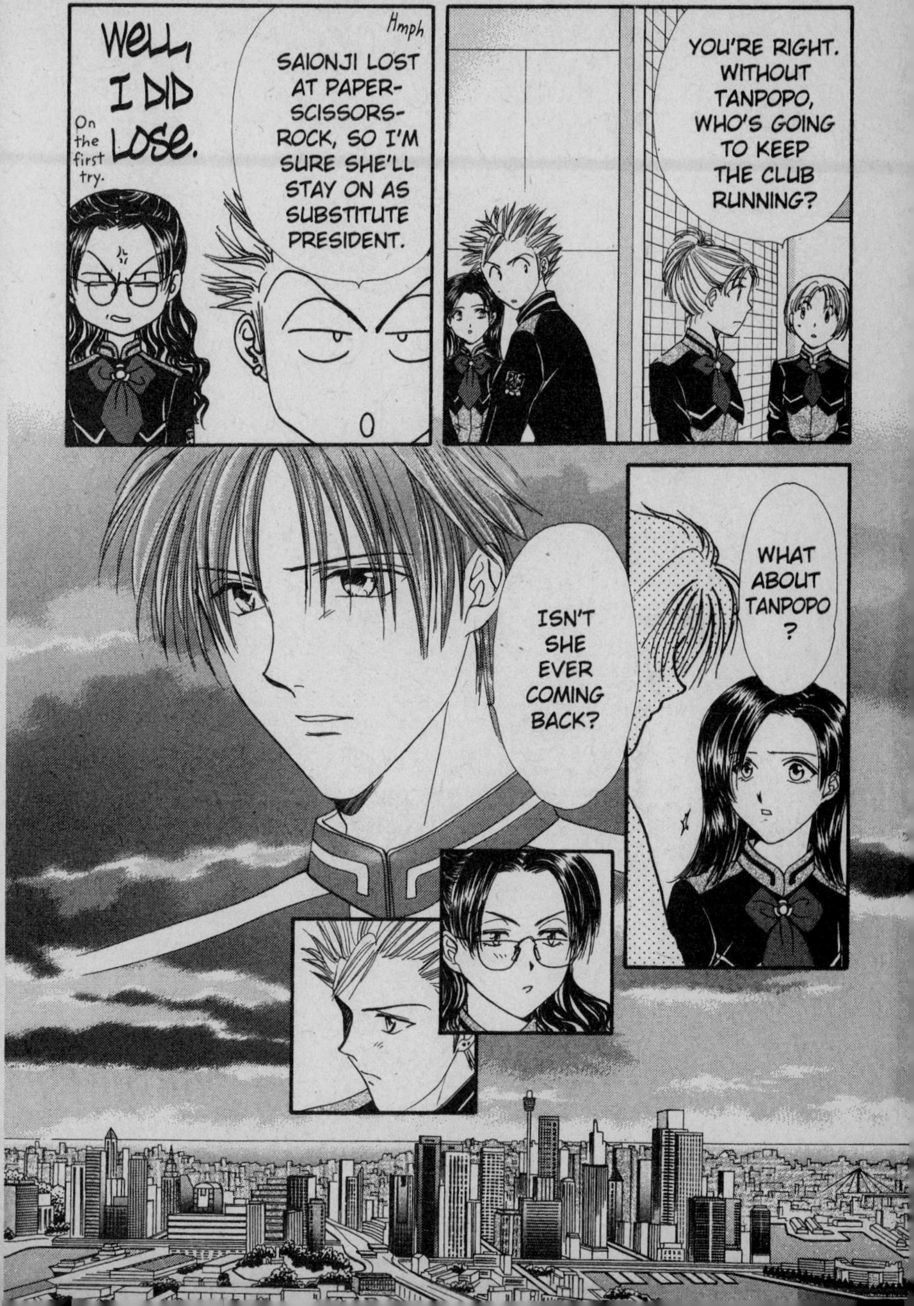
YOU'RE RIGHT. WITHOUT TANPOPO, WHO'S GOING TO KEEP THE CLUB RUNNING?
Hmph
SAIONJI LOST AT PAPER-SCISSORS-ROCK, SO I'M SURE SHE'LL STAY ON AS SUBSTITUTE PRESIDENT.
WELL, I DID LOSE.
On the first try.
WHAT ABOUT TANPOPO?
ISN'T SHE EVER COMING BACK?

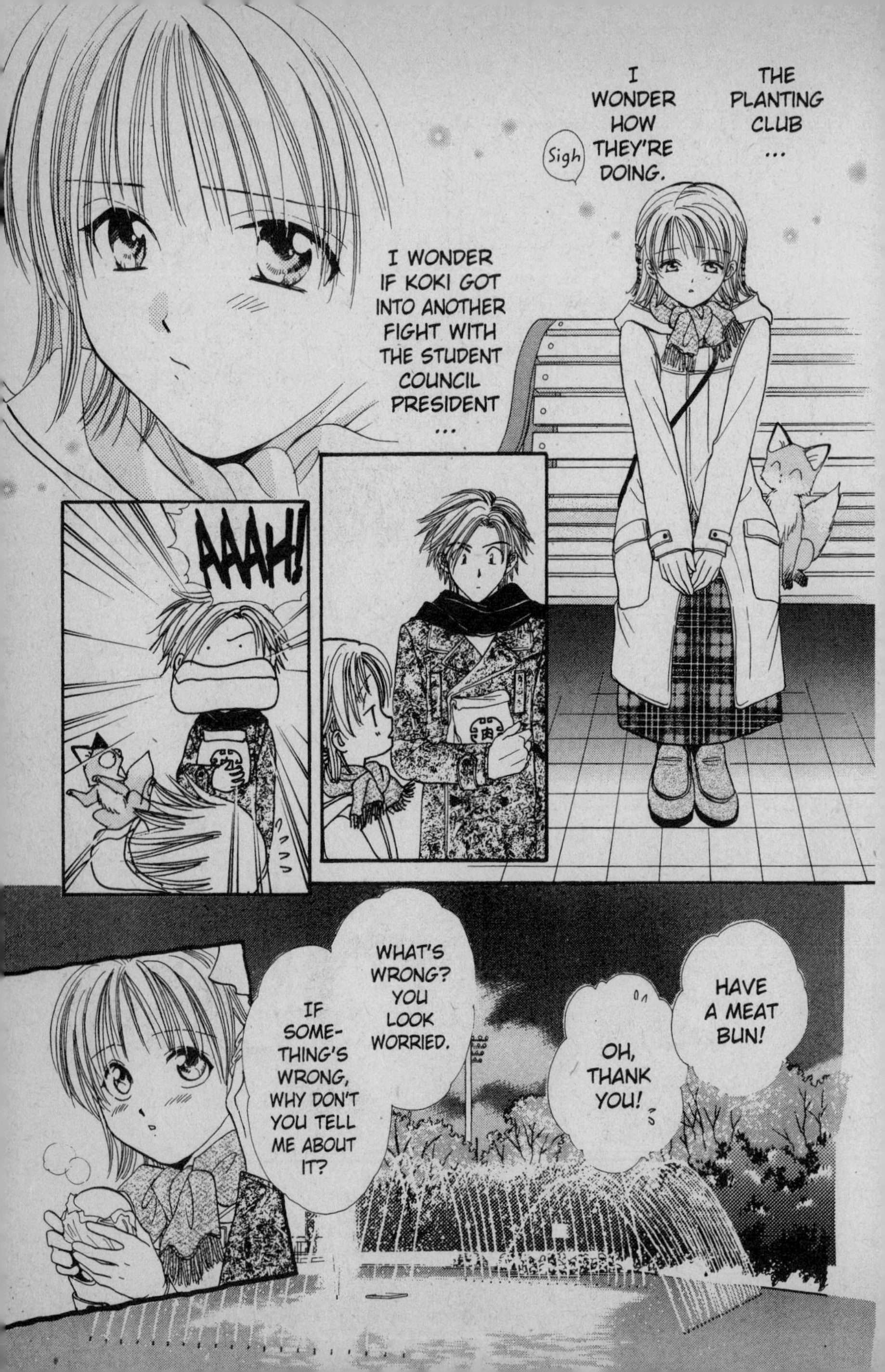
THE PLANTING CLUB ...
Sigh
I WONDER HOW THEY'RE DOING.
I WONDER IF KOKI GOT INTO ANOTHER FIGHT WITH THE STUDENT COUNCIL PRESIDENT ...
AAAH!
HAVE A MEAT BUN!
OH, THANK YOU!
WHAT'S WRONG? YOU LOOK WORRIED.
IF SOME-THING'S WRONG, WHY DON'T YOU TELL ME ABOUT IT?

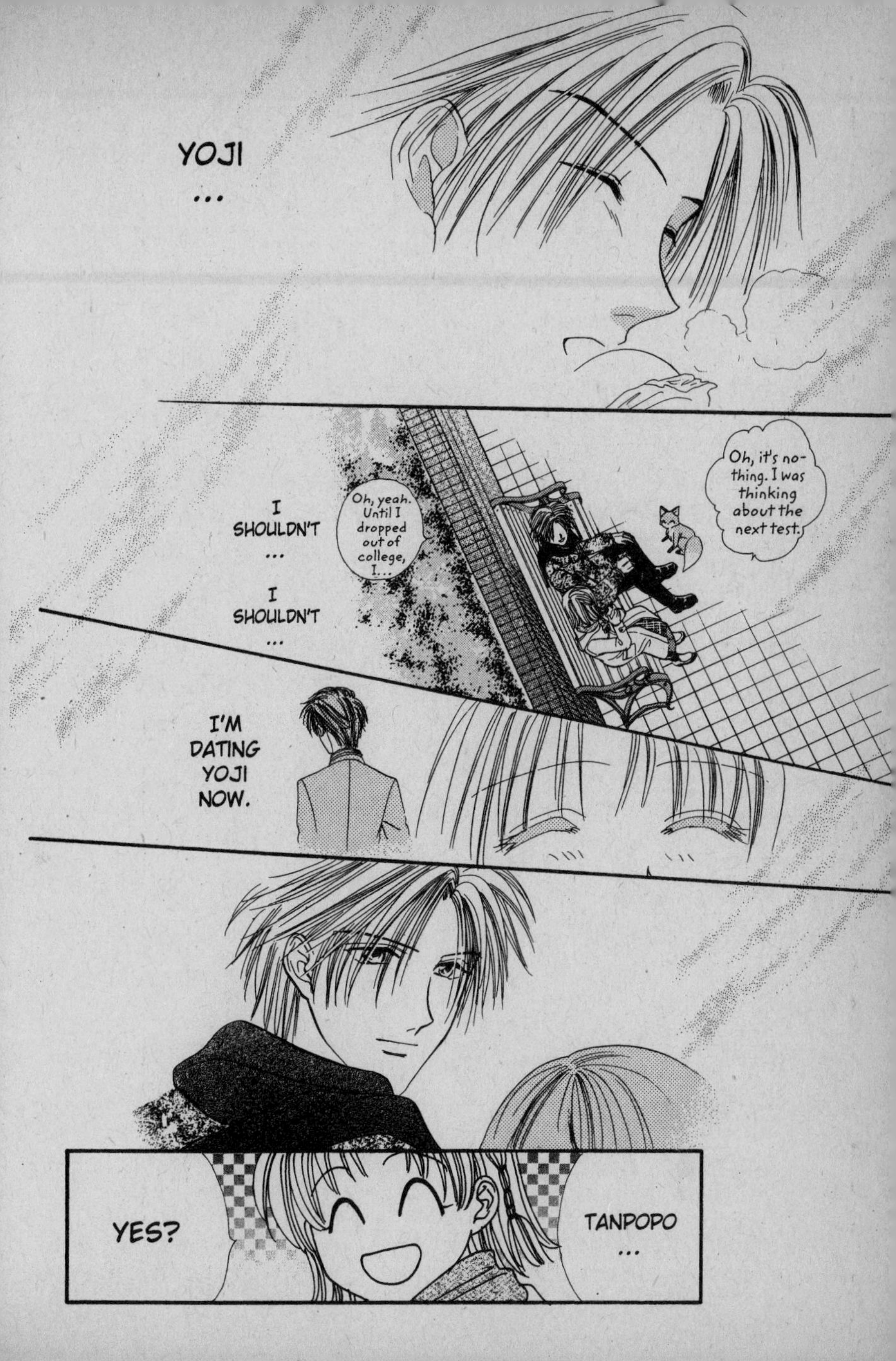
YOJI ...
Oh, it's no-thing. I was thinking about the next test.
Oh, yeah. Until I dropped out of college, I...
I SHOULDN'T ...
I SHOULDN'T ...
I'M DATING YOJI NOW.
TANPOPO ...
YES?

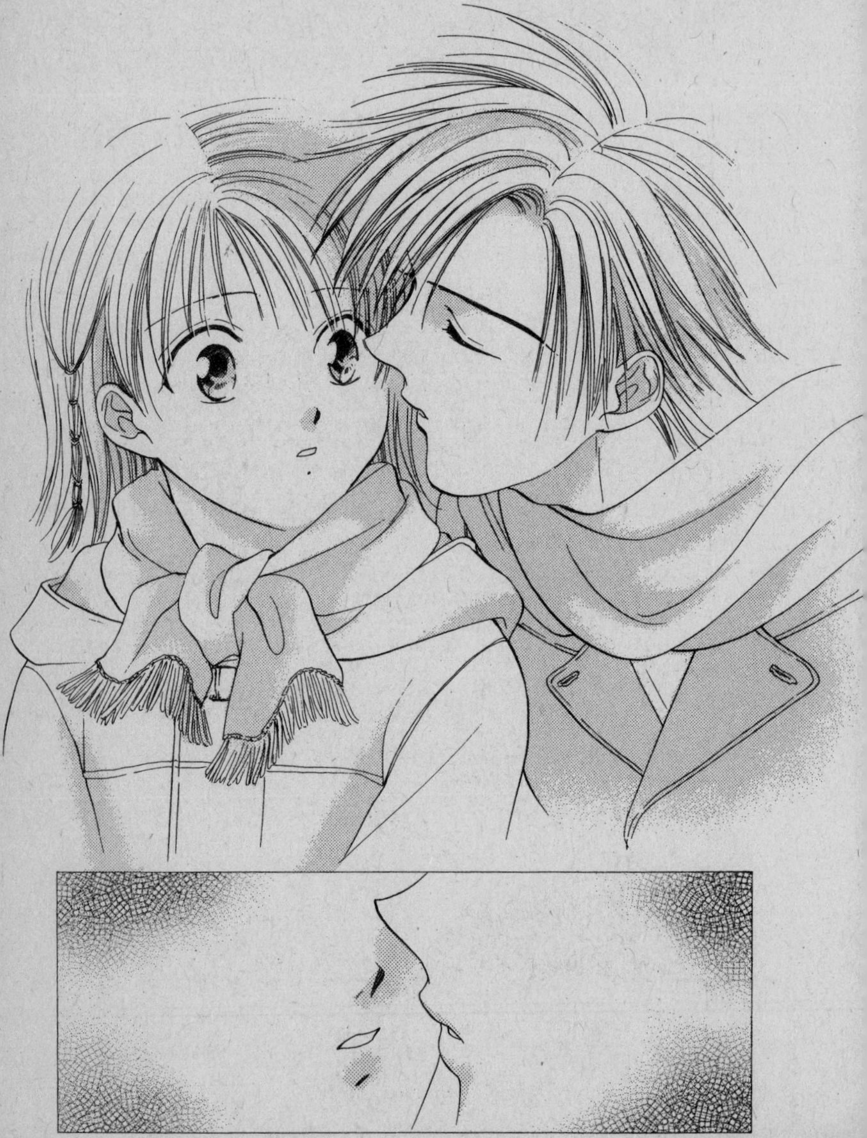

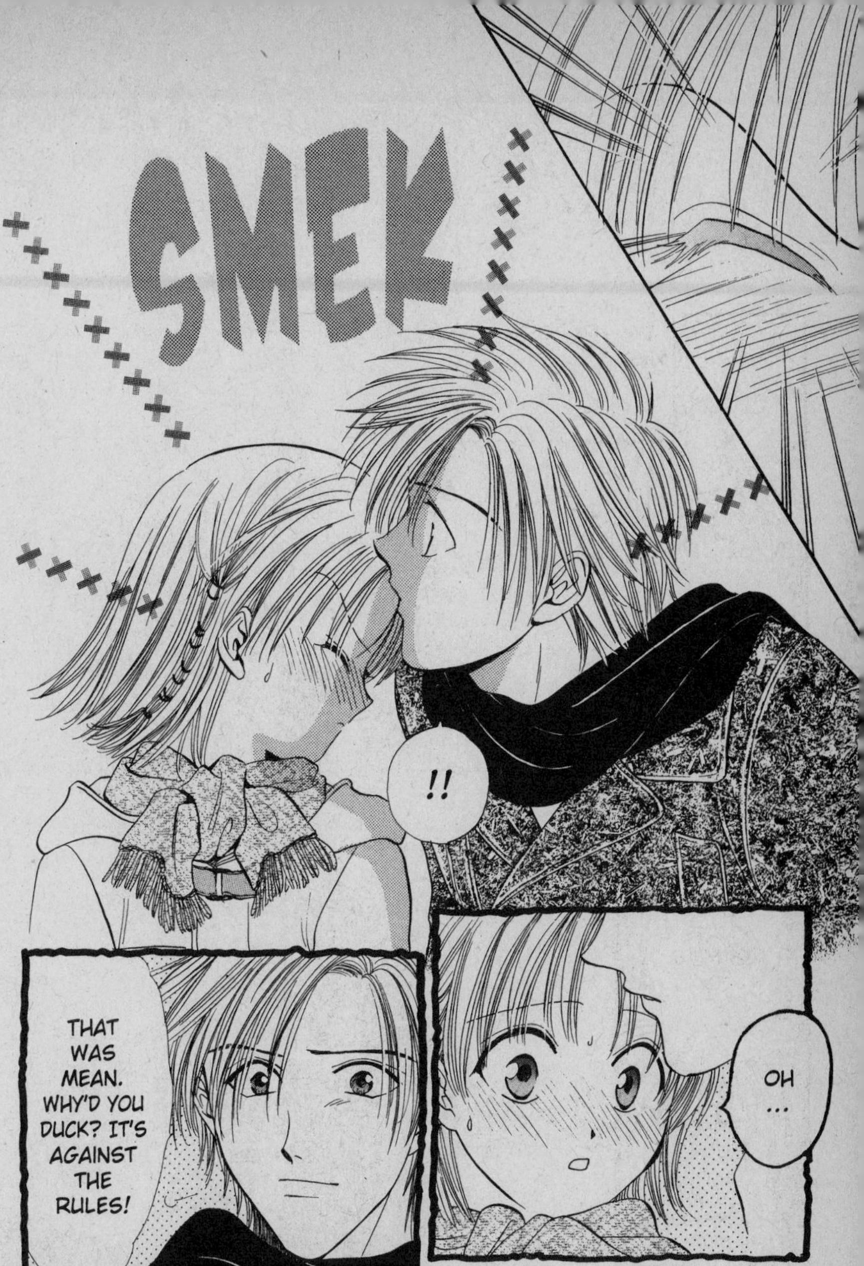
SMEK
!!
OH ...
THAT WAS MEAN. WHY'D YOU DUCK? IT'S AGAINST THE RULES!

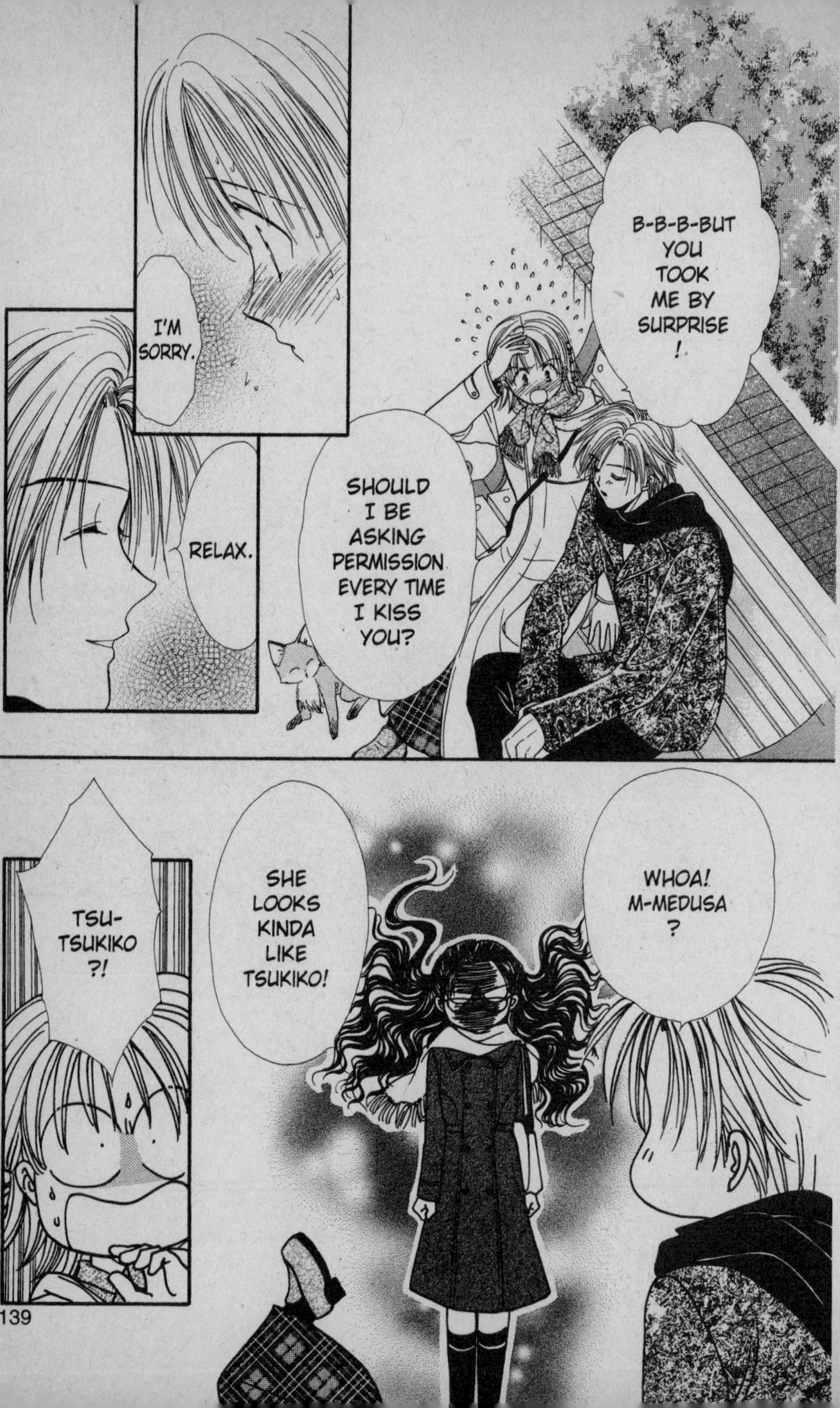
B-B-B-BUT YOU TOOK ME BY SURPRISE!
SHOULD I BE ASKING PERMISSION EVERY TIME I KISS YOU?
I'M SORRY.
RELAX.
WHOA! M-MEDUSA?
SHE LOOKS KINDA LIKE TSUKIKO!
TSU-TSUKIKO?!

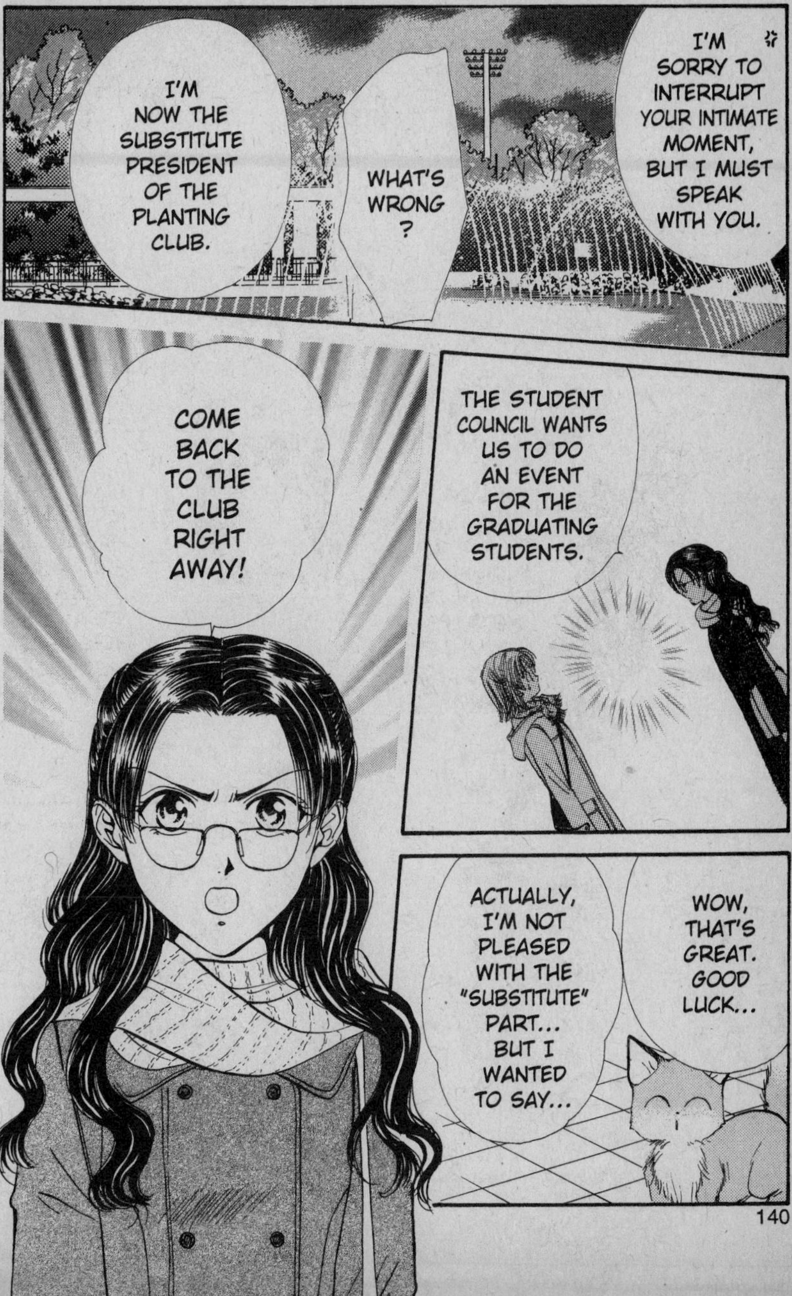
I'M SORRY TO INTERRUPT YOUR INTIMATE MOMENT, BUT I MUST SPEAK WITH YOU.
WHAT'S WRONG?
I'M NOW THE SUBSTITUTE PRESIDENT OF THE PLANTING CLUB.
THE STUDENT COUNCIL WANTS US TO DO AN EVENT FOR THE GRADUATING STUDENTS.
WOW, THAT'S GREAT. GOOD LUCK...
ACTUALLY, I'M NOT PLEASED WITH THE "SUBSTITUTE" PART... BUT I WANTED TO SAY...
COME BACK TO THE CLUB RIGHT AWAY!

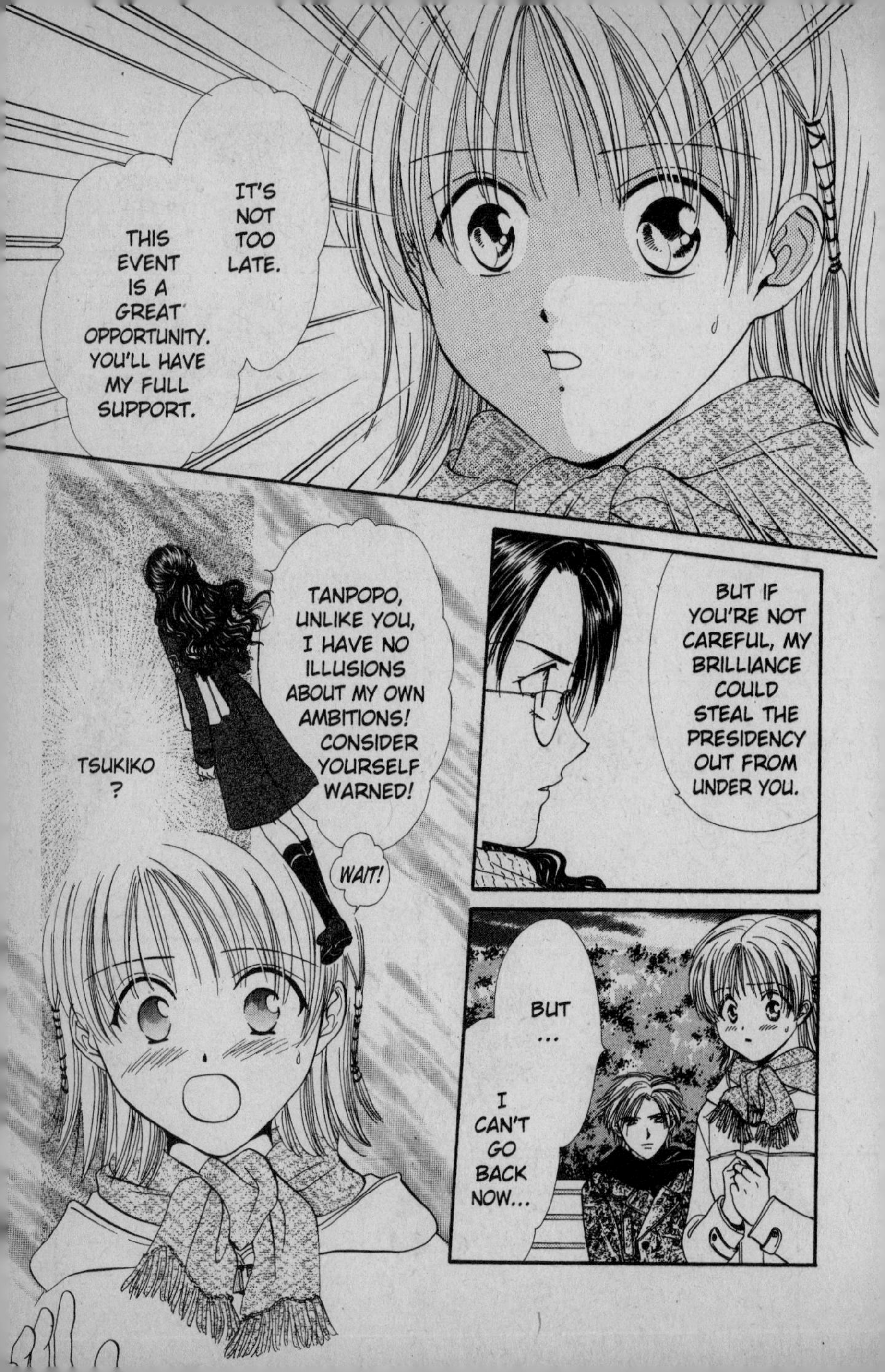
IT'S NOT TOO LATE.
THIS EVENT IS A GREAT OPPORTUNITY. YOU'LL HAVE MY FULL SUPPORT.
BUT IF YOU'RE NOT CAREFUL, MY BRILLIANCE COULD STEAL THE PRESIDENCY OUT FROM UNDER YOU.
BUT ...
I CAN'T GO BACK NOW...
TANPOPO, UNLIKE YOU, I HAVE NO ILLUSIONS ABOUT MY OWN AMBITIONS! CONSIDER YOURSELF WARNED!
WAIT!
TSUKIKO ?

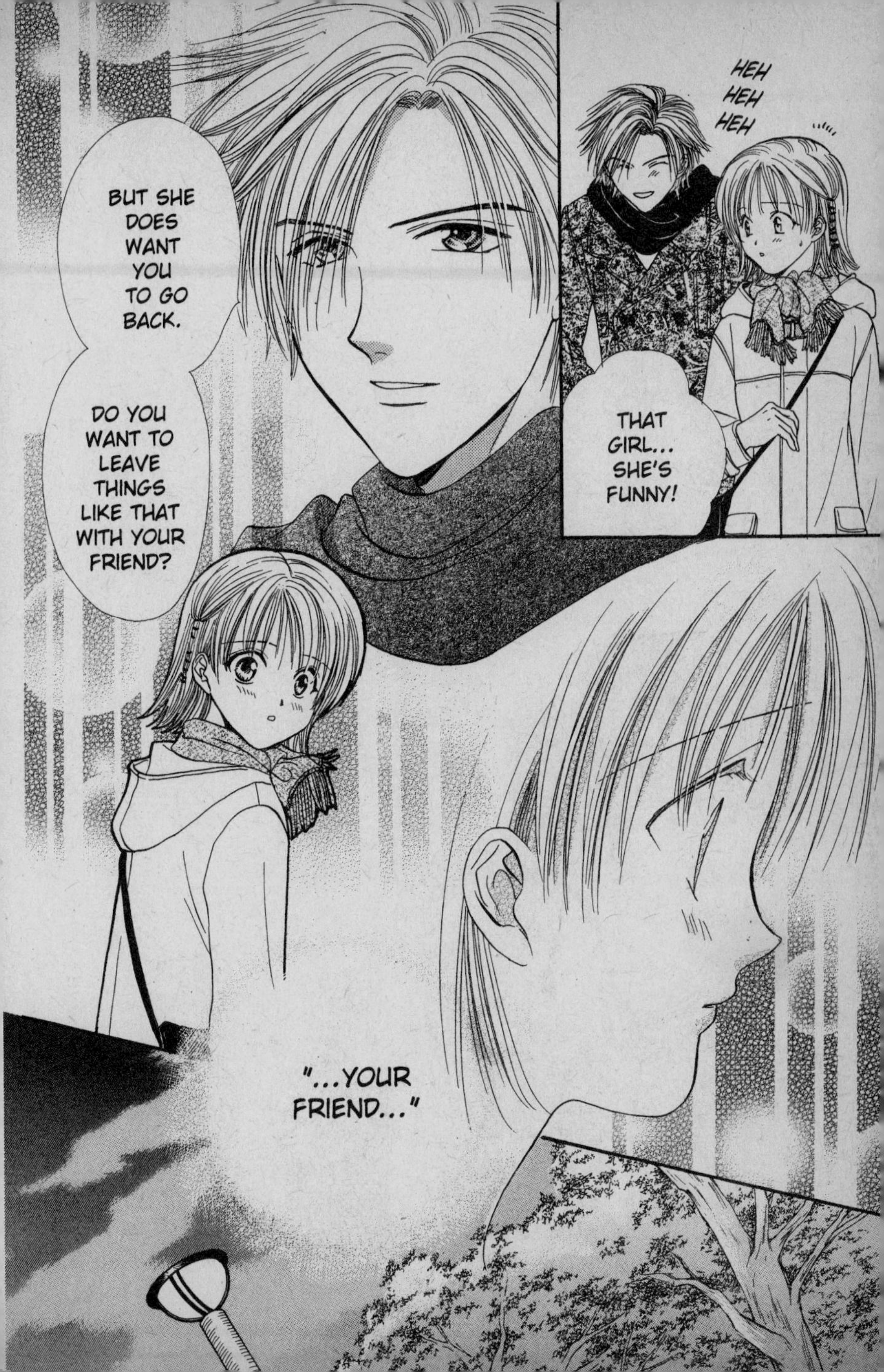
HEH HEH HEH
THAT GIRL... SHE'S FUNNY!
BUT SHE DOES WANT YOU TO GO BACK.
DO YOU WANT TO LEAVE THINGS LIKE THAT WITH YOUR FRIEND?
"...YOUR FRIEND..."

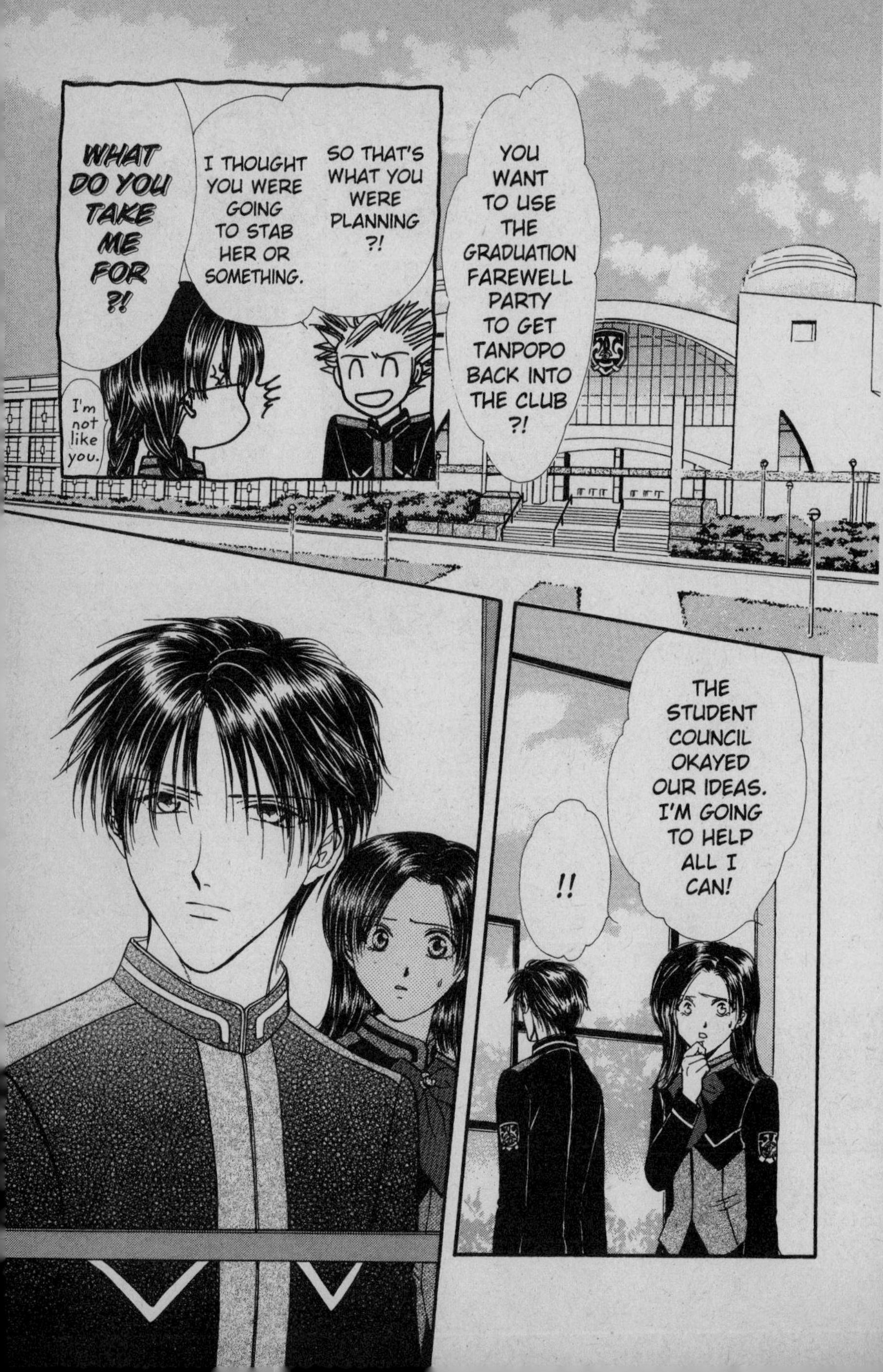
YOU WANT TO USE THE GRADUATION FAREWELL PARTY TO GET TANPOPO BACK INTO THE CLUB ?!
SO THAT'S WHAT YOU WERE PLANNING ?!
I THOUGHT YOU WERE GOING TO STAB HER OR SOMETHING.
WHAT DO YOU TAKE ME FOR ?!
I'm not like you.
THE STUDENT COUNCIL OKAYED OUR IDEAS. I'M GOING TO HELP ALL I CAN!
!!

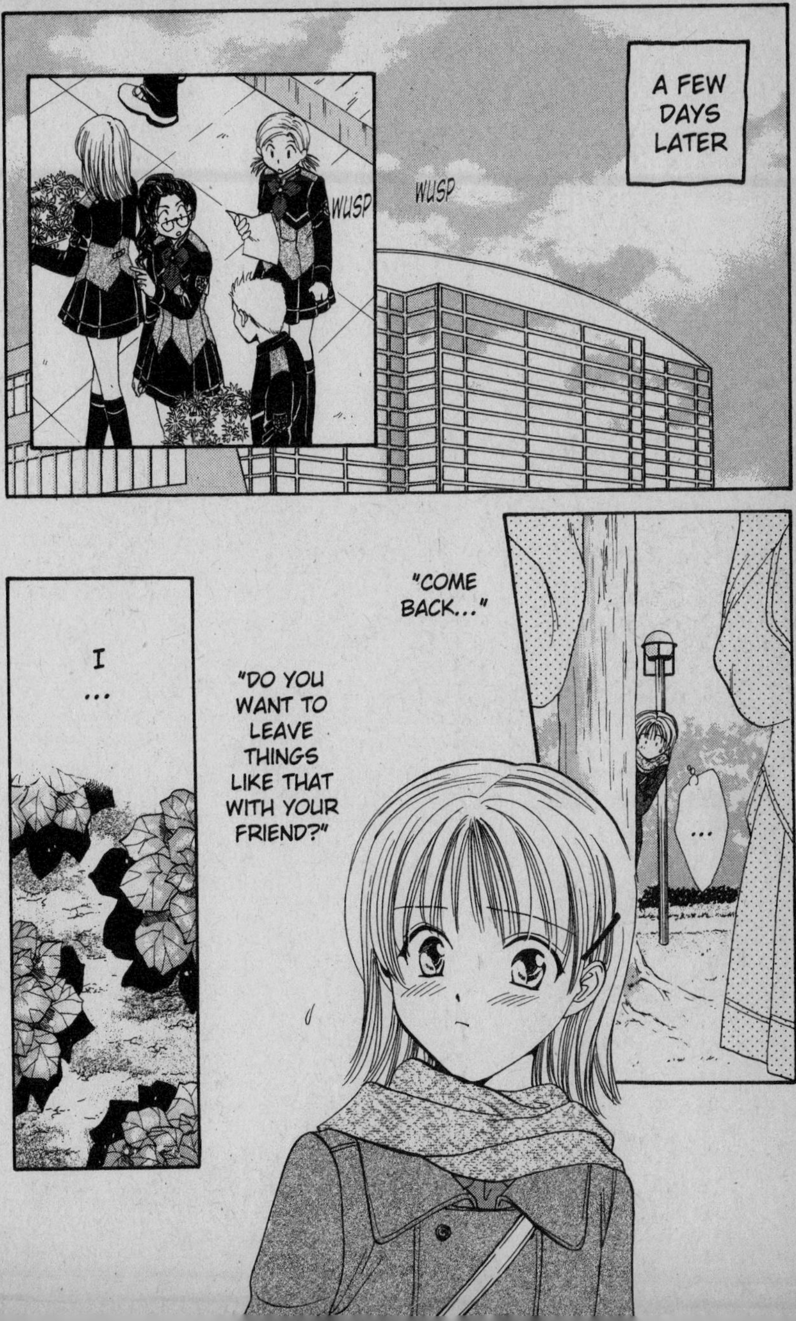
A FEW DAYS LATER
WUSP
WUSP
...
"COME BACK..."
"DO YOU WANT TO LEAVE THINGS LIKE THAT WITH YOUR FRIEND?"
I ...

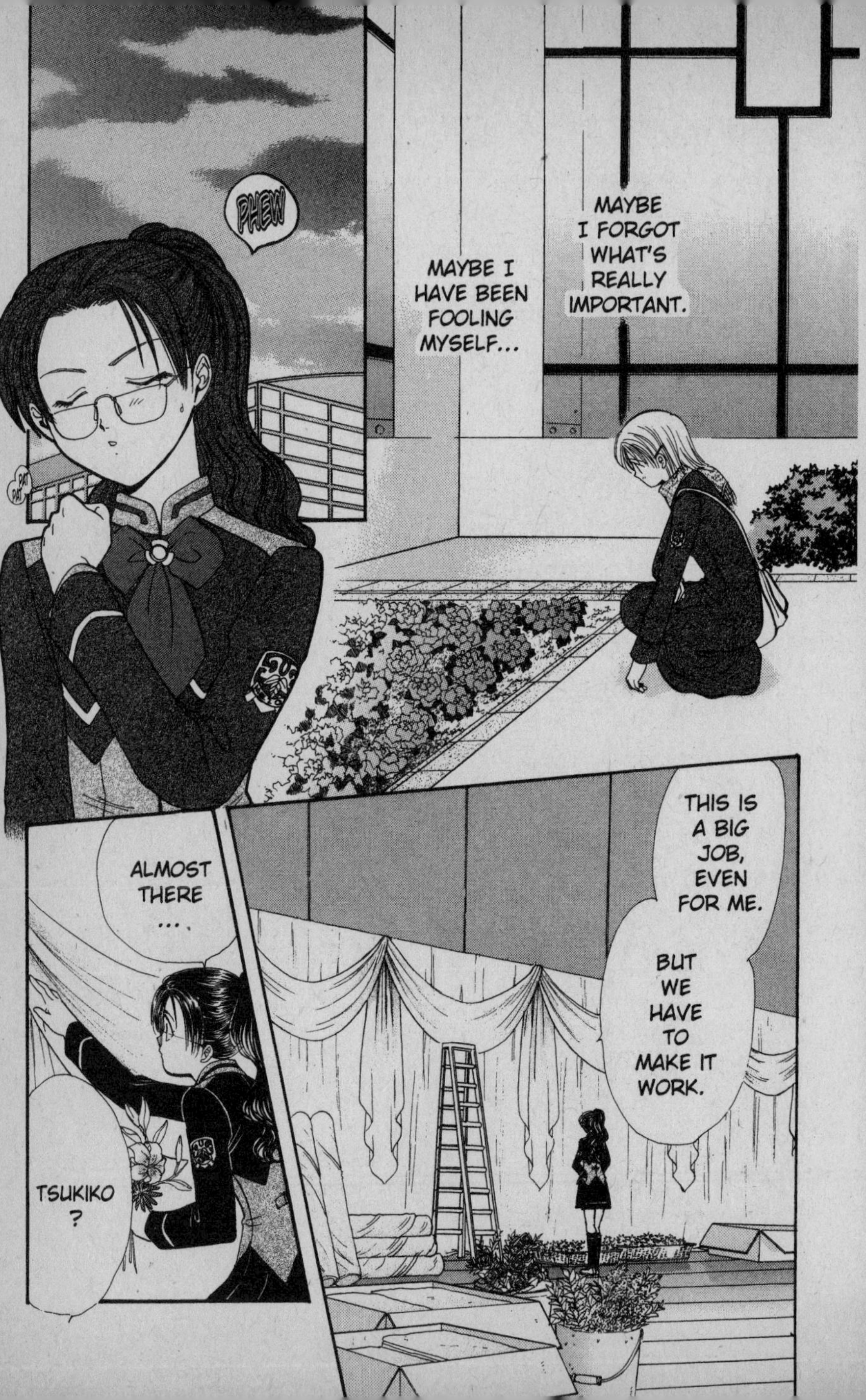
MAYBE I FORGOT WHAT'S REALLY IMPORTANT.
MAYBE I HAVE BEEN FOOLING MYSELF...
PHEW
PAT PAT
THIS IS A BIG JOB, EVEN FOR ME.
BUT WE HAVE TO MAKE IT WORK.
ALMOST THERE ....
TSUKIKO ?

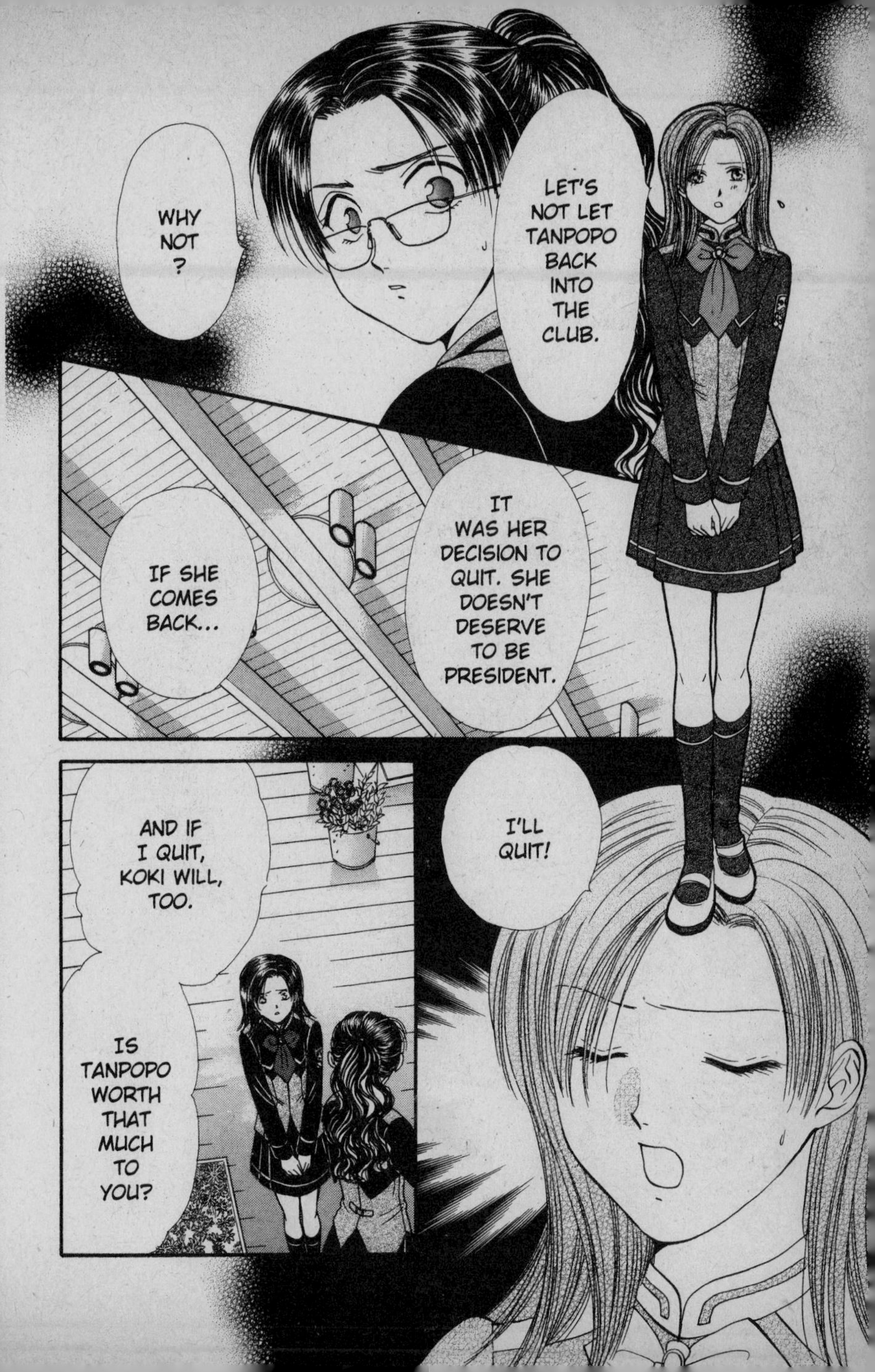
LET'S NOT LET TANPOPO BACK INTO THE CLUB.
WHY NOT ?
IT WAS HER DECISION TO QUIT. SHE DOESN'T DESERVE TO BE PRESIDENT.
IF SHE COMES BACK...
I'LL QUIT!
AND IF I QUIT, KOKI WILL, TOO.
IS TANPOPO WORTH THAT MUCH TO YOU?

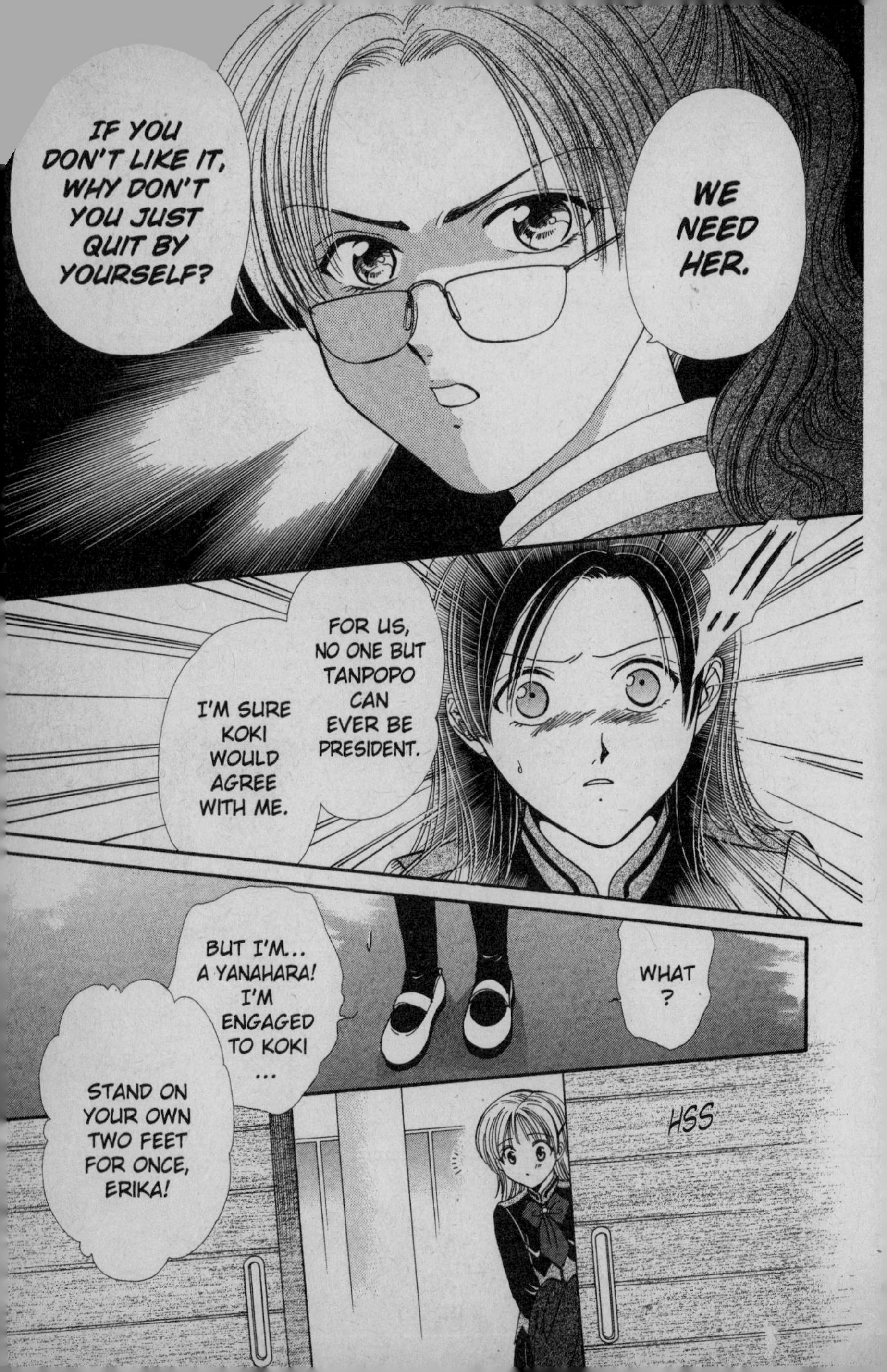
WE NEED HER.
IF YOU DON'T LIKE IT, WHY DON'T YOU JUST QUIT BY YOURSELF?
FOR US, NO ONE BUT TANPOPO CAN EVER BE PRESIDENT.
I'M SURE KOKI WOULD AGREE WITH ME.
WHAT ?
BUT I'M... A YANAHARA! I'M ENGAGED TO KOKI ...
HSS
STAND ON YOUR OWN TWO FEET FOR ONCE, ERIKA!

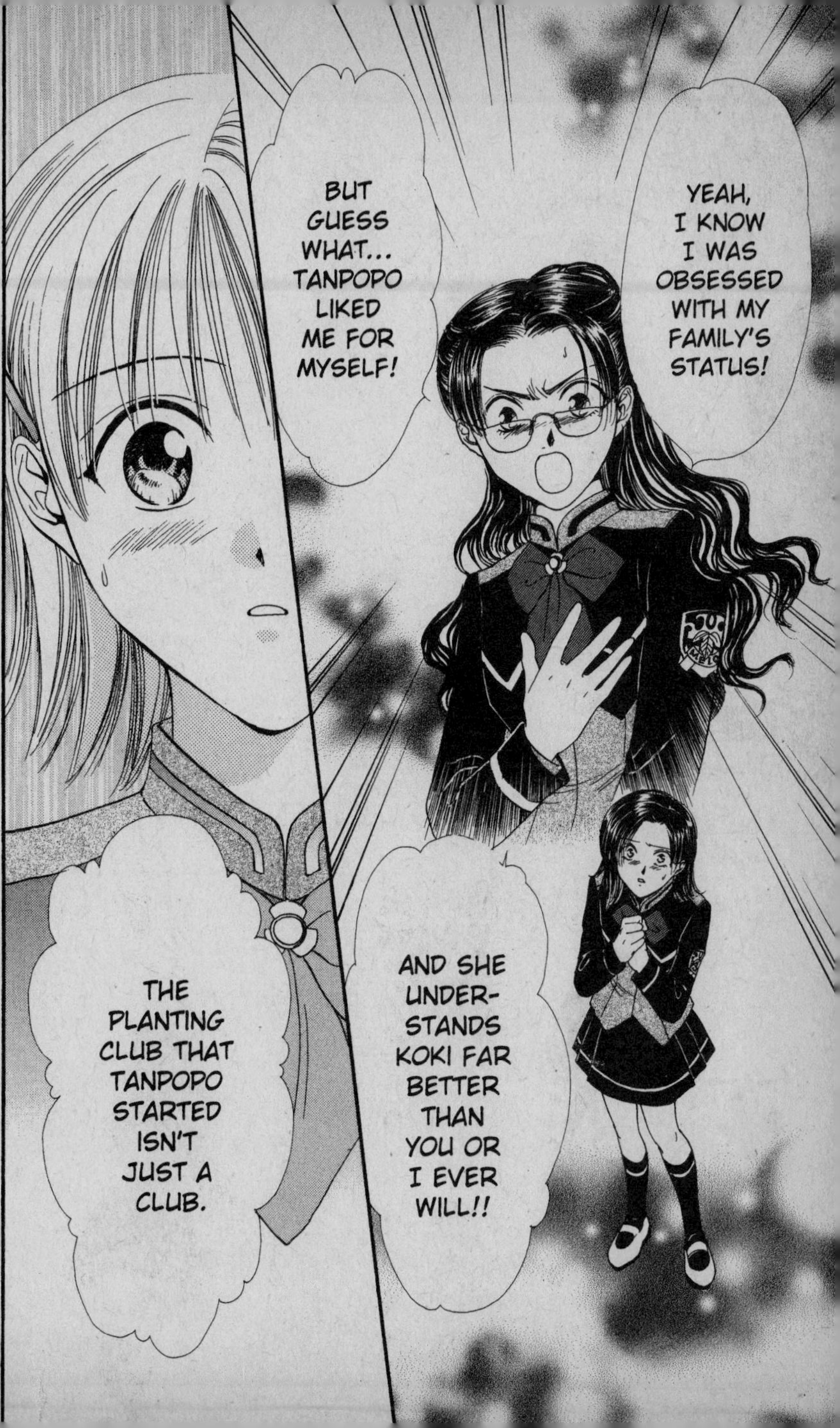
YEAH, I KNOW I WAS OBSESSED WITH MY FAMILY'S STATUS!
BUT GUESS WHAT... TANPOPO LIKED ME FOR MYSELF!
AND SHE UNDER-STANDS KOKI FAR BETTER THAN YOU OR I EVER WILL!!
THE PLANTING CLUB THAT TANPOPO STARTED ISN'T JUST A CLUB.

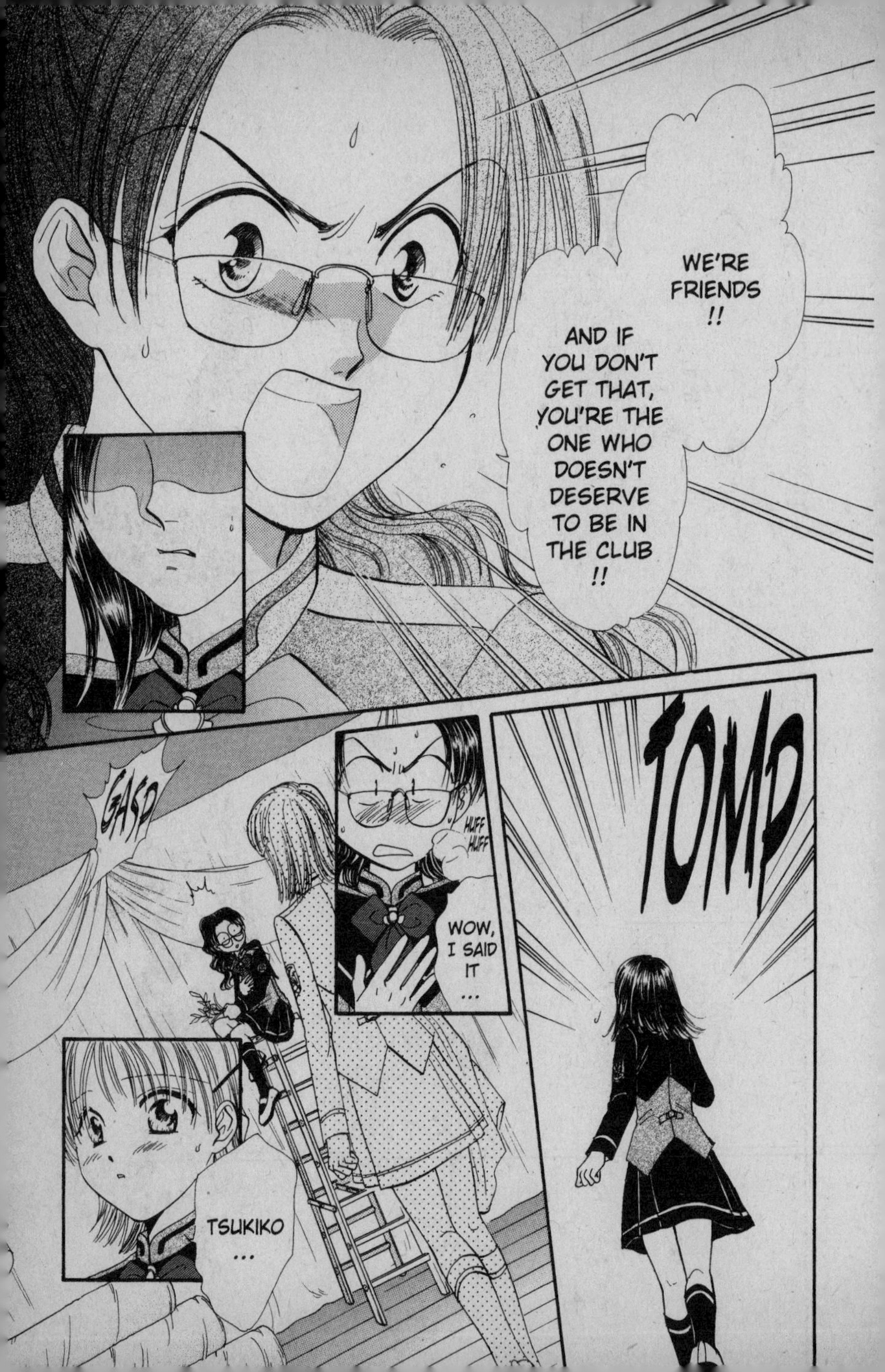
WE'RE FRIENDS !!
AND IF YOU DON'T GET THAT, YOU'RE THE ONE WHO DOESN'T DESERVE TO BE IN THE CLUB !!
TOMP
HUFF HUFF
WOW, I SAID IT ...
GASP
TSUKIKO ...

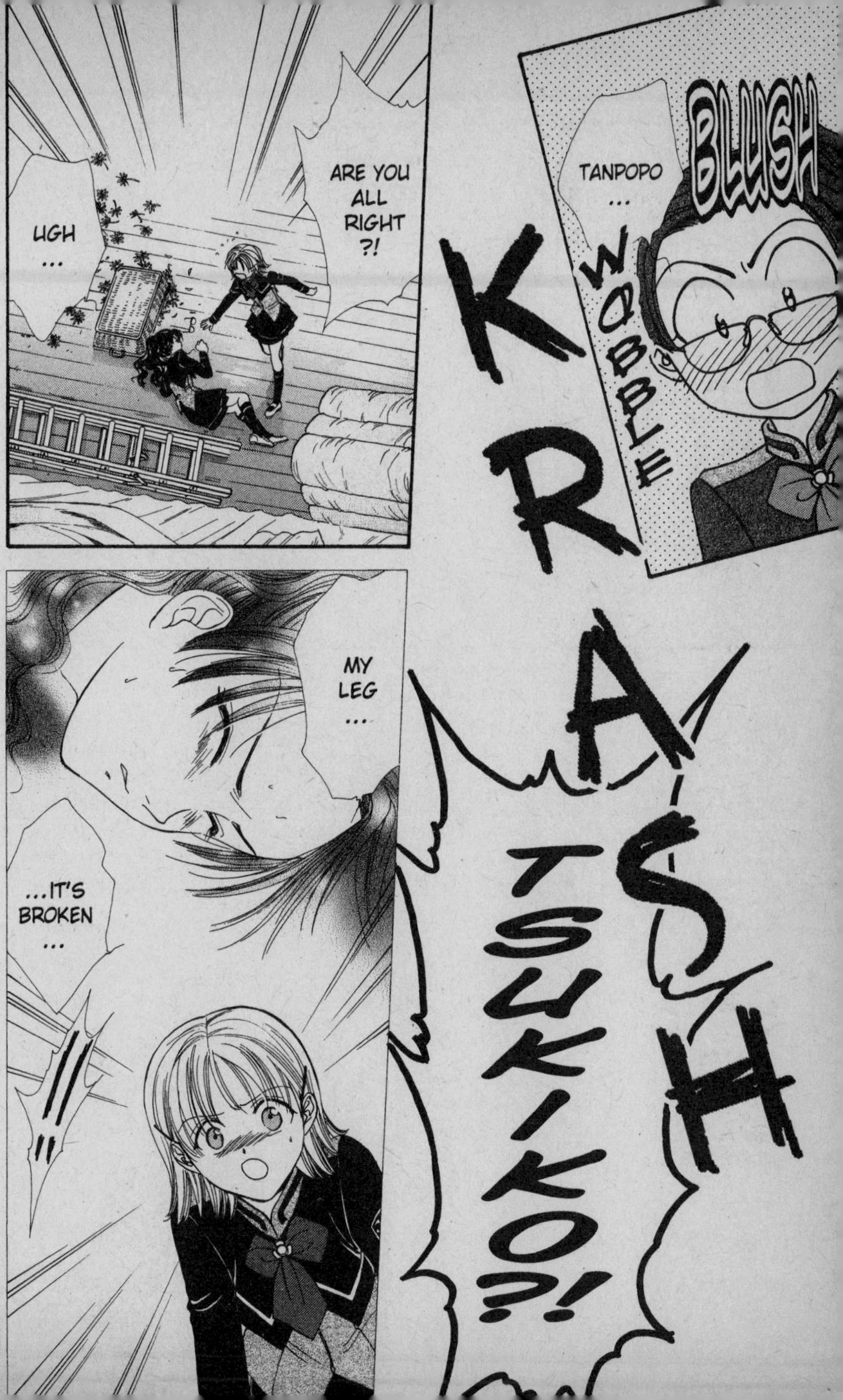

TANPOPO ...
BLUSH
WOBBLE
KRASH
ARE YOU ALL RIGHT ?!
UGH ...
MY LEG ...
...IT'S BROKEN ...
!!
TSUKIKO?!

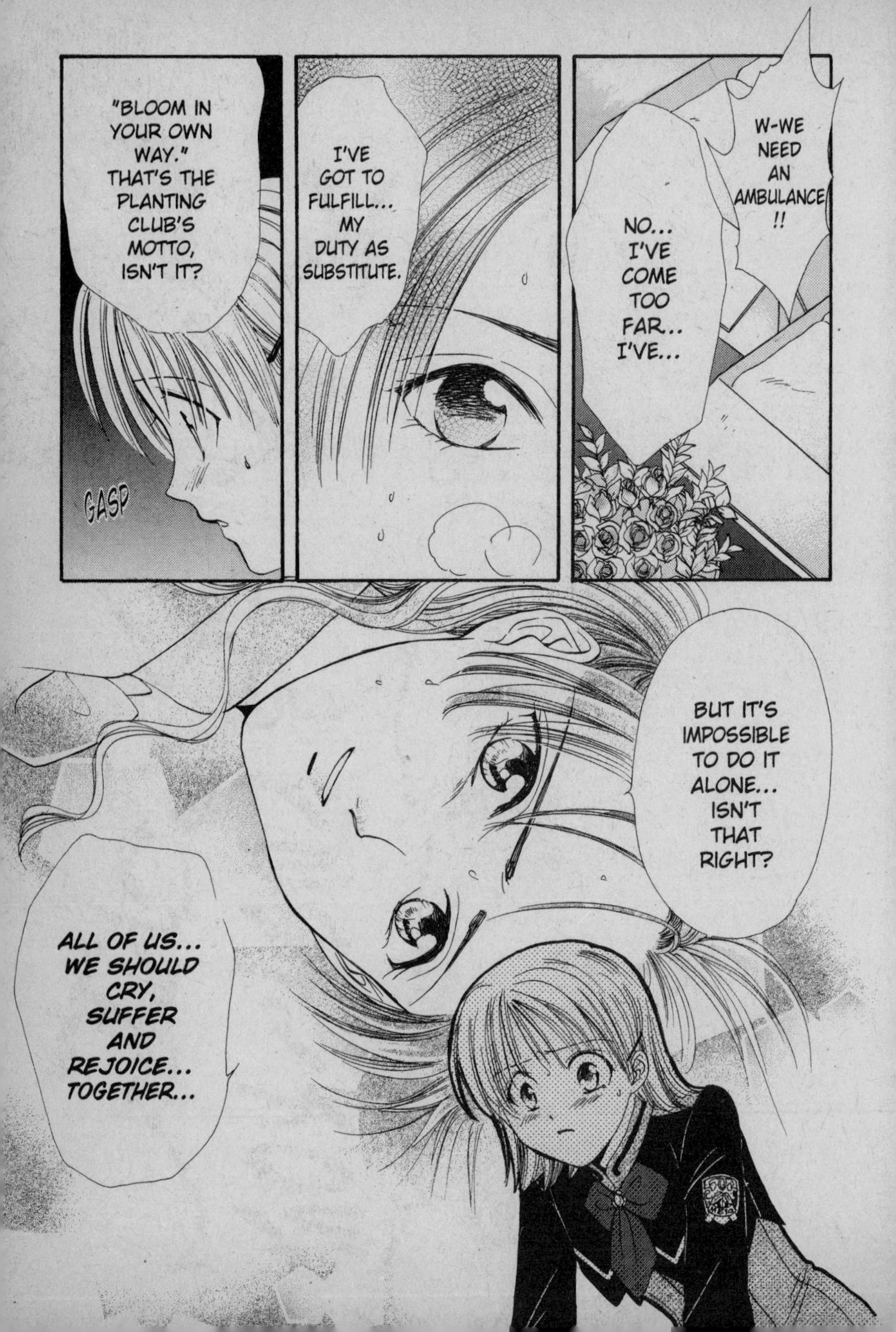
W-WE NEED AN AMBULANCE !!
NO... I'VE COME TOO FAR.. I'VE...
I'VE GOT TO FULFILL... MY DUTY AS SUBSTITUTE.
"BLOOM IN YOUR OWN WAY." THAT'S THE PLANTING CLUB'S MOTTO, ISN'T IT?
GASP
BUT IT'S IMPOSSIBLE TO DO IT ALONE... ISN'T THAT RIGHT?
ALL OF US... WE SHOULD CRY, SUFFER AND REJOICE... TOGETHER...

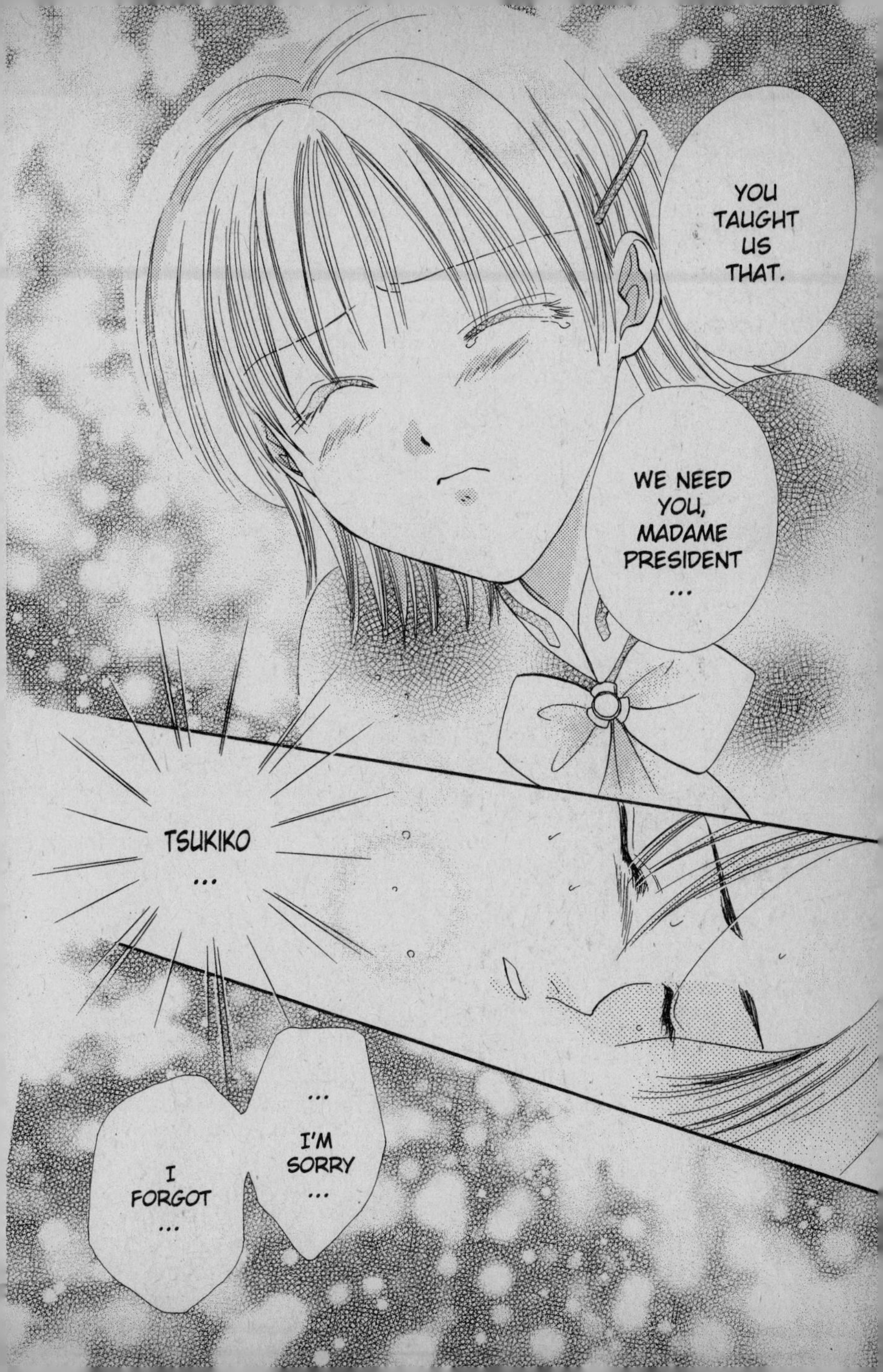
YOU TAUGHT US THAT.
WE NEED YOU, MADAME PRESIDENT ...
TSUKIKO ...
... I'M SORRY ...
I FORGOT ...

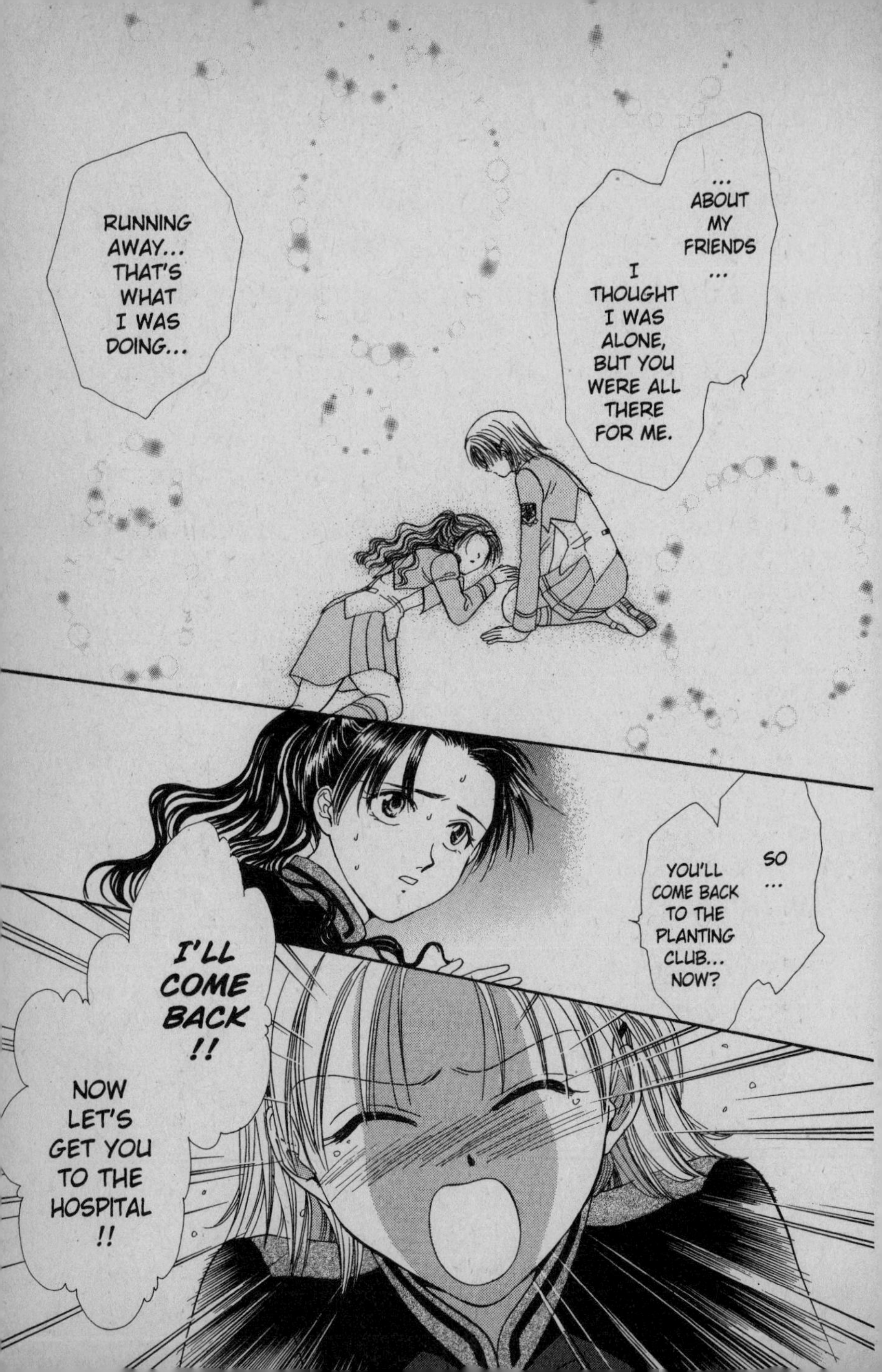
... ABOUT MY FRIENDS ...
I THOUGHT I WAS ALONE, BUT YOU WERE ALL THERE FOR ME.
RUNNING AWAY... THAT'S WHAT I WAS DOING...
SO ...
YOU'LL COME BACK TO THE PLANTING CLUB... NOW?
I'LL COME BACK!!
NOW LET'S GET YOU TO THE HOSPITAL!!

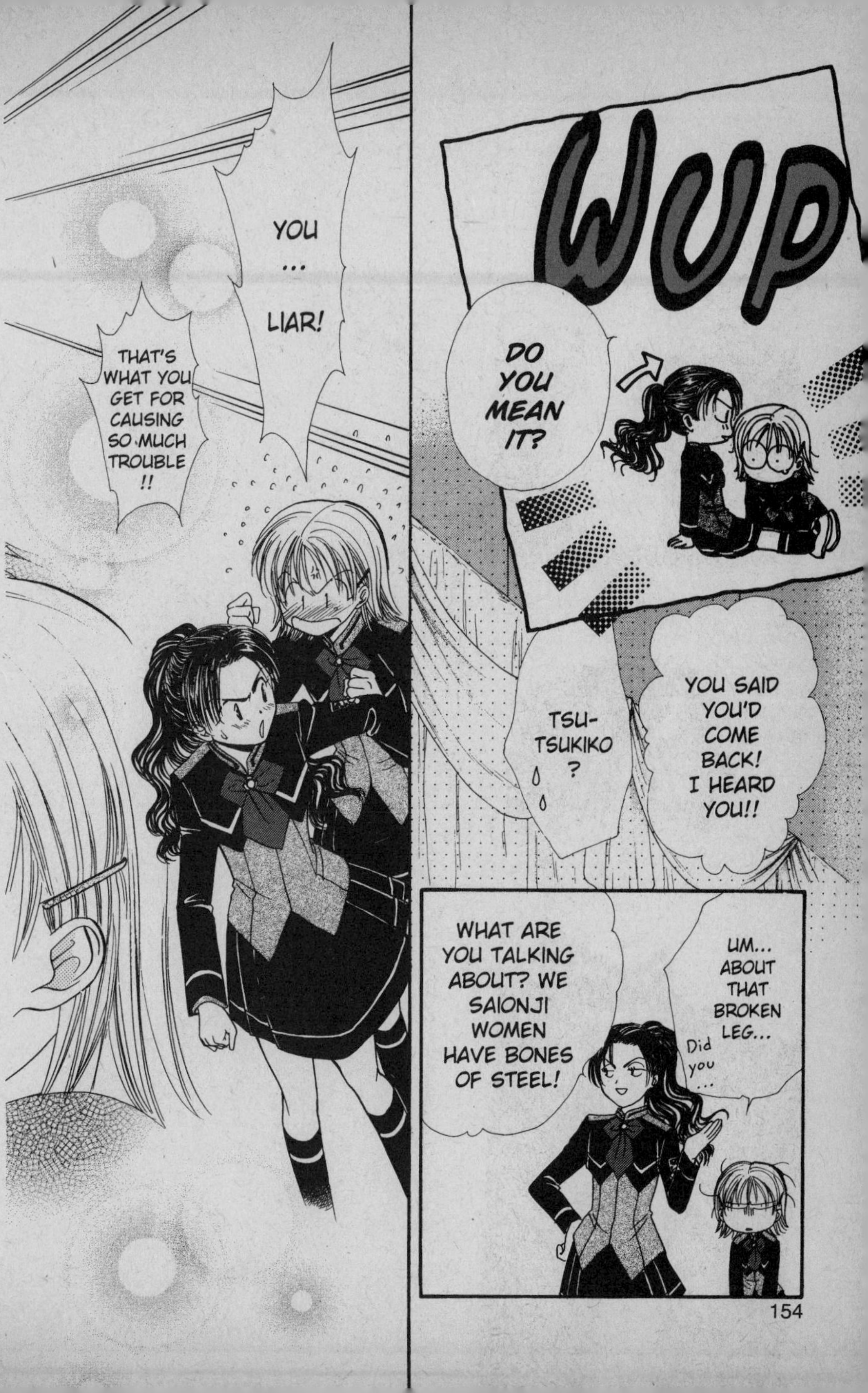
WUP
DO YOU MEAN IT?
YOU SAID YOU'D COME BACK! I HEARD YOU!!
TSU-TSUKIKO?
UM... ABOUT THAT BROKEN LEG...
Did you ...
WHAT ARE YOU TALKING ABOUT? WE SAIONJI WOMEN HAVE BONES OF STEEL!
YOU ... LIAR!
THAT'S WHAT YOU GET FOR CAUSING SO MUCH TROUBLE !!

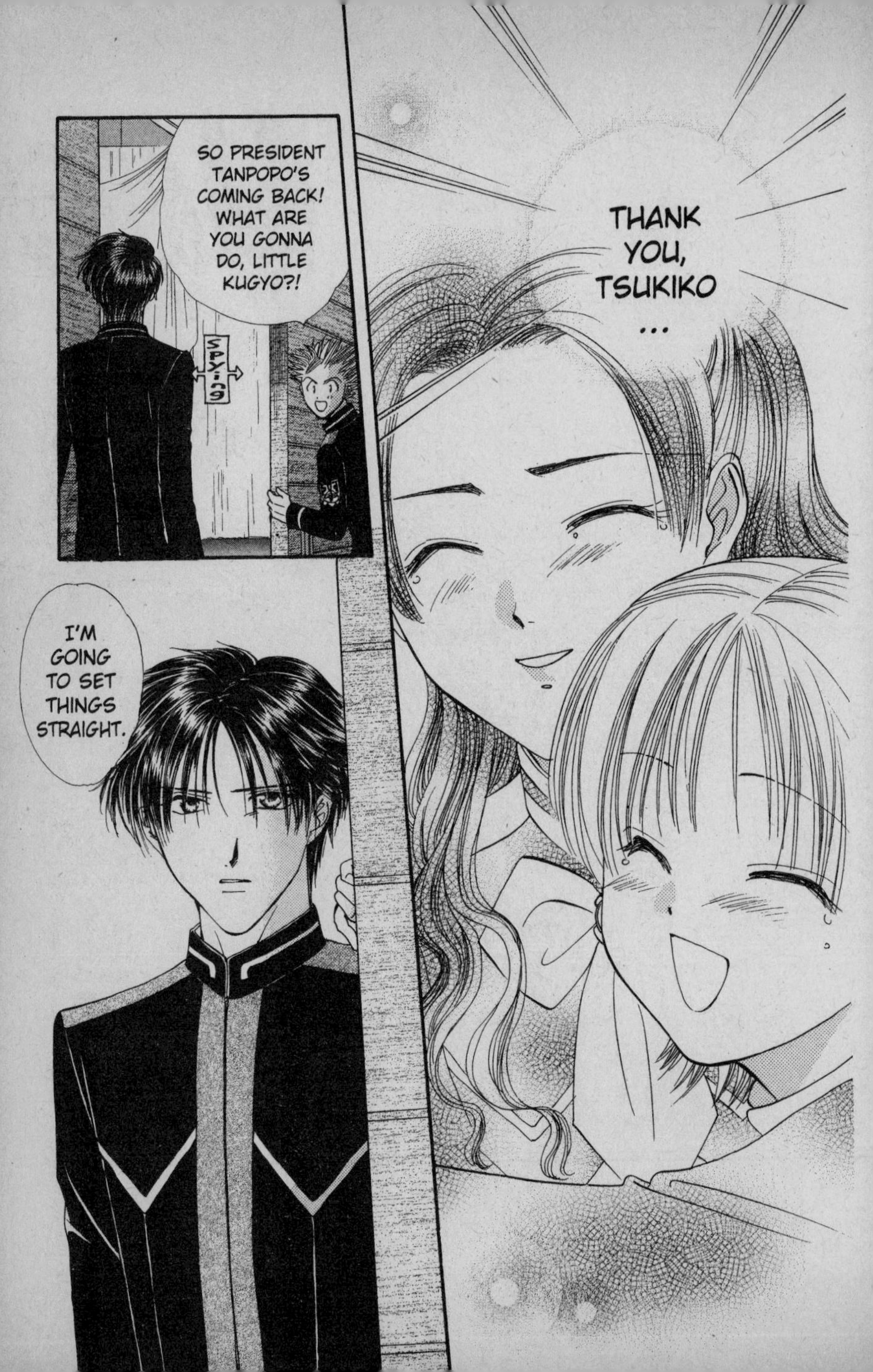
THANK YOU, TSUKIKO ...
SO PRESIDENT TANPOPO'S COMING BACK! WHAT ARE YOU GONNA DO, LITTLE KUGYO?!
SPYING
I'M GOING TO SET THINGS STRAIGHT.

A MINI-REPORT ON YŪ WATASE'S ACTIVITIES EARLY IN THE 21ST CENTURY

THE ANGOULEME COMICS FESTIVAL

JANUARY 24-31, 2001. (I WAS THERE FROM THE 25TH TO THE 28TH.)

I PARTICIPATED IN THE ANGOULEME COMICS FESTIVAL IN FRANCE.

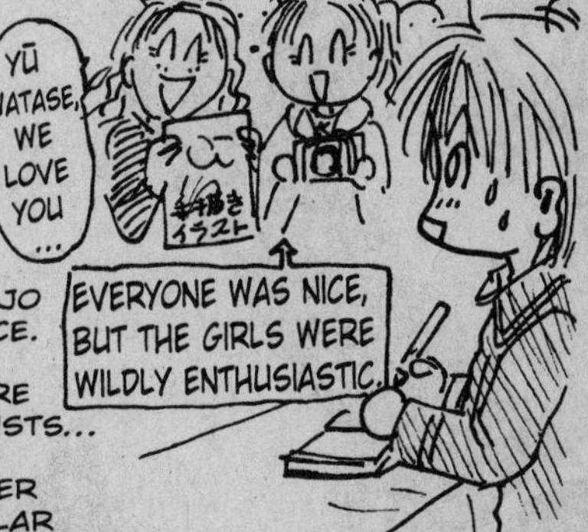
YŪ WATASE, WE LOVE YOU...
EVERYONE WAS NICE, BUT THE GIRLS WERE WILDLY ENTHUSIASTIC.

WELL...IT WAS SO CRAZY, I DIDN'T KNOW WHAT WAS GOING ON. BUT MY FANS IN FRANCE WERE AS ENTHUSIASTIC AS THOSE IN OTHER COUNTRIES. I WAS KISSED ON MY HANDS OR CHEEKS BY THE MALE FANS. ♪ COULD THIS BE THE PRIVILEGE OF A MANGA ARTIST? IT SEEMS *FUSHIGI YŪGI* WAS THE FIRST SHŌJO COMIC EVER TRANSLATED IN FRANCE. IT SEEMS THAT COMICS ARE THE DOMAIN OF BOYS THERE, AND THERE AREN'T MANY FEMALE COMICS ARTISTS... *AYASHI NO CERES* HAS NOW BEEN PUBLISHED UP TO VOLUME 4. OTHER GUEST ARTISTS WERE VERY POPULAR AT THE FESTIVAL, TOO.

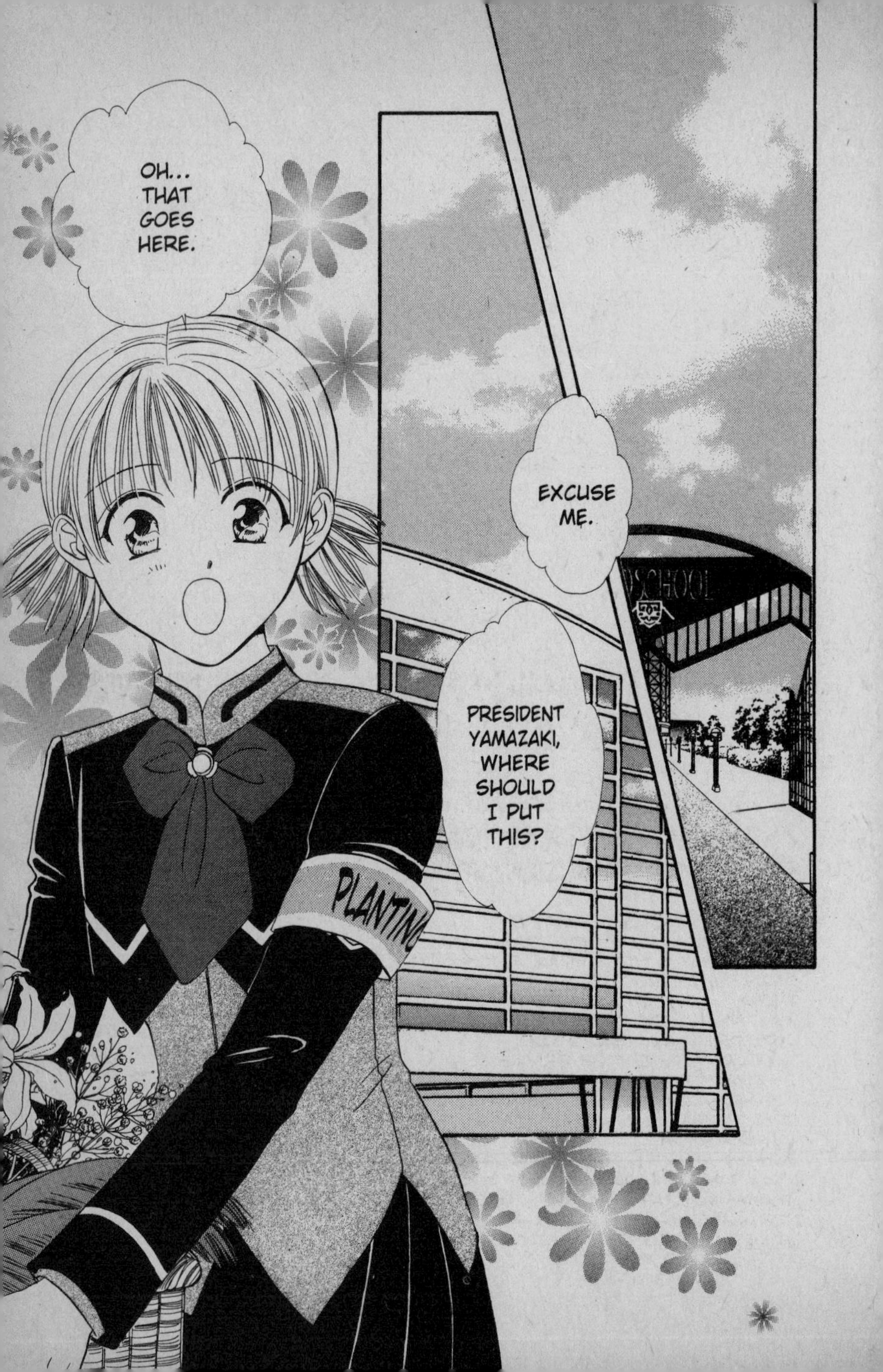
EXCUSE ME.
PRESIDENT YAMAZAKI, WHERE SHOULD I PUT THIS?
OH... THAT GOES HERE.

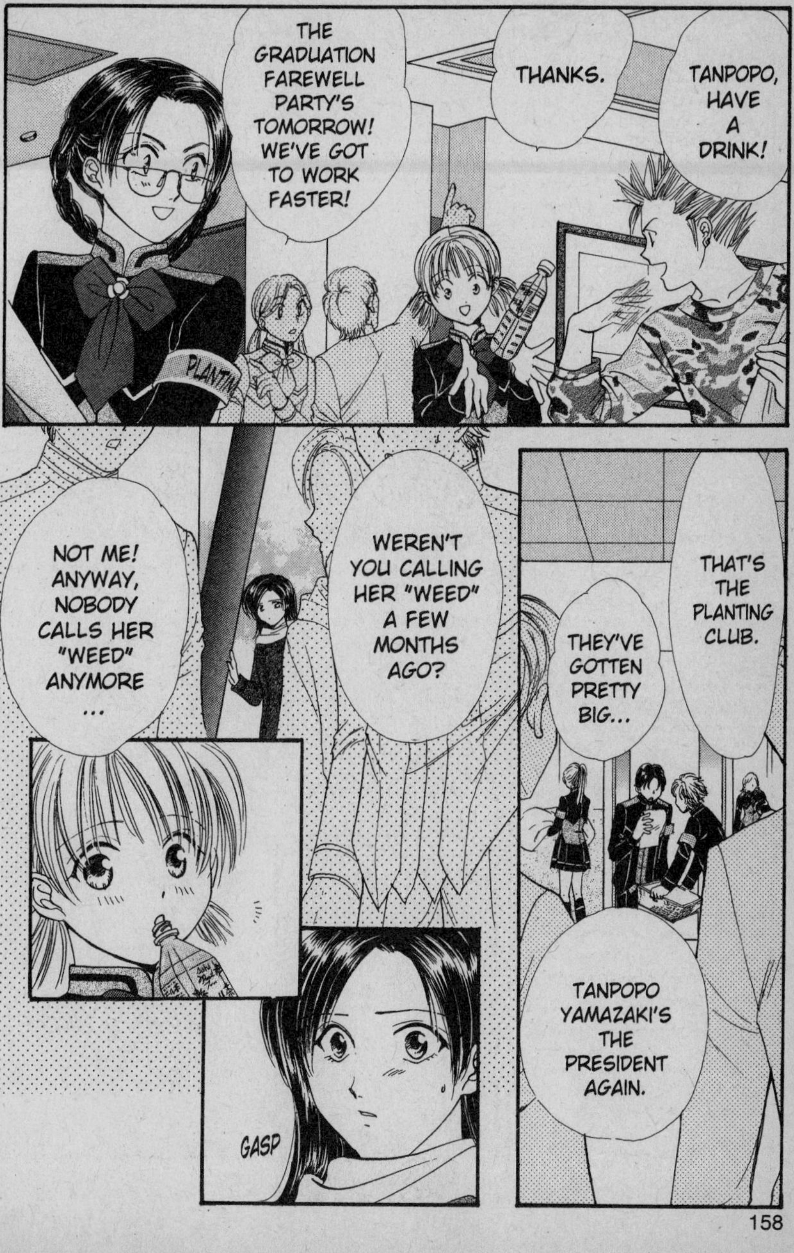
TANPOPO, HAVE A DRINK!
THANKS.
THE GRADUATION FAREWELL PARTY'S TOMORROW! WE'VE GOT TO WORK FASTER!
THAT'S THE PLANTING CLUB.
THEY'VE GOTTEN PRETTY BIG...
TANPOPO YAMAZAKI'S THE PRESIDENT AGAIN.
WEREN'T YOU CALLING HER "WEED" A FEW MONTHS AGO?
NOT ME! ANYWAY, NOBODY CALLS HER "WEED" ANYMORE ...
GASP

Perhaps it was a good thing that I got professional work before I could become an assistant, but they also say that you should suffer hardships while you're young! When I was a fledgling artist, I was pretty hard on the people who worked for me, but it's also a fact that I was working feverishly myself--almost to death. Goodness... Honestly, my body got worn out, and my pride got ripped to shreds. Why do I do this work when it's so unkind to my body?

Anyway, I'm very grateful to my assistants.

Oh, but although I have no experience as an assistant, when I first started, my editor (sorry, Mr. Y., I'm telling this story again) would reject the plot I worked so hard to think up, saying "Can't use this!" In my early days in Osaka, when I sent in a finished manuscript, he'd fill practically the entire copy with red marks (was he a Red-Pen Editor?), and I'd have to do the whole thing over! "Does the editor hate me?" "Is he harassing me?" (You're a lousy manga writer.) He was so strict and scary. Ah, now that I think back on it, what a gift that was!! I mean... Few people will bother to correct you so painstakingly. In the beginning, I thought, "I've got no talent," "I'm gonna quit being a manga artist." Things like that! Going home on the Bullet Train, I blinked back tears and felt depressed so many times. (Oh...I still do that. ^^) But I'm glad that I got to experience even a little of that hardship. (I don't really consider it a hardship, though.)

So that tough editor who used to be Watase's foster parent (I just think of him that way), after all these years, is my editor now. Tadah! (snicker) I feel like a fledgling writer again.

So! Now that I've started another new story, I must go back to my beginner's mind. (smile) Maybe I need to grow up.

The new serial will begin in the June 20 issue of **Shōjo Comics**. So **Imadoki!** will end with Volume 5... ^^

I'll be counting on your patronage again.

Until Volume 5, then... 4/8/01.

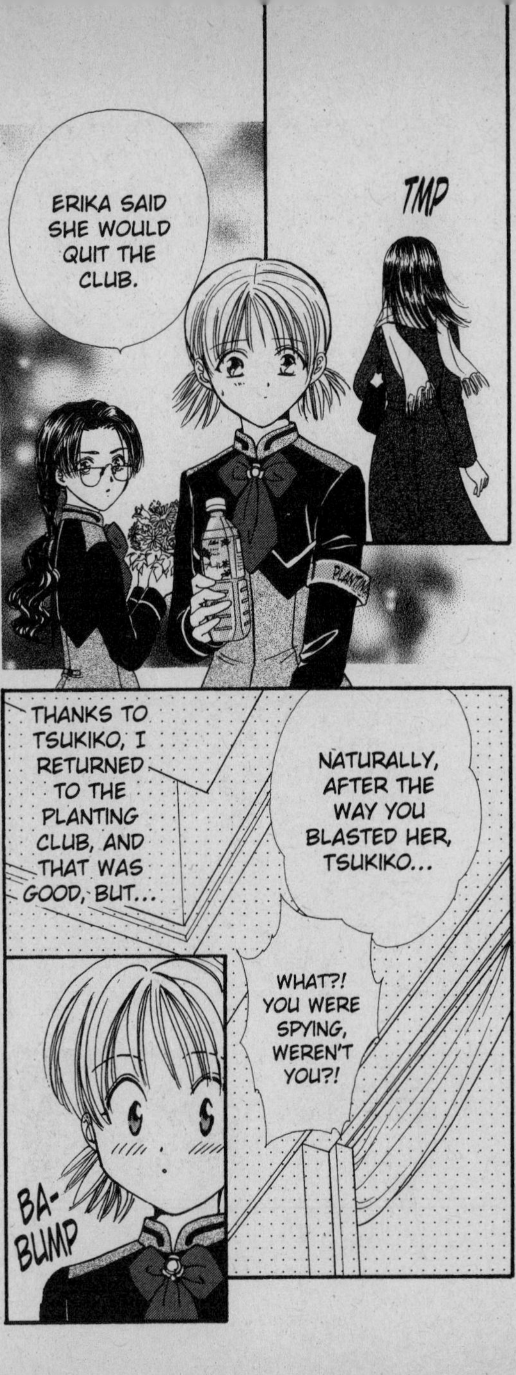
TMP
ERIKA SAID SHE WOULD QUIT THE CLUB.
PLANTING
THANKS TO TSUKIKO, I RETURNED TO THE PLANTING CLUB, AND THAT WAS GOOD, BUT...
NATURALLY, AFTER THE WAY YOU BLASTED HER, TSUKIKO...
WHAT?! YOU WERE SPYING, WEREN'T YOU?!
BA-BUMP

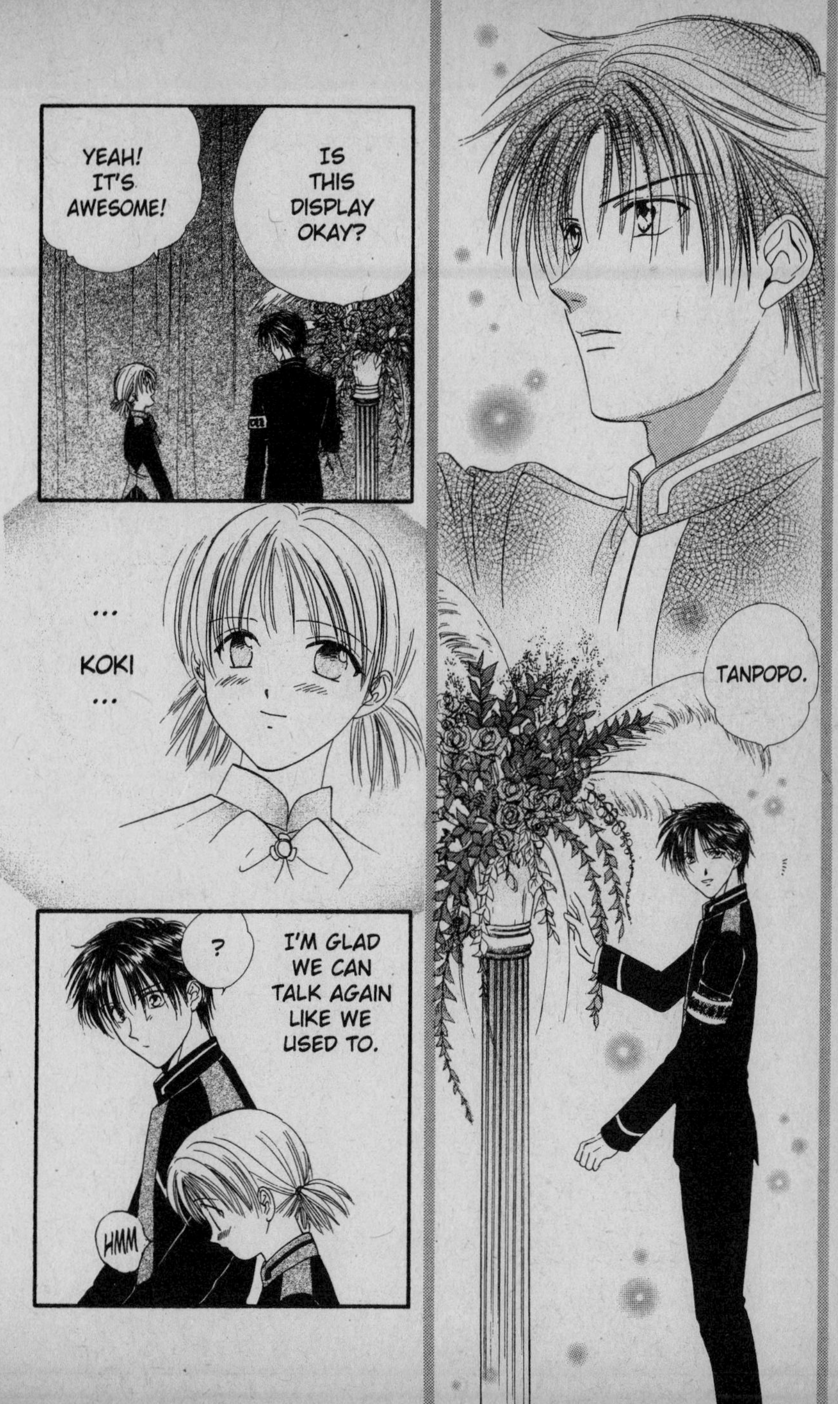
TANPOPO.
IS THIS DISPLAY OKAY?
YEAH! IT'S AWESOME!
... KOKI ...
I'M GLAD WE CAN TALK AGAIN LIKE WE USED TO.
?
HMM

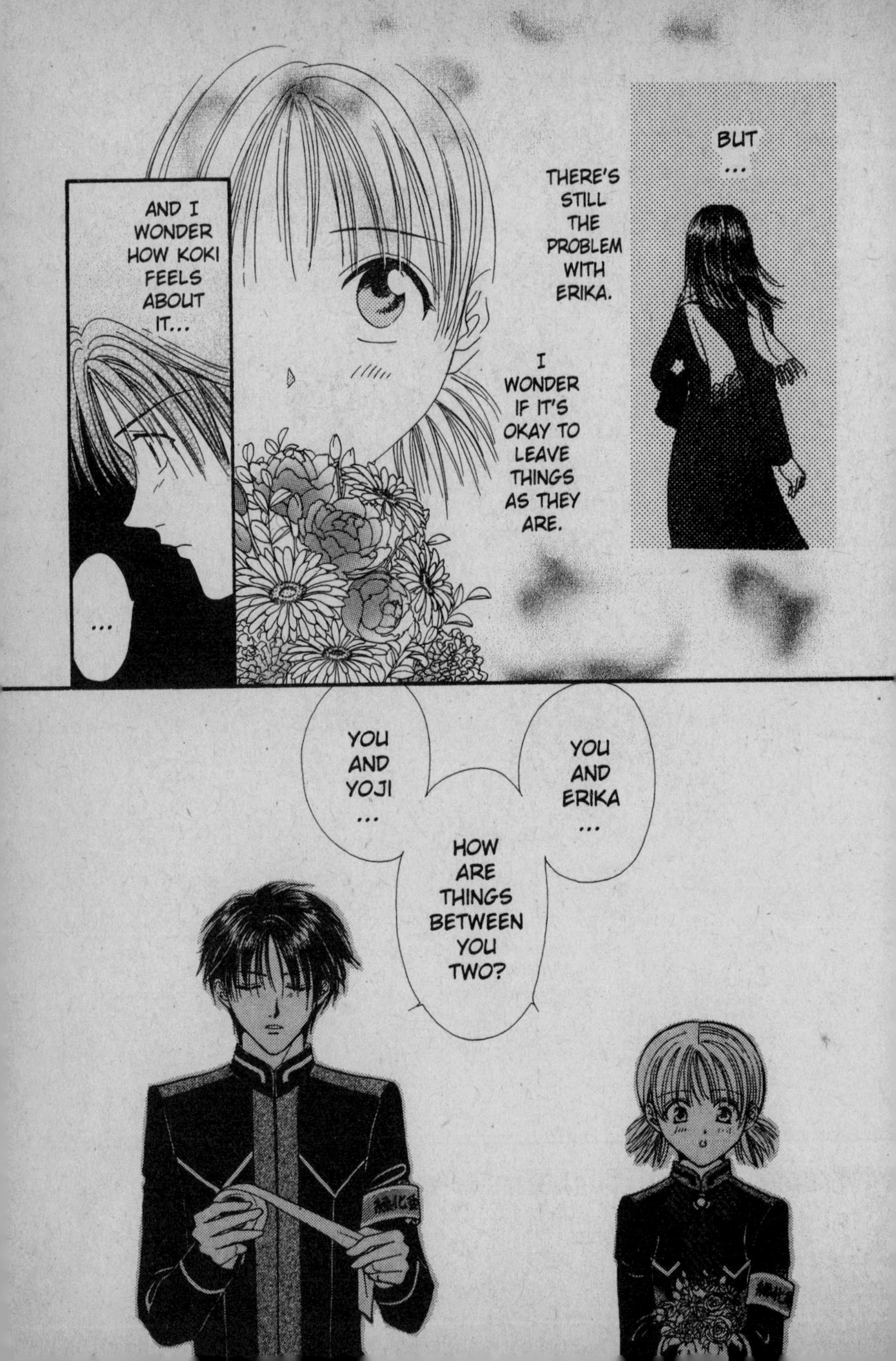
BUT ...
THERE'S STILL THE PROBLEM WITH ERIKA.
I WONDER IF IT'S OKAY TO LEAVE THINGS AS THEY ARE.
AND I WONDER HOW KOKI FEELS ABOUT IT...
...
YOU AND ERIKA ...
YOU AND YOJI ...
HOW ARE THINGS BETWEEN YOU TWO?

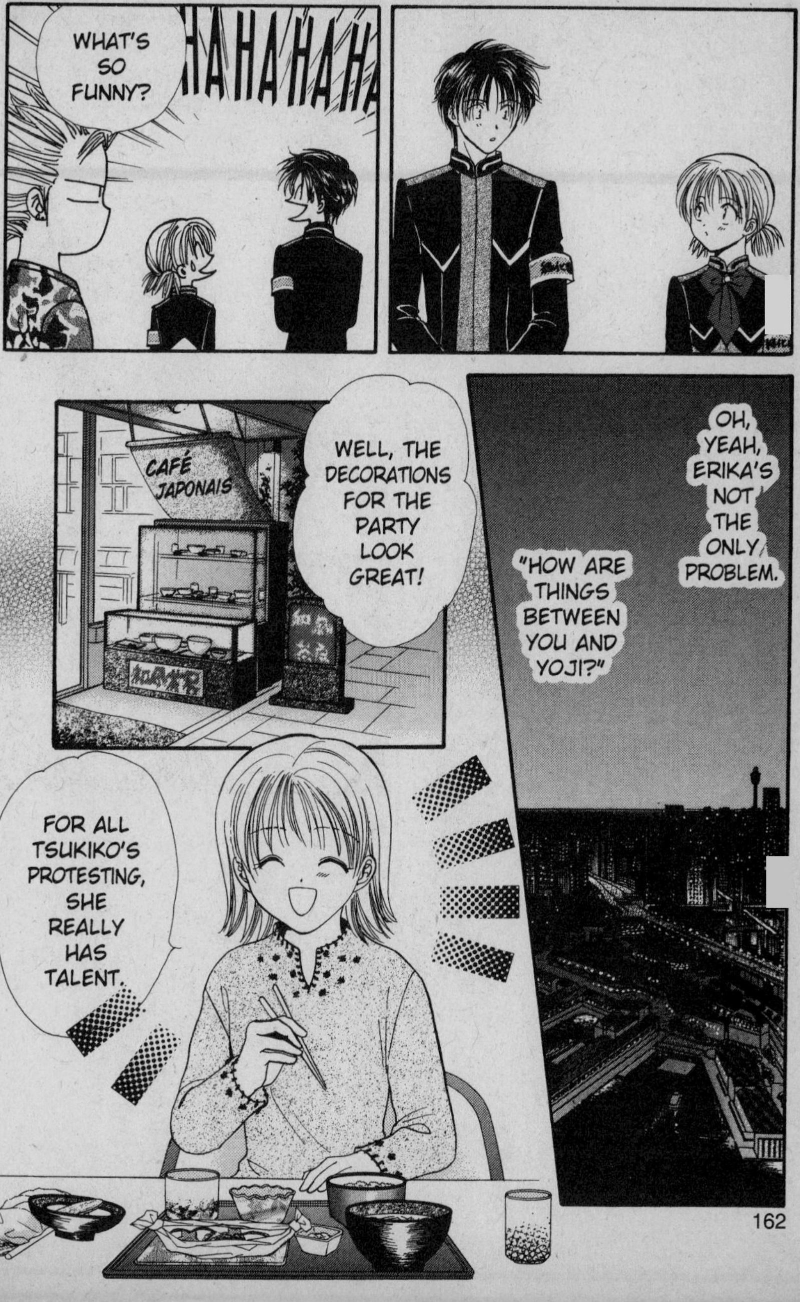
HAHAHAHAHA
WHAT'S SO FUNNY?
OH, YEAH, ERIKA'S NOT THE ONLY PROBLEM.
"HOW ARE THINGS BETWEEN YOU AND YOJI?"
WELL, THE DECORATIONS FOR THE PARTY LOOK GREAT!
CAFÉ JAPONAIS
FOR ALL TSUKIKO'S PROTESTING, SHE REALLY HAS TALENT.

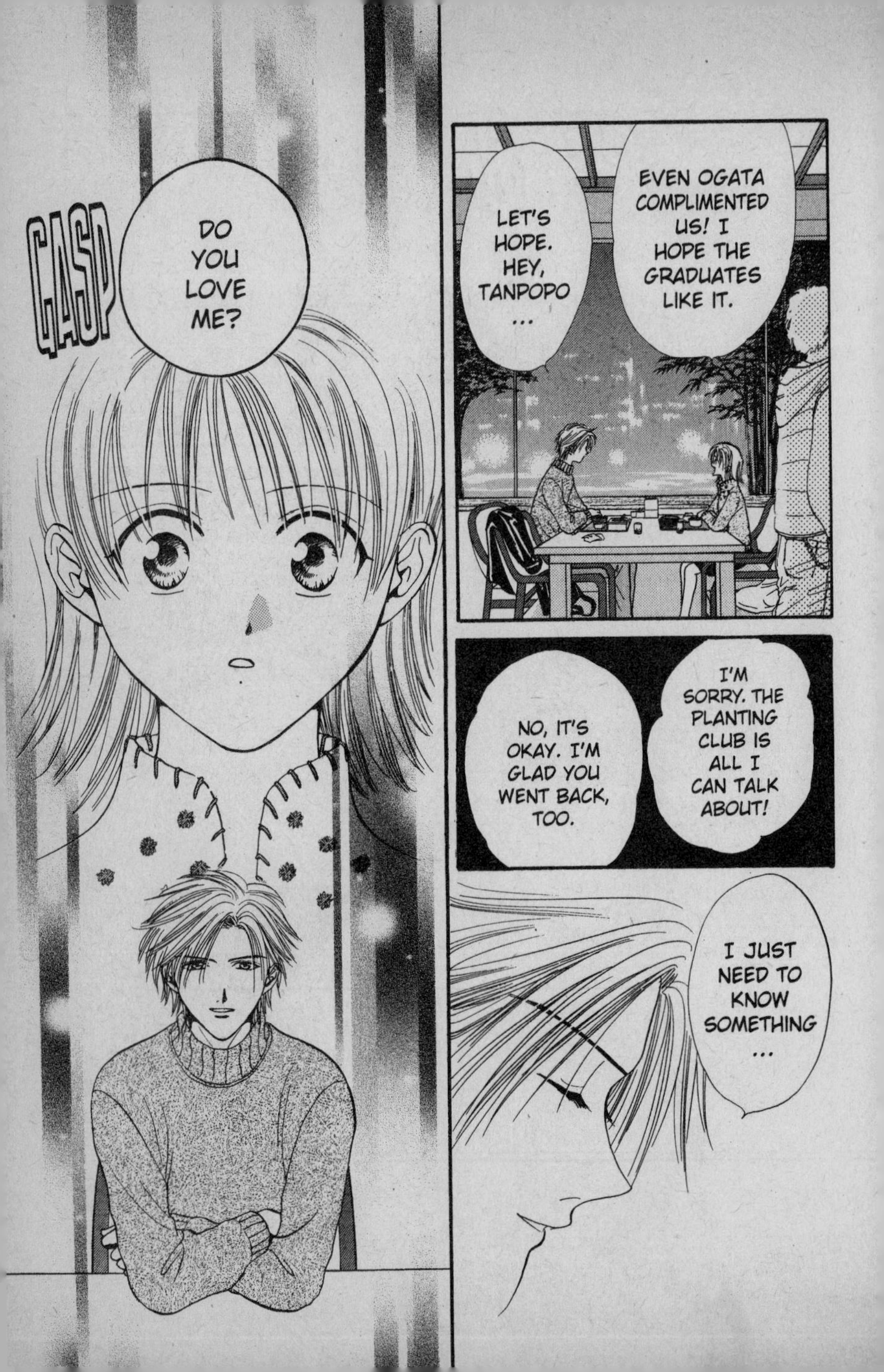
EVEN OGATA COMPLIMENTED US! I HOPE THE GRADUATES LIKE IT.
LET'S HOPE. HEY, TANPOPO ...
I'M SORRY. THE PLANTING CLUB IS ALL I CAN TALK ABOUT!
NO, IT'S OKAY. I'M GLAD YOU WENT BACK, TOO.
I JUST NEED TO KNOW SOMETHING ...
DO YOU LOVE ME?
GASP

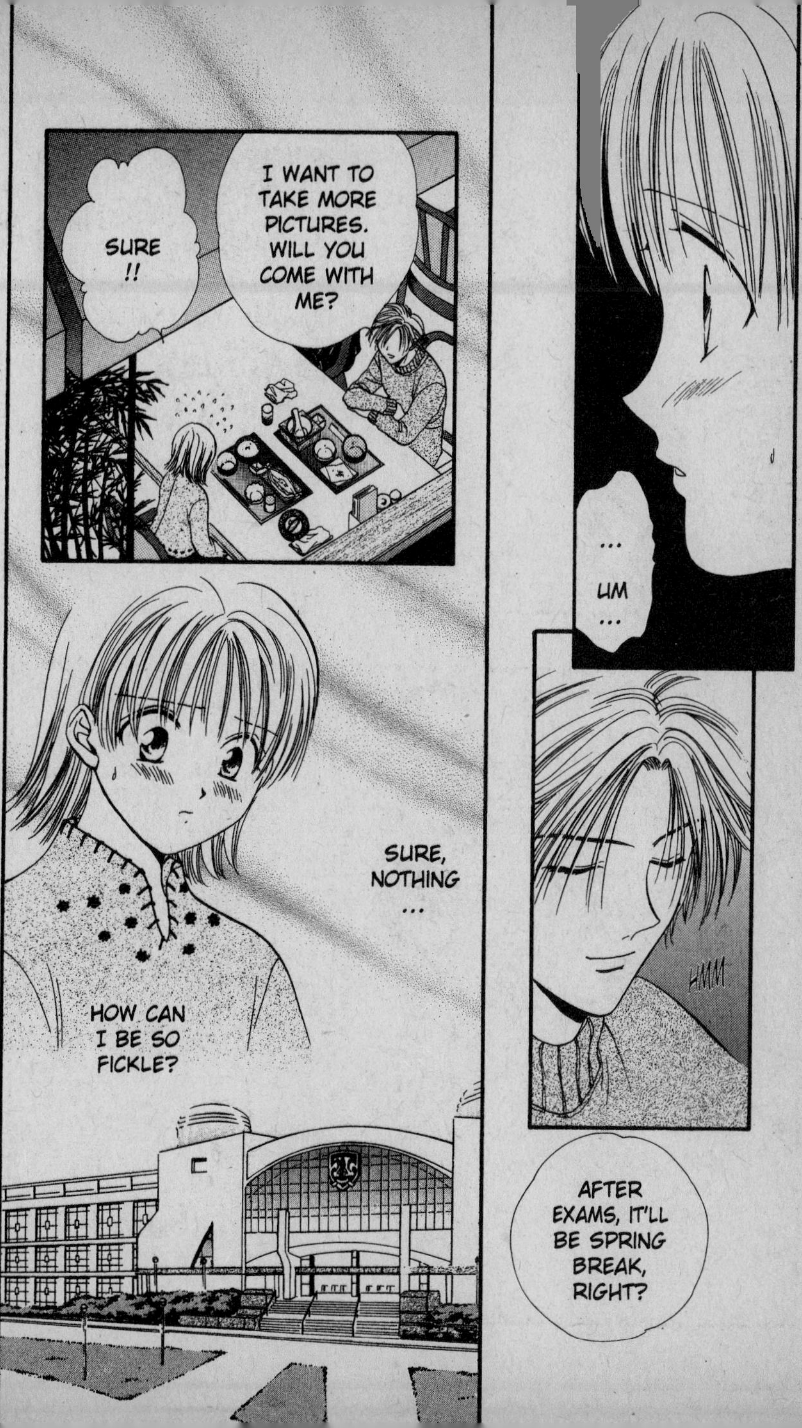
... UM ...
HMM
AFTER EXAMS, IT'LL BE SPRING BREAK, RIGHT?
I WANT TO TAKE MORE PICTURES. WILL YOU COME WITH ME?
SURE !!
SURE, NOTHING ...
HOW CAN I BE SO FICKLE?

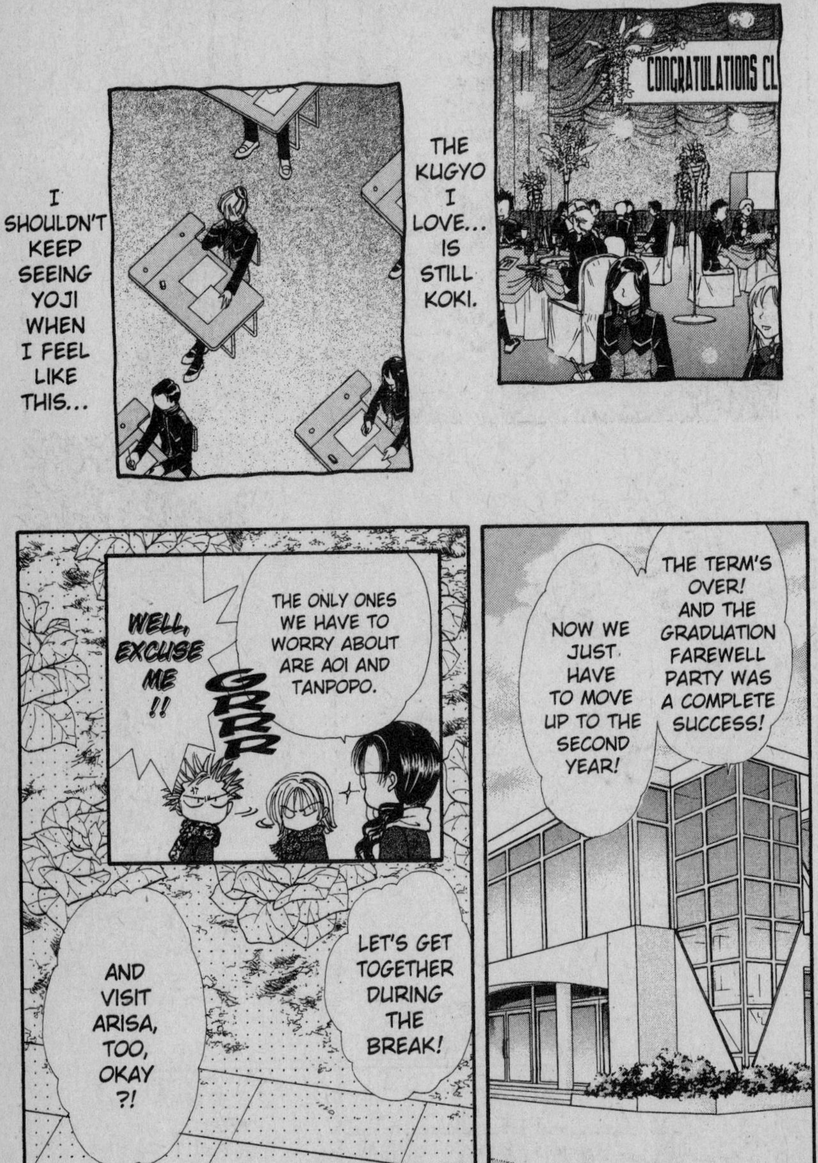
CONGRATULATIONS CL
THE KUGYO I LOVE... IS STILL KOKI.
I SHOULDN'T KEEP SEEING YOJI WHEN I FEEL LIKE THIS...
THE TERM'S OVER! AND THE GRADUATION FAREWELL PARTY WAS A COMPLETE SUCCESS!
NOW WE JUST HAVE TO MOVE UP TO THE SECOND YEAR!
THE ONLY ONES WE HAVE TO WORRY ABOUT ARE AOI AND TANPOPO.
WELL, EXCUSE ME !!
GRRR
LET'S GET TOGETHER DURING THE BREAK!
AND VISIT ARISA, TOO, OKAY ?!

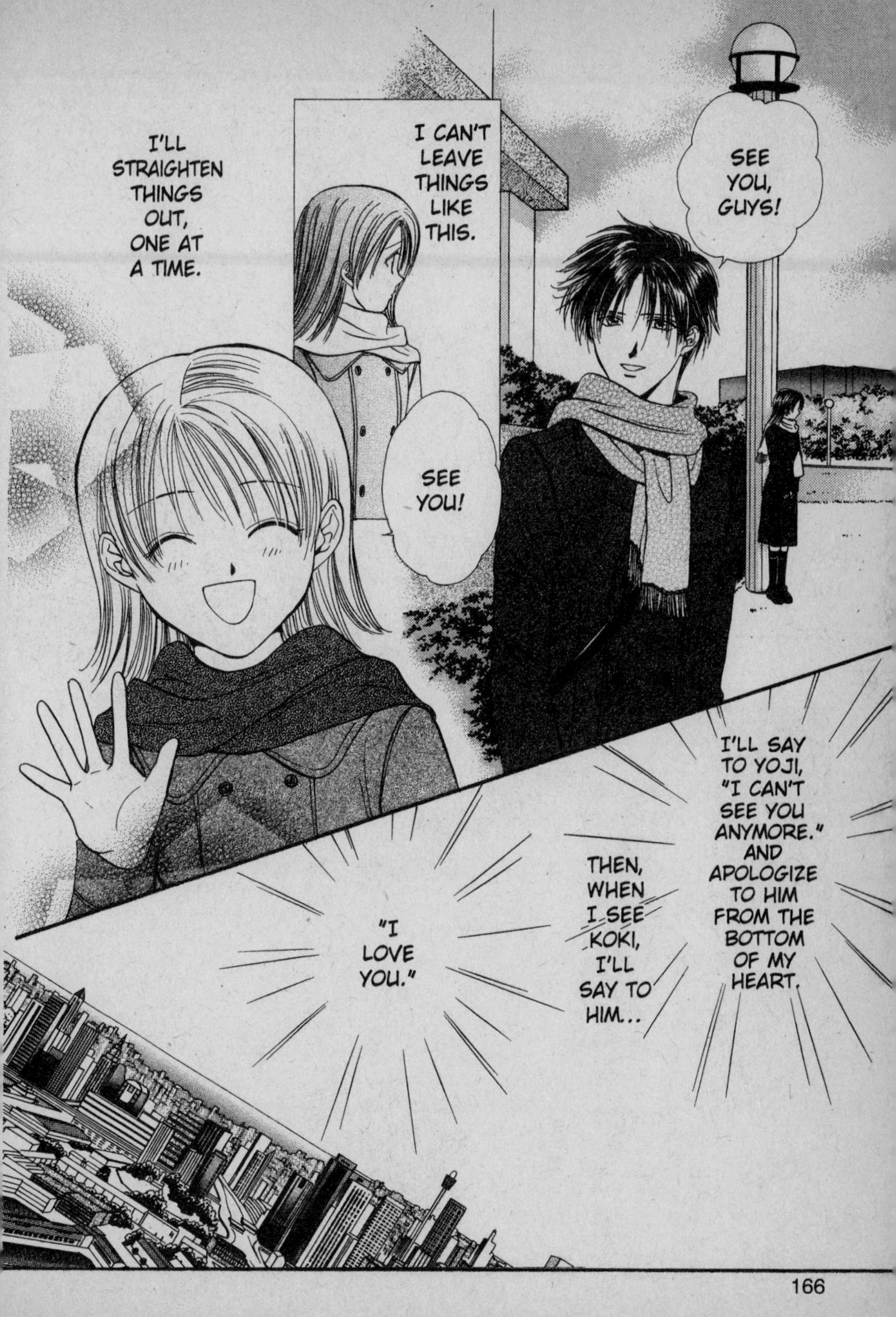
SEE YOU, GUYS!
I CAN'T LEAVE THINGS LIKE THIS.
I'LL STRAIGHTEN THINGS OUT, ONE AT A TIME.
SEE YOU!
I'LL SAY TO YOJI, "I CAN'T SEE YOU ANYMORE." AND APOLOGIZE TO HIM FROM THE BOTTOM OF MY HEART.
THEN, WHEN I SEE KOKI, I'LL SAY TO HIM...
"I LOVE YOU."

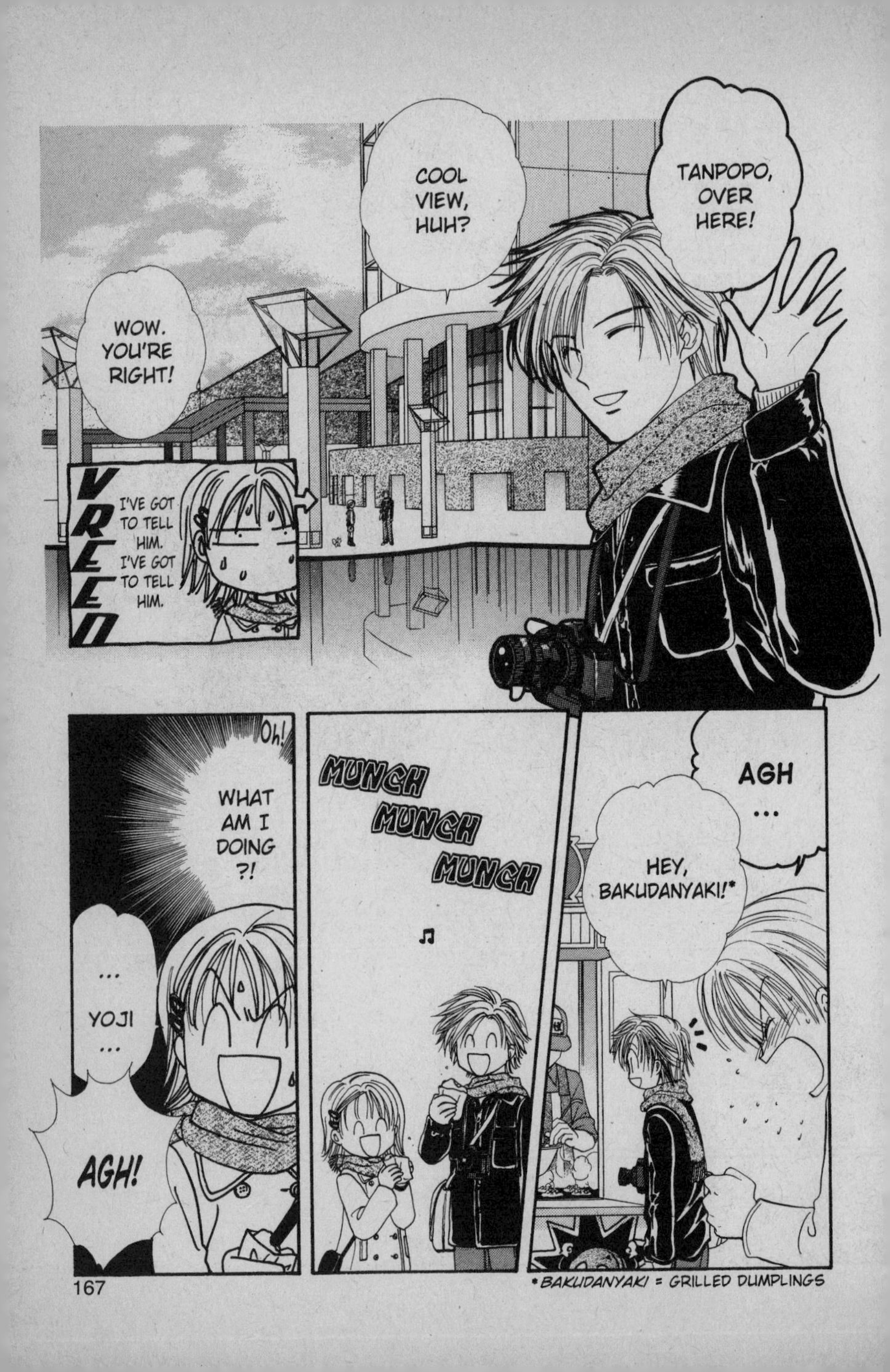
TANPOPO, OVER HERE!
COOL VIEW, HUH?
WOW. YOU'RE RIGHT!
VREED
I'VE GOT TO TELL HIM. I'VE GOT TO TELL HIM.
AGH ...
HEY, BAKUDANYAKI!*
MUNCH MUNCH MUNCH
♫
Oh!
WHAT AM I DOING ?!
... YOJI ...
AGH!

*BAKUDANYAKI = GRILLED DUMPLINGS

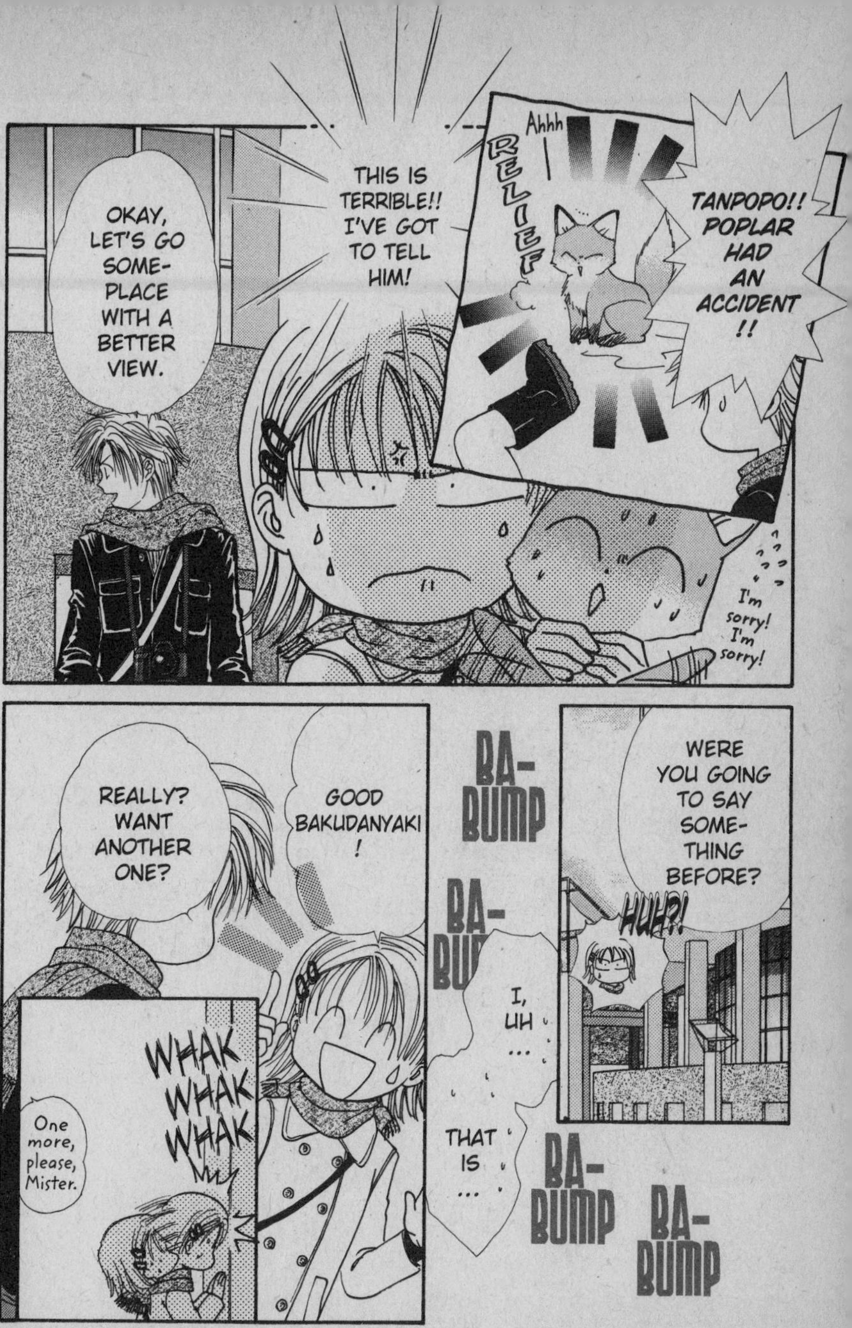
TANPOPO!! POPLAR HAD AN ACCIDENT!!
Ahhh
RELIEF
THIS IS TERRIBLE!! I'VE GOT TO TELL HIM!
I'm sorry! I'm sorry!
OKAY, LET'S GO SOME-PLACE WITH A BETTER VIEW.
WERE YOU GOING TO SAY SOME-THING BEFORE?
HUH?!
BA-BUMP
BA-BUMP
I, UH ...
THAT IS ...
BA-BUMP
BA-BUMP
GOOD BAKUDANYAKI!
REALLY? WANT ANOTHER ONE?
WHAK WHAK WHAK
One more, please, Mister.

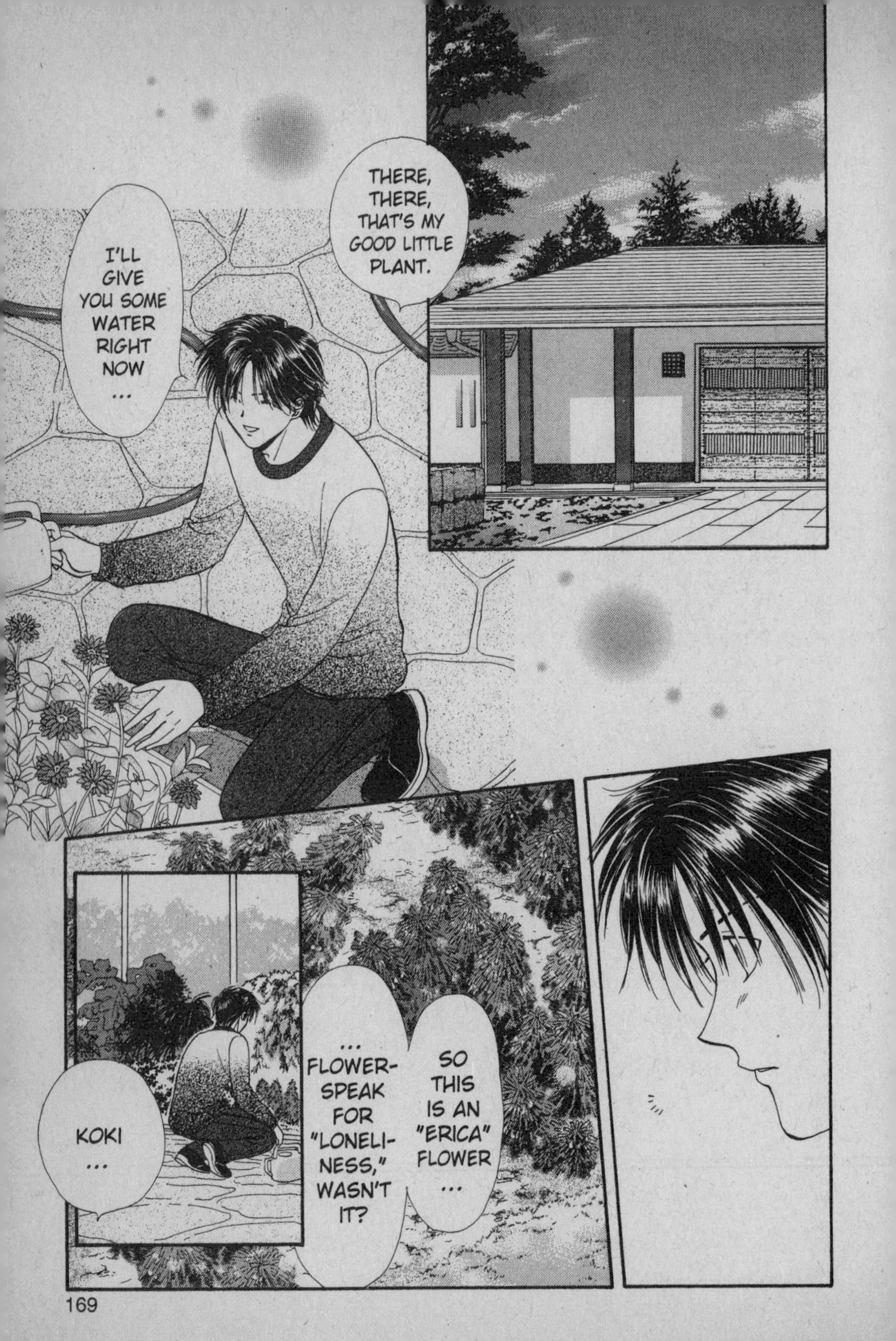
THERE, THERE, THAT'S MY GOOD LITTLE PLANT.
I'LL GIVE YOU SOME WATER RIGHT NOW ...
SO THIS IS AN "ERICA" FLOWER ...
... FLOWER-SPEAK FOR "LONELI-NESS," WASN'T IT?
KOKI ...

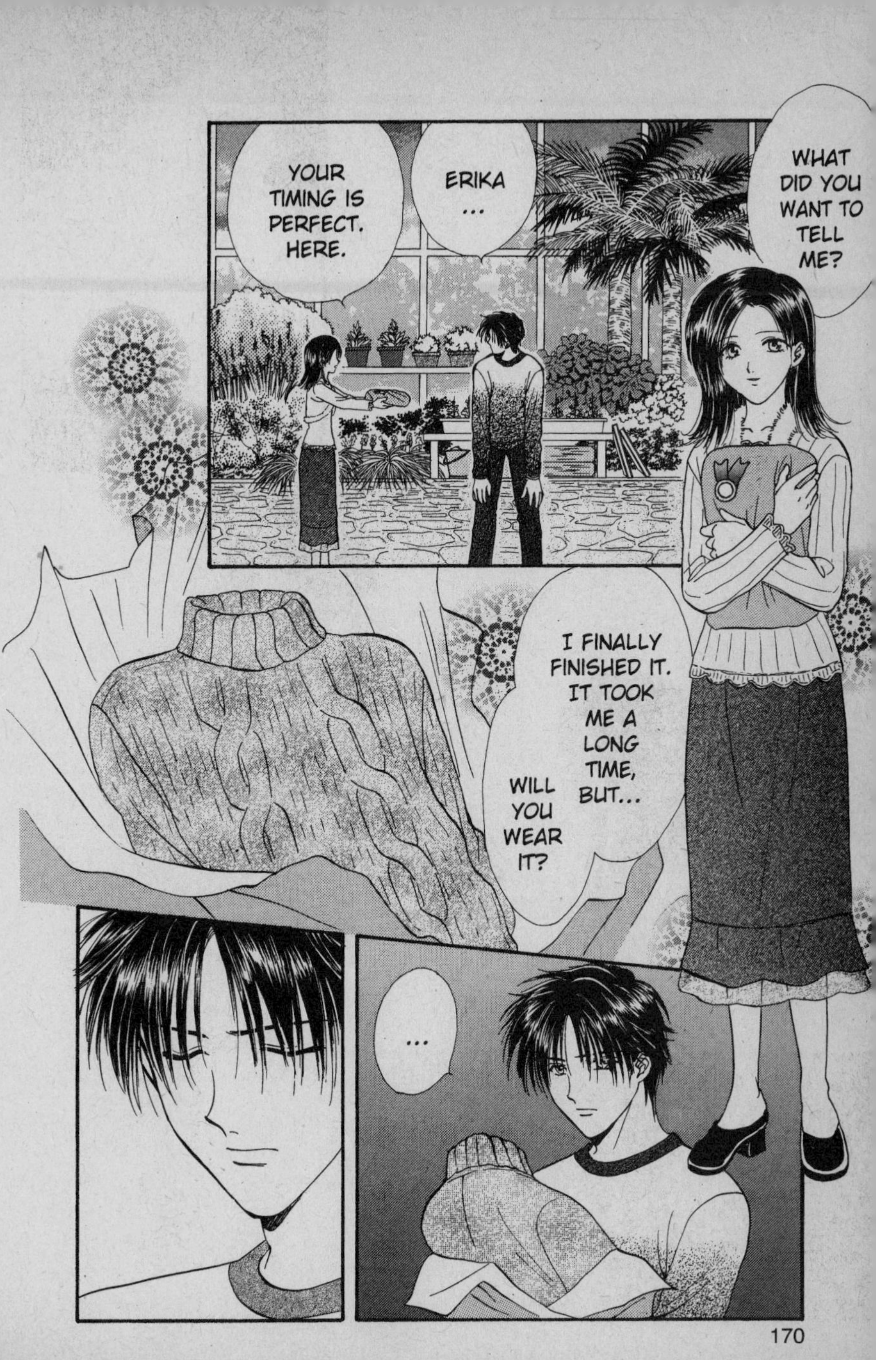
WHAT DID YOU WANT TO TELL ME?
ERIKA...
YOUR TIMING IS PERFECT. HERE.
I FINALLY FINISHED IT. IT TOOK ME A LONG TIME, BUT...
WILL YOU WEAR IT?
...

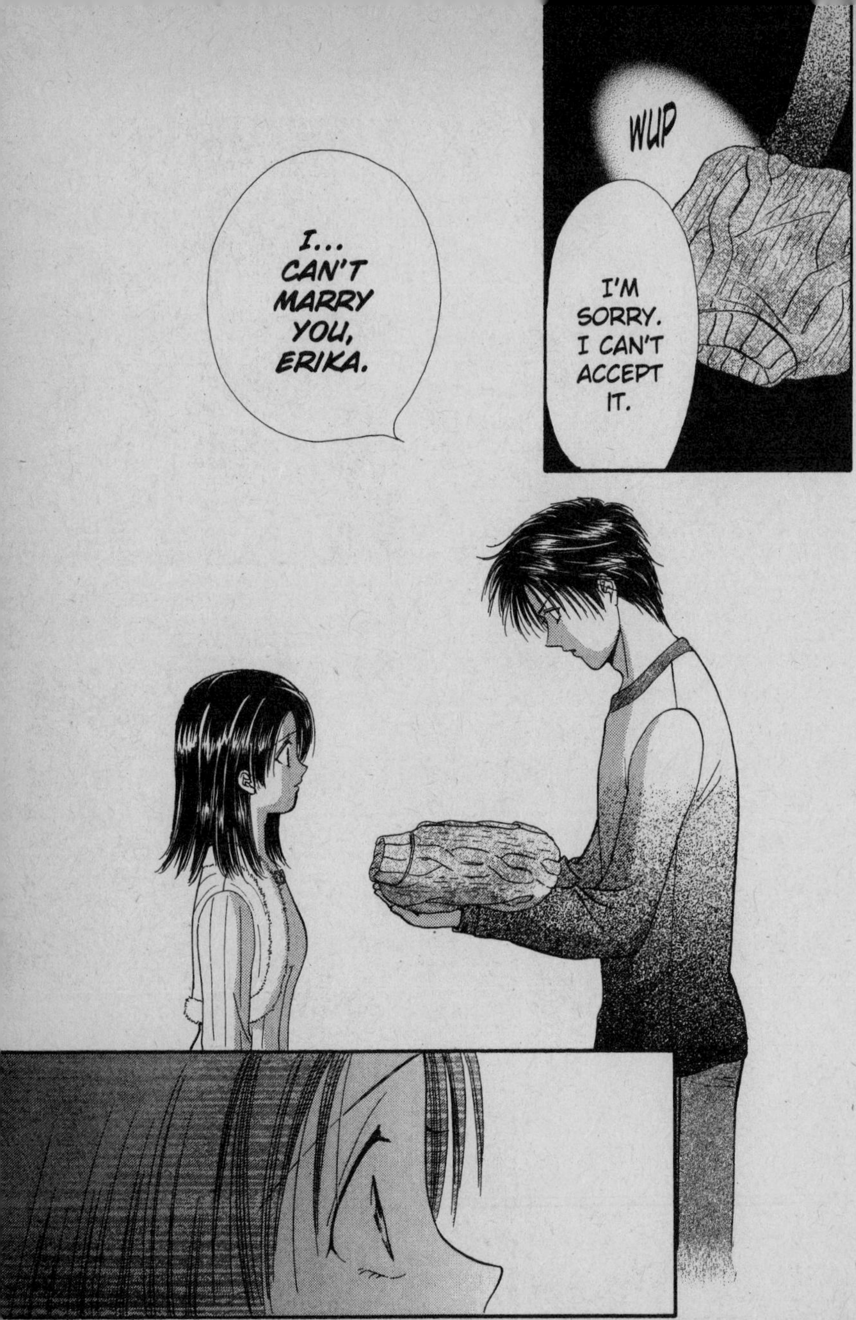
WUP
I'M SORRY. I CAN'T ACCEPT IT.
I... CAN'T MARRY YOU, ERIKA.

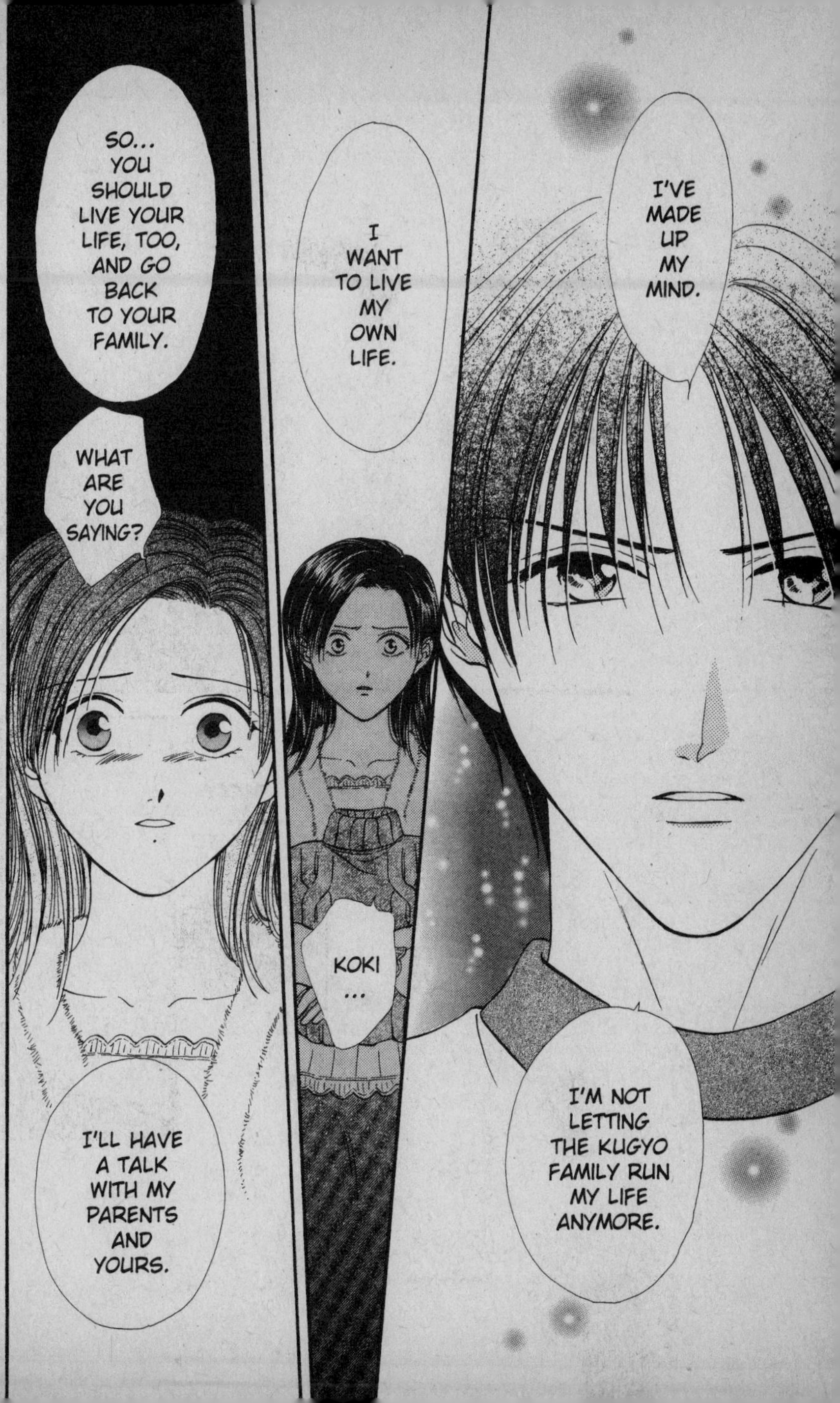
I'VE MADE UP MY MIND.
I'M NOT LETTING THE KUGYO FAMILY RUN MY LIFE ANYMORE.
I WANT TO LIVE MY OWN LIFE.
KOKI ...
SO... YOU SHOULD LIVE YOUR LIFE, TOO, AND GO BACK TO YOUR FAMILY.
WHAT ARE YOU SAYING?
I'LL HAVE A TALK WITH MY PARENTS AND YOURS.

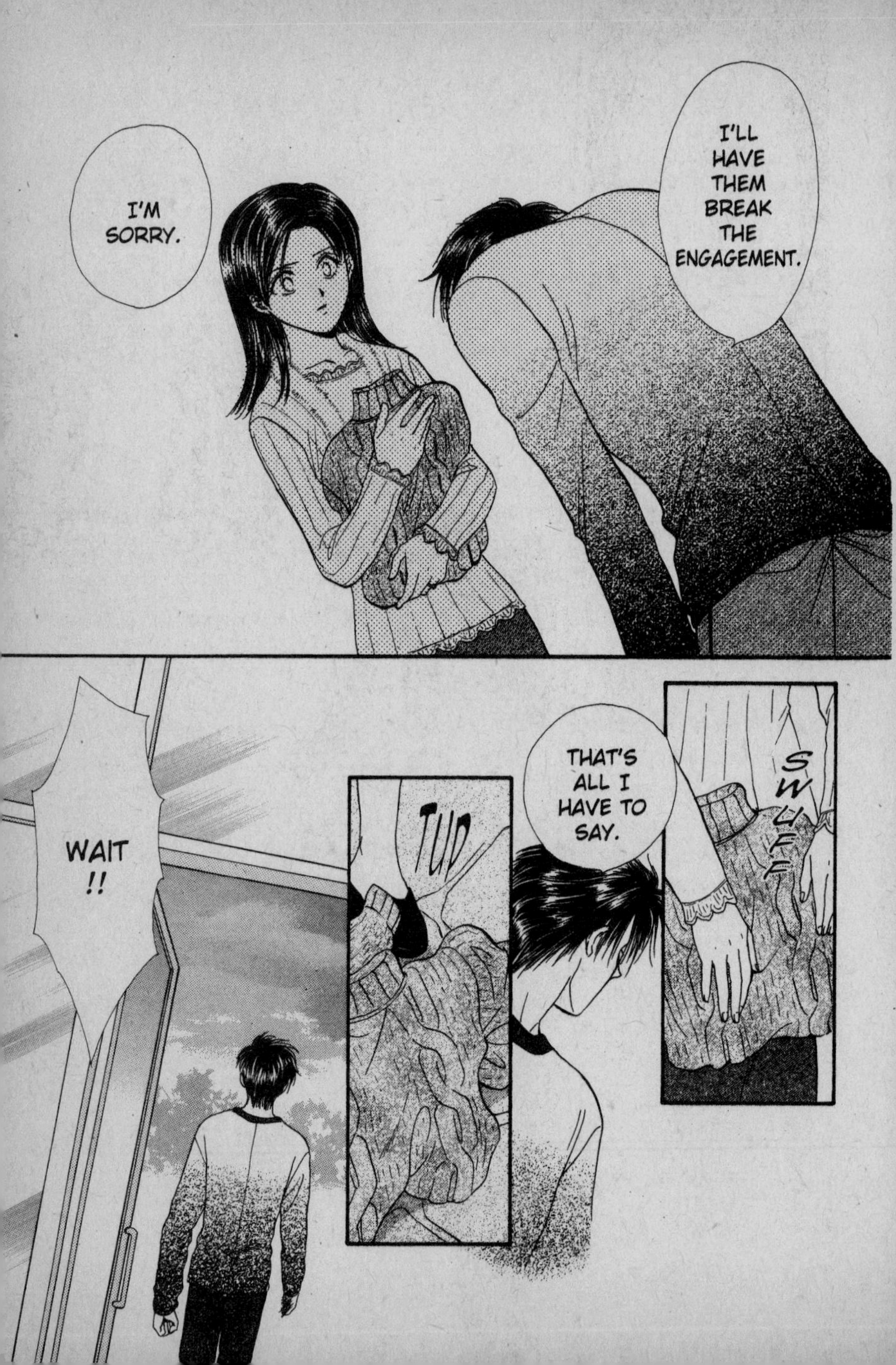
I'LL HAVE THEM BREAK THE ENGAGEMENT.
I'M SORRY.
THAT'S ALL I HAVE TO SAY.
SWUFF
TUD
WAIT !!

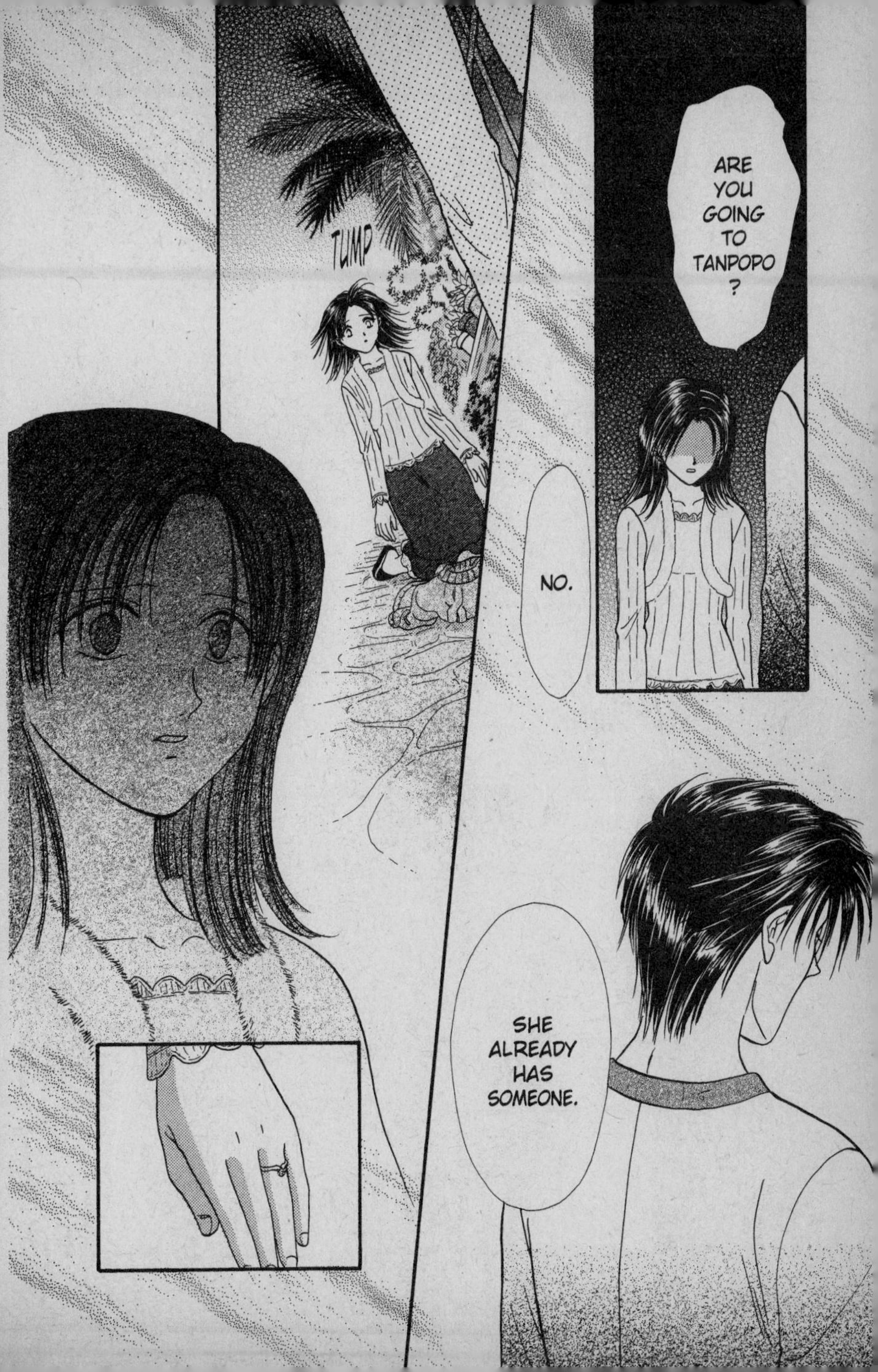
ARE YOU GOING TO TANPOPO?
NO.
SHE ALREADY HAS SOMEONE.
TUMP

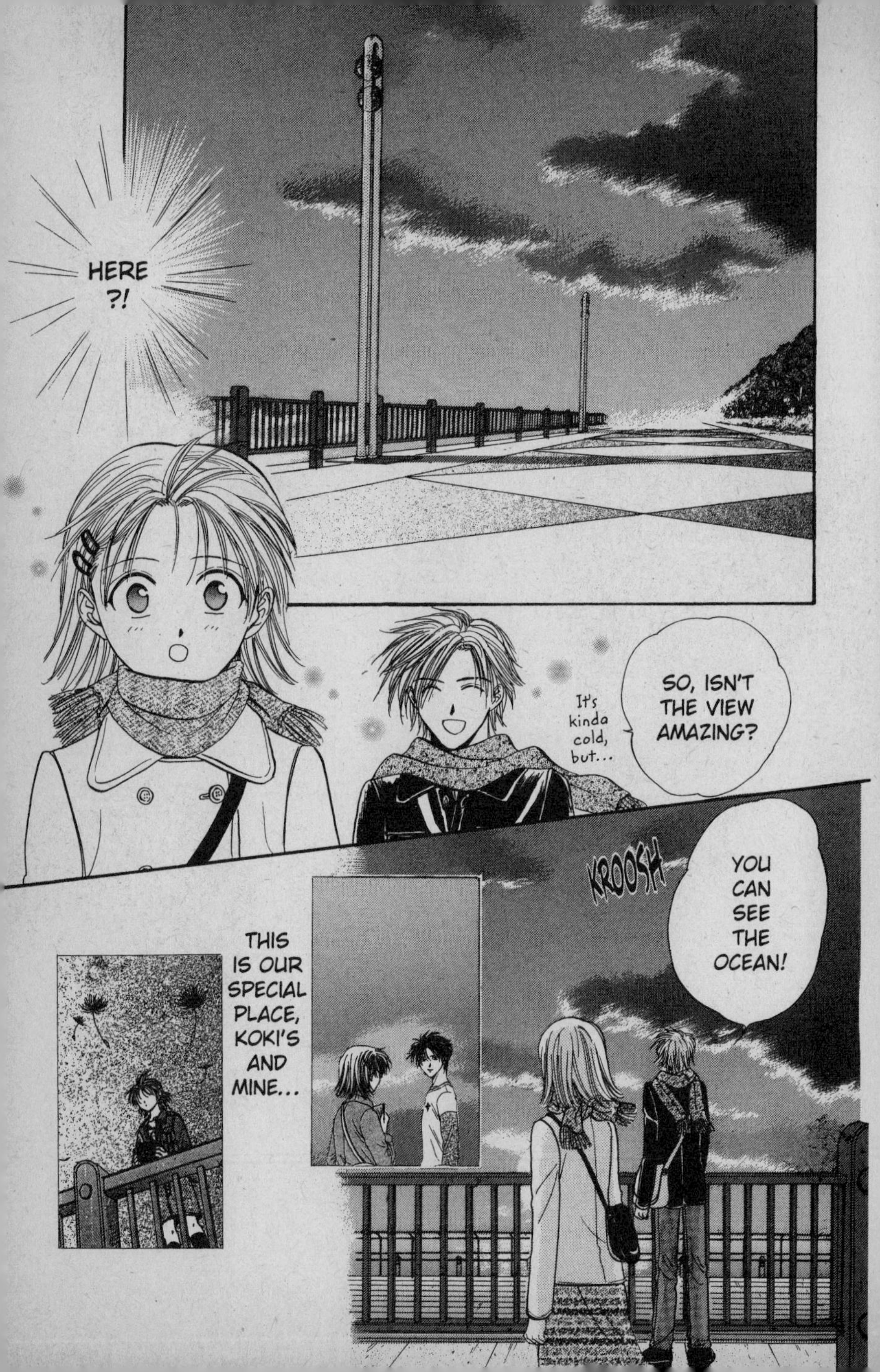
HERE ?!
SO, ISN'T THE VIEW AMAZING?
It's kinda cold, but...
KROOSH
YOU CAN SEE THE OCEAN!
THIS IS OUR SPECIAL PLACE, KOKI'S AND MINE...

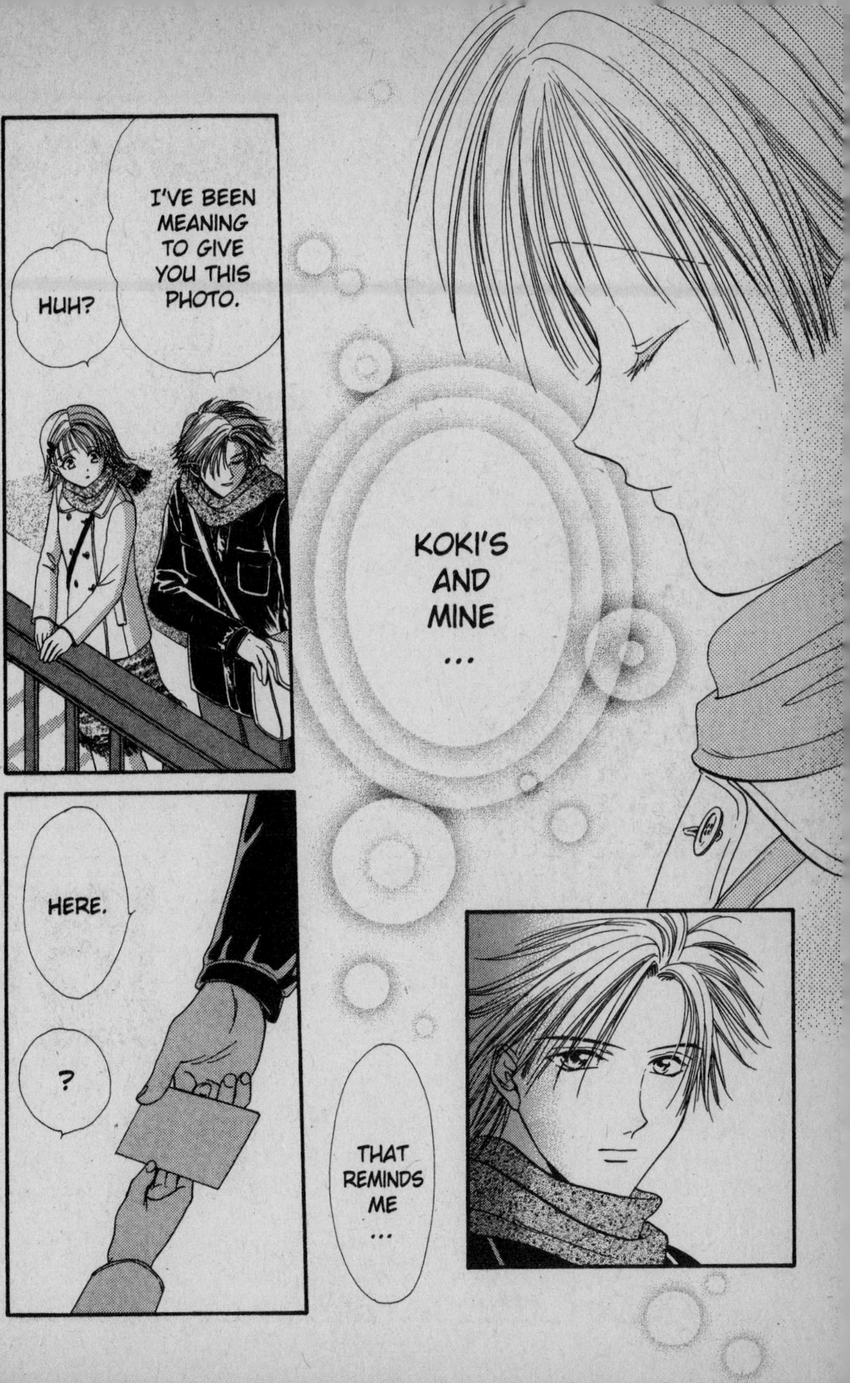
KOKI'S AND MINE ...
THAT REMINDS ME ...
I'VE BEEN MEANING TO GIVE YOU THIS PHOTO.
HUH?
HERE.
?

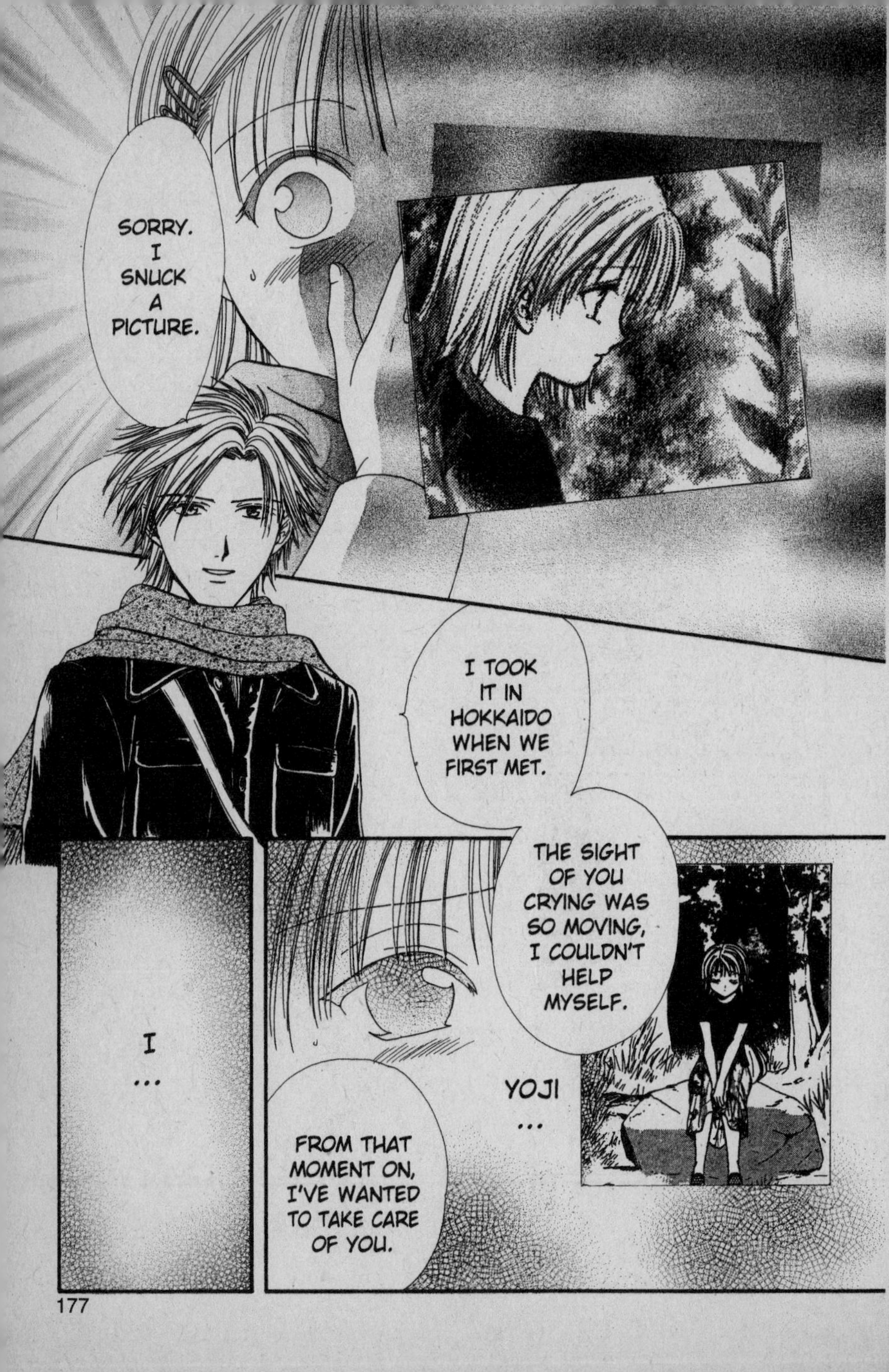
SORRY. I SNUCK A PICTURE.
I TOOK IT IN HOKKAIDO WHEN WE FIRST MET.
THE SIGHT OF YOU CRYING WAS SO MOVING, I COULDN'T HELP MYSELF.
YOJI ...
FROM THAT MOMENT ON, I'VE WANTED TO TAKE CARE OF YOU.
I ...

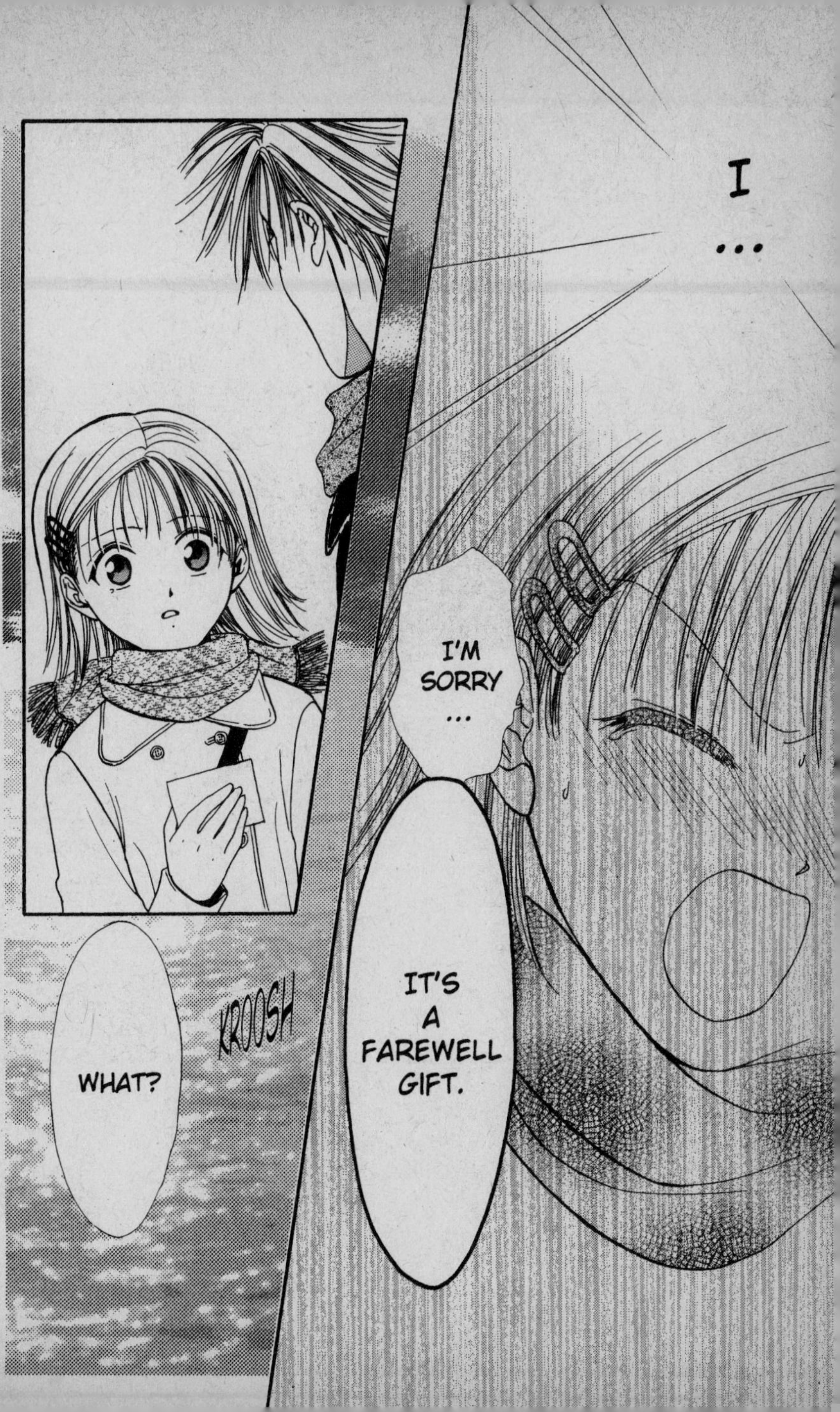
I ...
I'M SORRY ...
IT'S A FAREWELL GIFT.
WHAT?
KROOSH

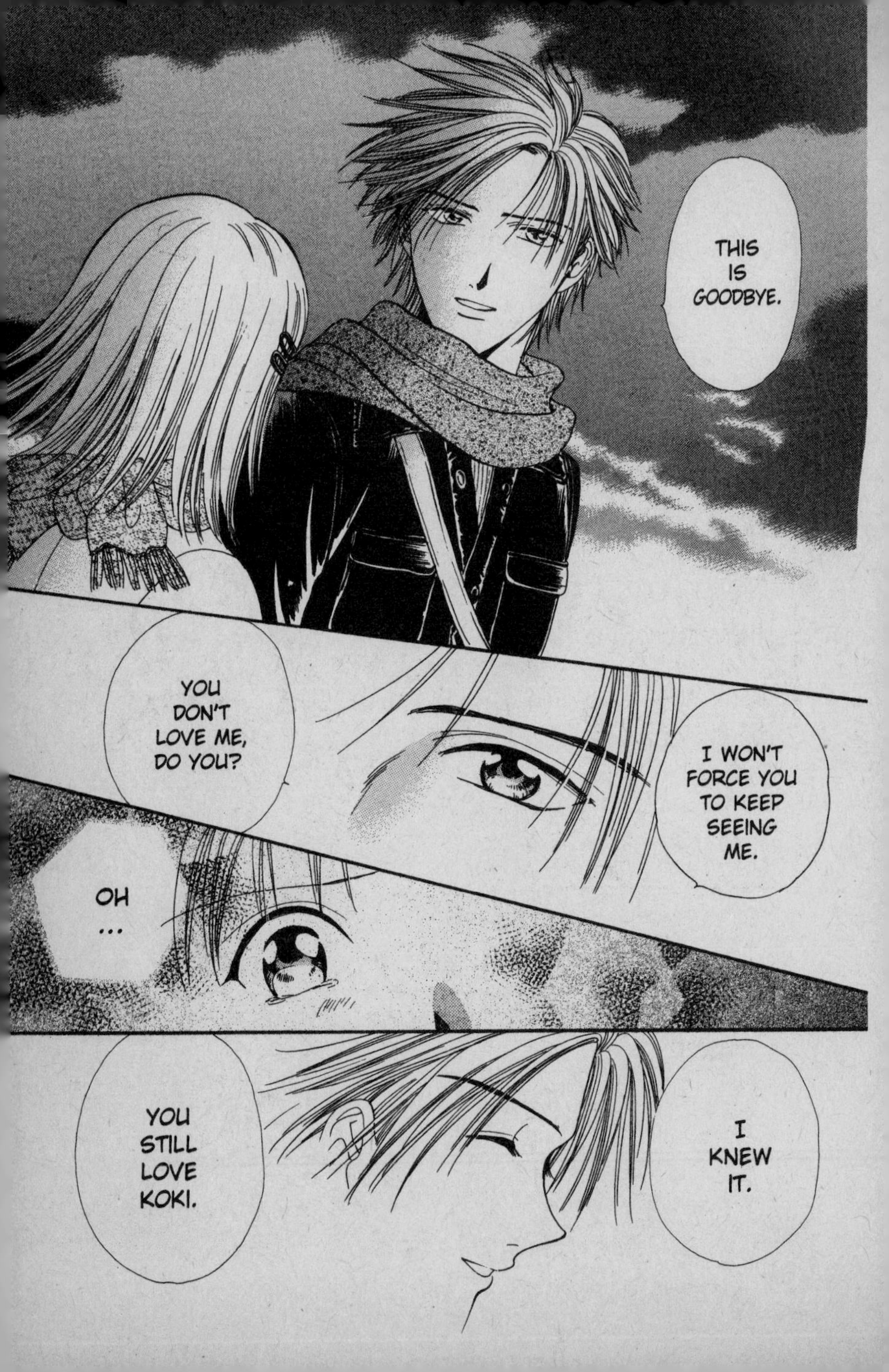
THIS IS GOODBYE.
I WON'T FORCE YOU TO KEEP SEEING ME.
YOU DON'T LOVE ME, DO YOU?
OH ...
I KNEW IT.
YOU STILL LOVE KOKI.

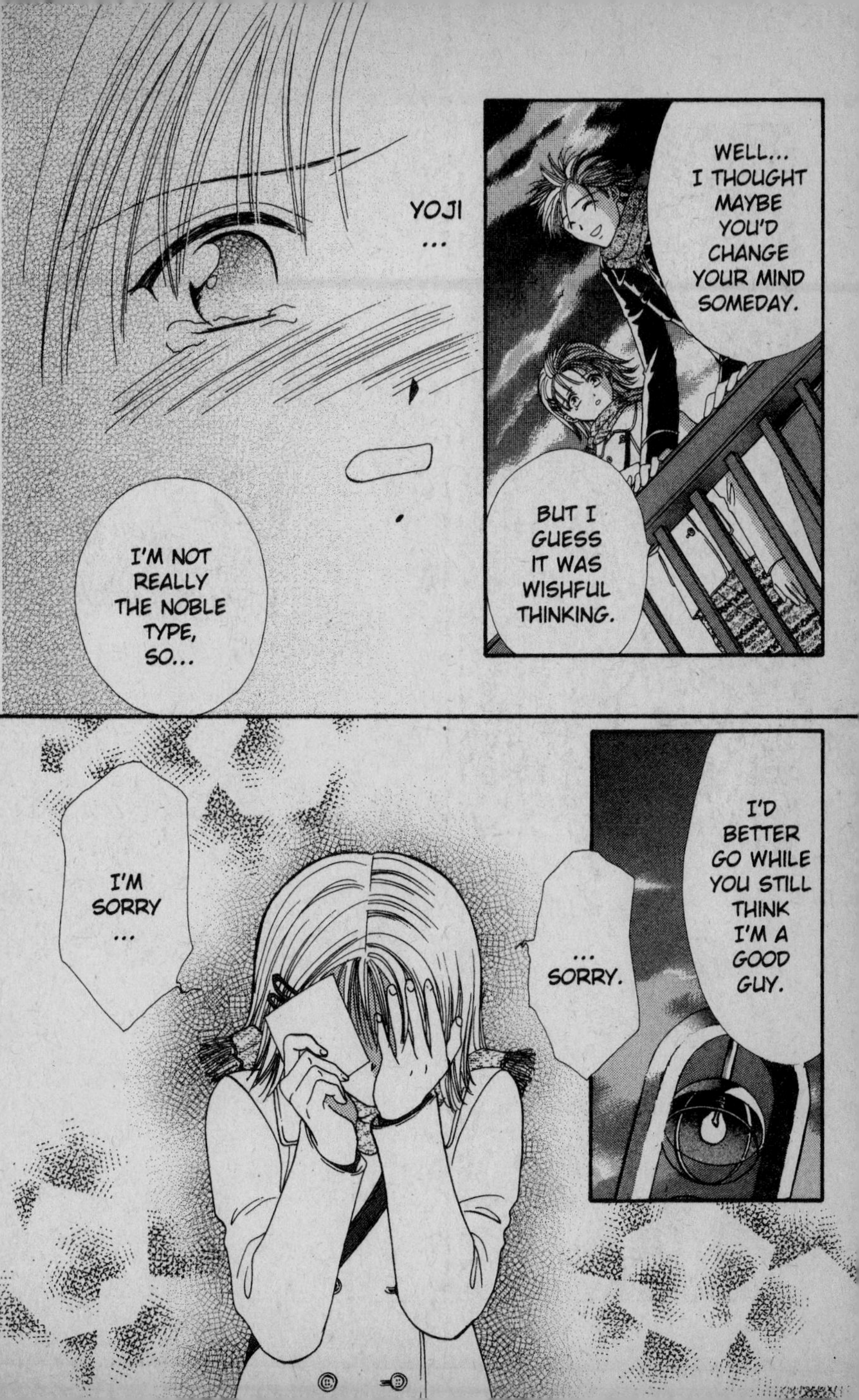
WELL... I THOUGHT MAYBE YOU'D CHANGE YOUR MIND SOMEDAY.
BUT I GUESS IT WAS WISHFUL THINKING.
YOJI ...
I'M NOT REALLY THE NOBLE TYPE, SO...
I'D BETTER GO WHILE YOU STILL THINK I'M A GOOD GUY.
... SORRY.
I'M SORRY ...

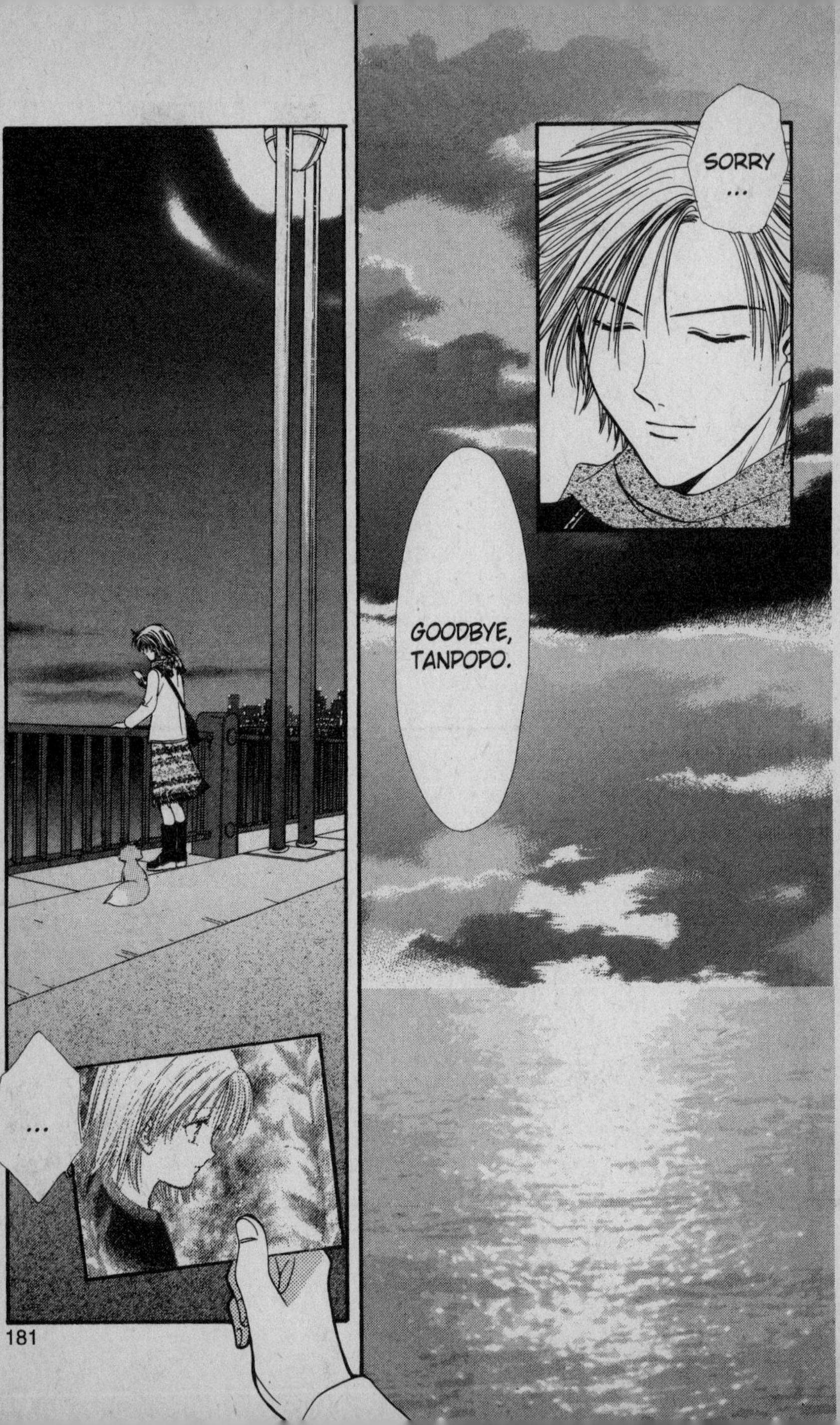
SORRY ...
GOODBYE, TANPOPO.
...

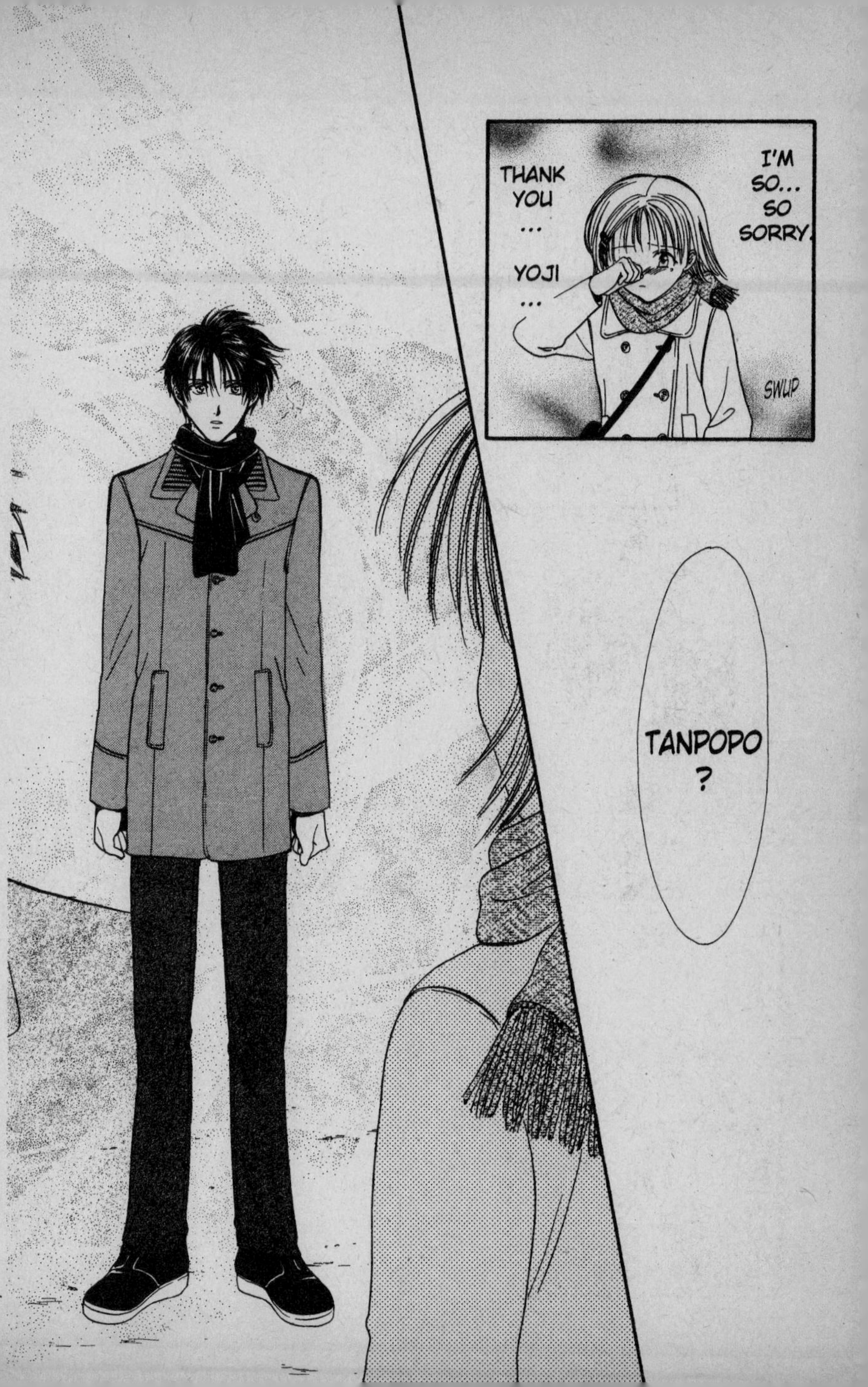
I'M SO... SO SORRY.
THANK YOU ... YOJI ...
SWUP
TANPOPO ?

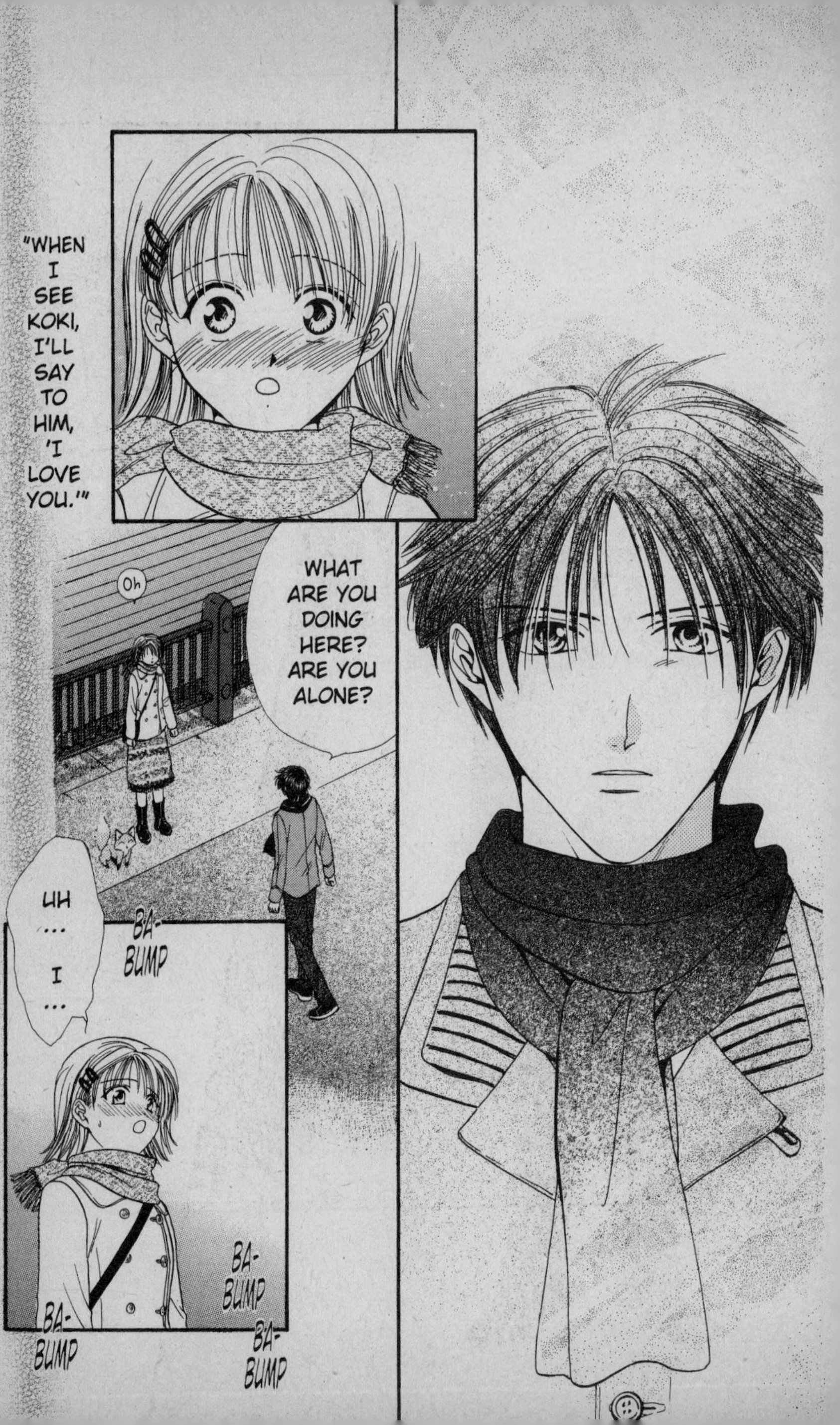
"WHEN I SEE KOKI, I'LL SAY TO HIM, 'I LOVE YOU.'"
Oh
WHAT ARE YOU DOING HERE? ARE YOU ALONE?
UH ... I ...
BA-BUMP
BA-BUMP
BA-BUMP
BA-BUMP

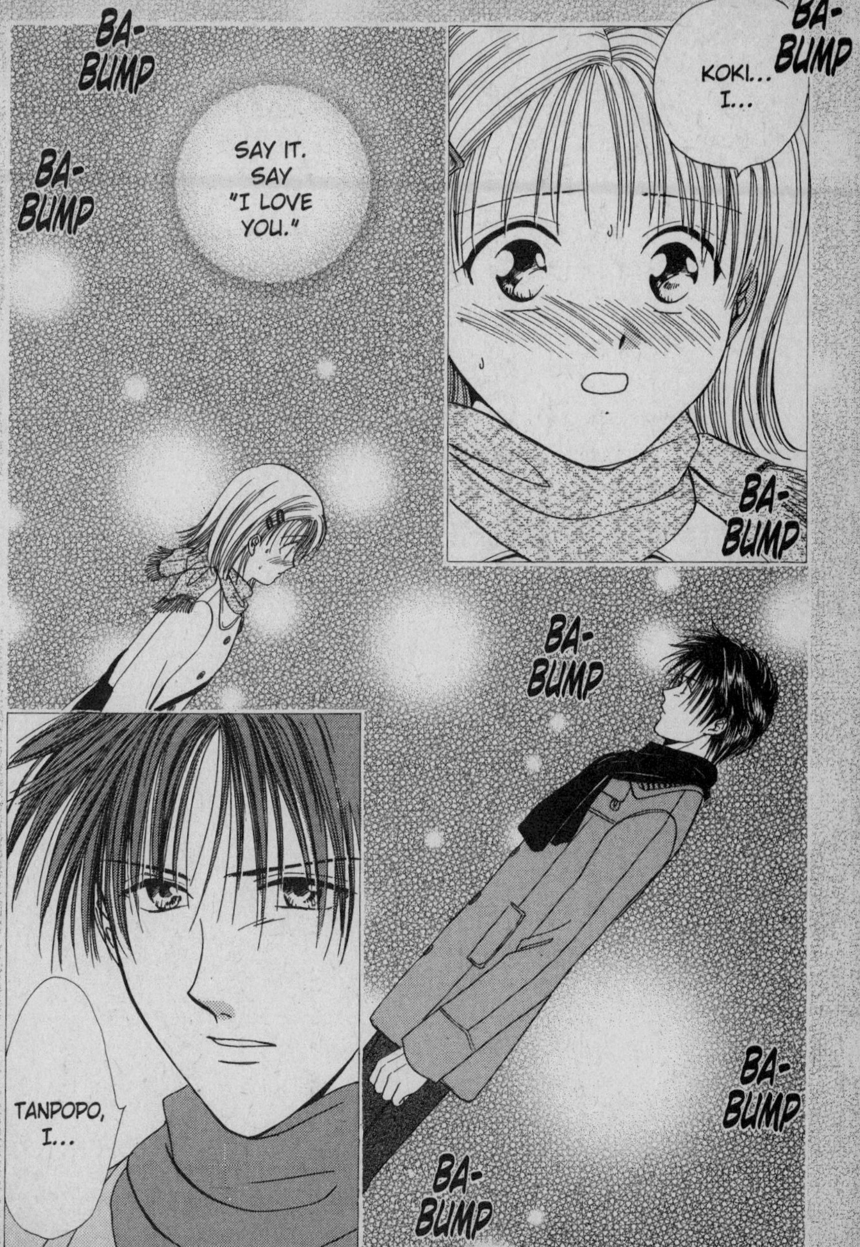

BA-BUMP
KOKI... I...
BA-BUMP
BA-BUMP
SAY IT. SAY "I LOVE YOU."
BA-BUMP
BA-BUMP
BA-BUMP
BA-BUMP
TANPOPO, I...

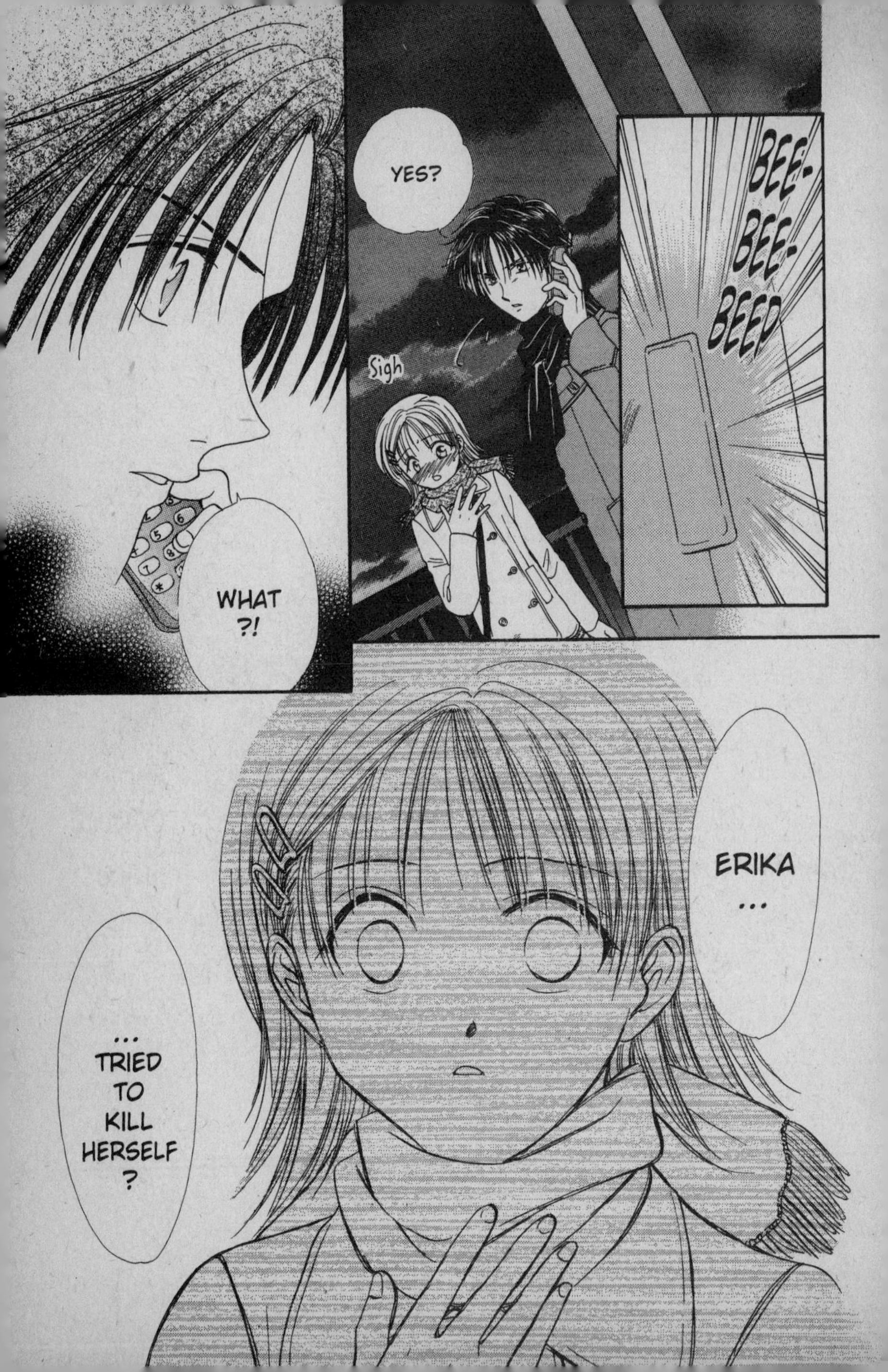
BEE-BEE-BEEP
YES?
Sigh
WHAT?!
ERIKA...
...TRIED TO KILL HERSELF?

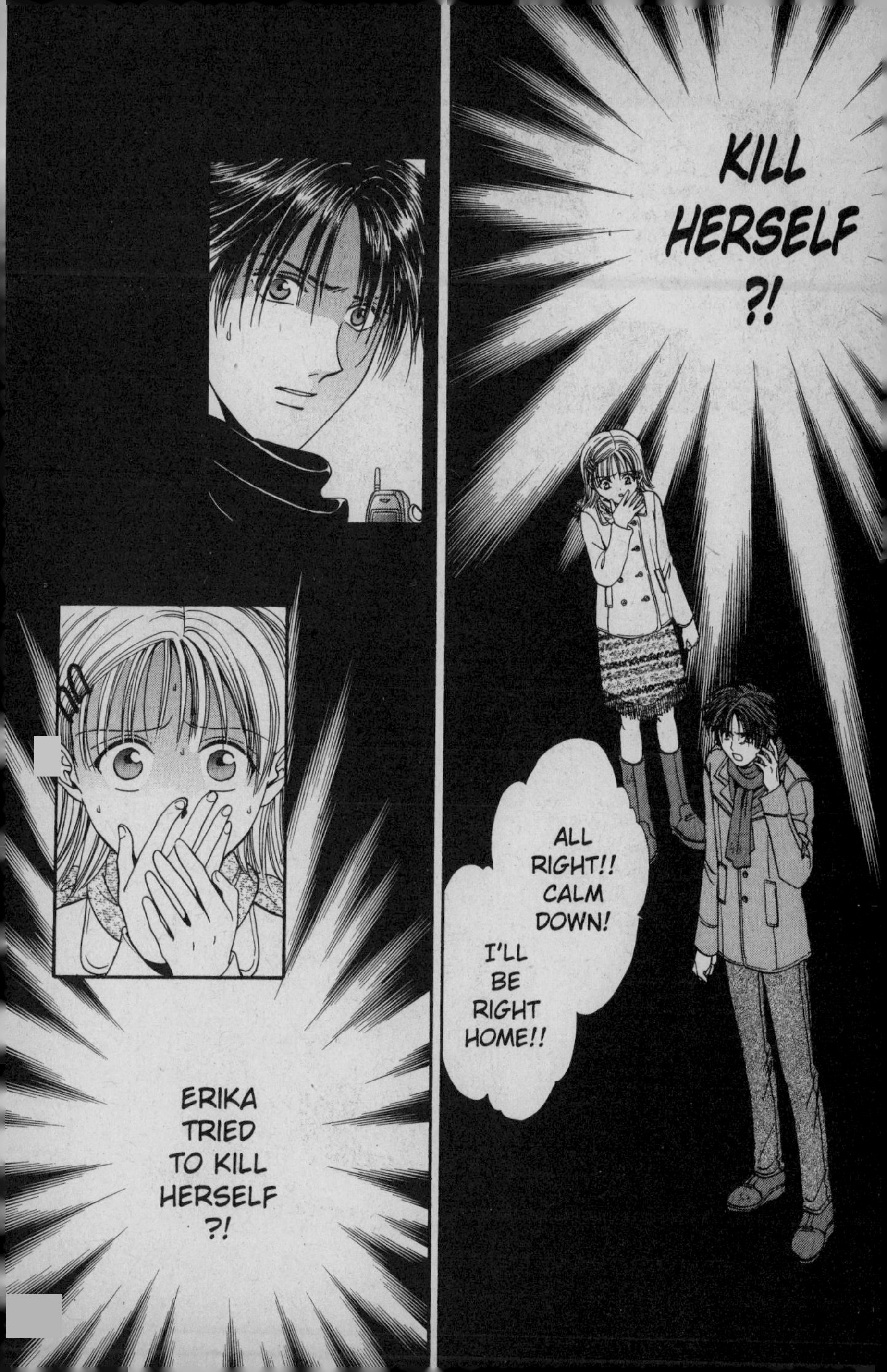
KILL HERSELF ?!
ALL RIGHT!! CALM DOWN!
I'LL BE RIGHT HOME!!
ERIKA TRIED TO KILL HERSELF ?!

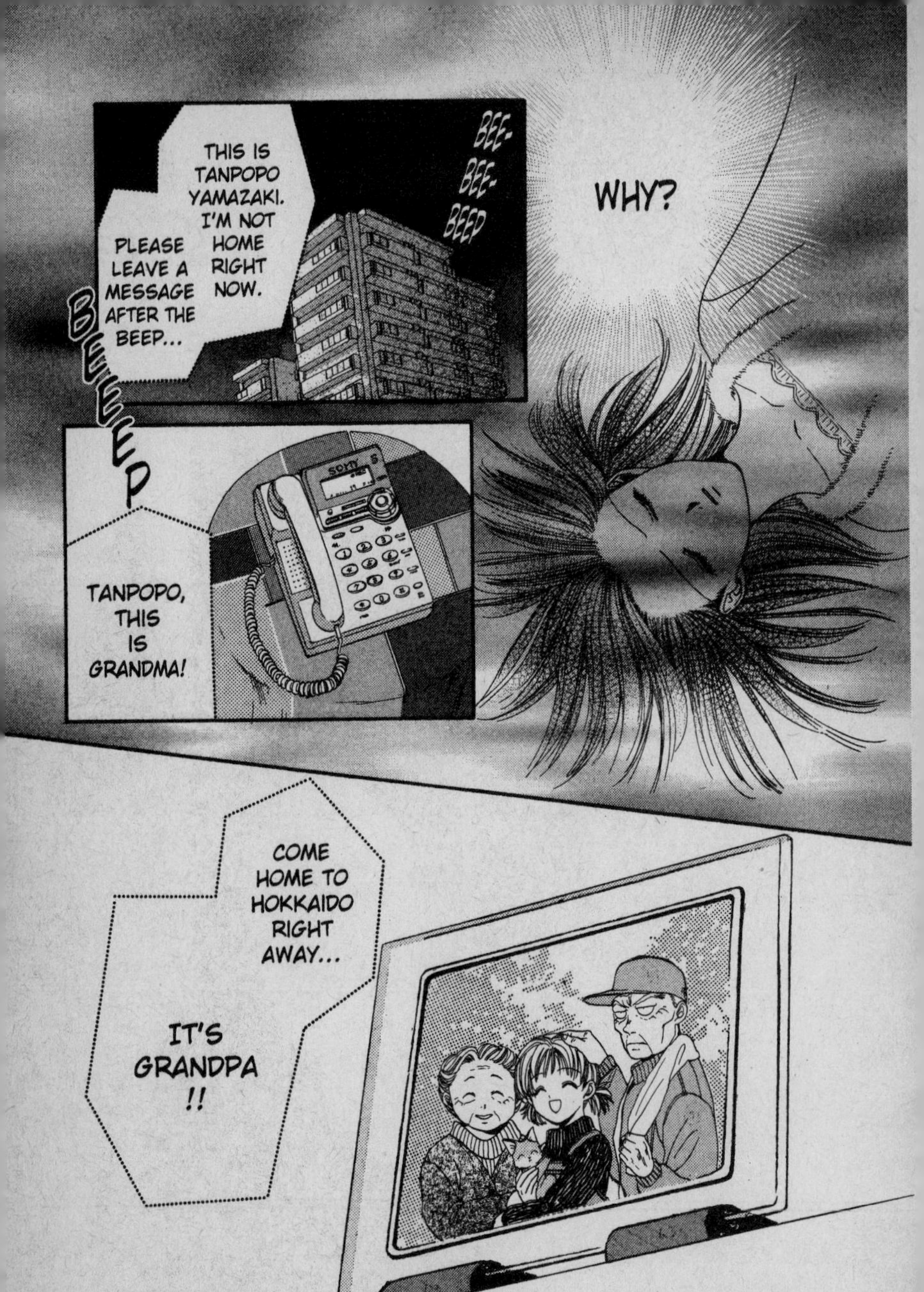
WHY?
BEE-BEE-BEEP
THIS IS TANPOPO YAMAZAKI. I'M NOT HOME RIGHT NOW. PLEASE LEAVE A MESSAGE AFTER THE BEEP...
BEEEEEP
TANPOPO, THIS IS GRANDMA!
COME HOME TO HOKKAIDO RIGHT AWAY...
IT'S GRANDPA !!

To Be Continued in Imadoki! Vol. 5

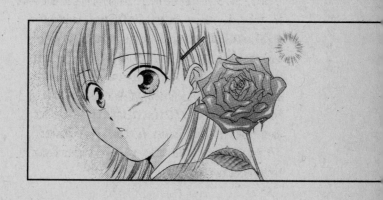

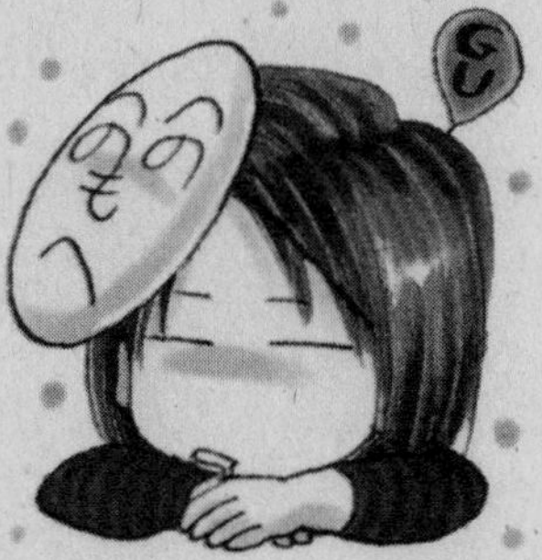
GU

Yuu Watase: Vital Stats

Yuu Watase was born on March 5 in a town near Osaka, Japan, and she was raised there before moving to Tokyo to follow her dream of creating manga. In the decade since her debut short story, ***Pajama De Ojama*** ("An Intrusion in Pajamas"), she has produced more than 50 compiled volumes of short stories and continuing series. Her latest series, ***Absolute Boyfriend***, is currently running in the anthology magazine ***Shojo Beat***. Watase's long-running horror/romance story ***Ceres: Celestial Legend*** and her most recent completed series, ***Imadoki!***, are published in North America by VIZ Media. She loves science fiction, fantasy and comedy.

EDITOR'S RECOMMENDATIONS

If you enjoyed this volume of IMADOKI! Nowadays

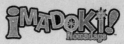

then here's some more manga you might be interested in.

Alice 19th
Yu Watase

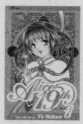

© 2001 Yuu Watase/Shogakukan, Inc.

Alice 19th

A chance encounter with a magical rabbit sets shy Alice Seno on the road to unlocking the power of the mysterious Lotis Words. One day, in a fit of frustration, Alice wishes for her pretty older sister to disappear—and she does! Now Alice must hurry to master the Lotis Words if she is to save her sister from the dark world that has claimed her.

Hot Gimmick
hot gimmick

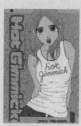

© 2001 Miki Aihara/Shogakukan, Inc.

Hot Gimmick

Sixteen-year-old Hatsumi Narita lives with her family in an apartment complex ruled over by the wealthy and much-feared Mrs. Tachibana. When the Tachibanas' domineering son, Ryoki, stumbles onto a Narita family secret, he agrees to keep it to himself—but only if Hatsumi becomes his "slave"!! Will her childhood crush, Azusa, be able to save her from Ryoki's creepy clutches?

UTENA

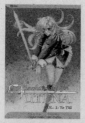

© 1996 SAITO CHIHO/IKUHARA KUNIHIKO & BE-PAPAS/Shogakukan, Inc.

Revolutionary Girl Utena

As a little girl, Utena was once saved by a beautiful prince and she's dreamed of finding him ever since. Now all grown up, she's vowed to follow him, even if it means becoming a prince just like him! Drawn to the elite Ohtori Private Academy, Utena is forced to duel for the hand of the mysterious Rose Bride in her search for her elusive savior.

Imadoki!
Nowadays
Vol. 4
Rose

STORY AND ART BY Yuu Watase
English Adaptation/Lance Caselman
Translation/JN Productions, Inc.
Touch-up Art & Lettering/Walden Wong
Graphic Designer/Nozomi Akashi
Editor/Yuki Takagaki

Managing Editor/Megan Bates
Editorial Director/Elizabeth Kawasaki
Editor in Chief/Alvin Lu
Sr. Director of Acquisitions/Rika Inouye
Sr. VP of Marketing/Liza Coppola
Exec. VP of Sales & Marketing/John Easum
Publisher/Hyoe Narita

Published by VIZ Media, LLC
P.O. Box 77010 • San Francisco, CA 94107

Shôjo Edition
10 9 8 7 6 5 4 3
First printing, December 2004
Second printing, February 2005
Third printing, August 2006

www.viz.com

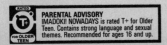

LOVE MANGA?
LET US KNOW WHAT YOU THINK!

HELP US MAKE THE MANGA
YOU LOVE BETTER!